COLLIE
PSYCHOLOGY
Carol Price

Inside the Border Collie mind

First published in 2013 by

First Stone Publishing

The Old Hen House, St Martin's Farm, Zeals,
Warminster, United Kingdom BA12 6NZ

Reprinted 2014. This soft back edition published in 2018.

Copyright First Stone Publishing and Carol Price, 2013 & 2018

Printed by Printworks Global Ltd. London & Hong Kong.

AUTHOR'S ACKNOWLEDGEMENTS

In writing this book I would like to express my gratitude to the following people: Ben Wilkes, of The Border Collie Trust, for his help with The Rescue Collie chapter – we must never forget all those dogs who lose their owners, or are just not lucky enough to find the right home the first time around. I would like to thank my vet, friend and fellow collie enthusiast Jill Matthews BVMS MRCVS for overseeing the health content of this book. Like me Jill now has four Border Collies. We just don't know when to stop. Thanks also to Heather Woodford, past winner of 10 Obedience CCs – including the Crufts Obedience title – for overseeing the Obedience section in Chapter 11 and to Wendy Beasley for her input on Working Trials in the same chapter. As far as I'm concerned Wendy is *the* expert on WTs as a pursuit. Finally, thanks to all those owners over past years who took the trouble to bring their collies to me for help. Without meeting them and you, and being continually faced with problems I had to find answers to, I would never have learned what I now know about the most remarkable dogs in the world.

YOUR DOGS, MY DOGS

To readers about to embark on this book I would like to say the following things. Border Collies are incredibly special dogs. Never take your own dogs, or everything that is so special about them, for granted. Appreciate what they give you, and bring to your life, every day. A dog's life can bloom and then flash by faster than you ever imagined.

To my own dogs I would like to say: Thank you for your patience, willingness and kindness, and for always believing in me and giving me your best, even when I don't deserve it. You are not always perfect, and neither am I, but together we work and still not a day goes by when I don't feel truly blessed to own dogs like you.

PUBLISHER'S ACKNOWLEDGEMENTS

Front cover photography © Nick Ridley (http://www.nickridley.com/); The publisher would also like to thank Carol Price, and Anne-Marie and Michelle Waugh (Chazak Border Collies) for help with photography.

ABOUT THE AUTHOR

Carol Price is a canine behaviourist, author and writer who has owned, trained, bred and worked with Border Collies for nearly 20 years. A former feature writer and commissioning editor on *The Sunday Times* (in London, UK), she has written for a wealth of national newspapers and magazines and is also author of the two best-selling books, *Understanding the Border Collie* and *Understanding the rescue dog*.

Today Carol's knowledge about dogs – particularly their psychology and behaviour – is much in demand. She is a regular contributor and advisor for both of the UK's top-selling dog magazines, *Your Dog* and *Dogs Today* and spends much of her professional time helping owners with problem dogs.

Carol has four Border Collies of her own. They keep her busy and fit!

CONTENTS

Introduction

THE UNIQUE BORDER COLLIE

Anyone who knows me or my work will be aware that Border Collies have been a massive part of my life for very many years now and, doubtless, a passion for them originated in my blood.

My Scottish and Welsh farming ancestors, on both sides of the family, owned and worked Border Collies, who were then simply known as 'sheepdogs'; animals who gave their all, rounding up livestock for their masters until the day they could run no more.

Today, I still cannot look at these dogs doing what they were bred to do without a sense of awe and admiration for their sheer beauty, athleticism and totally brilliant minds. There has never been a finer or smarter livestock herding dog in the whole of history, and probably never will be.

CHANGE AND CONFLICT

In recent decades the role and lifestyle of the Border Collie has undergone significant change, as more and more people have discovered the breed's exceptional trainability and range of talents. From being predominantly farmers' or shepherds' dogs, they have diversified into Sniffer dog and Search and Rescue work, moved into the pedigree show ring and become not only highly popular pets but also the must-have breed for anyone wanting to compete in pursuits such as Obedience, Agility, Fyball or Working Trials.

For the most part this transition has been successful, but at other times it has brought strife, as many less experienced owners, in particular, have struggled to understand the instincts and psychological complexities of these highly driven, sensitive and strong-willed working dogs.

Trouble often starts when owners try to impose expectations or lifestyles on Border Collies that are at odds with their inner genetic programming as sheepdogs, or view perfectly natural breed behaviour as a sign of bad character, or some sort of mental defect.

Certainly, in my work as a canine behaviourist, and Border Collie specialist, I see owners who fear that their dogs are 'not normal' all the time, simply due to insufficient understanding, or an inability to appreciate how much collies will vary as individuals, as a result of their background and breeding.

So many people never realise their collies' full potential, which is a tragic waste of a superb brain. If you imagine a collie's mind as a computer hard drive, with vast capacity and memory, the average owner may only fill a fraction of this during their dog's lifetime, for want of knowing how to better stretch or train him.

As highlighted later in this book, the more chance you give a collie to learn and be smart, the smarter he gets and the more he can do. Conversely, many collies only become problems due to a sustained lack of mental stimulation and occupation, or over-stimulation of the wrong kind.

GREATER UNDERSTANDING

Over a decade ago I wrote my first book, *Understanding the Border Collie,* from a belief that many of the people who acquired these dogs failed to fully comprehend what made them tick, and that a lack of sufficiently honest and helpful advice about the breed was making life so much harder for owners and their dogs alike.

In all the years that have passed since this first book, however, my knowledge of Border Collies has vastly increased through both necessity and an ongoing passion and fascination for the breed.

Through breeding and rearing my own dogs, living, working and training with them every day and constantly sorting out a wide range of behavioural problems or training difficulties in other people's collies, I have learned so many more invaluable things, which I would now like to share with you.

ANSWERS

So whether you are a would-be Border Collie owner, a less or more experienced one, a collie breeder, trainer or competitor, or just someone keen to get the best out of their dog in everyday life, this book is for you.

It will give detailed answers to the commonest questions, such as:
- Where do Border Collies come from?
- What makes them do what they do?
- What is 'normal'/abnormal behaviour in a collie?

Many collies fail to reach their full potential.

- Why are some collies so much more difficult or challenging to own than others?
- How do you find the 'right' collie?
- How and why do collies 'go wrong'?
- What makes them become aggressive?
- What's the difference between a 'bad' or 'aggressive' dog and one just misdirecting normal working instinct?
- Why do collies become fearful or 'manic'?
- Why do they develop obsessive patterns of behaviour?
- What are the secrets to raising a problem-free collie?
- What are the secrets to getting the best out of your dog in training and competition?

ALSO IN THIS BOOK

Such issues apart, there will also be some in-depth 'psychological profiling' of the Border Collie, to better explain some of the more mysterious – or exasperating – workings of his mind.

There is also advice on how to handle any less appropriate instincts or behaviours from puppyhood onwards.

The specific needs of rescue collies, and how to best manage their rehabilitation will also be covered, as well as how factors such as health, hormones, diet, exercise levels, different environmental stresses and (most of all) *you* may affect the behaviour of your dog.

To further help you, the second part of this book is entirely devoted to a comprehensive A-Z advice section which will, hopefully, address more specific queries or problems relating to your collie's behaviour.

I hope that what you learn from this book will enhance your life with your own dog or dogs. So now let us begin the journey of enlightenment.

Note 1: The term 'collie' in this book refers to Border Collie, whether a pedigree dog or not, unless otherwise specified

Note 2: Dogs in this book are universally referred to as 'he' or 'him' for reasons of simplicity, as opposed to any gender bias. Thus most text, unless otherwise specified, can equally relate to female dogs.

Chapter One

THE ORIGINS AND HISTORY OF THE BREED

Where Border Collies come from; what makes them the dogs they are

Genes are truly fascinating things. I think this every time I watch my own Border Collies doing what Collies do. Every time I see them racing down the beach in winter, trying to push back the roaring waves and flying foam with a deft snap and a charge, or stalk the dry sand whipped up into snaking rivulets by the wind. Or when they suddenly lock on to an object with an intense and almost trance-like glare, willing it to move just one fraction, in order that they may chase it down again. Or when they play together, endlessly tearing round in circles, because every time one dog tries to run away in a straight line, another will attempt to intercept him with a shoulder slam and grab of the neck.

For generation after generation, my dogs and their ancestors have been driven by the same genetic impulses and programming, of a kind that has made their breed the finest livestock herding dogs the world has ever seen. It is likely that your own Border Collie shares exactly the same kind of legacy. I am totally in awe of the Border Collie's speed, agility, stamina, intelligence and almost supernatural levels of responsiveness and intuition. But how did these unique dogs originate in the first place, and why?

THE EARLIEST SHEEPDOGS
From the time man first domesticated sheep, he has needed dogs to help him control them, guard them and move them over large distances to different areas of pasture.

Some of the earliest general stock dogs were used by Celts who settled in Ireland between the fifth and first centuries BC, and it is thought that they coined the 'Collie' term, which in their language meant 'useful'. Only much later was 'Border' added to this name to distinguish a particular kind of dog who worked sheep on the harsher terrain of the English and Scottish borders.

It is hard to know what the early sheepdogs looked like, when so few written or pictorial records were kept. The Romans have been credited with introducing to Britain dogs who possessed that mesmerising 'eye', or intense stare, so typically found in Border Collies today. They also had other skills which, over time and via selective breeding, continued the process of refining sheepdogs into ever more specialised animals.

EVOLVING THE MODERN SHEEPDOG
Despite early genetic additions to native British herding dogs, it has to be remembered that, even up to the 19th century, farmers and shepherds led pretty remote and isolated lives. With no motor vehicles or railways, it was hard for them to travel longer distances to visit each other in order to compare their dogs, improve them through skilful interbreeding, or learn new and better sheepdog handling skills.

The pursuit of sheepdog trialling had been well established in England, Ireland, Scotland and Wales since the 1870s, but these events tended to be somewhat more regional or local affairs. It was not until the development of far better transport links, particularly railways, that trialling enthusiasts from all over the UK and Ireland could meet together.

This gave everyone the chance to see which breed lines were producing the best working dogs which, in turn, had a massive impact on the quality of sheepdog breeding, as well as the development of a type of dog that was deemed most ideal for livestock work.

Old Hemp: Considered by many to be the father of the breed.

WHY ARE COLLIES BLACK AND WHITE?

Although today Border Collies can come in many coat colour variations, the commonest breed colouring remains black and white or black, tan and white (tricolour).

Over the years I have heard many theories as to why farmers or shepherds would favour such colouring in their dogs but, to my mind, this is looking at the issue the wrong way round. In other words, the specific character, behaviour and working traits shepherds persistently chose and bred from in their dogs dictated what colour they would be.

Several decades ago, the Russian geneticist, Dmitri Belyaev conducted an experiment which showed how the selection of specific behavioural traits in animals can affect or dictate their physical appearance. Belyaev ran a huge silver fox fur farm in Novosibirsk, but found that the foxes, despite being bred for 80 years in captivity, were still very difficult to handle and still behaved mostly like 'wild' animals, showing extreme nervousness or aggression around people. They would also panic easily, injuring themselves by running blindly into walls or suffocating from stress-induced over-heating.

He undertook a ruthless breeding programme, selecting initially only the 10 per cent of foxes who displayed tamer behaviour for breeding, and culling the rest. Within just 18 generations, he had produced not only naturally 'tame' foxes, but also other less expected physical changes in them such as floppy ears and piebald (i.e. black and white) coats and tails which turned up at the end. Moreover, they began behaving increasingly like domestic dogs – barking, seeking out their keepers, reacting positively to people and answering to their names when called.

Such an experiment not only suggests how domestic dogs may have evolved from wolves, through similar natural selection by man, over the centuries, but also helps explain why Border Collies might look the way they do.

For the full range of colours in the Border Collies, see Chapter Three.

THE ISDS

The body that has had the greatest impact on the breeding of modern Border Collies is the International Sheep Dog Society (ISDS), based in Bedford, England. Founded in 1906, its original aim was to promote the work of shepherds and establish better stock management through the constant improvement of the shepherd's dog (i.e. Border Collie).

For most, however, its greatest achievement has been recording and securing for posterity, in the form of Stud Books and pedigrees, the bloodlines of all the best working sheepdogs throughout the past century and beyond. Some of these records go back to the 1890s, and have proved invaluable, not only to farmers and shepherds, but also others most interested in collies with proven working ability.

The Border Collie is a truly British (and Irish) creation; a product of these countries' long rural and cultural history, and generations of skill in breeding dogs. All the world's herding sheepdogs descend from the original gene pool of British ISDS dogs.

If you have a pedigree Border Collie, then ISDS registered dogs will always feature in his history. *For more information on the ISDS and pedigree collies, see Chapter Three.*

THE TEST OF TIME

I am the kind of collie nut who never tires of reading and studying dog pedigrees. It is totally thrilling to me to know that my own dogs descend from some of the best sheep-working dogs ever seen, including Supreme International Champions. Similarly, I get a buzz looking at pictures of legendary past dogs such as Old Hemp (featured), a chief founding dog of the modern collie breed. Over a century on, and so many Border Collies today still look much the same as him, including some of my own.

There are very few other pedigree breeds now of which you could say the same; dogs whose essential design, character and function has remained so relentlessly unchanged over so many years.

RESPECT AND HARMONY

Hopefully, this chapter has given you a greater insight into your own dog's roots, and enabled you to gain respect for his history and genetic legacy.

Respect for who or what your dog is, and where he comes from, is a vital first step to owning Border Collies successfully. It is important to remember the massive contribution collies have made to our own survival over the years, ensuring livelihoods for people with no other source of income other than livestock. Even today, there is still no machine that can work and control sheep more successfully than a Border Collie, particularly over more treacherous terrain, and I am yet to meet a shepherd who thinks there ever will be.

I personally respect and admire Border Collies more than words can say and I know that this, ultimately, lies at the heart of my relationship with my own dogs. So please do the same and also appreciate, at the same time, how many of your collie's instincts or quirks, which may sometimes baffle or exasperate you, were put there for reasons which are not the fault of the dog.

If you do not respect your Border Collie, you will never get the best out of him and it will always be harder to progress on to that ultimate level of understanding, where you and your dog co-exist and work together in perfect harmony; an ambition which, I hope, is shared by all readers of this book.

Having explored where Border Collies come from, in the next chapter we will look at all the different instincts, behaviours and personality traits that can be typical in dogs with sheepdog genes.

THE BORDER COLLIE: A MASTERPIECE OF GENETIC DESIGN

Size: *Big enough to suitably elicit respect of livestock, but not so big that the dog becomes far less agile or energy efficient. Breed Standard ideal height: 53cm (21 inches) for males, bitches slightly less. Some collies are bred for greater size and power; others will be slighter but exceptionally agile. Shepherds will use different sizes and types of dog for different kinds of sheep work.*

Back/spine: *Highly flexible, affording maximum agility when twisting, turning, jumping or changing positions at speed.*

Tail: *Length and design of tail, with upturned flick at the end, provides optimum balance and braking power for the dog and also acts like a superb rudder, particularly when turning at speed.*

Hindquarters: *Strong, muscular, with long-boned thighs; the powerhouse of the dog.*

Coat: *Dense woolly undercoat and longer, waterproof top coat to keep the dog suitably insulated in all weathers*

Movement: *Loose jointed, effortless, tireless, superbly energy efficient.*

Feet: *Oval, strong, well arched, providing superior shock-absorbing qualities and sure-footedness over all terrains. Thick hair between pads affords additional protection.*

Chest: *Good size and depth of ribs, affording optimum lung and heart room for sustained speed and stamina.*

Head: *Strong skull. Muzzle tapers straight back into head. Anatomical streamlining then continues to flow down the sides of the dog – from the neck and shoulders to the tail – giving him superbly aerodynamic movement.*

Brain: *Exceptionally sensitive, responsive, reactive and intelligent.*

Ears: *Highly mobile, alert, responsive. Ears optimum size and shape to funnel in sound waves, minimise the risk of injury and prevent infection through poor ventilation. Dense hair round ears, flowing backwards, limits the entry of foreign bodies into the ear canal.*

Eyes: *Bright, keen, alert. Oval in shape and closely fitted into skull. No eyelid droop or other eye exaggeration that can present problems in other breeds.*

Nose: *Extremely sensitive, to track down the position of any straying livestock. The same tracking skills are now increasingly used in pursuits like Working Trials and Search and Rescue work.*

Neck, shoulders, forequarters: *Muscular, powerful and flexible. The dog must often transfer his whole bodyweight to his shoulders when landing from a high jump, or when heading off livestock with a barge or slam. Powerful, flexible shoulders also allow the dog to sustain a 'crouch' position low to the ground when stalk-herding sheep*

Muzzle/teeth: *Strong jaws of optimum length and structure. Perfect bite for grabbing or gripping livestock when required.*

Chapter Two

THE MIND AND INSTINCTS OF THE BORDER COLLIE

Understanding behaviour that is typical of the breed

I am often asked by owners, what is typical or 'normal' behaviour in a Border Collie, and what is not? So I hope this chapter will help in some way to answer this question. I also aim to explain why collies can vary so much as individuals, and why some dogs will always be so much more difficult or challenging to own. Let us begin with classic 'working' instincts or sequences that are present to some degree in many, if not most, Border Collies. These are a skilful genetic adaptation, refined over many generations, of predatory behaviour used by wolves. The genius of this adaptation lies in breeding dogs who display sufficient predatory behaviour to control livestock, but with the attack/kill part of their hunting sequence removed or sufficiently subdued, to prevent animals being harmed.

Another special feature of the Border Collie is his ability to be 'split minded'. In other words, he is able to stop a predatory motor sequence mid flow, in response to a

A collie with a good 'eye' has the power to hold sheep so they appear to be incapable of moving.

handler's commands. There are really not many other dogs who can do this.

Working instincts and behaviour in collies tend to follow a distinct pattern, as follows:

EYEING

The intense 'eye' or glare that collies fix on a target that either moves, or they want to make move, is one of their most famous features. The whole sequence of sheepdog working behaviour always begins with eyeing a selected object of focus.

Eyeing behaviour is not just a sign of the dog marshalling high levels of concentration. It will also be used as a way to pressurise or intimidate livestock into moving where the dog wants them to go. Most shepherds highly value a dog who not only has a strong eye, but also knows how to stay focused while using it.

A dog who begins with a good eye, but then runs straight into a chase, with no period of sustained concentration/focus wherein a handler can direct his next movements, is not much good. Similarly, some dogs can have too strong an eye. Once fixed on to a livestock target they then become almost mesmerised and rooted to the spot, thus entering a somewhat unhelpful state of stalemate, with neither dog nor sheep able to move.

Normal eyeing behaviour in collies should not necessarily be confused with more neurotic and endlessly perpetuated habits like shadow chasing (see page 15).

SUSTAINED FOCUS

As just highlighted, once a collie has fixed his eye on a target, there should then come a period of high concentration/focus. At the same time, the dog should remain receptive to your own commands.

If you are an experienced collie owner and handler, without sheep for your dog to fix his focus upon, then you know that keeping your dog's eye and focus exclusively on you, instead, is critical. It is also the starting point to both controlling his later behaviour and achieving ever higher goals in training.

If you do not work hard to both secure and sustain your dog's 'working' focus on you, from day one, then all too rapidly it will escape elsewhere on to any number of other targets instead (e.g. birds, other dogs, cars, trains, cyclists, joggers), with potentially dire consequences. *All these issues will be covered in far greater depth later in this book.*

STALKING

Once a collie has eyed and focused on a specific target, he may then start stalking it. In experienced sheep working collies, stalking will not necessarily move straight on to chasing. The shepherd may just want his dog to keep moving slowly and close to the ground, advancing stealthily

Once a collie has focused, he will stalk, gradually creeping up on his 'prey'.

The instinct to chase is never far from the surface.

A collie will adopt a pattern of circular herding to put the sheep under pressure.

The lunge/nip reflex will be used to reinforce the collie's power over the sheep.

up to the sheep in order not to panic them. The dog will be trained to do this.

In less experienced or less well trained collies, stalking can too often progress straight into all out chasing after a target – much to the owner's horror if the target in question happens to be a car or a train.

The stalking phase is probably the last point where, with moderate levels of recall training, as laid out in later chapters, you should be able to prevent your dog progressing into a chase. Beyond that, unless you have undertaken relentless and more advanced anti-chase training, as also outlined later in this book, the further and faster your dog runs towards his chase target, the less receptive he will be to any attempt on your part to stop him.

CHASING

Chasing is in a collie's blood. These dogs were born to chase things and it gives them a buzz. The more they do it the more they want to do it, until the behaviour can rapidly get to the point of all-out addiction.

The thrill collies get from running fast, and pushing their athletic abilities to the limit, is a quality that makes them excel at modern pursuits such as Agility or Flyball. The most dangerous thing you can do, however, is let your collie's chase instincts spiral out of control. Not only have umpteen collies been killed or severely injured through pursuing traffic or trains, but if your dog starts chasing other animals or people, neither he nor you will be very popular – particularly if he then progresses to herding and nipping them.

THE CIRCULAR HERD

Collies may chase and then herd, or just be quite happy to start herding, anytime, anything that is feasibly herd-able. This can include you, your family, your cat, your visitors, your neighbours, other dogs or, if they are really desperate, a toy or a football that you actually *allow* them to herd or play with. A typical redirected collie herding instinct is also to try to charge past and ahead of you through doorways, and then round back to eye or stalk you. It can become very annoying unless suitably addressed.

The main criterion for something a collie herds is that it moves or can be made to move.

Classic collie herding follows a 'round and round' ever-tightening circular pattern. This can make the victim, within the circle, feel very pressurised, persecuted, trapped and vulnerable, as it is meant to because herding – much like all sheepdog working behaviour – is simply a genetic adaptation of the way wolves hunt their prey.

Given the problems herding can cause with the wrong targets, it is yet another collie instinct that has to be got on top of, as early as possible, with the right training, as outlined later in this book.

THE BODY SLAM

Herding in collies can often progress on to the body slam, where the dog uses his shoulder and weight of his body to try to push back or turn round any animal who is trying to escape or run away from his herding circle. Alternatively he may use:

THE CUT OFF

This time the dog will get his head over an animal's shoulder and attempt to halt it from escaping by grabbing its neck with his teeth. Which brings us on to:

THE LUNGE/NIP

Of all the instincts that are misunderstood in collies, or misinterpreted as some clear sign of 'bad' character, the lunge-nip reflex probably has to come top of the list. Thus the roots and original working purpose of this behaviour is explained in extensive detail in Part Two of this book, under *Aggression,* as well as advice being given on how you can keep the instinct under far better control in your dog.

VARYING LEVELS OF INSTINCT AND DRIVE

So far in this chapter I have looked at the genetic instincts that dominate a Border Collie's life and which, to a considerable degree, will also shape his character. This is because you cannot divorce the working traits bred into a collie from the type of personality that usually goes with them.

Levels of working instinct can vary tremendously among collies, according to their individual genetic input. People who have previously owned pet collies with low working instinct and a pretty laid back approach to life can often have a very rude shock when the next collie they get is bred very differently; i.e. extremely highly tuned, in terms of working energy and drive, and thus a lot more challenging to live with as a social companion.

Conversely, if you are a keen canine competitor, used to a dog with extremely high levels of working drive and responsiveness, you can get a similar shock when the next collie you get is far less driven or responsive, and thus far more of a challenge to both motivate and train for competition work. (See, *Where does a collie's 'working drive' come from? Chapter Seven, page 70).*

Not all collies will possess, or develop, the entire repertoire of working instincts and behaviour – i.e. eye, focus, stalk, chase, herd, lunge-nip. In some dogs only one or two of these instincts may become very strong, whereas the rest are only minimal or non-existent. Usually this is down not just to the individual genetic make-up of a dog, but also how much opportunity he has had in life to rehearse and repeat specific instinctive behaviours and find them rewarding.

THE COLLIE PERSONALITY

In the previous chapter, I highlighted how the selection of specific instincts and behavioural traits in sheepdogs may have also governed their physical appearance, as behavioural and physical characteristics can be commonly linked together, genetically. Equally, the deliberate breeding, and magnification, of specific behavioural and psychological traits in sheepdogs will also have a significant influence on their individual personalities or characters.

Many of the problems owners face with collies result from working instincts or personality traits that have become misused, been misunderstood or mishandled, or which are just too over-tuned genetically for the dog to lead a balanced life; an issue I shall keep returning to throughout this book. Individual collie problems related to working instinct /personality will also be extensively covered in Part Two.

First, however, let us look at some classic personality/character traits found in many collies, as well as suggestions as to how these might have originated. They do not all appear in every collie, and in different collies, depending on their individual breeding, the incidence of these behaviours can vary from mild to extreme – but you need to know about them.

OBSESSIVE BEHAVIOUR

Obsessive behaviour is one of the commonest components of collie character and derives from their original need to be tireless workers –happy to keep performing the same livestock manoeuvres from dawn to dusk, day in and day out, with little let up in concentration or energy.

Obsessionalism is the hallmark of all the world's highest achievers. Be they Olympic athletes, top footballers or multimillionaires, there is something in their nature that drives them harder and longer towards a goal and beyond the point where others may falter or give up. In a dog who must not only physically out manoeuvre, but also psychologically out manoeuvre, other animals for a living – many of whom are much larger than himself – a certain obsessive streak is also vital. When he confronts an animal and makes eye contact, it must be with the sense that he will never be the first to give in or back down.

If you want a dog to train to a high level, or work in competition, then a certain degree of obsessionalism in his character is also crucial in order to sustain his motivation and performance. It is, however, a quality that can so easily escalate out of control in collies with the wrong breeding or handling. It can also affect the intensity of any other problem the dog may have – i.e. fear or aggression problems become more obsessive in nature.

DO COLLIES SUFFER FROM OCD?

It has long been my belief that the neurotic, endlessly repetitive patterns of behaviour seen in many Border Collies are linked to obsessive/compulsive brain function which is genetic in origin, and this seems to be backed up by modern research into human Obsessive Compulsive Disorder at Cambridge University in the UK.

Where once the condition was thought to have external or environmental triggers, such as trauma or stress, scientists found that human OCD sufferers not only had differences in brain structure, among areas which controlled thoughts and actions, but that this difference also ran in families.

Of course there are always degrees of obsessive behaviour. The key to a good collie is having a dog with sufficient drive to respond well to training, but not so over-tuned that he finds it hard to settle or rest, or develops maniacally repetitive cycles of working behaviour. It can be very hard to live with dogs like these.

For more on this subject, see Obsessive compulsive behaviour patterns and Self-mesmerisers in Part Two.

'MANIC' BEHAVIOUR
People who say their collies are 'manic' or 'hyper' often haven't lived with a more highly driven working dog before and thus are making a somewhat unreasonable assessment or comparison. Alternatively, there are owners who persistently over-stimulate their dogs, or allow them to self-stimulate – usually inadvertently – to the point where they are so continually charged with adrenaline that they lose the ability to ever fully settle or think clearly.

Collies can certainly be excitable dogs, with some – much like obsessive behaviour – being more genetically extreme on this front than others. How you handle this tendency, however, is crucial, beginning in puppyhood, with teaching dogs basic emotional self-control (see Chapter Five).

A vast number of collie problems arise from dogs never being taught, or being allowed, to attain and sustain a fully balanced state of mind, and there will be much more on this subject throughout the book.

MISDIRECTED WORKING INSTINCT
Other than traffic, trains, other people, animals or birds, some of the weirder targets you may find your collie directing his working instincts on to include:
- Dust
- Earth
- Leaves
- Sticks/branches
- Rain
- Moving water e.g. ripples, waves
- Hoses, lawn mowers, wheelbarrows
- Vacuum cleaners, brooms, mops

It is all normal, but undesirable. Your dog simply needs better training, as outlined in this book, and to be taught to use his working instincts and energies in a more positive way

'BULLYING', PUSHY AND MANIPULATIVE BEHAVIOUR
Collies excel at both identifying and exploiting weakness. When weakness is shown in another animal, or person, they see it as a green light to move in, snatch some kind of advantage and then push it home. They cannot help it. It is what they are programmed to do.

Different collies will exploit weakness in different ways; some will become psychologically manipulative towards owners, others may become physical bullies. This will happen if you make the mistake of letting your dog discover, early on, that both manipulation and aggression to secure some advantage, or make you back off, can be highly rewarding.

Once this lesson has been learned, it may not be long before your dog is ruling if not terrorising a whole household, or just picking on members within it whom they deem to be the weakest and thus most vulnerable to intimidation.

In general, I have found that male collies are more prone to aggressive bullying and bitches more prone to psychological manipulation, but there will always be variations and exceptions. Either way, as a collie owner, it is immensely important to understand the different ways you may exhibit weakness to your dog, and prompt him to take advantage of it. This will not only make life much more difficult for you, as the dog becomes more bullying, pressurising or unruly, but ultimately your dog will lose respect for you. This, in turn, will have an impact on how well he responds to you, or your commands, in later training.

Later in the book, there will be much more on dealing with bullying or pushy collie behaviour, as well as how to get your relationship right with your dog, whether you are just one person, or living within a household.

SENSITIVITY/REACTIVITY
The collie brain is a highly sensitive mechanism, driving not only the dog's extreme intelligence, but also his exceptional levels of reactivity/responsiveness; traits so valuable in both livestock work and competitive pursuits such as Agility.

The mental reactivity of collies is what allows them to turn or stop at speed, in response to a sudden command, with some always being a lot better at this than others. But with such sensitivity can also come some downsides, which may include:

FEARFUL AND PHOBIC BEHAVIOUR
Chief among the problems that come with heightened sensitivity is a greater vulnerability to the effects of stress, and a higher tendency towards fearful or phobic behaviour. Collies can be noise sensitive, but they can also be life sensitive – suddenly getting it into their heads that some particular sight, object or experience is highly threatening

and thus must be escaped or avoided.

Over the years, things that I have seen collies take fright of can include anything from food mixers, ceiling fans and fly swatters to people in odd-looking hats. If the dog has more obsessive overtones to his personality, such a fear can then rapidly take over his life.

The level at which any individual collie perceives threat, and subsequently reacts to it, tends to have a genetic setting. But over and above this, the way collies are raised and socialised when very young, and how they are handled by owners when they first show fearfulness towards something or someone, can be critical in minimising the problem, as outlined in Chapters Four to Six. For more on this subject see *Fears and phobias* in Part Two.

ANKLE-NIPPING

Some collie owners may find that their dogs develop a habit of nipping/grabbing their feet or ankles, or those of other family members, or visitors, and wonder if this is a sign of a bad or aggressive dog.

In most cases, it is merely a normal, instinctive reaction to sudden movement; e.g. a person walking quickly past the dog, triggering the lunge-nip restraining impulses that collies traditionally use on livestock. It is also more likely to happen when the dog is already in a more excited/aroused mental state.

Alternatively, when owners are standing still, collies may nip their ankles, shoes or trouser hems in order to goad or pressurise them into moving again. This will typically happen when you are out on a walk, and stop to talk to someone. It is yet another misuse/misdirection of working behaviour which must be addressed early on, as outlined in later chapters.

SHADOW CHASING

Collies fixating on shadows, reflections or torch beams to an obsessive degree, almost as if they were hypnotised, or hypnotising themselves, is not to my mind normal, or a typical adaptation of their working behaviour, if only because you can also see this form of compulsive neurosis in other breeds.

Undoubtedly factors such as stress, boredom or under-stimulation can exacerbate the frequency or intensity of this behaviour, as can owners, who start off encouraging it because they find it amusing, and then don't know how to stop it once it has taken over their dog's life. Personally, I still think the main trigger for this behaviour is a fault in normal brain function, and thus would not want to breed from any dog who displayed it.

ANTI-SOCIAL BEHAVIOUR

Beyond early puppyhood, some owners can find that their collies become increasingly more fearful, anti-social, or even aggressive, towards other dogs, or people they know less well, including visitors to the home.

Some collies are genetically more predisposed towards this kind of behaviour, once older. However, it can also result from a mismanaged earlier upbringing, and an owner's inability to understand how critical it is to keep collies socially tolerant and flexible throughout their lives. This is particularly important once they develop the instinct to react warily or negatively to anything new, as can typically happen beyond four or five months of age.

Ways of preventing this kind of behaviour in your collie will be outlined later in this book.

RESPONDING TO ONLY ONE MASTER

Very often you will hear it said that collies are 'one man dogs'; in other words, their natural instinct is to want to follow and obey only one master. On the face of it, this would be a logical trait to breed into a sheepdog, in order that his mind remains fixed entirely on his handler and his work.

Principally, however, I believe that collies – like most dogs – are drawn to the strongest and most stable source of energy in a household, and people with whom they forge a special social/working bond through shared experiences such as daily walks and training. It is unlikely that all members of a particular household would emanate the same level of strength, authority and stability to a collie, or spend as much time exercising and training him. This makes it easier for the dog to choose who it is most worthwhile, or important, for him to co-operate with. There will be far more on the subject of your relationship with your dog in Chapter Five.

A GENETIC BALANCING ACT

Throughout this chapter, I have introduced you to many of the working instincts and other genetic traits that shape the character and personality of the Border Collie, in order that you may better understand these dogs.

However, the most important consideration regarding all these instincts and character leanings in a collie, is that they exist in the right balance. There really is no better canine companion in the world than a well-bred collie whose genetic make up – in terms of health, temperament, looks and working ability – has been perfectly calculated. By contrast, when vital elements of breeding are not so well calculated, storm clouds of future strife can loom on the horizon.

The difference between people getting a 'right' or 'wrong' collie usually revolves around what they did not know about collie breeding or breeders when it mattered. So, hopefully, the next chapter will equip potential owners with all the knowledge they need to find that perfect dog.

Chapter Three

GETTING A BORDER COLLIE PUPPY

What to look for; what to avoid

Sometimes the worst thing that can happen to any breed is that it becomes popular, or fashionable, as the result of an idealistic image fixed in people's minds which individual dogs then struggle to live up to in reality. This is as true of Border Collies as any other type of dog.

People have seen these dogs artfully working sheep, or doing amazing things in Obedience and Agility competitions, and fallen in love with them – not realising how much of what they have seen is down to expert breeding, training and handling. They then think they can get any Border Collie from anywhere, and it will live up to all their expectations.

I am here to tell you that it will not – and why it will not – and what you need to know to avoid getting the wrong dog, beginning with a better understanding of the importance of genes.

It is vital to study your Collie's genetic relations so you have some idea of what he may inherit.

GENES AND YOUR FUTURE DOG

Genes do not just influence the way any animal looks, but also the whole way it behaves, and dogs are no exception to this basic fact of life.

There are things about dogs you can always change. You can alter or modify what is going on in a dog's external environment. You can manipulate external influences to shape what a dog learns. But you cannot change the way a dog is fundamentally programmed, genetically, to think, act or react.

People can be good at picking dogs according to their genetic physical appearance, but less good at picking them – or not picking them – on the basis of their genetic personality or character. Yet there is nothing about a dog that will more influence the quality of your future life with him than this.

Everything from the way a dog moves, barks and eats, to his individual fear or aggression responses, and how good or not he may be at specific work or competitive pursuits, will be governed by his individual genes. So you always need to look for a collie whose whole genetic make-up, including character and behaviour, is most in line with what you want from a dog.

The reason why so many people become unstuck with their choice of dog is because of their failure to see in him inherited character traits that will greatly influence the way he behaves in later life. They may also unfairly blame themselves for faults or problems in their dog which are chiefly genetic in origin. Sadly there are some breeders around who are only too happy for them to do this, as it lets them off the hook. (See *Genetically motivated behaviour*, in Part Two, for more on this subject).

GENETIC DIFFERENCES

Every day I see collies who are all so incredibly different, not just in the way they look but also in the way they behave, due to their specific breeding.
Some will be kind, willing, patient dogs who are naturally superb at Obedience but less suited to Agility. Some will be good at Agility, but too fizzy for Obedience. Some will be sweet-natured dogs who are great pets, but also lazy and not much good at anything work orientated. Some will be sharp, snappy, hyper and obsessive dogs who are brilliant at competition work but lousy pets. Some will be very biddable and passive. Others will be pushy, aggressive and anti-social. Some will be beautiful but nasty. Others will be less beautiful but adorable. Some are exceptionally laid back, others nervous wrecks.

The one thing I can guarantee about all these dogs is that, in their past history, they had relatives who looked and behaved in exactly the same way. The Border Collie gene base, compared to that of other dog types, is relatively broad, which is why it can throw up so many variations and extremes within the overall spectrum of breed appearance and behaviour.

GENETIC REGRESSIONS

Traditionally, shepherds also needed different types of collie to do different types of livestock work; for some tasks they needed a powerfully built, commanding dog to hold animals at bay, for others they needed a smaller, lighter, speedier and exceptionally agile dog to herd closely round animals without getting injured.

Some of the more challenging behaviour traits seen in collies today may have come from working dogs who originally founded the modern Border Collie breed. Others – especially heightened aggression, fear, nervousness and reactivity - may date even further back than that; i.e. to the wolves, from whom all dogs descend.

Returning to the Belyaev experiment I mentioned in Chapter One (where many of the more challenging fearful/aggressive traits found in farmed foxes were eradicated by highly selective breeding); it can be just as easy to reintroduce these 'wilder' qualities back into dogs simply through more careless, or shorter-sighted breeding practices.

WASTAGE

Border Collies as a breed today are also routinely over-bred and less wisely bred, and from such cynical mass production for financial gain, comes an inevitably high level of wastage; i.e. dogs who are so genetically unsound that they fail to make the grade as either working animals or pets.

Many of these intrinsically less sound dogs will be offloaded on to more naïve owners within the pet market, or end up in rescue centres at some later stage in their lives. Some can become so unpredictable and dangerous in their use of aggression that they eventually have to be euthanased, often causing much heartache for the owners concerned.

Thus for all the reasons I have now outlined, you must choose a collie puppy with great care, following the advice provided throughout this chapter.

PEDIGREE AND NON-PEDIGREE COLLIES

We will start your puppy search with the different kinds of Border Collies you can get, as people often wrongly believe that all collies are pedigree dogs, when they are not. There are dogs with working pedigrees, registered with their relevant national sheep dog societies (such as the International Sheep Dog Society in the UK), and dogs with breed pedigrees, registered with their national Kennel Club. There are also dual registered dogs, i.e., in the UK, collies registered with both the ISDS and the Kennel Club. See *Collie Classifications*, for more details.

DIFFERENT GOVERNING BODIES

The Border Collie is the only British breed ruled by two different governing bodies in the UK, with which they can be registered according to their breeding. Often people believe that Kennel Club pedigree collies are somehow different from ISDS ones, purely because those from show lines or stock, in particular, can have a more glamorous look. This is simply down to selective breeding for specific physical assets over generations. Even the poshest KC show collie still dates his original ancestry back to ISDS dogs.

UNDERSTANDING COLLIE CLASSIFICATIONS

ISDS WORKING SHEEP DOGS/BORDER COLLIES

Most top working sheep dogs will be registered with a body known as the International Sheep Dog Society (ISDS) in the UK, or similar sheep dog societies in different countries. Sheep dog societies serve a particularly valuable function in ensuring that the bloodlines of top working dogs are preserved. ISDS dogs in the UK were also the founding ancestors of today's Kennel Club registered collies. A Border Collie can only be registered with the ISDS if both his parents are also ISDS registered dogs, or 'on merit' through passing a specific ISDS working test, or if owners can provide other evidence of proven sheep working ability.

KENNEL CLUB REGISTERED BORDER COLLIES

Border Collies were first awarded pedigree recognition by the UK Kennel Club in 1976. They can only be registered as Border Collies with the Kennel Club today if they are already ISDS registered, or if both parents are already KC registered. Many ISDS/KC registered Border Collies today will be bred for purposes like Showing, Agility, Obedience and Working Trials. Dogs whose breeding qualifies them to be registered with both the ISDS and the KC are known as dual registered.

Elsewhere in the world, Collies may be registered with other national/regional kennel clubs, such as the American Kennel Club (AKC), but in other countries registration will be with a working organisation (see below).

COLLIES WORLDWIDE

Many countries across the world will have organisations which exclusively register working Border collies (as opposed to those registered with national Kennel Clubs or associations). They will also keep separate stud books for dogs of working origin or pedigree.

In the USA this organisation is the American Border Collie Association (ABCA); in Canada, the Canadian Border Collie Association (CBCA); in South Africa, the South African Sheep Dog Association (SASDA) and in Australia, the Australian Working Border Collie Registry (AWBCR).

NON-PEDIGREE COLLIES

A large number of collies fall into this category. They may look like any other Border Collie, but if they are not registered with either the ISDS or KC, or both, then they are not pedigree dogs in the true sense of the word. They may, however, be eligble to compete in events such as Agility, Obedience, Flyball and Working Trials. For example, in the UK they can be entered on to the Kennel Club's special Activity Register, which enables them to compete.

The pedigree Border Collie, registered with the Kennel Club.

A working dog registered with the International Sheep Dog Society.

A non pedigree collie can be registered with the Kennel Club Activity Register so he can compete in canine sports.

GENETIC PRIORITIES AND FAULTS

It is important to bear the genetic diversity of collies in mind when you are looking for a breeder, as breeders breed collies for very different reasons and purposes. This, in turn, will directly influence the typical look and character of the dogs they produce.

Most good breeders will have a well-defined idea of the kind of dogs they want to produce and plan their breeding programme accordingly. So, whenever you meet or talk to a breeder, ask them what their breeding priorities are. In my own case, for example, when breeding dogs, I place my genetic priorities in this order:

1. Joint first: Kind, bomb-proof temperament and optimum health status.
2. Good level of working ability/focus/drive/responsiveness, with no manic or overly obsessive elements attached to it.
3. Good looks.
4. Dogs who are either black and white or black, tan and white (tricolour). There are many other colour variations people may like or prefer in collies (see, *Does a collie's colour matter?* page 22). I am simply a stickler for dominant characteristics in dogs

I also favour dogs from pure English lines and like a high level of out-crossing in breeding stock; i.e. an interbreeding ratio of not more than 10 per cent. Ten per cent or less is also the same interbreeding ratio now recommended for pedigree dogs by expert advisors on the Dog Advisory Council in the UK.

The out-crossing fixation is probably a gut thing I inherited from my grandmother, a woman of considerable dog breeding experience. It was always her belief that the closer you bred dogs the more faults in health or temperament would eventually ensue; if not immediately, then somewhere later down the line.

RISKIER BREEDING

Elsewhere in the pedigree dog world, the closer breeding of related dogs (or line breeding) remains popular, as this practice is more likely to provide animals of a consistent type, in terms of the way they look or perform.

It is a form of breeding, however, that requires considerable skill and in-depth knowledge of the particular bloodlines used to do successfully, otherwise some less pleasant genetic skeletons could come rattling out of the closet, health or temperament wise, as already highlighted.

The same can be true when breeders turn a blind eye to some health or temperamental fault in a dog's line because it has some other attribute they desire to breed on, e.g. a talent for sheep work, a show-winning look or a Champion's title in some other competitive pursuit. It can be amazingly easy to ruin the health and temperamental quality of whole lines of dogs this way.

JOINING THE GENETIC DOTS

I cannot tell you how common it is for people to bring me seriously fearful/aggressive collies and then suddenly tell me: "Well, actually his mother/father was rather nervous…" Then why did you get this dog in the first place? People need to get a lot better at joining the genetic dots, *before* they acquire problem dogs from problem parents.

Friends and acquaintances who are avid Obedience/Agility fans also constantly complain to me about the number of foul-natured collies now being churned out for these competitive events. Of course, it may well be that the dogs in question are simply stressed out or badly handled. But a dodgier genetic temperament should not be the inevitable price you have to pay for having a collie who is good at competitive pursuits.

Plenty of breeders can, and do, produce good competition dogs with exemplary temperaments who do not try to take your dog's head off when you pass them at a show. Why not get your dog from people like this instead?

LASTING HARM

I would urge anyone involved in collie breeding to think hard about the longer term implications of using dogs, or lines, featuring anything other than predominantly sound health and temperament, whatever else they might have going for them. Once the damage is done, there can be a pretty massive fall out for the future owners of your dogs, not to mention the harm that can be done to your own reputation as a breeder.

Sometimes breeders may do their best to prioritise good temperament and health in their dogs, only to be sabotaged by the dishonesty of others. They may use stud dogs or acquire brood bitches, for instance, who carry faults in their lines that no one has told them about. I have every sympathy for them. But to know of fairly serious faults in dogs (including unsound temperament), and still breed from them, is unforgivable.

Of course, there will always be some element of risk and luck – good or bad – involved in all dog breeding, due to the often complex nature of genetic inheritance, and anyone breeding or buying dogs has to accept this reality. But the most you can hope for is that the breeder did everything in their power to produce only the healthiest and soundest of dogs.

Lowest of the low in the collie breeding world are those who do not actually have any genetic priorities at all. Their only priority is to make money out of dogs by breeding as many of them as possible, regardless of any suffering they inflict along the way. You must know about these people in order to avoid a disaster.

FINDING THE RIGHT BREEDER

One of the most frustrating things that happens, when you are trying to help people track down a good collie breeder, is that they will say: "oh so and so got his collie from a pet shop", or so and so's collie emerged for sale out of the gloom of some stinking barn, crawling with fleas, or whatever…and yet: "he turned out to be *a lovely dog*".

Inside you want to scream because I cannot tell you how lucky this is. Luck-wise, this is the equivalent of stepping out on to a busy motorway and not being hit by a car. Most people are not so lucky when they get collies from such places or backgrounds. Most people end up with dogs who have serious health problems, or serious psychological and behavioural problems – or all of these things. Trust me, I deal with these dogs all the time.

You cannot divorce the quality of the dog you get from the quality of the person who has bred him, and raised him during his most formative weeks of life.

If you are really lucky, you will know someone personally who breeds fantastic Border Collies. Over time you have got to know both the breeder and his or her dogs and everything about them strikes you as ideal. They are healthy, happy, sweet-natured dogs, raised and owned with love and devotion. Thus, getting a puppy directly from them is a virtual no-brainer. Alternatively, you may come across somebody with a really lovely collie and ask them where they got it from. This will, hopefully, lead you to a breeder who produces equally lovely collies related to the one you saw.

If you are not so lucky on either front, you must proceed with greater caution. Having already covered where you should not get a collie from, let us now consider other options.

FARMS

In the main, it is not advisable to get a collie puppy destined to be a pet from a working farm – not to be confused with the puppy farms/mills mentioned later on page 27 – unless you really know the farmer and his dogs well, and the puppy in question *has been raised in a domestic home* (a vital consideration). This is because if the puppy comes from working parents, he is more likely to have a stronger working temperament and character.

Many problems seen in farm bred collies, turned pets, can arise less from genetically dodgier temperaments than insufficient understanding of the dog's inherent working psychology and instincts, and lack of training by an owner from puppyhood onwards, of a kind outlined in later chapters. But, all in all, they can be harder work.

Increasingly today, owners are developing a keen interest in working their collies with sheep, and there are now many training courses where they can do this. If you are such an owner, a dog from a working background may be your best bet, as long as he has a temperament you can live with the rest of the time, when he is not working.

Sometimes Agility or Obedience enthusiasts will get collies from farms in the belief that this, in itself, should guarantee them a dog with great promise in these disciplines. Not necessarily. A dog with a long genetic history of working sheep is not the same as a dog with a long genetic history of being good at Agility or Obedience, as this usually calls for some extra level of refinement in his breeding.

A farm-bred or ISDS dog may not possess the more glamorous physical features seen in collies from show lines, as they have fundamentally been bred for what they can do, as opposed to how they look.

VARYING QUALITY

Farm-bred collies can vary greatly in overall quality. If sheep farmers, for instance, have produced puppies from top ISDS working dogs, is it likely that they would be selling them off cheaply at their gates to all comers? They will be selling them instead to other farmers or shepherds, often for a considerable price; sheepdogs of the highest calibre can now command prices of over £6000 in the UK. They are, after all, about the most vital asset a shepherd can own.

A lot, if not most, collies sold off cheaply at farm gates tend not to be ISDS registered dogs. They may not even descend from parents who are good sheep workers, but failed sheepdogs instead, who are only being bred from to make some extra cash. Some of these failed sheepdogs may have rearing backgrounds and temperaments that will completely ill-suit them to life as a domestic pet. Sometimes puppies advertised at farm gates as 'Border Collies' will have a father who is not even a pure Border Collie at all, and if you never see him, you will never know. So please do be aware of all these considerations.

PEDIGREE BREEDERS

By now you may be thinking, well perhaps I should go to a breeder of Kennel Club registered pedigree dogs instead, as a safer bet. But is it? Not always. One of the biggest misconceptions held among the public is that a KC pedigree dog is somehow a naturally superior product to a non-pedigree dog.

Certainly, as I write, there are no compulsory requirements, in terms of health tests, quality of rearing environments etc. laid down by many national kennel clubs (including the UK's) as a condition for dogs being registered with them, and no inspection programme by the KC of pedigree breeders' establishments. There are schemes where individuals can sign up to a commitment to superior standards but this – again, as I write –remains voluntary, as opposed to compulsory.

HOW TO USE YOUR COMMONSENSE

When looking for a pedigree Border Collie puppy, it is assumed that you have already decided what role you want

DOES A BORDER COLLIE'S COLOUR MATTER?

Collies today can vary enormously in coat length and texture, and also colour. Over and above the more traditional black and white or tricolour (black, tan and white) dogs, there are also red and whites, red and blue merles, sables, and dogs with diluted coat colourings such as blue or 'lilac'.

The trouble with more novel collie coat colours is that people can view these superficial characteristics in a dog as a higher priority than far more important considerations, such as his overall health and temperament.

Black and white.

Over the years I have heard many theories linking different collie coat colours to different kinds of temperament. Some of the less usual colours in collies, especially sable, can be astonishingly beautiful, but a dog's beauty should never distract you from the quality of what is going on in his head. Of course, it's always possible to have more unusually coloured collies with superb temperaments and robust health – as the classic old saying goes: 'no good dog was ever the wrong colour'.

Blue and white.

Tricolour.

Blue merle

Red merle

Red and white.

Sable.

Blue sable.

COLLIE HEALTH SCREENING

Collies in the main are a relatively healthy breed but can suffer from some hereditary disorders you should know about. Those that can be tested or screened for in dogs are:

- Hip dysplasia
- Deafness
- Collie Eye Anomaly
- Primary Lens Luxation (PLL)
- Central Progressive Retinal Atrophy (PRA)—Recently reclassified in collies as Retinal Pigment Epithelial Dystrophy (RPED)
- Predisposition towards glaucoma (Gonioscopy testing)
- Ceroid Lipofuscinosis (CL)
- Trapped Neutrophil Syndrome (TNS)

All the above can be tested for in the parents of puppies. Puppies still need to be tested individually for deafness. If breeders have done such tests they should be able to show you proof in the form of original documentation from the relevant testing organisations or individuals. For far more detail on all these conditions, plus others suffered by collies, see Chapter Twelve.

words, '*health*' and '*temperament*'. Never mind what the puppies' relatives have won at shows, or what colour they are, or how near a breeder happens to live to you. Nothing will have a greater bearing on the life you will have with a dog than how healthy he is and how essentially sound his temperament is. So look particularly for a breeder's emphasis on these two all-important criteria – and the more emphasis the better

The health status of dogs can be backed up, to some extent, with relevant certificates or screening results, although not all important hereditary conditions in collies can, as yet, be tested for (see *Collie health screening*, opposite). The trouble, of course, with advertisements or websites declaring that dogs have been 'bred primarily for good temperament' is that just about every breeder says this, including those who have bred some of the most unsound dogs I have ever met.

This suggests some breeders are either not being too truthful, or they do not know how to breed dogs of truly sound temperament, or that they have lived so long with temperamentally unsound dogs they can no longer recognise what a sound one is. Either way, you will need to visit a breeder yourself to make sure.

FIRST IMPRESSIONS
The first contact you have with a breeder can be very significant. If you ring up a breeder and the very first thing they tell you is how many puppies they have got for sale, and how much they cost, this is not very promising, as it is rather indicative of where their priorities lie – i.e. making money. Thus it would be wise not to go any further. There will be other, better breeders.

The first thing any good breeder should want to talk about is *you*. They should want to know things like whether or not you have owned a Border Collie before, how much you know about the breed in general, what provisions you will make for a dog's overall daily care, exercise and training, and how long the dog is ever likely to be left alone. They will want to know if you have young children, other dogs or animals, whether you have a garden big enough for such an active dog, and whether that garden is escape proof.

The list of enquiries should go on and on and, ideally they may also want to come to vet you and your home personally. Please do not be offended. This is a sign of someone who really cares about their dogs, which often, in turn, can be reflected in the quality of them, too.

HOME REARING
If you want a Border Collie to live with you in your home, make a point of asking the breeder where he or she mainly keeps and raises their puppies – i.e. outside or inside their home. If it is outside, this is not the breeder for you, as puppies raised inside a home will always have a massive

this dog to fill in your life – i.e. show dog, Obedience dog, Agility dog, personal companion, family pet – or a combination of these things. This, in turn, should determine the kind of breeder you start looking for, as different pedigree breeders may specialise in dogs for different functions.

Your next step may well be to get a list of recommended breeders from a local breed club or society, or to comprehensively surf the Internet. In the latter case, guess what? There are breeders' websites galore. Everybody seems to have exactly what you want and everybody seems to breed the most wonderful, amazing Border Collies in the world.

This is not so helpful. So next look for those two magic

advantage over those raised outside when it comes to making well adjusted domestic companions.

You do not want a collie puppy who wets himself or has a near nervous breakdown the second anyone opens a cutlery drawer, puts on the washing machine or TV, or brings strangers in through the front door, simply because he has not experienced such things during his earliest weeks of life.

Even if a breeder says he or she 'regularly brings puppies into the house', this is not good enough – at least not for me.

VISITING A BREEDER

Once you have had a promising first phone call with a breeder, the next step will be to visit them. You need to know the kind of conditions and environment in which any future puppy of yours will have been raised. There can be a tendency in adverts, and on websites, for people's dogs to be photographed beautifully groomed and against a backdrop of spacious rural splendour. Then you visit them and find the same dogs shoved into kennels and crates all over the place, in rather less spacious surroundings and in somewhat less good fettle.

If you arrive at a breeder's premises and find umpteen stressed and noisy dogs packed into indoor crates or cramped outdoor kennels and living in fairly squalid conditions, you may sensibly conclude that this kind of battery farm background is not one you would want any dog of yours to come from. So do not go any further. Find another breeder.

I cannot tell you how common it is for people to visit a breeder with an absolutely filthy living environment – dirt and dog muck everywhere, every available surface covered in clutter and grime, pups sitting in their own urine, stale food and dirty water, flies buzzing around (you are getting the picture) – and *still* think this is an okay place to get a dog from. Are they *mad*?

The first thing such an environment tells you about the person in charge of it is that he or she is not overly bothered by basic principles of hygiene and order, which are critical factors in the healthy rearing of any animal. Moreover, if he or she is so sloppy about such fundamentally essential things, how much more care and effort are they likely to have put into other equally crucial concerns that cannot be so easily spotted by the naked eye – such as the optimum genetic selection of the puppies' parents, relevant health screens undertaken on these parents, painstaking early socialisation of the puppies, or even just regularly worming them?

WHY WE CAN'T RESIST PUPPIES

As soon as you enter a place as described above, it is best to make your excuses *quickly* and leave. Do not hang

around to meet the puppies because as soon as you see them, you will forget about the kind of place they are coming from, and what impact this is likely to have on them later as individuals. Or you may feel a desperate need to rescue them.

Why do so many sensible people lose the logical part of their brain when faced with cute, fluffy puppies, and especially those with a more pathetic looking air? The answer is simple – oxytocin. Oxytocin, sometimes referred to as 'the cuddle chemical', is the hormone responsible for parental nurturing behaviour in animals, and dogs have been found to trigger the production of it in humans. This is what gives people that gooey, affectionate and protective feeling when handling puppies.

It is also a reaction less scrupulous breeders will exploit, and why they want you to come and look at puppies as soon as you arrive. Good breeders do not do this. Good breeders will not let you see puppies until they have first given you a grilling, in order to gauge your suitability for one of their dogs.

If there is one extra thing I cannot bear about bad breeders – and you will often witness this stunt among puppy farmers – it is the way they go around feigning mock affection and concern for their dogs, for the benefit of would-be buyers. Any fool can see through it – you just have to look at the fear and apprehension in their dogs' eyes. But it is still a truly nauseating spectacle. I guess they must just not do oxytocin on any level.

THE PRICE OF PITY

The urge to rescue a neglected, timid and sad little puppy raised in dire circumstances can be very strong. People may wonder: what is going to happen to him if I don't take him? It is a real moral dilemma which I completely understand, especially if a breeder tries to ramp up the emotional blackmail by threatening to destroy any unsold puppies, which is not unknown.

But also consider, what is going to happen to the puppy if you *do* take it? It could develop health or behavioural issues which break your heart. Further, the more puppies an unscrupulous breeder can sell and offload in this way, the more they will keep breeding, and the more suffering will be visited on other dogs.

There is really only one way to end this kind of dilemma, and that is to stop allowing the wrong people to breed dogs.

GOOD AND LESS GOOD PEDIGREE BREEDERS

In the main I would divide pedigree collie breeders into the following four categories:
• First, there are wonderful, dedicated people who care desperately about the quality of their dogs, and the homes they go to, and do everything in their power to

get their puppies off to the best possible start in life.

- Second, there are people who might start off with the best of intentions, but then become overwhelmed by the ever-increasing number of dogs they keep or amass. As a result, they lose their ability to rear or care for them all sufficiently well. Similarly, the more dogs they produce the less fussy they are able to be about the homes they go to.
- Third, there are other fairly well meaning people who simply lack the knowledge or skill to breed and rear consistently high quality puppies.
- Finally there are people who care a lot less, and will happily compromise the physical and psychological welfare of dogs in order to fulfil their own personal needs and ambitions, including stark financial gain.

MORE SUITABLE BREEDERS

After warning you away from less good breeders what, by contrast, should you be looking for in a more suitable breeder? What are the more telltale signs, in other words, of a *good* breeder, on top of an aforementioned keen interest in your own suitability for one of their pups before they allow you to see them?

Well, the home does not have to be pristine and spotless, as, goodness knows, raising puppies takes a lot of time and can be quite a messy business. But you do want to see good basic standards of hygiene applied to the area where a bitch is kept with her puppies. Bedding should be clean, and the puppies should also be clean – not caked in stale food, faeces or urine. Similarly, any puppy wee or poo should be instantly cleaned up.

THE LOVE

Most of all in a breeder, you want to see that the *love* is there. You want to see someone who has a really close, caring and affectionate relationship with any resident dogs they possess.

A person who really cares about their dogs will go on and on about them; why they are so special, why they chose the dogs they did to breed from, what health screening procedures have been done on them, how they intend to socialise their puppies. In fact, rather than having to ask a breeder endless questions, you might have difficulty getting a passionate breeder who cares for their dogs to shut up, such is their enthusiasm for what they are doing.

I really like this in a breeder. I like someone who shows a real passion not just for their own dogs, but for their breed as a whole. By contrast, I do not want to see a breeder who is principally interested in making a sale, or who reacts to your questions with impatience or irritability.

THE REACTION OF THE PUPS

I want to see a breeder, additionally, who shows real respect, affection and consideration for the mother of their puppies, and the puppies alike. Watch carefully. Are the puppies clearly thrilled to see the breeder and visitors walk into a room, or do they look quite wary, subdued or overly submissive? Obviously the pups would have to be over a month old for such reactions to be most evident.

If the pups look wary or barely register the presence of the breeder and visitors, this makes you wonder how much positive interaction they have had, to date, with people – apart from being fed.

Happy, healthy, well-socialised little Border Collie puppies should go berserk with excitement when they see their breeder, especially if they are bringing some new playmates – i.e. visitors – in tow. This is because all their previous experiences of the breeder, and visitors, have been nothing but positive, and they have learned to find the company of people highly rewarding.

THE MOTHER

Much is often made of the fact that you should always see the mother, with her litter of puppies, because her behaviour – either nervous or aggressive – could be an indication of her offspring's future temperaments.

There is certainly an element of truth in this, but there are also other things to bear in mind. The first being that pregnancy, and the exhausting daily process of feeding and nurturing young puppies – especially a particularly large litter – can place enormous stresses, both physical and psychological, on a bitch. If you add to this the huge hormonal upheaval that is going on in her body after having pups, then you cannot always expect to see any dog in this situation at her best, or most sociable.

I actually think it's quite understandable for a bitch to look wary when strangers come to handle her puppies, especially while they are still very young and vulnerable i.e. under a month old. Overt aggression by a mother dog towards visitors who approach, however – such as teeth baring, growling and snapping – is a far less desirable thing to see as, apart from anything else, it is not the best kind of example she could be setting her own puppies.

To get a better idea of a bitch's true temperament, ask the breeder to take her away from her puppies for a little while, to give her a break, and in order for you to see how she behaves with you when the puppies are no longer there. If she looks much chirpier, and comes to greet you in a confident and friendly manner, with her tail wagging, it is likely that she is normally a pretty sweet-natured dog If she remains highly aloof and nervous, however – or worse still, is aggressive in any way – this is not the kind of temperament you want to see in the mother of a puppy you are thinking of acquiring.

THE FATHER

Mothers, however, it should always be remembered, are only one part of a much bigger genetic picture, as far as puppies are concerned. What about the father of the litter?

I am frequently amazed at how little interest or curiosity many owners possess about the father of a litter of puppies. After all, he has contributed 50 per cent of his own genes to them, and thus is just as likely to influence how they turn out.

If you are really lucky, a breeder will own the mother and father of a litter, and you will be able to meet both of them. You will see what kind of temperament they both have, as well as the overall 'look' they possess which, in turn, will give you a better idea of the kind of dogs they are likely to produce.

If, as is more often the case, the sire of the puppies is not owned by the breeder, you should ask to see a photo of him, and also his pedigree (more on reading pedigrees later).

Also ask for the phone number and/or email address of the owner of the sire, so that you can gather more detail about the kind of dog he is, as well as the type of puppies he may have previously produced. Most good breeders will offer you this information without you having to ask.

WHERE NOT TO GET A COLLIE PUPPY FROM

Be wary of getting a collie puppy from any of the following sources:

FROM A PET SHOP/STORE

Chances are that the puppy in question will have been transported many miles there from a puppy farm, or puppy mill as they are known in the USA, and will have had the most appalling start in life. Puppy farms are grim, commercial establishments where bitches are often kept in dreadful conditions, purely to turn out litter after litter for cash. Many puppy farm-bred dogs develop serious health and behavioural problems due to being the products of persistent interbreeding or over breeding, twinned with hideously deprived and stressful early upbringings. They also have a far higher risk of early mortality for the same reasons. The most troubled and psychologically damaged collies I have ever seen have all come from puppy farms

THROUGH SMALL ADS IN LOCAL OR TRADE PAPERS

Approach with caution, as these can just be another way puppy farmers offload their stock. Be particularly suspicious of anyone offering a wide number of puppies for sale of whatever colour/sex you like. Be even more suspicious if they offer to deliver a pup to your door, or to meet you with it somewhere like a motorway service station. This is a classic ploy to stop you knowing the appalling place your pup really came from, or seeing that its mother is a pitifully undernourished and unkempt wreck who spends her time

Puppies are irresistible, but you must not let your heart rule your head.

knocking out puppies for money in a filthy, dark shed, or that she is a dog with a seriously unsound temperament (is it any surprise?) – or all these things together.

THROUGH AN AD ON THE INTERNET

Again, approach with extreme caution. Is the advertiser a recognised/recommended pedigree breeder? Do they offer you a dog, no questions asked? This is not good. Can you visit the puppy's family and see where and how he is being reared? If not, then again this is not good. Sometimes people use the Internet to offload, for money, dogs or older puppies that have proved to be a problem. I know a couple who got an eight-month-old collie puppy this way. Within days he had badly attacked them both and the original owners refused to take him back or refund their money. Eventually they were forced to euthanase the dog and it broke their hearts. So do be warned.

DOMINANT AND RECESSIVE CHARACTERISTICS

It is equally important to see and know about other relatives of a Border Collie puppy because one of the best bases on which to choose a pedigree dog is according to the laws of genetic probability; i.e. the sort of dog that is most likely to be produced by two genetic lines.

What I mean by this is that in every line of dogs, types of dogs will emerge who are more typical of that line than others, and are therefore genetically *dominant*. Other types may crop up on a far less frequent basis within the same lines and these, by contrast, will be viewed as more genetically *recessive*. Recessive traits in a line can include anything from a more unusual coat or eye colour to the whole nature of the way a dog behaves.

Where people often go wrong in choosing puppies – or parents of them, come to that – is not understanding enough about dominant and recessive genetic characteristics in lines of dogs.

A breeder can make the mistake of thinking, for instance, that a particular dog – in terms of looks, temperament or working ability –is a dominant (or very common) example of his line when he is, in fact, a far rarer, or more recessive, phenomenon. This means that less dogs of his type will be produced genetically in a line, and more of another type, which may have less superior looks, temperament or working ability.

STUDYING GENETIC RELATIONS

A classic example of misjudging or misunderstanding dominant/recessive features in dogs' genetic lines is when people mate, for example, two Show Champions together or two Obedience Champions, imagining they will automatically get similarly exceptional offspring. They are then very disappointed when more mediocre puppies ensue, which happen to be far more typical of, or dominant within, the lines the parent dogs came from.

Without trying to blind anyone with science, I cannot stress too strongly how much you can improve your chances of getting a really great dog through seeing as many of his immediate genetic relations first. This means on both sides of the family tree – not just mother and father, but also grandparents, brothers and sisters, cousins, aunts and uncles. The more related dogs you see with qualities you desire, on top of the basic essentials of sound health and temperament, the more likely it is that you will end up with a dog with similar characteristics.

Most good breeders with any real pride in their dogs should willingly aid you in this research, putting you in touch with the right people, as well as people who own other puppies they have bred, so that you can compare notes. If, alternatively, they show no interest in helping you on this front, you would have to wonder why, or what they might be trying to hide.

THE PUPPIES

Now let us look in more depth at individual puppies themselves.

A normal sized litter for a Border Collie is usually between four and seven puppies. This does not mean you cannot get great puppies from smaller or bigger litters. The snag with a smaller litter is that, with fewer litter mates, puppies do not always get the best grounding in how to communicate and socialise competently with their own kind.

This is particularly the case when there is only one puppy in a litter. Alternatively, if you have only two puppies in a litter, one will inevitably be a stronger character and become the top dog while the other assumes the role of the underdog. The adoption of these roles so early in life could govern much of how these puppies relate to other dogs when they are older and throughout the rest of their lives.

A really good breeder will be alert to these potential problems, and will do much to overcome them through skilfully controlling the social development of the puppies they have from day one – a vital subject I will cover in depth a bit later.

No matter how many collie puppies there are in a litter, all of them should look happy and in the peak of good health

GOOD AND BAD SIGNS IN PUPPIES

WHAT YOU WANT TO SEE:
- Puppies raised in a loving, warm, clean and cosy domestic home.
- Tremendous affection between breeder and their dogs.
- Lively, wriggly, chunky, well-nourished puppies with bright eyes and sleek, glossy coats.
- Perfect bites. A perfect bite in a puppy, or dog, is when the top incisor teeth just overlap the lower ones and the top and bottom canine teeth neatly interlock in a 'scissor' fashion. A bad mouth, e.g. cleft palate or undershot/overshot jaws, is a serious fault in a collie, leading to potential pain and discomfort, excessive drooling and trouble eating. Note: If a puppy is born with a bad mouth, it will not correct itself when the adult teeth come through. Beware a breeder who tells you otherwise.
- Puppies showing a clear willingness to meet visitors and interact and play with them.
- Puppies showing no evidence of worms, fleas, diarrhoea or eye or nasal discharges.
- Plenty of space for the puppies to play in and sources of stimulation – e.g. toys, items to chew.

WHAT YOU DON'T WANT TO SEE:
- Undernourished, weak-looking puppies.
- Puppies with dry, dull and poor quality coats.
- Puppies caked with their own urine or faeces.
- Puppies with eye or nasal discharges.
- Puppies with light and bloated – as opposed to firm and rounded – tummies, which is indicative of worms.
- Puppies who are listless, lethargic or excessively timid.
- Puppies who are uneasy about interacting with people or being picked up by them.
- Puppies who do not seem at ease in their domestic home environment. Is it likely they have been reared outside

instead, and just brought indoors for the benefit of visitors?

- Puppies and resident dogs who show wariness or fear towards a breeder.

ASSESSING PUPPY TEMPERAMENTS

When acquiring a puppy, most people have an idea of whether they want a dog or bitch. Each can have different plusses and minuses as they grow, in terms of how they behave, as well as other issues discussed in more detail later (see Chapter Nine).

Over and above this, however, there appears to be a modern preoccupation with would-be owners doing their own puppy temperament tests. They may have heard advice, for example, that if you pick the really outgoing puppy in a litter who rushes towards you, this could turn out to be a very dominant or strong minded adult dog. Conversely, if you pick the shy puppy who runs off and hides when you visit, this could prove to be a rather nervous adult dog.

The problem I have with such advice is that it begins with the presumption that such extremes of temperament are inevitable, if not normal, in a litter of pups, when I don't think they should be. I have bred a number of Border Collie puppies, but never yet had one who *doesn't* rush up to new visitors with great excitement, or one who shows the remotest concern when they approach. Can they all be intrinsically dominant when merely weeks old? I don't think so. Confident maybe, but who wouldn't want or expect that in a Border Collie?

MERITS OF THE CONFIDENT PUPPY

If you are seeking a dog to work in competition, confidence is the first thing you want to see in him when young, as well as a noted keenness for human interaction; for example a puppy who keeps coming to you for attention, and who brings toys to you to share with him. Dogs who make highly positive associations with people, very early on in life, will always be easier to train.

A confident puppy is not the same as one who is bullying and domineering; this should really be fairly clear to see, as should an exceptionally nervous puppy. For instance, a classic, bullying puppy will be constantly pushing other litter mates around and refusing to share things with them. But over and above these obvious character traits, I do not think anyone can know a litter of puppies better than the person who bred them and lives with them 24/7.

If I wanted a fuller temperamental assessment of a puppy in a litter, I would ask his breeder. If you feel that what a breeder is saying is at odds with what you are seeing, take a more experienced dog person along with you to make a better judgement.

Like many breeders, I am always more than happy to let a would-be owner do their own special temperament tests on my puppies, providing they do not cause any distress, and make their individual assessments. But I remain sceptical as to how accurate these can ever be in predicting a dog's future character. This is because so many of the events and experiences that ultimately shape a dog's character occur over a far longer time span; i.e. at least up to, if not beyond, adolescence. How an individual puppy is reared and handled by a new owner can also make a massive difference.

PLAY BEHAVIOUR

People will often get unnecessarily alarmed, or misjudge the true character of puppies, through not appreciating the part aggression can play in their early discovery behaviour. It is only through lots of teethy grabbing, tumbling and horseplay with other puppies that puppies learn vital life lessons such as bite inhibition. Other puppies will tell them, with a squeal, when they are biting too hard and this sets limits on how they interact with other dogs later.

The same is true when puppies keep nipping people's hands or clothes; it is purely instinctive behaviour that can easily be curtailed with the right approach, as outlined in the next chapter.

Puppies need to keep doing and trying behaviours which produce consequences they can then learn from; play aggression is part of this. Collie puppies in whom aggression becomes a more serious issue will be covered in the next chapter. Also note there is extensive advice on aggression in collies in Part Two of this book.

POSSESSIVE BEHAVIOUR

If possible, try to see the behaviour of puppies when they are feeding collectively or playing with toys. Puppies who are happy to share food or toys without conflict are always a good sign. By contrast, puppies who become extremely aggressive and possessive and fight over these things are a less good sign. It is something a breeder should always look out for, and address appropriately (see *Aggression* in Part Two).

THE EARLY FEAR PERIOD

It can be easy for people to misjudge a sound puppy as being nervous through not knowing enough about young dogs' first or earliest fear periods. Though fear is a vital survival response in all animals, the instinct to react fearfully to new or strange things is not something they are actually born with. Instead, fear perceptions and reactions will begin kicking in at different times in different animals, according to their normal phases of early psychological and social development.

Typically puppies enter their first fear period at around six to eight weeks of age, though in collies I believe this often begins earlier. This first onset of a fear response in puppies prompts them to react more warily to newer sights, sounds and experiences.

If you are not sure how much of a puppy's behaviour is down to the effects of this normal developmental phase, which is transient in most cases, and how much is indicative of his true character, then try to see the puppy first at about a month old, and then at regular weekly or two weekly intervals. This will give you a much better idea of his normal character. There will be much more on first and second fear periods in collies in later chapters.

THE IMPORTANCE OF EARLY SOCIALISATION

As previously mentioned, collies, as a breed, are not the most naturally sociable of dogs, and can be easily unnerved by experiences that other less sensitive breeds might take in their stride. The fear response can kick in very young – well under six weeks of age – and once a collie pup has had a bad or frightening experience, he can stubbornly retain it in his mind.

It is possible such traits in collies originate from the wolves they evolved from, and with which they can share so many similar characteristics.

THE VITAL EARLY SOCIAL WINDOW

The onset of fear behaviour in wolves is thought to begin when they are around 19 days old. Studies have shown, in turn, that if they are not introduced to people before this time, they will forever after be wary or fearful or them.

Domestic dogs, in general, are thought to have a much longer time window for forming new social relationships – i.e. from two to 16 weeks of age. This is also the optimum time for them to successfully integrate into a particular living environment and develop relevant social skills. In collies, however, I have seen this time window close much earlier than in other breeds and similarly, as just mentioned, the fear response will kick in that much earlier.

Thus, if collies are destined to be pets, not only do their genes need to be slanted towards more trusting/outgoing behaviour, but their socialisation can also never begin early enough. Virtually from the moment the pups are born they are learning, and a breeder's job is to start them learning the right things at the right time.

A BREEDER'S RESPONSIBILITY

It seriously concerns me how often both breeders and owners alike will assume that the socialisation of a dog is primarily an owner's responsibility. It is not. A breeder will have a puppy for eight weeks or more before he goes to a new home. These earliest weeks of life comprise the most crucial first phase of a dog's social development, wherein lessons he is taught, or not taught, may critically affect his later behaviour and ability to psychologically cope with the life that lies ahead of him.

Puppies who go to new homes without first experiencing important early life lessons often do so completely handicapped, and in an ongoing state of insecurity, stress, panic or fear.

For instance, I think it is totally unacceptable that a puppy's first experience of car travel – and possibly car sickness – should be twinned with owners coming to take him to a new home, which is a big enough trauma in itself. If you add to these twinned traumas the fact that the puppy may also be going through his initial early fear period, you get a picture of the potential psychological damage that can be inflicted on a young dog in a very short space of time.

As outlined in the next chapter, breeders who do not give their puppies the right start in life make it that much harder for owners to settle them into their new homes and lifestyles. Some collies never fully recover from the impact of poor socialisation during their first months of life. That is why it is so vital.

HOW GOOD SOCIALISATION WORKS

The art of socialising puppies during their earliest weeks of life does not lie in just aimlessly exposing them to a wide range of experiences, but also in being conscious of what you want them to *learn* from these things, and then doing your best to ensure this occurs.

Some breeders can be highly skilled at this process, but others may not fully understand how dogs learn, or the lessons that are the most critical at a very young age. Thus, what a breeder may *imagine* he or she is teaching a puppy from a set experience, and what the puppy *is* actually learning, can be very different things.

The more you understand about what good early socialisation for collie puppies requires, the better you should be able to spot a breeder who does it correctly or not, as the case may be.

NO GUARANTEES

Please be aware that while a star-studded pedigree of wall-to-wall Champions suggests that your puppy could inherit similar looks or talent, it is still no automatic guarantee. Exactly how the genetic dice will roll in any litter can still be a highly complex issue to predict. Sometimes the most stunning or brilliant of parents can produce some pretty mediocre offspring, and vice versa.

OTHER CONSIDERATIONS

Before acquiring a puppy, check with the breeder to see if any restrictions or conditions have been imposed. For instance, a breeder might retain KC registered ownership of a puppy despite selling it to you, or may endorse the dog, prohibiting you from registering any future offspring from him or her with the Kennel Club. The breeder might also prohibit you from exporting the dog.

If you have acquired a bitch puppy, the breeder may want to enter into a breeding terms arrangement, whereby they

Look at the litter as a whole, and then focus on the individual puppies.

can have the dog back to have one or more litters, at an agreed time. Make sure you are happy about this. A lot of owners can feel okay about it when they first get a puppy, only to change their minds when the time to breed from her is imminent!

THE DANGERS OF GETTING LITTERMATES

Buying two puppies from the same litter is something I would warn owners against.

If the puppies are of the same sex, they could end up fighting endlessly as they get older in a battle for highest status. Or the most dominant puppy could continually bully and oppress the weaker one.

Additionally, two littermates of the same sex, or different sexes, have a tendency to form their own little special pack, with an owner becoming less important to them as a result. This can have a disastrous impact when it comes to their future training. The more time the puppies are allowed to spend together, the more likely it is that this will happen. Unless you house, exercise and train the puppies entirely separately during at least their first eight to 12 months, they will also become increasingly dependent on each other psychologically, and have hysterics whenever you try to separate them.

It is always best to leave a six month gap, at least, between getting one puppy and another, and ensure that when you do this, each dog clearly sees you as the boss, and forges his or her primary bond with you.

Any half decent breeder should know full well the risks involved in getting two littermates together, and warn you against such an undertaking.

WHAT AGE SHOULD YOU GET A PUPPY?

People often agonise about the right age at which they should get a puppy. Everywhere you go you probably hear different views or theories.

To my mind, many collie puppies go to new homes when they are far too young – i.e. only six or seven weeks old. Sometimes this is simply down to a breeder being anxious to offload them, but there are also people who really seem to think that getting a collie puppy very young is vital if they are to get him most successfully fixated on them for training and competition work.

But what about what is actually best for the puppy? Even at eight weeks old, you are still taking a puppy away from his mother and littermates before he has had adequate time to fully develop his canine identity and social skills. Unless he goes to a new home where there are a range of different dogs to teach him important social lessons, this increases the chances of him being more anti-social towards other dogs later in life.

Many studies over the years have revealed that puppies removed from their mothers and littermates before eight or even 10 weeks of age can display far more severe behavioural problems when older. These can range from more phobic behaviours to heightened aggression towards other dogs, as a result of developing insufficient canine social and communication skills when younger, including

VITAL FIRST LIFE LESSONS

This is the early socialisation programme that I give to all my own puppies:

(1) Puppies destined to be pets should be raised in the home; preferably somewhere near or adjoining the kitchen, source of most of the noisiest gadgets (e.g. washing machines, dishwashers, tumble driers, food processors etc.) and general hullabaloo in any household.
The lesson learnt from this is: That a human home environment, awash with activity and particular noises, is the most normal place to be.

(2) Puppies should start life in a big and cosy indoor kennel, with their mother. This is their basic den. The door to the kennel is always left open. The only time it should be shut is when you go out for short periods or at night – once the puppies are weaned and mobile – for their own safety. You may also need to shut the kennel for short periods during the day so that the puppies can be free of ongoing stimulation and are able to rest properly.
The lesson learnt from this is: That indoor kennels are places of comfort and safety. If the puppies go to new owners who want to use the same kind of kennel in the same way for their dog until he is older, they will immediately adapt and feel at home. If not, that is their choice. But it will always be much harder for a puppy to adapt to an indoor kennel without any previous experience of one.

(3) From two to three days old onwards, puppies should be handled first by visitors known and trusted by their mother, providing they have all followed suitable hygiene precautions.
The lesson learnt from this is: The scent of different people, and the sensation of being picked up, is a normal experience – even before puppies can see or hear

(4) Again, from days old onwards, puppies should get used to having their feet, ears and mouths inspected daily.
The lesson learnt from this is: Such experiences are a normal and completely non-threatening part of life.

(5) From three to four weeks old onwards, more and more different people, of all ages and sexes, should come to visit the puppies, and play with them on a one-to-one basis.
The lesson learnt from this is: Being around people, and interacting with them, is highly rewarding.

bite inhibition. Any sudden change in environment can also be harder for very young dogs to cope with, psychologically.

Such factors apart, I also do not like puppies leaving home before they have had their first vaccinations and time to get over these in a familiar environment. Nor do I think that puppies should be vaccinated for the first time until they are eight weeks old, or even older, due to the risk of these vaccinations conflicting with existing maternal immunity.

If, however, you vaccinate a puppy for the first time just after he has gone to a new home, he will already be in a stressed state from the upheaval, and thus have a heightened chance of a bad reaction. Also, why make a

puppy leave home just as he is entering the heights of his first early fear period?

LEAVING LATER

To my mind, 10 to 12 weeks is a far better time for puppies to leave home, having already had their first vaccinations. The only time you would need to take a puppy away earlier, for his own good, would be if his breeder was completely neglecting his earliest socialisation. But then, why would you really want a puppy from someone like this?

Ultimately the quality of a puppy's earliest and ongoing socialisation with his breeder, as opposed to his age, is

6 From four weeks old onwards pups should have their first experience of wearing a collar, and soon after, walking on a lead, with the use of lots of treats, praise and encouragement.
The lesson learnt from this is: These things are a normal part of life.

7 Also from four weeks old onwards, puppies should be taught that when they come to you – or another person – in response to a certain sound, e.g. "puppies come!", something good will always happen, such as a meal, a treat, a new toy, a game or another visitor to play with. They are also taught that in order to have these good things they must first sit, when someone says "sit" and wait for a short period when someone says "wait".
The lesson learnt from this is: The basic beginnings of 'recall', 'sit' and 'wait' commands, plus that concentrating on people and co-operating with their commands, will always be highly rewarding.

8 Also at a month old onwards, pups should begin basic toilet training. They are taken out into the garden every half hour, plus after a sleep, meal or play session, so that they are most likely to be in the right place when they 'go'. A command is also attached to action, e.g. "be clean!" and a treat, plus praise, while they are actually relieving themselves
The lesson learnt from this is: There is only one really correct place to go to the toilet – and that is outside.

9 Also at a month old onwards, each pup should be taken out separately in the car, at least once every day, for a short outing, initially with his mother.
The lesson learnt from this is: Being in a car is a normal every day experience. I always take each pup out separately, with his mother and/or another adult dog, so his reactions are guided by their confidence, as opposed to being influenced by a more fearful littermate.

10 Finally, also at a month old onwards, each pup should be taken out daily, and separately, to see the whole wide world outside: to meet other dogs, animals and people, and experience traffic, trains and a massive array of different sights, sounds and events that make up the every day human world. Taking a puppy out separately, or initially with a confident adult dog, will allow him to absorb the confidence of others and, again, not be influenced by more apprehensive littermates. Obviously pups are carried, and cannot go on the ground, when out, until they have finished their vaccinations
The lesson learnt from this is: All these things are normal life experiences.

usually the best indicator of how well he will settle in a new home. I have had puppies go to new homes at 10, 14 and 16 weeks old, and all have settled in brilliantly from day one, and formed wonderful bonds with their new owners.

As for the fixation issue, I rescued a Border Collie at 13 years old who fixated on me, more or less, from the moment I got her. Equally I have had another bitch from birth who took up to 10 months to acquire the same level of focus on me, despite 10 times the amount of work being put into achieving this. So this consideration usually has less to do with age, and more to do with individual dogs, and handling skills.

YOUR FUTURE DOG
Hopefully, this chapter will have given you all the information and advice you need to find the best possible collie puppy. Never forget how vital it is to get your choice of dog right, nor what heartache can await those who get it wrong

If your sights have been set on a rescue collie, these dogs will be covered in Chapter Ten. If you already have a collie puppy, and want to know the best way to train him, and rear him into a sound adult dog, the next three chapters are for you.

Chapter Four

EARLY REARING

Starting off the right way with your new collie puppy

Many of the more troubling behaviour issues found in adolescent or adult collies date back to wrong lessons they learned during their earliest months of life. Owners frequently fail to understand how much of what their collie puppy learns is down to them, and the quality of their earliest training and guidance, and through not better controlling what their dog learns when young, they subsequently lose control of the way he behaves later on.

It is also not helpful that Border Collies have a reputation for being easy to train, because this can make many owners over-complacent about their dog's earliest training, believing, usually erroneously, that any less desirable behaviours or habits picked up in puppyhood can be easily reversed later on.

In truth collies are not so much 'easy to train' as exceptionally quick learners, which is somewhat different. It means that they can learn the wrong thing just as quickly as the right thing. Moreover the speed with which a collie puppy can learn wrong behaviour, and subsequently ingrain it, can be so fast that owners often fail to see it happening before it is too late. They can then be left struggling to understand why a dog, who is supposed to be so 'easy to train', behaves so badly.

UNDERSTANDING THE MIND OF YOUR YOUNG DOG
In a young collie puppy you are typically faced with a highly sensitive and reactive dog who has a keen eye for any weakness in your handling, but also a capacity to be greatly harmed, psychologically, by any badly managed fear experiences, or owners who are too harsh or aggressive in their treatment.

When you add to this a developing range of working instincts, which can readily attach themselves to inappropriate targets, and a dog who is not always the most naturally sociable of breeds, then it is clear that young collies must be raised with some care in order to emerge as problem free adults, in whom you have developed and consolidated only the breed's virtues and most rewarding characteristics. But it can be done!

The aim of this chapter is to highlight how much wrong or bad behaviour you can prevent your young collie learning during his earliest days with you, through a greater insight into his developing mind. The next chapter will then look at how you can establish the best possible relationship with your dog, and handle his ongoing social education.

EARLY TRAUMA
Your insight into your collie puppy's mind cannot begin soon enough; i.e. from the moment you first bring him home. For us, getting a new collie puppy may be highly exciting, but what about the psychological impact this event has on the dog himself?

In leaving all that is familiar behind, there will inevitably be a degree of trauma involved, and the less well socialised the puppy has been prior to you bringing him home, the greater this trauma is likely to be.

If, for instance, you have a puppy who has not been sufficiently familiarised with car travel, prior to you getting him, then he might do anything when being driven home from shake, whine and howl to urinate, defecate or vomit – all classic signs of a young dog experiencing immense distress and anxiety. It is not the best way for any puppy to begin his new life, yet all of this trauma could have been avoided had his breeder just given his very earliest socialisation a bit more effort and consideration.

By wrapping your puppy snugly in a blanket, and getting someone to hold him on their lap for the car journey home, you can significantly reduce this trauma.

OTHER EARLY ANXIETIES
If your collie puppy was not initially raised in a domestic home, then other early anxieties should be expected once he is placed in a new environment that is totally alien to him. Everyday household items from radios and washing machines to running taps and banging cupboard doors could cause him intense unease, as he is being introduced to these things just as his mind has begun the process of reacting fearfully to less familiar objects or experiences.

Some collie puppies, raised in more confined or deprived circumstances, can freak out when they first see things like

The young Border Collie's mind is highly receptive to new experiences.

the sky above them, or even grass, and reactions like these always give you an idea of just how limited your dog's earliest socialisation must have been.

Puppies who have been well bred, reared and socialised by a breeder do not behave in the way I have just described. There may be mild apprehension, curiosity and fascination when coming to a new home, but never outright terror. In general, the older an under-socialised collie puppy is when you get him (i.e. 12-14 weeks plus), the more effort it can take to integrate him harmoniously into his new life with you.

MANAGING EARLY FEAR

If you have a collie puppy who reacts very nervously when you first bring him home, it is important to handle this correctly.

Should he, for instance, run off to hide in places, such as under a table or behind a cupboard, and does not want to come to you when you first call him, leave him be. He is

making it clear he wants to be left alone in a place where he feels safe and can psychologically regroup. Never, ever keep pressurising a puppy in these situations to come out to you or, worse still, try to physically drag them out to be sociable.

This is exactly the kind of owner behaviour that can first trigger defensive-aggressive responses in many collies. The dogs then learn to use the same defensive behaviour, in later life, when faced with any sense of challenge or threat.

Your puppy should eventually come out of his hidey-hole when he feels ready. At this point, praise him really well for showing confidence again, and perhaps give him a tasty treat to reinforce this good behaviour.

MORE 'MANIC' BEHAVIOUR

Some collie puppies in new homes may behave in a very 'manic' way which makes it difficult for them to settle. Owners may read this as a sign of happiness and excitement. It can also, however, be a classic sign of stress. Collies learn very early in life that firing adrenaline into their

THE REFUGE ZONE

A safe, enclosed, den-like place of rest is an essential consideration for all Border Collies. A blanket placed over the top and three sides of the crate is vital in providing a sense of security.

It is vital that all collies, from early puppyhood onwards, have a special place of refuge where they can rest or sleep undisturbed. This is because they can be excitable dogs prone to over-stimulation from ongoing environmental noise and activity. So the busier and noisier your household, the more critical this refuge zone is.

Also be aware of how many problems in collies can be caused, or exacerbated, by the dog being denied his own private place to settle in peace. A puppy's indoor kennel or crate in his own quarters can be ideal for this initially (see Using And Abusing The Indoor Kennel, page 39).

Alternatively, if you do not want to use an indoor kennel, put your puppy's bed somewhere as enclosed as possible - under a table for example - to give him the same sense of safety. Dogs instinctively seek out small spaces to retreat to in the home, as these are modern equivalents of the dens their ancestors used. Ideally, any spot chosen should be enclosed over the top and round three surrounding sides. Whenever a puppy goes to this place he should also be left alone by all household members so he can rest in peace, until he ready to be sociable again.

systems, and keeping it there, is the best way to displace any more uncomfortable feelings such as insecurity or anxiety.

In Part Two (see *Self-stimulators*), there will be far more on this phenomenon, but for now let us concentrate on making your new puppy feel less stressed.

The worst thing you can do with a puppy who quickly becomes manic in a new home is to stimulate him still further with endless games and fuss. You may hope this is going to 'make him tired later' but, in fact, it will do quite the reverse. The more adrenaline you allow your puppy to produce, the longer he will take to wind down again, and the more stressed he will be. This, in turn, can compromise his immune system and makes it more likely that he gets ill.

Manic puppies, nervous puppies and, in fact, *any* collie puppy will benefit enormously from having their own special, quiet place where they can settle and rest in peace

when desired (see *The Refuge Zone, above*). This is where you should place your puppy whenever he gets into an over-excited state, in order that he may calm down.

AN EDUCATION INTERRUPTED

What must always be considered when taking a young puppy away from his family, to live with people, is that this interrupts his whole education as a dog.

A puppy begins his life with his own species, learning dog language, communication and social skills and then suddenly, at a critical stage in his social development, this stops, and he finds himself with a new species which does everything very differently.

About the same time as we typically acquire puppies, they are also in the process of forming their most important social attachments and relationships. If we keep a puppy primarily in the company of human beings during this period, he may form good relationships with the people involved, but may lose his ability to be just as much at ease, socially, with other dogs.

Similarly, if a puppy spends the same developmental period chiefly with other dogs, and not people, this will lessen his ability to be at ease with human beings – and particularly less familiar ones – later in life. I see many collie puppies like this, and they often prove very difficult to train.

The need for dogs to be socially bilingual – just as much at ease with the company of other people or dogs – is a peculiarity of the way we own the canine species. But it is also a critical factor for owners to be aware of, and work at, throughout their dog's earliest puppyhood if they want to raise him to be the most successful and adaptable of social companions in later life.

LIMITS AND BOUNDARIES

Another thing that is important to remember about a dog's early education among his own species is that dogs set limits on a puppy's behaviour from very early on. A mother or another adult dog will very quickly let a puppy know when his behaviour is out of line or disrespectful and correct him with an appropriate growl or snap. If he really keeps pushing his luck, the adult dog may then progress on to pinning him down to the floor by his neck, until suitable submission or 'respect' is shown.

Adult dogs in puppies' families do these things instinctively, not because they want to bully smaller and younger animals, but because they want to teach them the behaviour required of them to live harmoniously within a canine pack.

Human beings are not always as successful at educating puppies. We do not always place the right kinds of limits and boundaries on a puppy's behaviour, or consistently enforce rules. We are also emotionally inconsistent – sometimes over-indulgent, sometimes over-harsh – leading to confusion and insecurity in a young dog's mind.

We do not always correct puppies at the right time or in the right way. We do not always reward at the right time or in the right way. We are not always persistent enough in training, ensuring that any command we give a young dog is always followed through, or complied with, and such lack of resolve on our part can quickly signal weakness for a puppy to exploit.

We do not always make it clear what lessons we want puppies to learn from specific experiences. We imagine, instead, that they should just know things they cannot possibly know.

You cannot blame a dog for the way he behaves if you were in charge of his education and failed to teach him any better.

YOUR DOG'S EDUCATION

Exactly what you want your collie puppy to learn – and just as importantly, *not* learn – then take on into his later life, should be considered before you even bring him home.

The most crucial thing to start with is his basic *social* education. As continually stressed in this book, collies are not always the most naturally outgoing of breeds, socially, and thus have to be equipped as early as possible to deal with the social demands we will make of them throughout their lives.

You begin your collie puppy's social education by integrating him harmoniously and respectfully into a human pack, as outlined in this chapter, and constantly expose him to car travel and daily outings that will boost his general social confidence.

Thereafter you must establish the best possible relationship with him as his protector, mentor and leader. This includes teaching him the difference between right and wrong behaviour and how you expect him to behave in the home.

TIME ALONE

As part of his all around early education, I can never over-emphasise how vital it is to teach him to cope with regular periods on his own, from day one – both at home and in the car. This is because collies, as a breed, are highly prone to becoming emotionally over-attached to their owners. This, in turn, can lead to greater trauma when they are separated from owners later.

If you make your collie puppy rest in his own quarters, away from you, not just at night but also for other regular periods during the day or evening, while you are still at home, he will learn to cope far better, emotionally, with being separated from you later.

Also apply the same exercise to your car, if you have one. Every day put your puppy in the car for a short period of time on his own to rest. Always choose a time when he is tired. Do not, however, leave him in the car during hot weather, as young puppies can rapidly over-heat.

If you have a collie already suffering separation issues, see *Separation Distress* in Part Two.

CONCENTRATION, SELF CONTROL AND CO-OPERATION

Your dog's early social education should also involve learning basic concentration and emotional self-control. In addition, he must be encouraged to focus any working drives on you. Once you add helpful co-operation tasks, such as 'watch me', 'sit', 'down', 'wait', 'stay', 'recall' and 'retrieve', to the early educational curriculum, you already have a dog far better prepared to take into the outside world for further social or more formal training.

Too many people, alas, think their collie puppy's whole

education begins with a first trip to a training class. This is because they do not understand the difference between teaching a dog set tasks or exercises and equipping him with essential life skills.

GROUP AND HOME TRAINING

If you take a collie puppy to a group training class without already having built a strong personal bond with him, or taught him how to focus on you through distraction, or equipped him with the social confidence to deal with such an otherwise pretty unnerving environment with lots of dogs, people and noise, then there is a high chance that this outing will be a disaster. Psychologically, your puppy will just not be sufficiently prepared for such an experience.

So owners be aware. You always start your collie puppy's social education first, before moving on to any other types of training. Doing it the other way around will never work so well. This said, group training classes simply may not suit a lot of collie puppies, and particularly more nervous or sensitive dogs who are easily unnerved or distracted by noisy and stimulating environments.

If this is the case, then you may benefit from much of the early home training advice laid out in the next chapter. Remember it is always easier to teach puppies new things in the least distracting environment possible. You can then keep reinforcing the commands or exercises you have taught your puppy in many different, or progressively more distracting, environments which will make his overall training more solid and reliable.

YOUR COLLIE'S EDUCATION

Your collie puppy's early social education should include these 10 critical lessons:
- Integrating respectfully into a human pack or household.
- Learning and complying with a set daily routine, including periods when the dog must spend time on his own.
- Coping with car travel and the outside world environment.
- Building the right relationship with you.
- Understanding right and wrong behaviour.
- Basic house manners – including toilet training and respect for items and territory which belong to you.
- Focus training and learning emotional self-control.
- Early co-operation training.
- Polite behaviour towards visitors to the home.
- Correct social behaviour towards other dogs and people when out.

Note: Some of the above lessons will be covered in following chapters.

EARLY MISTAKES

In the last chapter I outlined some of the vital early life lessons I begin teaching my own collie puppies when they are just weeks or even days old, in order to begin their social education as early as possible, and to ensure that they integrate smoothly into their new homes.

If your puppy has come from a breeder who put similar effort into his early social education, you simply carry on the good work when you bring him home. If the breeder has not put in this kind of effort – which should be evident from some of the more fearful behaviour described earlier in this chapter – then you might have to start his social education almost from scratch.

Either way, one of the biggest mistakes that can be made with a new collie puppy is to allow him full access to the whole home and garden from day one. In so doing you are giving him a privilege he is too young to handle correctly and which he may, in true collie fashion, go on to exploit.

Giving your puppy free access to the whole of your home from day one also gives him the opportunity to do things such as chew or destroy items that are valuable to you, or go to the toilet on your best carpets. You are then likely to get cross, which will cause him distress. If you start to get physically or verbally abusive at this point, out of frustration and anger, some collie puppies may resort to defensive/aggressive behaviour out of fear.

The longer a puppy has access to the whole of your home, the more he can also grow in territorial confidence. He may begin to steal possessions belonging to household members and run off with them as trophies. The more people chase him to get them back, the more fun he has and the more power he feels.

TAKING OVER

Worst scenario of all, your puppy may eventually feel the need to take over all the home territory and start aggressively guarding things such as chairs, sofas and beds or other strategic areas such as stairways, hallways and the area around your front door (a problem discussed in far more depth in Part Two under *Aggression*).

Once controlling the front door area he may then try to intimidate visitors that come to your home. He may also become aggressive when household members try to physically move him out of the main home area and into another room or place.

Your puppy is simply responding to the opportunities you have given him to gain an upper hand in your pack. Why put a puppy in a situation like this, where he can make so many mistakes in such a short period of time – some with potentially very serious consequences? You may well have a collie puppy who shows no signs whatsoever of being aggressive or manipulative in your home environment, but you will not know this until you have got to know him far better.

Keep remembering that it will always be easier to relax rules with a puppy who you have previously been firm with, should his behaviour warrant it, than to start being firm with a puppy you have previously been indulgent with, because he will have already spotted your weakness and will not forget it.

OTHER DRAWBACKS

Also understand that by allowing your puppy to go anywhere in your home from day one, you have immediately conceded a highly symbolic advantage in terms of establishing your own status in relation to your dog. If your puppy is able to see that you command a far bigger territory than he has access to – i.e. the whole of the house – this immediately has bearings on your level of status and authority in relation to him.

If your puppy already has access to your entire home, you cannot use the privilege of entering your territory as a reward for good behaviour, as outlined in the next chapter. Dogs who have constant access to owners and the whole home from day one are also, as previously stressed, far more likely to suffer from separation issues later on.

ORGANISING YOUR PUPPY'S QUARTERS

The most effective way to start off a collie puppy's new life with you is to set aside a specific household area for him, which is easy to keep clean, and where there are very limited things for him to damage or destroy. If things are left out for a puppy to chew or destroy, it is your fault, not his, because puppies have no concept of the value of anything you own and simply know no better.

A typical area for your puppy's initial quarters would be a kitchen and/or back room leading immediately into the garden, as close access to outside should help speed up your puppy's toilet training. You can limit your puppy's access to other parts of your home through installing one or more dog gates, as necessary.

It is also a good idea to initially fence off a specific part of the garden for your puppy, to reduce destruction to plants or other outdoor items, and minimise the risk of him chewing or consuming something poisonous.

Just through these simple early steps alone, you will drastically reduce the number of conflicts you have with your puppy over mess and destruction, as well as all the emotional upset that so often goes with them.

Only once your puppy's toilet training is reliable, and he has learned sufficient respect for owners' rules and authority, as outlined in the next chapter, can you begin inviting him into your territory for progressively longer periods.

RESTING AND SLEEPING

You will need to establish your puppy's sleeping area – or aforementioned refuge zone – within his own quarters. This is the place where he will sleep at night, and also where you can put him for regular periods in the day to wind down and rest.

Some owners may prefer to keep their new puppies in an indoor kennel in their bedroom over the first night or two, while the puppy is likely to be most distressed. The puppy and his kennel can then be gradually moved further away from the bedroom each night, until he finally becomes established in more permanent quarters downstairs.

The only drawback with the above strategy is how hard some owners can find it to move their puppy into downstairs quarters once they have set the precedent of having him sleep with them in their bedroom. However, I would urge them to persist with gradually moving him – even in the face of much protest whining, because unless you get a puppy used to resting and sleeping in his own quarters from early on, and teach him that being separated from you for routine periods is a perfectly normal part of life, you could be storing up bigger troubles for your dog, and yourself, when he is left alone in the future.

USING AND ABUSING THE INDOOR KENNEL

Indoor kennels can be ideal for puppies to rest and sleep in, as well as acting as a wonderful place of sanctuary and safety for them. Too often today, however, these devices are being abused, with both puppies and adult dogs being imprisoned in them for appalling lengths of time, simply to suit an owner's convenience.

Other than overnight when they are sleeping, a puppy should not be left in an indoor kennel, with the door shut, for more than two to three hours at a time, and then only after an activity period and toilet opportunity. At around 10 or 11 months of age, I usually dispense with a puppy's indoor kennel altogether, once all his basic house manners are in place.

Owners who are barbaric enough to leave a puppy or adult dog shut in an indoor kennel for far longer periods – or even while they are at work all day – will often tell you that their animals 'cope'. But this is because they do not know the difference between a dog who is genuinely coping, psychologically, and one who is simply exhibiting classic 'learned helplessness'; a syndrome present in many, if not most, domestic dogs to some degree and which will be covered in more detail at the end of the next chapter and elsewhere in this book.

You do not have to be a genius to work out that any animal who is confined in a small space for a long time is suffering. Any parent who did this to a child would be prosecuted for cruelty.

A puppy who has not been raised in an indoor kennel from very early on may have real problems adapting to one later. In which case you could set up a refuge area somewhere else, such as under a table – generally the quieter and more enclosed the spot the better.

The drawback with not having an enclosed space like an indoor kennel for your puppy is that you will not be able to keep him safe when you are out or not watching him, or be able to limit any destructiveness to the same degree. If you do use an indoor kennel, it is vital to cover the top and three surrounding sides of it with a blanket to make it more like a den, and leave cosy bedding, toys and chew items inside. Leaving a dog in an uncovered cage, by contrast, makes him feel incredibly vulnerable and thus far more stressed.

To further encourage positive associations, always feed your puppy inside his indoor kennel.

BONDING

Once your collie puppy is installed in his own quarters, it is important that owners and all household members spend as much time as possible bonding with him on a one-to-one basis. The best way to do this, early on, is through having lots of fun games and to play together with toys. You can use these toys, as well as the environment of shared play, to begin teaching your puppy basic exercises, manners and the rewards of co-operation, as outlined in the next chapter.

As stated previously, collies have a reputation for being one person dogs. While it is true that a collie can often be more attached and responsive towards one particular member within a household, it is usually the person who spends the most time with them early on, and who also undertakes the majority of their training and daily walks.

If you want a collie to have the same level of responsiveness towards all members of a household, then they must all spend equal time bonding with him as a puppy, as well as training him and taking him out on walks later on.

COLLIES AND CHILDREN

I once read an apparently 'expert' dog book which stated: *"Border Collies, with their tendency to 'herd' children, make good family pets."* It made my hair stand on end. Was the author aware of how many collies are discarded as family pets each year because they are doing just too *good* a job of herding the children?

An excited collie chasing small children round a garden tends to be driven, unfortunately, more by the instincts of the fox in the hen run than nanny in the nursery. Small children give the dog the idea they are prey-sized because they move at his eye level. The more they run and scream, the more adrenaline rushes into the collie's body and the more excited and determined the chase becomes.

While few collies would ever intentionally attack a child, some get so over-aroused by the chase that, in their heightened excitement, the possibility of nipping or knocking over a youngster can arise.

Scenarios like this explain why so often it is said that collies are actually not good pet dogs to have with young children. But it still ultimately depends on the nature of the dogs and children concerned.

TEACHING CHILDREN RESPECT FOR DOGS

Some children are naturally gifted with dogs. Even when still quite young, they know how to treat them with appropriate kindness, calmness, compassion and respect, especially if they have also been relentlessly taught these things by their parents. Children and parents like these have every chance of making a great success of any dog they own.

Other children, however, are a total nightmare. There is nothing that makes my blood boil more than the sight of children being allowed to torment dogs, be it their own or someone else's – constantly screaming and shouting, or getting the dog to sit 50 times in five minutes, or dragging and yanking him around by his collar.

How could their parents let them do this? This is torture for any dog. Rescue centres are full of dogs with signs above their kennels saying: 'not to be homed with children', and this is why.

Some collies have got much lower thresholds than others when it comes to reacting defensively in situations of pressure, over-arousal or perceived threat. Do be aware of this. Teach young children to treat your collie puppy with respect and to never unnecessarily wind him up or disturb him once he has gone to his refuge zone. Also encourage your children to bond with your puppy on a one-on-one basis and train him to respond to specific commands – as outlined in the next chapter.

LIVING WITH OTHER DOGS

If you have other dogs in your household, prior to getting a collie puppy, I cannot overstress how important it is to spend as much separate time as possible with your new puppy away from these dogs, from day one. Not only train and play with him separately, but also take him out with you daily on his own for a walk, even if this walk is relatively short.

This is how you begin the process of making a collie primarily bond with you, readily focus on you and be most responsive to your commands. It will also give you the best chance when out – as detailed in Chapter Six – of shaping his individual social behaviour, rather than letting him hide behind another dog, or the rest of your canine pack, or pick up bad habits from them.

The length of time you need to spend training and exercising a collie puppy on his own with you, before integrating him back into a pack with another dog (or dogs) can vary from six months to a over a year. If you have done things correctly during this time, then no matter how many dogs you later take out with your collie puppy, he will still always respond first and foremost to you and your commands.

Interactions between a puppy and children should be closely supervised.

FIXATING ON OTHER DOGS

If, instead, he starts to fixate more on your other dog or dogs – either at home or when out – and becomes less responsive to you, then you know you will need to spend more time with him on his own again.

If you do not spend all this valuable one-on-one time with a collie puppy, away from your other dog or dogs, at the stage in his life where he is making his most important social relationships, he may build a stronger social attachment to another dog instead. This will make it far harder for you to train him later. He is also more likely to have hysterics when you try to separate him from the other dog.

Additionally many collie puppies, if left too lengthily with other dogs, can begin to make them the target of their more obsessive working focus and instincts; i.e. they will continually eye, stalk and herd them. This can become incredibly tiresome for both you and the 'herded' dogs alike.

If you are ever to keep a collie under the best possible control, and train him to the highest level, the only target of his obsessive focus should be *you*. How you achieve this will be outlined in the next chapter.

THE IMPORTANCE OF ROUTINE AND TOILET TRAINING

It is incredibly important to establish a daily routine for your puppy from day one. Routines make animals feel secure and give them the mental wherewithal to distinguish between active and non-active parts of the day and thus settle more readily during the latter. If, by contrast, your puppy never knows what is going to happen when, or gets intensely stimulated at less predictable times of day, he will never settle so well due to an ongoing sense of anticipation.

Every household will have its own routine but, over and above this, the regular needs of your puppy have to be considered. For instance, the less frequently he is given a toilet opportunity outside, the longer it will take to toilet train him and the more likely he is to have 'accidents' indoors.

As highlighted in the last chapter, the only reliable way to toilet train a puppy is to take him outside as often as possible and wait until he performs. While he is actually going to the toilet, immediately attach a command to this activity, and then give him a tasty treat and much praise.

If he starts going to the toilet in the wrong place, i.e. inside, immediately put him outside to finish, then praise and reward him as before. If you are too late to stop him going in the wrong place, or do not see him do it, just quietly clear it up. Do not get angry with your puppy, as he will not make the connection between his earlier mistake and your disapproval. Puppies also become highly insecure when an owner's hostility towards them appears inexplicable or unpredictable.

So many dogs become more devious or neurotic about their toilet habits when older as a result of associating human punishment with this activity when younger. Do not make this mistake.

Without essential early bonding between you and your puppy, there is a real danger that he will focus on anther dog in the family, rather than you.

Capitalise on all learning experiences, as long as they are positive.

PLAY TIME

As previously outlined, you must also set aside regular one-on-one daily play sessions with your collie puppy. This is where the whole bonding process with your puppy starts, and where you can also give him much vital early training, as outlined in the next chapter.

When you have your regular daily play sessions with your collie puppy, make sure you bring in special toys he will not see any other time, as this will increase his enjoyment at being in your company and also increase his motivation to co-operate with you. There will be more important advice on collies and toys in the next chapter.

CAR TIME

Take your collie puppy out at least once a day, every day, in the car, as car travel is likely to be a regular part of his future life. When you take your puppy out in the car it is best to secure him to a tie point that keeps his eye level well below the car windows. This minimises car sickness and also limits his ability to learn bad habits such as flying at car windows and/or barking at passing traffic.

For more detailed advice on any car related concerns in your collie, see *Car problems* in Part Two.

TRIPS OUT

Again, from the moment you get him, you should give your collie puppy at least two trips out each day to different places. He needs to meet other people and dogs and generally absorb everything that goes on in the outside world before he has a chance to become more fearful about these things. In Chapter Six, I will outline how you can best manage your puppy's social training in the outside world.

Day in and day out I meet owners who tell me their collies are fine within the home environment, but become aggressive, or start mentally falling to pieces, as soon as they leave it to go out on walks. This can sometimes be down to an earlier fright when they were out that was not correctly handled, but more often it will simply be down to the dog totally lacking in social confidence because he was not exposed to the right things at the right time, and in the right way.

A common reason why puppies do not get this exposure

sufficiently early is that owners mistakenly believe their dogs cannot go out until they have completed their vaccination programme at around 13 weeks of age. This means they are keeping their puppy in relative isolation at home during his most critical early period of social development.

If you get an under-socialised or completely non-socialised collie puppy at around 12 weeks or older, you can have similar problems later trying to make him feel at ease with a wealth of new sights, sounds, experiences and social encounters within the outside world.

As highlighted in Chapter Three, my own collie puppies first start going out, and travelling in the car, at around a four to five weeks old. The most important consideration with puppies who have not completed their vaccination programme is that you do not put them on the ground anywhere where there might be a risk of infection from other dogs – e.g. pavements or common exercise areas. But you can still carry them around, as much as possible, to meet other people and see other dogs and encounter traffic and busy high streets.

It is important to keep remembering that the younger your collie puppy is when you introduce him to new things, the more he is likely to take these in his stride later.

DOWN TIME

As well as establishing a regular routine for mealtimes, playtimes, toilet opportunities, and daily trips outside the home, it is also vital to establish regular down times when your puppy rests and sleeps during the day and evening. The more routine these rest periods become, the more likely it is that your puppy will settle. These down times will also give *you* an opportunity to have a rest from your puppy!

Puppies need a lot of rest and sleep to grow both mentally and physically. Much like young children, they can also be at their most manic when they are most tired. The best time to settle a puppy is when he has had an activity period or outing, a meal and a toilet opportunity. When a rest period is due for your puppy, do not do anything to further stimulate him – such as playing with him, making a fuss of him or giving him a new toy. The less stimulation he gets, the quicker he will wind down.

You can then put your puppy in his refuge zone to rest for an hour or two. If you are putting your puppy into an indoor kennel to rest, then it is vital that you always *invite* him into this place, by first throwing in a toy, tasty treat or chew item. As he goes in to get these things say: "in your kennel" gently, then praise him with "good boy!" as he settles down with the thrown item. This way, your puppy has made a choice to co-operate with you by going into his kennel, and he has found such co-operation rewarding.

Never *physically force your puppy into an indoor kennel* before shutting the door on him. The combination of a sudden loss of control and your hostility can be a very frightening

experience for a puppy. He may panic and act in a defensive-aggressive way through fear. He may also become increasingly reluctant to go inside his kennel again. The latter is also likely if you leave him in his kennel too often, and for over-lengthy periods.

HOW DOGS DEVELOP A SIEGE MENTALITY

People who have a larger amount of land have a tendency to neglect their collie puppy's early socialisation, because they think he doesn't need to go out elsewhere for walks. Then they wonder why they end up with a dog who becomes progressively more anti-social towards other people or dogs visiting their home.

The purpose of taking your young collie puppy out regularly to different places is not just to exercise him, but to teach him social tolerance and flexibility. So no matter how much land you have, in order to teach him such social adaptability, and avoid him developing a more troublesome siege mentality later on, you must keep taking him out while he is still very young and keep inviting people and dogs to visit your puppy at home for plenty of positive interactions. Also be aware that good socialisation for dogs – particularly breeds like collies - must be a constant, ongoing process. If you do not continue to expose your collie, throughout his lifetime, to positive visits from people and other dogs, as well as trips beyond the home, his social tolerance and confidence can quickly start to diminish at any age.

STARTING AS YOU MEAN TO GO ON

Hopefully, this chapter will have provided you with some basic early measures to settle your new collie puppy most successfully into your home and begin your relationship on the soundest footing.

I am sure there are some people who will read this chapter and consider my recommended early approach towards collie puppies as somewhat strict or even over-pessimistic. It is easy to think this way if you have never had a problem collie, whose stressful or even dangerous behaviour stems directly back to the way he was raised.

In my role as a behaviourist, however, I deal with collies like this all the time. Their problems have sneaked up subtly on owners, then escalated to a level that has driven them to despair. And I feel I owe it to owners like these to try to explain why they may have lost control of their dog's behaviour.

Appreciate that every collie you own is likely to be different from the one you had before. The more you are able to anticipate the kind of future problems he could face you with, the better placed you will always be to nip them in the bud.

Even if your collie never gives you problems, you can only gain from raising him to be the most respectful, well-behaved and rewarding of companions, as outlined in following chapters.

Chapter Five

EARLY TRAINING

Getting your relationship with your dog right; spotting and preventing early problems; teaching basic manners, exercises and self control

Once you have settled your collie puppy into his new home, the next critical thing to get right is the quality of the relationship you establish with him. If you intend to work your dog in competition, or train him up to a fairly high level, this is all the more essential. The same is true if you wish him to be the most well balanced of social companions. Your dog must not only respect you, and respond happily and readily to your commands, but also see you as the main point of focus and guidance in his life.

Strangely, at least to my mind, people do not always think very hard about the nature of the relationship they intend to establish with their dog. Once they get their puppy home, there is a tendency to wait until the dog does something and then react to it on an *ad hoc* basis, rather than already have in mind an agenda for how they want their dog to behave.

The readiness of owners to be controlled or influenced by their own behaviour seldom goes unnoticed by collies. If you give a collie the chance to train *you* into doing things *his* way – for want of stronger or better guidance – he will always take it. The more intelligent and strong minded the dog, the more reluctant he will be to suffer fools gladly and the more ready he will be to exploit perceived weakness in your level of authority or resolve.

KNOWING WHO YOU ARE TO YOUR DOG

People's relationships with their dogs are often sabotaged by their inability to see themselves as their dog sees them. We have a tendency to project our own emotional needs and agendas on to dogs, and are unable to disentangle our true relationships with them from the demands of our own egos, which includes a perceived sense of natural superiority.

Simply through the act of acquiring or buying a dog, we imagine this gives us an automatic right to be respected and obeyed as a superior being. Alternatively, in showering a dog with a wealth of unearned privileges, we may expect him to show his gratitude by complying with whatever we ask him to do.

Misguided notions like these are what fuel all the anger, frustration, distress or resentment owners so often feel towards dogs when they fail to meet their expectations. The stark reality is, however, that dogs cannot know our expectations because they cannot think like us.

Neither do they – nor can they – know that they are 'owned' by us. To dogs, we are simply fellow pack beings they share their lives with, and the way they relate to us is according to how we relate to them at any given time. If we are strong and benign, they will follow and co-operate with us. If we are weak, they will not. If we are cruel and aggressive, they will not trust us.

BEING THE PERSON YOUR COLLIE NEEDS YOU TO BE

I am a strong believer that dogs need, if not crave, leadership from their owners. They also inherently sense that their own survival rests on the quality of this leadership, which is why they may keep testing your fitness to hold this all-important role in their lives.

Certainly, one of the earliest and best lessons collies ever taught me was that if I did not become the person they needed me to be as their boss or leader, I would be punished for it – and some dogs would punish me more than others. If I was emotionally over-indulgent they would not see this as a sign of me being a lovely person. They saw this instead as a sign of weakness they could exploit with increasingly more manipulative behaviour. It also made them less responsive and more insecure.

If I did not consistently and persistently follow through every command I gave my dogs until it was complied with, they increasingly defied, disrespected or ignored these commands because, again, they saw this as a clear sign of weakness on my part. If I did not *look* like I meant it when I corrected them for something, they would not take me seriously. If I lost my cool in a challenging or worrying situation, they lost their cool as well. If I got impatient, frustrated or angry in training, they would mentally shut down and retreat from wanting to work with me, which is completely understandable. If I persistently took their co-operation for granted, they could become resentful.

If I could not make a dog feel safe, I could not stop him from behaving aggressively, to protect himself, in situations where he felt this was necessary.

Border Collies taught me, ultimately, that they will only view you as a leader when you behave like one.

KNOWING WHAT YOU ARE SAYING TO YOUR DOG

The process of evolution, and being raised with people from a very young age, has given domestic dogs a heightened ability to read human emotions and physical gestures. They will, for instance, understand immediately what a human being means when he or she points to something for them to approach, whereas a wolf will not.

But still a vast part of the way dogs relate to us is governed by our use of eye contact, individual body language and energy. It can be helpful to be far more aware of these things, and the effect our own behaviour can have on dogs.

MAINTAINING CALM BEHAVIOUR

By avoiding glaring or over-challenging eye contact, keeping our voices low and calm and making our movements slow and deliberate, we have the highest chance of keeping a dog in a correspondingly balanced and calm state. View this as an approach to master most of the time with your collie.

From this approach, now consider how little you have to change in order to alter your dog's behaviour. As soon as your movements become more animated and/or jerky, your dog may become more unsettled or excited. This is even more likely if your voice also rises in tone or pitch.

TRIGGERING PREDATORY RESPONSES

Dogs instinctively react this way to any sudden eruption of frantic energy in other dogs or people, because it can signify the beginning of pre-hunting, rallying behaviour (where dogs deliberately excite themselves to raise aggression levels), or some immediate threat looming, either to themselves or to the stability and harmony of the pack they live with.

The combination of animated body movements and a louder or more highly pitched voice tone can also trigger lunge-nip working responses in collies. This is why owners who over-excite their collies in training, or in adrenaline charged pursuits like Agility or Flyball, so often end up getting nipped by their dogs. Excitable young children can also trigger similar responses.

TRIGGERING THREAT RESPONSES

Now let us propose you direct a more glaring and intense eye contact towards your dog, move challengingly into his space, stiffen your body and lean right over him. All these things are typically done by an owner who is angry with their dog, and thinks they are disciplining him, when in fact such behaviour evokes an instinctive threat response from him instead – i.e. flight, fight or freeze.

When threatened by owners like this, some dogs may try to run away/escape and hide, some may resort to defensive aggression, and others will initially freeze then adopt excessively submissive behaviour, i.e. cowering, avoiding eye contact, rolling on to their back and lifting a hind leg. This latter behaviour is most typical in dogs who have highest levels of *learned helplessness (see p 59);* i.e. dogs who have least confidence in their ability to escape or resist an owner's control.

When a dog reacts to your anger by freezing, then showing submission, please never think – as so many owners do – that this is a sign of the guilt they feel about some previous misdemeanour. It is merely a sign of their desperation to appease your hostility.

TRIGGERING MANIPULATIVE OR 'BULLYING' BEHAVIOUR

As consistently highlighted in this book, collies are highly attuned to patterns of weakness in other animals, and will take advantage of them. Such weakness in owners is typically signalled to the dog when they allow him to dictate or control their actions via a variety of pressurising behaviours, e.g. staring, whining, barking, pawing (also see *Manipulative behaviour* in Part Two).

If continually successful with these manipulative strategies, some dogs may then gain sufficient confidence to move on to more overtly intimidatory behaviours – e.g. growling, nipping – to get their own way. This is the typical progression of collies who turn into household bullies.

It is essential not to let your young collie dictate your actions in the above mentioned ways, and also make it clear to him, from day one, that you control his movements, rather than the other way around, as outlined more fully in *Collies and movement sensitivity, page 49.*

TEACHING RIGHT AND WRONG BEHAVIOUR

The earliest test of your relationship with a new collie puppy comes when you try to correct him for wrong behaviour. In this respect, it is critical that he begins his relationship with you accepting your right to correct him, but in a way that preserves his respect for you and does not make him feel frightened or threatened, as previously outlined.

Many people let undesirable behaviour in puppies flourish too long, out of a belief that they are unable to consciously control their actions, or are too young to be taught right from wrong. Not only is this untrue, but it can also lead to bigger problems in the future. After all, if you cannot get your collie to respect your correction and authority when he is a very young puppy, he is even less likely to do so as he gets older and becomes a lot more confident about challenging you.

RESPONDING TO A THREAT

Not 'guilty', just scared – How dogs instinctively use submission tactics to defuse hostile body language in owners.

An owner's hostile body language and eye contact immediately unnerve this collie.

He first attempts to defuse conflict by avoiding eye contact.

When hostility persists, he turns his head away in a more submissive gesture.

Then he moves to an even more placatory pawing and face licking.

As tension persists he lies down and averts his head.

Total submission: lying on his back and offering up his belly.

In this sequence the owner used only her body language to elicit this instinctive, threat-defusing response in her dog.
No words, sounds, commands or verbal cues were used.

GIVING A CORRECTION

Typically an early correction will need to be given to your puppy for something such as nipping your hands or clothes or chewing something inappropriate. This is all perfectly natural, exploratory behaviour for collie puppies, but their teeth can be incredibly sharp and destructive.

One of the biggest mistakes people make, when puppies nip them, is to yell or scream or become highly animated. As previously outlined, all these things can trigger predatory or defensive responses and thus further excite a puppy to nip longer and harder.

Traditional advice for early nipping behaviour is to yelp loudly like another puppy would, to indicate that he is being hurt. This can work for some collie puppies but, sadly, it can simply encourage the bully in others to nip even more.

The best way to correct your puppy is via a better understanding of how dogs – and collies in particular – respond to different types of body energy and movement.

MAKING YOUR PUPPY STEP BACK

When your puppy nips, you will need to move forwards towards him in a calm but purposeful manner, and in a way which makes him take a few steps back. As he is stepping back, maintain a steady eye contact with him and say your correction word firmly, e.g. "*hey!*". Then stay completely still; do not do or say anything more that might provoke or frighten him. I also like to point to a puppy to reinforce with a body signal that I am correcting him.

If your puppy does not accept your first correction, and keeps trying to come forwards towards to nip you, repeat the process, remembering to keep calm, silent and absolutely still after you have corrected him, held his eye contact and made him step back.

Once your puppy has stepped back and stopped nipping, while maintaining eye contact with you, he has accepted your correction. At this point, completely relax your body posture, break eye contact and use words he will ever after associate with reward and 'right' behaviour, e.g. "*good boy!*". You can then give him something more appropriate to target his teeth on, such as a puppy chew or a toy. Do this every time he nips until he gets the message. The earlier and better your correction is each time, the sooner this behaviour will stop.

WHY ISN'T IT WORKING?

If your puppy is not getting your correction message, it is probably because the energy and eye contact you are using to move your puppy back, in an authoritative way, is not convincing enough. It could be that you are frightening your puppy into more defensive reactions with a lot of extra verbal shouting or over-hostile body language and eye contact (i.e. glaring, instead of a calm, steady gaze). Or you are not remembering to keep absolutely calm and still once

you have given your puppy a correction.

As soon as you get your level of authority and energy, and accompanying body language just right for this exercise, your puppy should move back and stop nipping without looking frightened or threatened.

Follow exactly the same procedure should your puppy begin chewing something inappropriate like a door-frame or a plant. Before you correct him, first find something more appropriate for him to chew. Walk up calmly but authoritatively to your puppy, in the same way as before to make him move away from the 'wrong' object he is chewing. As he is moving away say your correction word – "*hey!*" – then praise him for complying and give him the alternative chew item.

Through these simple early methods you quickly teach your puppy two distinct commands and approaches, i.e. "*hey!*" and "*good boy!*" which define for him when he is doing 'wrong' or 'right' things.

TEACHING BASIC HOUSE MANNERS

Once your puppy has learnt the specific cues for wrong or right actions, you can use these lessons to manage his later behaviour.

When, for instance, you start inviting your puppy into the rest of your home territory, you can correct him each time he begins chewing the wrong things or doing anything you find undesirable. But you should also do your best to praise him fulsomely each and every time he is behaving well. Also remember to keep sticking to the same basic correction and praise methods. If you keep changing the way you react to your puppy's behaviour, you will simply confuse him.

If your puppy keeps misbehaving when you correct him within your home territory, you can attach a more negative consequence to this by banishing him straight back into his own quarters. Be careful how you do this initially, however. If you suddenly grab your puppy, he could become frightened and defensive. Alternatively, he could try to stop you returning him to his own territory by running away. The more you chase him, the more fun he has each time, because now he is controlling your behaviour and movement rather than the other way around.

If either of these things happen, it is more sensible to keep a collar and short line on your puppy for his initial excursions into your territory, so you can calmly remove him, whenever necessary, without picking him up or grabbing his neck. Also see, *Using the shorter and longer line, p 49.*

OTHER GOOD MANNERS: "BACK" AND "OFF!"

Your puppy should also be taught to move back automatically and respectfully for you when you open the dog gate to enter or leave his quarters, and not try to barge past you through the gate or jump up at you.

To teach this, proceed as follows, again using your body language and energy in the right way. If you enter your puppy's quarters and he tries to barge through the gate past you, calmly move right in front of him, block him and then keep walking *forward* into him, giving him the correction command – "*hey!*" – that makes him step back. As he is stepping back, say the word "*back*". Then praise him for his co-operation, "*good boy!*".

When you are leaving his quarters and open the gate, block him again if he tries to go past you. This time move *backwards* into him, while giving the correction command, to make him step back. As he moves back, say the word "*back*" again. Then praise him for his co-operation.

If your puppy jumps up at you, move forward in a way that pushes him back off you. Remember to use only the forward momentum of your body energy to push your dog back in this way and *not your hands or arms*. Also do not be over-aggressive; move forward in a calm but determined way. Then stay absolutely still and quiet. As your forward movement pushes your puppy off, say the word "*off!*" as he is *actually moving off you*. Do not say "*down!*", as so many owners do. "*Down*" is a completely different command, as outlined later in this chapter. The more you say "*off!*" as you move your puppy off you in this way, the less he will jump up at you.

Once your puppy knows the command "*back*" and also stops jumping up when you say the command "*off!*", ask him to "*sit*" and "*watch*" you (these exercises appear later in this chapter, page 53). Always praise your puppy fulsomely for moving *back,* or *off* you, and then *sitting* and *watching* you, on command. From time to time, give him a treat or a toy after praising him, to further reinforce the right behaviour. Later on you can use these same commands to stop him jumping up at visitors or other people when you are out.

"QUIET!"

Collie puppies can yap and bark a lot, especially when they get excited. It is pretty normal behaviour, but can get out of hand – at which point, you need to know how to stop it.

To do this, first have a selection of tasty treats around and wait until your puppy is actually barking or yapping. While he is barking, hold up a treat for him to see and smell. Keep this treat held between your fingers in a pinching motion. Your puppy cannot eat the treat and bark at the same time, thus he must stop barking for a moment in anticipation of eating it. The moment he is quiet, even for a second, say "*quiet!*". Then immediately praise him – "*good boy!*" – and let him have the treat.

Keep doing this until your dog realises that a pinching motion from you, held above his head, and the command

"*quiet!*" means he should stop barking. Be very careful to only give your dog a treat while he is still quiet, or you will quickly ruin this exercise. Your dog must always be quiet when you say "*quiet!*" and remain quiet when you praise him and give him the treat.

Keep practising this, each time trying to get your puppy to stay quiet just that little bit longer before praising and rewarding him. You can also add the "*sit*" and "*watch me*" exercises after a "*quiet!*" command to keep your puppy quieter for longer.

Like all focus exercises, of a kind laid out in greater detail later, this one loads a reward on to correct behaviour – i.e. not barking – and also helps to teach your puppy greater emotional self-control. If you shout at your puppy aimlessly when he barks, you have simply rewarded this behaviour instead with your attention. Or he may think you are 'barking' as well, and thus joining in with his behaviour.

CUEING HUMAN CONTACT

If you have a collie puppy who has been used to being handled and picked up by people since he was very young – i.e. only days or weeks old – he will be less likely to react adversely to this when you bring him home.

However, a collie puppy without this kind of very early exposure to human contact may panic if you suddenly grab him to pick him up. He may growl or react defensively out of fear. This is perfectly normal behaviour for a young puppy who suddenly feels threatened, but not ideal in a dog you wish to raise as a bombproof social companion.

For this reason, if you have a collie puppy who reacts like this, get into the habit of having a tasty treat with you each time you wish to handle him and pick him up. First get his attention by saying his name, then show him the treat and say a word which alerts him to the fact that you are about to pick him up – e.g. "*hup!*". As you pick him up immediately praise him, "*good boy!*". Put the treat in his mouth, *before* he has a chance to react aggressively, and as a reward for letting you handle him in this way.

By cueing your puppy with a special word every time you wish to pick him up – as opposed to suddenly surprising him – and rewarding him for complying, you should soon overcome any worry he has about this kind of human approach.

Get into the habit of regularly holding your puppy's collar, and simultaneously giving him a tasty treat. This will progressively diminish any sense of worry or threat he may have about this kind of approach from people.

COLLIES AND MOVEMENT SENSITIVITY

It is important to understand how sensitive collies are to the movement and body energy of other animals, including humans. This is what makes them such incredibly responsive dogs in training; able to interpret and react to even the slightest physical moves or gestures we make.

Similarly, in their working role, you will constantly see a collie use energy and movement to their advantage – applying relentless forward momentum to wear down the resistance of livestock and thereafter control where it goes.

A collie's approach conforms to the basic law of nature in which the stronger or higher force always makes the weaker or lesser force move or retreat, just as higher-ranking dogs show their authority over lower-ranking dogs by controlling when and where they move.

Once a collie has worked out that he can make something move – be this another person, animal or even traffic – then he sees what he has made move as the weaker force. This is why, when you correct your dog, it is important to also make him move back, even just a step or two. Similarly, when your dog jumps up at you, you should make him not only move off you, but also go back a few steps. Such gestures are highly symbolic, i.e. you, as the stronger force, have made him move, as opposed to the other way around.

Once you have made your dog step back, it is also important to keep absolutely still, and thus block further attempts by him to move you out of your space. Throughout this book I will highlight how much you can control your dog's behaviour simply through improved use of your body language and energy.
Note: Noise is also a form of palpable movement/energy to a dog, i.e. reverberations which move towards him at different levels of force and volume. This is why collies are equally sensitive to sound – a subject that will be covered in greater depth throughout this book.

NOT LIKING A COLLAR

If your puppy has not been used to wearing a collar, prior to you getting him, be aware that he could react very badly until he has had greater time to get used to it. I have seen collie puppies go absolutely berserk with Oscar-winning hysterics when a collar is first put on them, particularly if the pup is older when he first experiences it. Others will take it in their stride.

It can be hard to predict, in advance, how an individual puppy may react to their first experience of a collar. But if your puppy does have hysterics, you must completely ignore him until he calms down.

Alternatively, you can try to distract him with a fun game until he has completely forgotten about it. Get into the habit of putting a collar on your puppy just before he has a meal, to build up a more positive association.

USING THE SHORTER AND LONGER LINE

When trying to encourage a puppy into desirable patterns of behaviour, a shorter and longer line attached to his collar can be of much use to you.

The shorter line is one you can use simply to remove your puppy, without aggression or conflict, from your main home territory and back to his own quarters. By using this line you avoid any sudden grabs to his neck which could frighten him or trigger a defensive reaction. You do not need to get an expensive lead for this; a simple bit of string or washing line will do just as well.

The longer line is one you will use to improve your dog's response to commands such as recall or retrieve, as outlined later in this chapter. You can get longer training lines from most pet stores.

GROOMING AND OTHER HANDLING

In order to keep your puppy healthy, he has to get used to you doing things such as grooming him, cleaning and inspecting his teeth and ears and clipping his claws. If his breeder has not already got him used to these procedures, again he may react adversely and find such intimate contact and manhandling by humans threatening, or perceive them as an attempt to dominate him.

Human infants often struggle when adults try to dress them, bath them or cut their hair, trying to resist the control of others. But parents still have to persevere. It's much the same with puppies. You must not let your puppy make you stop these vital health and hygiene procedures by employing tactics such as hysterical whining and writhing, or biting.

It is usually much easier to sit down, gently turn puppies on to their backs and hold them between your legs to do things like ear inspection, teeth cleaning and claw clipping, as this kind of position and restraint often has a subduing effect on dogs.

It is also important to remain calm and purposeful while persisting with these procedures, but never be aggressive or frightening to your puppy. Never try to soothe your puppy or give him attention when he is protesting, as this will only reinforce such behaviour and spur him on to continue it.
When your puppy stops protesting, praise him well for his co-operation in letting you handle him and also give him a treat. If you carry on doing these things regularly, in the same way, your puppy will eventually get used to them. He will put up less and less resistance each time, as he will realise that this is the key to getting them over and done with more quickly.

My own dogs are so used to teeth cleaning/claw clipping procedures by adulthood that they not only relax but can actually doze off into a snooze while I am doing it.

You must, however, instantly and continually correct –

PLEASE NEVER DO THIS!

I have never quite understood why some owners – and predominantly male ones it seems – have a compulsive desire to engage in rough and tumble games with puppies on the floor or ground, in a way which puts owners in a submissive position to their dogs.

You may notice that when young collie puppies do this with each other they get progressively more excited and a lot of teeth get used. The more excited they get, the harder they can bite – only they have lots of thick fur round their faces, necks and limbs, and you have not.

I cannot tell you how many collies' aggressive careers with people began with these kinds of stupidly provocative games in puppyhood. Biting or nipping for a collie puppy cannot sometimes be okay, when you want to play like this, and at other times be wrong. Biting people must always be wrong, full stop.

"*hey!*"– a puppy who tries to bite you while you are grooming him. If he still persists you may need to tie him up to something by his collar in order to complete the process in a quiet but purposeful way. It is not the nicest or most ideal option – but neither is having a filthy, matted dog you cannot groom.

Puppies or dogs who learn that aggression or hysteria will allow them to avoid being groomed or handled by people can also be a total nightmare to take to the vet.

EARLY AGGRESSION

If you do not follow the early handling advice laid out in this chapter and instead simply back off when a collie puppy reacts aggressively to you, you have taught him a very bad lesson. But please, as ever, remember the difference between simple play nipping in a puppy, which is perfectly normal, and a puppy showing clear hostile intent.

If a puppy can intimidate you when only months old, how much worse will his behaviour become as he gets older and even more confident about challenging you?

Sometimes initial play biting can escalate into more hostile aggression in a collie puppy simply because the owner handles him in too aggressive a way. This frightens the puppy into a more defensive response. Once he realises that this more hostile reaction can make an owner back off, he has also learned a very bad lesson.

POSSESSIVE AGGRESSION AND STEALING

Some collie puppies can become highly possessive about their food, and may react aggressively when owners approach them while they are eating.

They can also become highly possessive about objects such as toys or items they have stolen from you, particularly if you are unwise enough to allow them regular access to such things in the first place. For more advice on these issues see *Aggression* and *Stealing* in Part Two.

GETTING HELP

Whatever the initial cause or trigger, I cannot over stress how important it is to take a very serious view of any genuinely hostile aggression in a collie puppy the first time you see it. Do not imagine, as so many owners do, that this is simply a one off event or that he will grow out of this type of behaviour in time. He will not. He will go on being aggressive as long as aggression is proving rewarding for him as a strategy.

Many owners make early puppy aggression worse because they misunderstand the cause of the behaviour, or mishandle it by reacting aggressively to the puppy's hostile behaviour. If you have any doubts about your ability to deal with your puppy's aggression, I urge you to seek professional help for the problem as soon as it first arises. Do not wait until this behaviour has become progressively more ingrained.

Note: There is extensive advice on all types of aggression in collies in Part Two.

PUPPIES WHO DO NOT UNDERSTAND HUMAN AFFECTION

Collie puppies who come from more socially deprived or isolated backgrounds can have lots of gaps in their earliest social education, which only become apparent when they go to their new homes. Some, for instance, have no idea what toys are, or how to play with people. Others will not understand the human concept of affection; i.e. a person approaching to stroke and cuddle them. As a result, the puppy may feel greatly threatened by this kind of behaviour and react defensively.

This can prove highly upsetting for owners, as sharing

affection is, for many, one of the greatest pleasures of owning a dog. It needs to be understood, however, that while most domestic dogs have psychologically evolved to the extent where they can tolerate, or even enjoy, human expressions of affection, not all dogs will have evolved as far as others on this front. A dog's tolerance and enjoyment of human displays of affection can also depend on how early on in his life he was introduced to this kind of behaviour.

When a puppy reacts adversely, early on, to affectionate approaches from people, great patience may be required until you have built a far more trusting bond. This includes making no sudden approaches towards him which might frighten him, and always calling him to you, to share a more affectionate moment. Your puppy should make it clear when he feels ready for this.

Puppies who are extremely wary or nervous of human approaches should also, initially, be exclusively hand-fed. In other words, instead of feeding the puppy in a bowl, set aside his daily food allowance and encourage him to come to you, or another household member, for every piece he eats. This way your puppy will learn to find human interactions highly positive and rewarding experiences.

DEVELOPING WORKING INSTINCT

As your collie puppy grows, the level and strength of his individual working instincts will become increasingly apparent to you. Classic eyeing and stalking behaviour can be seen in some collie puppies when they are only six to eight weeks old. In other dogs similar instincts – along with the desire to chase and herd moving objects or other animals – can manifest themselves somewhat later.

Either way, as soon as these instincts appear in your young collie, and particularly if there seems to be a more obsessive edge to them, you must know how to get control of them as soon as possible. If you do not do this, then very quickly your dog will begin targeting his eye-chase-herd instincts on to a wealth of inappropriate targets, ranging from birds and traffic to runners and cyclists. In all the excitement engendered by a chase, he may also start nipping as well. The more of a buzz he gets from such activities, the less responsive he will be to you and the more you will lose control of his behaviour. You never want this to happen.

THE OBSESSION TARGET AND THE HANDLER

Control of working instinct in collies has to start with the understanding that these dogs must have an obsession target in their lives, i.e. an object on which all their working focus will primarily be targeted. The stronger the level of working instinct in the dog, the more essential this is.

Even when deeply focused on an obsession target, collies still have a special ability to divert their concentration back and forward from this to a handler and his or her commands. It is a form of highly evolved mental functioning that makes them so good at what they were originally bred to do.

When a collie is working, the sheep are his obsession target and the shepherd is his handler. Obviously, as a pet owner, you will have no sheep or other more legitimate targets for your collie to direct his instincts on to. This means you not only have to become the authoritative handler in his life – but also the obsession target as well.

Becoming this all important obsession target for your young dog begins with giving him all those early, and previously mentioned, one-to-one play and bonding sessions, plus the kind of focus training laid out in this chapter. If you do all this well and then move on to the more advanced training outlined in Chapter Seven, you will always be able to keep your collie's working instincts and behaviour under your control.

FOCUS TRAINING

All training of dogs has to begin with teaching them to concentrate on you on command. After all, if you cannot teach a dog to focus on you, on command, how on earth can you teach him anything else?

Many people do not understand that owner focus, along with emotional self-control, are things you have to teach dogs, through the right kind of early training. They are not skills or responses you should expect them to just naturally master on their own. As your collie grows, there will be umpteen different sights, sounds and smells competing with you for his attention. There will also be the aforementioned risk of his attention switching rapidly off you and on to moving chase targets instead. That is why you can never start the mission to hold and sustain your dog's focus and concentration on you early enough.

EARLIEST FOCUS AND SELF-CONTROL EXERCISES

When my puppies are really young and all yapping and jumping about like maniacs to get out of their big indoor kennel, I just stand there completely silently holding one finger in front of my face. Simply through not moving or saying anything, one by one they all eventually become quiet again, while simultaneously watching me and my finger. As they do this I say: *"watch me"*, immediately praise them and then let them out to play.

I do the same thing when I am feeding them. I simply hold their communal feeding platter in one hand, while pointing up a finger in front of my face with the other, and stand completely still watching them. At first they are all whining and yapping and jumping up but eventually, just through me remaining totally still and quiet, they all eventually become quiet again and watch me. At this point, again, I

The Collie has the ability to focus very intently. Your aim is to make sure that focus is on you.

say: *"watch me"*, immediately praise them and give them their food.

Every time I do these things, the puppies get quicker and quicker at responding to *"watch me"*. I find such early exercises fascinating on several fronts. First, it shows how effectively you can stop, or abort, more agitated or unstable forms of energy in dogs simply through staying absolutely still and quiet yourself. Second, it shows how early you can begin teaching dogs very basic lessons in emotional self-control. Third, it shows you how quickly collies can learn that sustaining focus on a person can be a highly rewarding strategy in life.

HOW TO TEACH 'WRONG' EARLY BEHAVIOUR INSTEAD

If, by contrast, I had let the puppies out of their kennel or fed them while they were still in a highly vocal and excitable state, I would just be reinforcing and rewarding that kind of behaviour instead. The same would be true if I had given them any kind of verbal/physical attention for being in a more excitable state of mind.

I recommend you try these very early kinds of focus/self-control exercise with your own puppy. They will initially demand great patience from you, because when a puppy is noisy and boisterous it can be very easy to crack

and say something or do something, or just give him what he wants to shut him up. Unfortunately, this is exactly how you quickly teach him the wrong behaviour by making it rewarding. You also begin process of undermining his respect for you, because you are showing him that you do not have greater mental strength than him; a key ingredient of convincing leadership.

The last thing you want any young collie to learn is that you will always be the first to crack, or give in, whenever he exerts the slightest psychological pressure on you.

'WATCH ME'

As just outlined, when you have finally got your puppy to wind down, through staying still or giving him a correction command (*hey!*), and he is concentrating on you, remember to attach words to this activity that he will remember later on, i.e. *"watch me"*. At the same time, give him a body signal, such as the finger held in front of your face that I use, to further reinforce this command in his head.

Inside the hand with the finger pointed you should also place a treat or a small toy. As soon as you are able to hold your puppy's concentration for just five seconds, while you say *"watch me"*, then praise him well for his co-operation and let him have the treat or toy.

Note: In this exercise, your puppy should really be focusing on the imagined (or real!) reward you have in your *hand,* with the pointed finger, when you ask him to 'watch' you, instead of watching your *eyes.* This is because in the canine world, persistent and lengthy eye contact can be read as challenging or threatening.

'SIT' AND 'WATCH ME'

Next, move on to getting your puppy to *sit* and watch you. To teach him to *sit* hold a toy or treat in your hand. Let your puppy see the toy or treat before you hold it up. Any time he tries to jump up and grab it, hold it higher away from him so he cannot get it. Eventually he will sit and the *instant* he is sitting say the word: "*sit*", then immediately praise him – "*good boy!*" – and let him have the treat or toy to play with.

Keep practising this exercise until your puppy can sit reliably on command. Also add a body signal to the verbal cue, "*sit*", such as your arm sweeping up, which will make the command even clearer for him.

Next, ask your puppy to *sit,* but this time keep the treat or small toy in your hand while you point your finger up in front of your face and say: "*watch me*", as before, while he is watching you and not moving. As soon as he does this for around five seconds, immediately praise him and then reward him with the treat or toy and a game.

When this is going well, ask him to sit and watch you for 10-20 seconds before praising and then rewarding him. Then get into the habit of asking your puppy to sit and watch you in the same way before any of the following:

- Before a game with a toy
- Before a meal
- Before giving him any kind of treat
- Before a trip out for a walk
- Before opening a gate or door for him to go through.

This way you not only continue to teach him that focusing on you will always be highly rewarding; you also keep building up his levels of emotional self-control in situations where he could otherwise become highly excited. The more rewarding a controlled state of mind becomes for a dog, the calmer a dog you will raise.

LOW CONCENTRATION

Some collie puppies can start out with appallingly low levels of concentration. Often this is because they have inadvertently, in the past, been rewarded for more excitable behaviour. Alternatively they may have been rewarded too often and too quickly for expending very little co-operative effort – e.g. just sitting without

prolonged focus on an owner as well. This means that if the dog does not immediately get a reward for just sitting, he rapidly loses interest in remaining engaged with his owner.

Although completely the fault of the owner, this is still pretty spoilt and disrespectful behaviour. If this sounds like your collie puppy, you will need to make him work and concentrate much harder in the future in order to access any of the good things in life – which, of course, you totally control.

'DOWN'

It is vitally important to teach all collies the '*down*' command and then later the '*down on the move*' command (see Chapter Eight), which will basically serve as the future brakes on your dog when he is out and you desperately need to stop him chasing something.

For young puppies, '*down*' is an exercise you can use to make them settle, or stop them doing anything you don't want them to do, especially if you add a "*watch me*" command once he has laid down, or the '*wait*' or '*stay*' commands as outlined (see below).

To teach '*down*', proceed as follows. First get a tasty treat and make your puppy *sit.* Once he is sitting, let your puppy smell the treat but keep it in your hand. Place your hand with the treat between his front legs, but keep one finger pointing towards the ground. As your puppy bends down to sniff the treat pull your hand back, so he slides his legs down and forward to get at the treat you are holding. The moment he has slid completely to the ground say: "*down*", praise him well – "*good boy!*" – and give him the treat.

By keeping a finger pointing to the ground in this exercise, your puppy will eventually be able to read from this body signal, as well as the verbal cue "*down*", that you want him to lie down. Keep practising this exercise until you can get your puppy to lie straight down on command, without always having to start from the '*sit*' position. Each time he does it praise him well and then reward him with either a treat or a toy and a game.

'WAIT' AND 'STAY'

I always start teaching '*wait*' and '*stay*' as two different commands for my dogs. In '*wait*' I want the dog to stay still until I ask him to do something else – e.g. come to me, or pick something up and bring it to me. In '*stay*' I want the dog not to move from where I have put him until I come back and give him a release command.

Such differences will be important if you wish later to pursue a discipline such as Competitive Obedience. I also think they result in far less confusion for the dog.

When training '*wait*', I ask the puppy to sit *next* to me and put a hand in front of his face while I am standing next to him as an accompanying body signal. With the hand still in front of his face and my back to the puppy, I then take one step *forward*. If the puppy does not move I immediately say: "*wait*", then step back to him and praise him – "*good boy!* – and reward him with a treat. Then I aim for more and more steps away from the puppy while he remains still, always saying "*wait*" while he does so, before going back to praise and then reward him.

Only when his '*wait*' is really reliable will I then ask a puppy to come to me after he has waited, or go and bring something to me.

Stay is quite different. In this exercise I ask the puppy to adopt a specific position – i.e. *sit* or *down* – before walking *in front of him* and holding my hand *up* as the accompanying body signal. I then take one step *backwards*, away from him, while still looking at him. If he does not move I say: "*stay*". Then I go back to him, stand next to him, and wait *at least another three to five seconds* before touching him on the shoulder and saying: "*okay!*". This is the release command I will thereafter give my puppy to tell him the exercise is finished. I can then praise and reward him fulsomely.

Gradually you can work at getting your puppy to *stay* for longer and longer on command. You can also extend the period between returning to him, and releasing him from the command, to 10 seconds or more. This stops a puppy moving before you return to him, or as you return to him. Also, once a puppy knows what '*stay*' means, he will not be anticipating you calling him to you, and thus move too quickly because of this.

If your puppy moves when you have asked him to "*wait*" or "*stay*", keep placing him back, gently, in the spot where you originally left him and start again. Do not get angry and aggressive about it, you will just unnecessarily upset him. But do be persistent, because if you let your puppy get away with moving just one or two steps forward when you have asked him to "*wait*" or "*stay*" he will keep doing it and his responses to these commands will never become fully reliable.

Note: The only time I use a release command – "*okay!*" – to end a *wait* exercise is during more advanced *anti-chase* and other movement control training, covered in Chapter Eight. The release command in this case is only ever *verbal* – i.e. I do not touch the dog as well to release him, as I would do with a normal *stay* exercise.

RECALL

Recall is an exercise that so often goes wrong for owners because they do not understand the need to condition a 'returning response' into a dog, with the right early training, *before* they go out and let him off a lead.

In other words, when you first go out and let your puppy off his lead, you are relying on his immature owner

dependency to keep him near you, as opposed to good training. However, as your dog gets older, more confident in himself and more distracted by other things, including targets on which to focus his working drives, the battle to keep his attention focused on you is progressively lost.

Good recall responses begin with all the early play and training work you do with your puppy, where you teach him that focusing on you and co-operating with you will always be highly rewarding. Beyond that, you will also need to devise a special word or sound – which could be a whistle or just a particular way of calling his name – that your puppy will also quickly associate with a highly rewarding experience.

If, for example, your recall word is "*come!*", you should say this, in a highly encouraging and inviting way, in the following situations:

- Before a game with your puppy
- Before you give him a meal
- Before giving him a treat
- Before a trip out for a walk

The more you do this, the more he will respond quickly and enthusiastically to your recall sound. If he does not come quickly, keep a long line on him for this exercise. You can then reel him to you in an inviting manner, with your recall sound, so that he can keep associating both the recall sound and the act of returning to you with a reward. Remember to only say your recall sound/command to your puppy *while he is actually returning to you*. Otherwise you will quickly teach him, instead, to ignore you while you make this sound – a very common owner mistake that can lead to ever poorer recall responses later, once the dog is let off a lead.

Never use your recall sound/command in any kind of negative context –i.e. when you want to do something like groom or bath your puppy or clip his nails, or tell him off for some misdemeanour. You will quickly undo all your earlier hard work building more positive associations and the overall effectiveness of this command.

When practising recall with your puppy when you are out, always wait until his attention is either on you or not directly fixed on something else before calling him. When dogs are sniffing something or locked into an encounter with another dog they will not come so readily to you because they are otherwise distracted.

I also like to add a distinct body gesture – both arms raised up in the air – to reinforce the *recall* command, as this works particularly well when recalling dogs from some distance away. All my dogs are trained to respond to both an individual and collective *verbal* recall command, but the arm gesture itself, from a distance, signifies recall to all of them.

A puppy's concentration will improve the more often you ask him to focus on you.

There will be more on recall training and recall failures in following chapters and also Part Two.

'GIVE'

It is extremely important to teach young puppies that giving you things, on command, will always be highly rewarding. Not only does this minimise the chance of your dog stealing things and running off with them, and maybe then even guarding them from you, but it is also – along with *recall* – a vital component of a more formal retrieve exercise you may wish to do later.

Teaching a puppy to '*give*' you something is actually pretty simple if you go about it the right way. You can start teaching it during one of your early play and bonding sessions.

First, place a tasty treat in one hand and a toy in another. Throw the toy for your puppy. Once he has got the toy in his mouth, hold on to it. Do *not* tug or pull the toy, as this will encourage your puppy to hold on to it harder. Next, show him the tasty treat in your other hand. As he lets go of the toy to eat the treat say: '*Give*!' Then immediately praise him – "*good boy!*" – before letting him eat the treat and give him the toy back. This way you have taught him that giving you things will always be highly rewarding.

Keep repeating this exercise, always remembering to say "*give*" as he is actually letting go of something in his mouth for you. Then immediately praise him for this, let him have the treat and give the item back to him. When you want to end a play session, ask him to '*give*' the toy back to you. Thereafter praise and reward him for this with a treat, but do not give him the toy back. When your puppy grabs something in his mouth that you do not want him to have,

ask him to "*give*" this to you as before, and praise him when he does, but also regularly attach a jackpot reward to this kind of co-operation, like several very tasty treats and a highly prized toy.

This will always highly motivate him to return things to you, even if they are not always given back to him. If you begin this exercise when your puppy is very young you will never have any problems getting anything from him in response to the '*give*' command.

RETRIEVE

A basic retrieve exercise entails putting several commands together. If you ask your puppy to "*sit*" and "*wait*" before you throw something for him to retrieve, that is already two commands. You will then need to attach another command for him to leave your side and run to the thrown item – e.g. "*go get it!*". When your puppy picks up the item in his mouth, this requires another command – e.g. "*hold*" – to reinforce the action. You will then need a *recall* command to get your puppy to return to you with the item, and finally a "*give*" command to get him to hand it over to you.

So what you may regard as just one exercise is actually *six* different actions for your puppy, all of which first have to be separately trained in, and then put together. In Competitive Obedience there are actually several more aspects to this exercise that your dog will need to learn (see Chapter Eleven on competition training).

If you are having trouble getting your puppy to return to you with thrown items, keep him on a long line for this exercise, and encourage him back to you as laid out in the earlier *recall* training.

THE USE OF HAND SIGNALS AND BODY LANGUAGE

Because dogs are primarily tuned into our body language, as opposed to our verbal language, it always helps to accompany any verbal command you teach your young collie with a physical gesture as well. Recapping on exercises mentioned previously in this chapter, these are as follows:

A correction: You make your dog move back using your body energy, while also pointing at him and maintaining eye contact.
Back and off: You make your dog move back, or off you and back, using your body energy.
Quiet!: You hold out your fingers in a pinching motion.
Watch me: You keep a finger pointed up in front of your face while you stand still.
Sit: You sweep your arm and hand upwards.
Down: You point a finger to the ground.
Wait: You hold your hand in front of your dog's face while he is next to you.
Stay: You hold your hand up in front of your dog's face while you are in front of him.
Recall: You raise both your arms up in the air.

Once your young collie has learnt all these exercises really well, he should be able to respond to just a hand signal or verbal command, instead of both at once. If you later use primarily verbal commands it is still very important to keep using additional hand signals/body language every so often for training exercises as these will be useful when you are working a greater distance away, or when your dog is older and his hearing becomes less acute.

COLLIES AND TOYS

Collies can quickly get obsessed with toys, which to some extent is what you desire. This is because toy chasing can replace, in your dog's mind, the buzz he would otherwise get from working sheep. Through controlling access to toys, you thus control your dog's visual attention and working drives and become, as previously outlined, both the handler and the obsession target in his mind.

Many collies will eye and herd or 'circle' their owners, when they have toys, which is a classic example of this. Or they may eye and herd owners just in anticipation of getting a toy.

Golden rules about toys and collies are:

• First, the toys must always belong to you. You always begin any game and decide when it ends. Once you end the game, you must remove the toys and not let your dog pressurise you either psychologically (with whining, barking or staring) or physically (by nipping you or your clothes) into further play. This makes you look weak and your dog will never stop the habit as long as you allow him to get his own way.

• Second, decide your own rules of play. Always make your dog do something for you - e.g. get him to place a toy in your hand and then sit or lie down – before you throw it for him. Do not allow your dog to just dump a toy at your feet and then whine or bark for you to throw it for him again. This is how you become your dog's personal toy slave. It is weakness again.

• Third, in similar vein, never throw or give your dog toys just for the sake of it; always use them as training currency – i.e. in return for a good behaviour or response to a command. The more you do this the better his responses to your training will get.

• Fourth, do not use endless toy throwing as an easier and lazier alternative to distance exercise or other mental occupation for your collie. This is how you create a mush-brained dog who begins every outing totally hyped up and obsessive about a toy and goes home in much the same frame of mind. It is not healthy and your dog could easily get injured through putting such repetitive strain on a body that simply is not fit enough. Fitness only comes via other, better forms of exercise such as distance and gradient work to increase stamina, agility and heart/lung function.

• Finally, never throw a toy for a dog who has just got out of a car. This increases the chance of injury even more as his muscles and joints have not warmed up. Always intersperse toy throwing with exercises such as 'down' and 'stay' or scent tasks (see Chapter Eight) which will restore a bit of calm to his brain. Keep remembering that an over-excited collie never thinks straight.

HOW DOGS LEARN

It can be hard to most effectively train your collie without a good enough understanding of how dogs learn.

Dogs learn from the immediate consequences of their actions. If the action in question has positive consequences – i.e. proves rewarding – they will want to repeat it. If instead there are more negative or unrewarding consequences to the action they will not want to repeat it.

In a quick-thinking breed like collies, this learning process can literally occur in a split second. Thus the better you are at attaching an instant rewarding consequence to a 'right' action or behaviour in your dog, the better a trainer you will be, and the quicker your dog will learn desirable things. If you are slower in timing your consequences to actions, your dog may not learn so fast, or he may learn wrong lessons through you inadvertently attaching a reward to an undesirable behaviour.

It is important to understand that dogs think in pictures and contexts. This means that they begin associating a specific behaviour or exercise with a specific context, such as your home. If you want your dog to respond just as well to a specific command or exercise wherever you are, you must teach and reinforce these things in a multitude of different places and contexts to make them most reliable. *Also see Bomb proofing your training.*

Your body language and mental state can also affect how your dog views the training process, for better or worse. If you approach training in an aggressive, impatient or hostile manner, you are immediately attaching negative associations to a process that you need your dog to find rewarding. So never train your dog when you are feeling stressed, tired, unwell or if you are simply in a bad mood.

DO NOT UNDERESTIMATE YOUR PUPPY'S BRAIN

All the basic training exercises I have so far outlined in this chapter have been taught to my own collie puppies by the time they are 10-12 weeks old. You should never underestimate how early in life collies can learn things, and the earlier right lessons or good behaviours are programmed into their brains, the more likely it is that these will endure into adulthood.

Many people attempt to start training their collie – in terms of just basic co-operation tasks – far too late into puppyhood, out of a belief that their dog was not ready to learn such things any earlier. Newsflash! Collies start learning things from the moment they are born. By failing to take charge of this learning process early on, you miss out on that period of your dog's life when he is most receptive to the absorption and retention of desirable behaviours.

You also leave a vacuum in his head that can be filled with a wealth of undesirable behaviours instead. The longer you leave a puppy to experiment with undesirable behaviours and find them rewarding, for want of better guidance, the more ingrained these will become and the harder they will be to change as he grows.

Also be aware that the quickest way to teach a dog to be disobedient is to not teach him first that co-operation will always pay.

BOMB PROOFING YOUR TRAINING

You can teach all the exercises I have outlined in this chapter at home, initially, and/or anywhere else where there is the minimum amount of distraction for your young dog. Only once your puppy responds reliably to all the exercises in situations of minimum distraction, then start practising them more and more when you are out in busier places. Do them in as many different places or contexts as you can, at the same time gradually increasing the level of distraction your puppy is exposed to, while still maintaining his focus on you.

This is how you bomb proof your dog's training, and make it work just as well wherever you are. If, by contrast, your puppy only associates responding to set tasks in the environment of home, or a training class, he will start thinking that everywhere else he can behave differently, or do what he likes.

Beyond a certain age, and once they have learned a wide range of exercises, I only ever train my dogs when they are out – e.g. at a local park or on a walk. You also never stop training a dog; constantly reinforcing specific commands through regular practise, and with the intermittent attachment of rewards. It is a process that needs to be continued throughout your dog's life to retain the most reliable responses.

HOW AND WHEN TO USE PRAISE AND REWARDS

Whenever you are teaching your collie a new exercise, it is very important not only to use praise and rewards with the right timing, but also in the right order.

Let us imagine that you are teaching your young collie to *sit*. First of all you need to do something to actively encourage or invite this action, such as hold a treat or toy above his head. Then you need to immediately attach the verbal command ("*sit!*") and hand signal (arm sweeping up) to this action as your dog *actually sits*. While he is *still* sitting, you must then praise him – "good boy!" – *before* giving him the treat or toy as a reward.

By working in this order, your dog will eventually come to associate your praise with a reward. Such conditioning means that, later on, your praise, in itself, will be viewed as a reward. If, by contrast, you get into the habit of giving treat or toy rewards first, and then praise him for doing something, your verbal praise will become far less important to him, and less of an incentive for his co-operation.

Later on you may also end up with a dog who will not co-operate with you until he first sees a toy or treat in your hand. So always remember to do things in this order:

- Invite the behaviour (e.g., *sit* or *down*).
- Put a command/hand signal to the behaviour *while* the behaviour is still being performed.
- Praise your dog *while* the behaviour is still being performed.
- *Then* reward your dog with a treat or toy.
- Apply the same principles to all your training.
- Also be aware that continually over-rewarding dogs for any act of co-operation can actually diminish, as oppose to enhance, their responses to exercises over time. After all, the easier it is to get a reward from an owner, the lower the motivation for a dog to try harder to earn it.

The best ways to use rewards are as follows:

- When you are first teaching a dog a new exercise. In this case, use them – after praise – each and every time your dog performs a new behaviour correctly or, if it is a more complex exercise, every time he moves nearer to your ultimate training goal. This will act to reinforce the new behaviour.
- Once your dog knows an exercise well, then mostly use praise alone to reward him for responding. Only add additional rewards such as treats or toys intermittently, after praise, to keep his motivation high, and especially when he does an exercise particularly well.
- Regularly add a jackpot reward (i.e. much praise, followed by several delicious treats and a favourite toy) to a particularly good training response. This will also keep your dog's motivation to co-operate with you really high.

EARLY TRAINING MISTAKES

If you are a relative novice at dog training, and training collies in particular – they always react so much faster to any handler error – then it is both likely, and understandable, that you will make some mistakes early on.

Such errors include not building a good enough early one-to-one bond with your dog, which will always inspire greater focus and co-operation from him, or inadvertently attaching commands and rewards to wrong behaviours. Classic examples of this are:

- Saying *"sit"* and praising and rewarding your dog with a treat *as he is getting up from a sit*, as opposed to *remaining* in a sit.
- Praising and rewarding a dog for '*staying*' after he has moved forward.

- Praising and rewarding a dog for *lying down* as he is getting up, as opposed to while he is *still lying down*.
- Saying *"sit down"*, which is actually two different commands at once. Also see *How and when to use praise and rewards, page 57,* and further advice on training problems in Chapter Seven.

As previously outlined, always train in a good mood and make every training session fun, because any 'bad' or hostile emotional energy you display could make your dog mentally shut down, lose confidence, or come to view all training as a negative experience.

You also need to know when to *stop* training. By making your dog repeat the same commands again and again, he may become progressively less enthusiastic or, again, lose confidence out of a belief that he is constantly getting something wrong. Always end training as soon as your dog has given you one good response to any exercise and while he is still clearly very keen to do more. Training should always be viewed by your dog as a fun experience you regularly treat him to, as opposed some ghastly affliction you make him endure.

The more I train dogs the more I have also realised that it is the quality, rather than quantity, of the teaching you give them which underlies consistently good performance.

WALKING PROPERLY ON THE LEAD

For reasons I forever fail to understand, owners never teach their young dogs to walk properly on the lead from day one, thus rendering future outings with them a constant source of strife. They may then move on, in desperation, to employing a vast array of different choking/restraining devices on their dog, which add even further misery to his whole lead-walking experience. I do not feel that dogs should have to be half strangled or trussed up like kippers, just in order to keep them walking by your side. They just need to be better trained.

Lead pulling can be very damaging, longer-term, for a dog's neck and windpipe. It can also be very bad for you, placing great strain on your wrists, shoulders, neck and back. So why not just put a bit more effort into preventing this habit developing in the first place?

Begin by understanding why a dog pulls on the lead. It is not because he is bad or being deliberately un-co-operative, but because he wants to get to somewhere or something faster than you can walk. When he tries this, you may then pull him firmly back on the lead by his neck. The more you pull him back, the more he tries to pull forwards to escape the pressure you are applying to his neck. It's a vicious circle.

MAKING PULLING UNREWARDING

As long as a dog finds that pulling enables him to move

forwards faster than he would if he did not pull, he will keep on pulling. So the answer to this is to make pulling forward on the lead totally unrewarding for your dog.

There are two ways to do this. You can try stopping dead, each and every time your young dog walks ahead of you and makes the lead tighten, and correct him for this action – "*hey*"! Then immediately make him come back to you and sit for around 10 seconds before moving on again. Alternatively, stick your leg out in front of your dog to stop him, every time he tries to pull ahead of you on the lead. At the same time give him a correction – "*hey!*" – for this wrong action.

Whichever method you prefer, it is also extremely important to keep praising your dog – "*good boy!*" – and rewarding him with the occasional treat for walking in the right place, i.e. by your side. Asking your dog regularly to "*watch*" you while he is out walking on the lead can also help to keep him in the right position.

Continual persistence with this exercise is also the key, until you have finally conditioned your dog into the right behaviour. It is only by failing to be persistent and consistent with this type of training that allows dogs to keep finding the lead-pulling habit rewarding.

USING YOUR TRAINING

Once you have taught your dog the separate exercises outlined in this chapter, you can then string them together, in a manner of your choosing, to best control his behaviour – e.g. *recall* followed by *sit,* followed by *watch me.* Or *down,* followed by *wait,* followed by *recall.* All that matters is that you have taught each individual exercise correctly to your dog, before joining it up to another one.

These early taught exercises in basic focus and co-operation will also make all the difference at home, or out, when you have to manage your puppy in different social situations, as outlined in the next chapter.

'LOYALTY' – OR LEARNED HELPLESSNESS?

For me, no chapter outlining the nature of relationships between humans and dogs would be complete without recognition of the psychological syndrome of learned helplessness.

Humans can suffer from this, and so can dogs. Basically, it describes the mindset of an animal who feels powerless to control his own life or escape situations that may be stressful or harmful to him. It explains why people feel unable to leave abusive relationships or retaliate against their abusers, or why people taken hostage can become ever more compliant towards, and psychologically or emotionally dependent on, their captors.

In modern domestic dogs, learned helplessness may have become more prevalent or widespread a syndrome simply through selective breeding; i.e., the constant favouring by man of canine companions or workmates that were more easily trained and bent to their will. You do not find this same behaviour so prevalent in wolves. Wolves are not easily trained and whatever confined space you put them in, they will never stop trying to escape.

The state of captivity, which most domestic dogs are subjected to by humans very early on in their lives, further encourages a more helpless mental state and perhaps also better explains why dogs can remain so apparently loyal to people who treat them badly. They have actually become conditioned to believe that there is no other option.

THE BEHAVIOURAL FALL OUT

If not sufficiently understood and handled, learned helplessness can have a significant behavioural fall out on dogs, depending on how well, or not, they can adapt individually to the state of captivity and the imposition of relative powerlessness over their lives. Some may become extremely agitated and aggressive, others distinctly withdrawn or depressed – all symptoms you will see in dogs who have been ill-treated and/or confined in smaller spaces like kennels over a long period of time.

The syndrome can also lead to dogs who feel totally unable to solve any problem in their lives without human help or intervention, and more extreme forms of separation anxiety.

The intrinsic psychological helplessness of dogs can too easily be exploited by any of us. Typical examples of exploiting learned helplessness in dogs is when owners leave them for hours on end in confined conditions, with no thought given to the psychological suffering this causes them. Or when dogs are subjected to abusive training, handling or lifestyles simply to satisfy the demands of their owners' egos or personal ambitions.

WOULD YOU LIKE IT?

A simple test of whether or not you are exploiting your dog's more helpless position is to ask yourself: how well would you cope with the demands or lifestyle you inflict/impose on him on a daily basis? If you would not like it, there is your answer.

Also bear in mind – as outlined in *Stress and stress related problems*, in Part Two – that a dog who is not coping well psychologically will not necessarily display behaviours or symptoms that an owner is able to read as stress-related.

MINIMISING THE MORE HARMFUL EFFECTS

You can minimise the more harmful effects of learned helplessness in dogs in many ways. First, by giving them a good life with plenty of daily exercise and outings to offset the stresses of captivity. Second, teach your dog to cope

Clear signals are invaluable in the learning process.

When teaching Down, use a hand signal with your finger pointing downwards.

The hand signal for "Wait".

The hand signal for "Stay".

early on with regular separation from you – as outlined in the last chapter – and never make this separation too long.

Third, always try to give your dog the feeling that he is making his own choices, as opposed to having his every thought and action rigidly controlled by you – as nothing is more damaging than this, longer term, to his inner sense of confidence and overall psychological health.

MAKING CHOICES

Providing it does not put your dog or anyone else in any immediate danger, let your dog sometimes experiment with a wrong behaviour first, if he wants to, before offering a right option that he will always find more rewarding. Through being given the freedom to make choices, your dog regains some sense of control over his life. Encouraging your dog to solve his own problems without your intervention (e.g. scent and search tasks, as outlined in Chapter Eight) will also boost his confidence and his belief in his own abilities.

Most of all, always be a benignly protective force in your dog's life. There may be times when you will need to be strong and firm with him, in order to teach him behaviour that will keep him safe and afford him the highest quality of life, but do not abuse your power.

BULLYING AND PUNISHMENT

The verbal and physical punishment and bullying of dogs is a classic human abuse of power. People will target their anger and frustration on to dogs through hitting them and shouting at them, in a way they would never do if the dogs in question were able to retaliate or escape their control.

Collies, in particular, are so easily damaged by harsh treatment of any kind. But physically unleashing anger or frustration on to an animal who is smaller than us, and unable to retaliate or escape our control, also demeans us, as human beings. We need to be better than this, and we can be.

A dog needs to see in us something that readily inspires him to follow us, without fear or hesitation. As soon as you become verbally or physically abusive to your dog, you break this essential bond of trust. You put doubt in his mind and cross a line which transforms you from a worthy leader to an everyday bully.

Allow your collie to sometimes make choices so that he does not become too dependent on you.

Bullies in the canine world – as in the human world – are those that are not good enough to be natural leaders. True leaders are strong and inspire trust, whereas bullies are essentially weak and instil fear. Understand that difference, because dogs always do.

Chapter Six

ONGOING SOCIAL TRAINING

How to raise a dog at ease with his world

In the last chapter, I explained how vital it was to establish the right relationship with your collie as his leader, protector and mentor. I also outlined the kind of focus and co-operation training exercises a puppy needs to learn *before* being exposed to some of the greater social challenges facing him in the outside world.

If you do not build this respectful bond with him early on, and teach him how to respond to set commands in different situations, he will always be far less prepared for, or able to cope with, these things later. You will also, as a result, find it harder and harder to control his behaviour.

In this chapter, I shall now show you how you can progressively stretch your collie puppy's social flexibility and tolerance with the right handling and training.

VISITORS TO THE HOME

Even before facing less familiar people, dogs and experiences in the outside world, one of the first bigger social tests for many growing collie puppies can be visitors to the home.

A lot of owners will tell you that their collies were quite friendly with people visiting their home when they were very young but, thereafter, they got increasingly anti-social, reacting to less familiar visitors with anything from obvious wariness to outright aggression.

In fact, there is a perfectly rational explanation for this. The visitors the dog was fine with were introduced to him at the stage in his development – typically below 16 weeks – when he was most amenable to making new social relationships. By contrast, visitors who were introduced to him later on coincided with his development of both territorial behaviour and more fearful/defensive responses towards strangers.

It is important to understand how instinctive it is for dogs, as pack animals, to evolve an 'us and them' mentality beyond a certain age. In other words, people or dogs they meet and socialise with at an early age become regarded as part of their pack, whereas people or dogs they meet later are deemed *outside* the pack, and thus more likely to pose a threat.

SOCIAL CONDITIONING

Human beings, without more intense social conditioning

and exposure from a young age, can have similar attitudes towards strangers when they are older. This is because, much like dogs, we have an inherently tribal mindset as a species.

Dogs have to be socially conditioned, from early puppyhood onwards, to accept less familiar visitors in the same way. If your collie puppy came from a more socially deprived background and/or has a greater genetic tendency towards territorial or 'fear of the new' behaviour, he is likely to react more adversely to less familiar visitors as he grows, unless you follow the training guidelines laid out in a moment.

If your puppy is not so genetically fearful or territorial, and/or was exposed to new visitors constantly throughout his early puppyhood and beyond, in ways that always made their presence highly positive and rewarding for him, he is far less likely to have the same kind of anti-social problems later in life.

CONTROLLING HOUSEHOLD TERRITORY

As highlighted in Chapter Four, where a lot of people go wrong with collie puppies is allowing them free access, from day one, to important household territorial areas, such as stairways, halls and front or back doorways, where owners leave the home and visitors will enter it.

As a puppy grows in confidence and develops both working and territorial instincts, he may then seek to take over these areas and control them. He may herd and nip household members or visitors who attempt to pass through these areas or react towards them in an aggressive way.

This would not have happened had owners and other household members laid better claim to these important areas in the home from day one, through keeping their puppy in separate quarters.

Also be aware of how incredibly easy it is to inadvertently reward undesirable behaviour in your dog towards visitors – i.e. barking, growling – through simply giving him *attention*, as opposed to a swift correction ("*hey!*"). This includes talking to your dog in a scolding tone to make him stop, or trying to reassure him that a visitor is harmless, etc.

As soon as your dog sees how important his negative

reaction towards visitors appears to be to you, this is all the more reason for him to repeat it. It is much better to train him, as early as possible, to have much more positive attitudes towards visitors or strangers, as now outlined.

BEWARE THE DOWNWARD SPIRAL

The emphasis I have placed in this chapter on properly conditioning collie puppies to tolerate and behave respectfully towards visitors is because problems with this issue can so rapidly spiral out of control.

Too frequently, I come across cases where a collie's aggressive behaviour towards visitors has escalated to the extent where it can place a whole household under siege. Because of their dog's hostile behaviour, owners invite fewer and fewer people to visit them, meaning both they, and their dog, become ever more reclusive in their habits. This, in turn, makes the dog even more aggressive to those few visitors who do come, such has his social tolerance diminished by this stage.

The downward spiral begins with the dog being allowed, when younger, to dictate the terms for how visitors should be encountered, and the owners allowing their dog's aggressive behaviour to then restrict the way they lead their own lives. You must never let this happen.

If you cannot correct a young puppy for wrong behaviour towards visitors, and train him to behave in a more acceptable and desirable way, the challenge to change him will become ever greater as he gets older and is increasingly confident in his use of aggression to control other people's actions and lives.

THE 'GO SEE!' COMMAND

The '*go see!*' command is one of the best things you can teach any young dog, *before* he reacts over-fearfully to new people, dogs or things. This is because, if taught correctly, the command will condition him to approach new situations in a more confident way.

To teach it, proceed as follows. When you give your puppy a meal, and have made him *sit* and *wait* first, next release him to eat the food by pointing to the bowl and saying "*go see!*" as he approaches and goes to eat the food.

Next, get into the habit of regularly putting a treat on the floor and making him *sit* and *wait* first. Then point to it and release him to eat it with "*go see!*" as before. Then do the same with every toy you give him – say "*go see!*" as he runs up to get it. Practice these things every day. Remember to always praise your dog, too – "*good boy!*" – every time he runs up to something when invited, to reinforce his confidence.

LESS FAMILIAR OBJECTS

When your puppy is responding really well to this exercise, you can try something a bit more testing, like a stranger object. Lay an item such as a mop or coffee jar on the floor, with a tasty treat or favourite toy – whichever works best – right next to it, and ask him to "*go see!*" this unfamiliar object. If he rushes up to it confidently, praise him – "*good boy!*" – just before he eats the treat, or gets the toy.

If your puppy hesitates or freezes, it is vital *not* to keep saying "*go see!*" as you will be attaching this command to a more fearful response. Also do *not* try to coerce or cajole him into approaching an object he is wary of, as this will also reinforce more fearful behaviour. Just wait quietly and be patient. If your puppy slowly goes up to the object after initially hesitating, and then gets the treat or toy, say "*go see!*" only *as he is actually eating the treat or grabbing the toy*.

If your puppy is very hesitant, put a treat or favourite toy half way between him and the strange object and ask him to "*go see!*" the treat or toy instead. Then work on getting the treat or toy nearer and nearer to the strange object until your puppy is happy to "*go see!*" it when it is right next to the strange object.

Every day, try to introduce your puppy confidently to at least three new and unfamiliar objects in this way.

The "go see" command allows you to control greetings at a distance.

WHY THE 'GO SEE!' COMMAND WORKS, AND DOESN'T WORK

If used and trained correctly, the 'go see!' command can condition young dogs (who might otherwise be wary) that what they are about to approach will always be safe and have a positive and rewarding outcome.

However, it is also a command that is incredibly easy to corrupt, or render useless, by incorrect timing or application by owners. So follow these golden rules:

- Only ever say "go see!" as your dog is confidently approaching something or someone or just before he gets the reward (i.e. treat or toy) for his confident approach.
- NEVER say "go see!" when your dog is looking remotely hesitant or fearful.
- Similarly, never give attention/verbal assurance to a dog who is acting in a fearful way.

If your young dog has already made a negative or fearful association with something the 'go see!' command in itself may not work, especially if it is still at the very early stages of being conditioned into his mind. You will have to go back to the earlier exercise where you very gradually put a treat nearer and nearer to what he is scared of, while asking him to "go see!" it.

When you later go out with your puppy and attempt to use the 'go see!' command to introduce him to new people, dogs or objects, it is also vital that none of these will be harmful or frightening to him in any way, which will simply undermine his faith in both the command – and you. If you have any doubts at all about who or what you are asking your puppy to approach, do *not* use the 'go see!' command.

GREETING VISITORS TO THE HOME

Once your puppy is responding really reliably to the 'go see!' command at home when asked to approach a variety of unfamiliar things, try using it when visitors come.

First keep a jar of tasty treats by the front door and also put two of your puppy's favourite toys in the room where your visitor will go. As soon as the doorbell rings, or a visitor is heard arriving, shake the jar of treats for your puppy to hear, then give him a treat. This will give him a very early positive response to visitors arriving. Your puppy should also be in his own quarters when they arrive.

When your visitor comes in, ask him/her to initially ignore your puppy. As outlined before, your puppy should never get the idea he is so important, within the household, that visitors greet him first, or that all of you care so much about his reaction to visitors coming.

Once your visitor is sitting down and settled, put the jar of treats next to him/her and wait until your puppy is quiet. You should never let a dog that is in an excitable mental state greet a visitor. When your puppy is quiet, go to get him from his own quarters, attaching a line to him. Bring him in to the room where the visitor is and ask him to "sit" and "wait". Open the

treat jar and give a treat to your visitor. Then ask your puppy to "go see!" him or her. If he goes confidently, praise him really well – "good boy!" – just before he gets his treat from the visitor.

KEEPING THINGS CALM

If your puppy is friendly and well behaved, he may play with the visitor, using his favourite toys. If he misbehaves in any way – e.g. extensive play nipping or jumping up – instantly correct him: "hey!" If he will not stop at this point, return him to his own quarters to reinforce your disapproval.

Never be aggressive or hostile when you banish your puppy. Always act in a calm, quiet but resolute way. Once you have returned your puppy to his quarters, wait until he is quiet again – banishment may have provoked a tantrum of frustration – before bringing him back to meet your visitor again, with praise and another treat when he responds to "go see!".

Allow your puppy to stay with the visitor and keep praising him – "good boy!" – as long as he is behaving well, using an immediate correction – "hey!" – and banishment each time he misbehaves. He will soon understand the behaviour he has to display in order to stay with you and your visitor. He should also gradually see visitors coming as a highly rewarding event.

It is very important, however, to know when banishment is the right or wrong solution for managing your puppy's behaviour towards visitors. See, *Puppies who prefer banishment*, page 65.

BUILDING UP YOUR DOG'S TOLERANCE

When training your puppy to be more confident with visitors, start teaching visitor greeting rituals with people your puppy already knows really well. Get other household members, for instance, to regularly ring the doorbell as pretend visitors, then go through the exercise I have just outlined every time. Then ask neighbours and friends to visit, always doing the exercise in the same way.

It must also be made consistently clear to your puppy that *you* control all access to, and departures from, pack territory and that all visitors belong to *you*. Thus you, alone, will dictate how they should be greeted and treated. By taking charge in this way, you will help your dog to relax because now he has got someone he respects to handle this otherwise potentially worrying experience for him.

VISITING WORKMEN

Visitors such as postmen, builders, deliverymen and window cleaners often alarm dogs because their status seems so unclear. They have a habit of coming and going, and are not always being greeted like other visitors within the core territory of the home, so are they friends or intruders? The uncertainty prompts a dog to bark and react with hostility – whereupon the workman so often leaves again. This typical sequence of events, unfortunately, leads a dog to think that his aggression has made a less welcome or obvious social visitor depart. And the more often this happens, the more confident the dog becomes about being aggressive again whenever similar visitors appear.

You must nip such behaviour in the bud. Once again, take control of greeting workmen yourself and swiftly correct your puppy – "hey!" – for showing aggression. Also get the treat jar out again. Ask your puppy to "go see!" a workman or postman and give him a treat to give your dog. The earlier you begin this kind of conditioning with your puppy, the greater his social tolerance will be towards visiting workmen.

As ever, it is you who has to set down the rules for how your puppy greets all types of visitors. Do not let him take over and make wrong decisions that then turn into more undesirable and ingrained reactions.

PUPPIES WHO PREFER BANISHMENT

Sometimes banishment is the right solution for your puppy's wrong behaviour towards visitors, and sometimes it isn't. It usually depends entirely on the individual dog.

If you have a puppy who generally desires to be centre stage in your household, and control everything that happens within it, then banishment will be a deterrent for bad behaviour. The same is true if your puppy's aggressive behaviour towards visitors has become an attention-seeking ploy. As previously outlined, hostile behaviour towards visitors can so easily become ingrained through owners reinforcing it with attention.

As a general rule, this type of dog is most likely to have a frustration tantrum – i.e. much furious whining or barking – when you banish him because, in so doing, you are depriving him of the level of control and attention he desires. That is why it serves as a deterrent.

However, the one thing you need to look out for, early on, is the exceptionally wary/fearful collie puppy who uses aggression simply to make the visitor problem go away. By banishing a dog like this and removing him from visitors, you are actually *rewarding* him for his hostile behaviour.

RELIEF WHEN BANISHED

A classic indication of this is that the dog will not show any frustration behaviour when banished. If anything, he is intensely relieved to be removed from visitors and, thus, he may show reduced anxiety when banished or even settle down quietly.

A puppy like this has to be completely ignored by visitors (i.e. they shouldn't talk to him, touch him, or make eye contact with him) from the moment they arrive. This immediately removes the pressure in the dog's head about what visitors may do to him when they come.

If the puppy chooses to retreat into another place away from a visitor, leave him be. If he shows any signs of fear, the owner must completely ignore this. If he shows any signs of

confidence, an owner should praise him well. Simple steps like these, early on, could do so much to stop the hostility of fearful puppies escalating out of control.

Most of the visitor aggression/control problems I have just outlined tend to occur once a collie puppy gets older – aged 16 weeks plus. That is why the earlier training/conditioning is so essential to avoid these things happening.

If your puppy is showing excessive aggression towards visitors, for whatever reason, do seek expert help as soon as possible, as other measures/behaviour strategies may be needed to combat the problem.

Note: The whole subject of Aggression in collies is covered in depth in Part Two.

THE OUTSIDE WORLD

Many young collies' problems can begin and end with experiences that occur in the outside world, beyond the familiar home environment. Alternatively they stem from the outside world coming *into* the home environment, in the form of visitors, as just outlined. In both cases the problems in question arise from their growing awareness of the concept of threat.

This is all the more likely in dogs who have not been systematically exposed to visitors and outside world experiences from the time they were very young puppies, or not been taught how to deal with them by their owners. Stronger or more extreme fear reactions in collies towards newer or stranger things will very often also have some significant genetic factor involved.

Such considerations apart, much of the unease young dogs can feel beyond the relative safety of the home environment is not just to do with developing a fear response towards less familiar things, but also their sheer inability to see their surrounding world as we do.

A WORLD WITHOUT LOGIC

As human beings, we can rationalise everything that is going on in our world. We know why everything from thunder and fireworks to the local council dustcart exist and why they are also not essentially harmful to us. Similarly, through prolonged social exposure and conditioning, we learn to tolerate meeting, and being surrounded by, a massive array of other human beings we might not know, yet still not automatically assume they will be a potential threat to us.

Dogs, by contrast, are essentially creatures of instinct, and thus cannot rationalise their reaction to potential external threat in the same way. They can be trained and socially conditioned to cope better with otherwise threatening things, as outlined in this chapter, but it is beyond them to know the logical explanation as to why so many weird looking or sounding things exist in our world, because their brains don't function at that level of reasoning.

This lack of reasoning power, in turn, means that when a

dog is suddenly faced with something strange – be it a sight, sound, object, person, animal or experience – he has one of two choices. He can either inherently trust that something is safe, or fear that it is not – and then react accordingly. Recent studies have also suggested that a dog's tendency to see his surrounding world in an optimistic or pessimistic light can have a high genetic component; a subject covered further in Part Two under *Separation distress*.

WHY SOME DOGS COPE BETTER THAN OTHERS

When breeding dogs, I always look specifically for collies who have a naturally more trusting, biddable and outgoing genetic temperament. This same inherited quality then becomes obvious to me in their offspring when the puppies are only five or six weeks old. This gives me confidence, in turn, that they are going to grow into dogs destined to be socially successful and at ease with their future world – although the quality of how they are raised and trained by new owners is also a vital consideration.

In other collie puppies I often see different things, ranging from a clear reluctance to socially engage with strangers to more extreme reactions to novel external experiences. These can range from a hesitant, freezing body language to shaking and shivering, and a tail clamped between the legs. Puppies like these will always have to be more expertly and extensively socialised, and socially conditioned, to avoid more serious future problems.

When looking at anti-social and problematic adult collies it can frequently be hard to establish how much of their behaviour is down to basic genetic input and how much stems from poor early socialisation when they were very young puppies – i.e. under eight weeks of age. This is because the dogs with the poorest genetic temperaments, and the dogs with the worst earliest socialisation, are usually one and the same creature from the same bad breeder.

TEACHING YOUR PUPPY TO COPE

Good ongoing socialisation of a young collie puppy, within the outside world, consists of progressively stretching what he can encounter without feeling fear. As constantly stressed, it is also incredibly important never to reinforce fearful responses in your puppy by giving them attention. In trying to soothe anxious puppies as if they were children, owners constantly reinforce fear.

Always take tasty treats with you when you take your puppy out, and every time he passes something new without looking fearful, reinforce this behaviour by praising him –*"good boy!"* – and giving him a treat. If he looks worried, *totally ignore him.*

Be very careful about your timing, however, as often owners will give puppies a treat, by mistake, when they are looking worried or fearful. Remember, the only thing you ever want to reward in your puppy is *confidence.* You want to condition this response into your dog, time and time again, every time he

goes out. Always approach trips to the outside world in a very happy and confident manner yourself, too, as your puppy will pick up on this.

STAGE MANAGING EARLY SOCIAL ENCOUNTERS

One of the earliest sources of unease or fright for young collie puppies, if not correctly handled, can be encounters with strange people or dogs when out. It is incredibly important not only to understand why these can go wrong, but also the need to deliberately stage manage all your puppy's early social encounters so that he only ever learns the right lessons from them, and continues to grow in confidence.

If, like so many owners do, you let a collie puppy run ahead to meet a strange person or dog first, some potentially bad things can happen.

First, if the person or dog gives your puppy a fright, you will not be able to stop this bad lesson being learned.

Second, in allowing your puppy to race up to a strange person or dog first, you are also not behaving like his protector and leader, but a mere pack follower, trotting along behind, letting him take the first hit of any social encounter that goes wrong.

Both the above shocks can immediately make your puppy feel more vulnerable. He may lose faith in your ability to protect or adequately guide him when other encounters with strangers loom. Strangers may also come to be associated in his head with worry and mental pressure, and mental pressure, as you now well know, triggers defensive patterns of behaviour in collies.

If your puppy becomes aggressive to strange people or dogs through worry or lack of confidence, and learns that this makes them go away, or prompts you to let him keep avoiding them, you have then sown the seeds of a potentially serious problem.

BETTER CONTROL OF SOCIAL ENCOUNTERS

To avoid the kind of problem I have just outlined, the answer, as ever, lies in better all-round early training and social conditioning. You must also teach your puppy to remain '*close*' to you, on command, whenever you are out and people or dogs approach. Begin training this with your puppy kept on a long line if, off lead, he will not immediately come to your side when called.

In order to encourage your puppy to stay next to you in response to the word '*close*', take the all-important tasty treats out with you. Always start this training somewhere where there are no people or dogs to distract your puppy.

One of the earliest bits of preparation I do for this exercise is to regularly praise and reward a puppy *just for looking at me* when we are out. As soon as he looks at me I say *"good boy!"* and give him a treat. If he is on a line and stops for a moment to look back at me, I do the same thing. This continues the process of conditioning your dog to keep focusing on you through any surrounding distraction, and I recommend you do this with your own puppy.

TEACHING THE 'CLOSE' COMMAND

From this step, then regularly encourage your puppy to come to your side, using the line for this, if necessary. As soon as he is close to you say the word *"close"* and then praise him – *"good boy!"* – and reward him with a treat. Once this is going well, ask him to come *"close"* whenever you see another person or dog approaching. Your puppy needs to learn that when you do not give him the *"go see!"* command, which means that the dog or person is safe for him to approach, he must stay *"close"* to you instead and just pass by ignoring them.

If your puppy tries to shoot ahead of you when you have asked him to stay *"close"*, immediately give your correction *"hey!"* – and also quickly stick your foot out in front of him to stop him. When he returns to the '*close*' position, say the command again, praise him well – *"good boy!"* – and reward him with a treat. It is also important to give your puppy a verbal release command – such as *"okay!"* – which tells him when he can move away or ahead of you again, after passing other people or dogs.

You now have the training and conditioning required to stop your puppy running up ahead of you to strangers. Practice this relentlessly, until you can get your puppy to come and stay *"close"* to you on command while he is off the line as well as on it. If ever your puppy's response to *"close"* deteriorates once he is off the line, put him back on it and continue training and conditioning, as before, until it improves again.

GETTING YOUR PUPPY USED TO STRANGER AND LOUDER NOISES AND TRAFFIC

Collies can be a particularly noise-phobic breed, and for this reason it is essential that they get used to a wide range of louder or stranger noises while they are still very young.

Do your best to take your puppy out in your arms as soon as you can – even before he has finished his vaccination programme – and expose him to as many new and louder sounds as possible, including passing trains, noisy building sites and traffic.

The younger puppies are when exposed to louder and stranger noises, the better they tend to cope with these things when older. I begin this process with my own puppies when they are about four or five weeks of age.

The worst thing an owner can do when a collie puppy first shows apprehension about a certain noise, is try to verbally or physically soothe and comfort him, which simply reinforces their young dog's anxiety. As ever, any anxious behaviour in your puppy should be totally ignored and attention given back to him only when he returns to a more confident frame of mind.

As collie puppies get older and develop working instinct, the visual and auditory overload brought about by oncoming traffic can suddenly start triggering stalking and defensive (i.e. lunge-nip) patterns of behaviour. This must be rectified with the kind of training outlined in later chapters, to avoid it becoming a more obsessive habit.

See Part Two for extensive advice on phobic behaviours in collies, including extreme reactions to noise.

STRETCHING YOUR PUPPY'S SOCIAL SKILLS

While it is important to train your young collie puppy to avoid social encounters with people and dogs you do not know well, it is equally important to build up his social skills and confidence with other people and dogs that you know will be friendly and provide positive and rewarding experiences for him.

Start with friends and other people you know well and meet while you are out. Instruct your puppy to *"go see"* them, and give these people a tasty treat to give him. Then praise him – *good boy!"* – for showing confidence just before he eats it. Also visit shops or other places where there are people you know will be friendly and welcoming to your puppy.

Note: It is very important your puppy sees that treats other people give him always come from *you*, otherwise, when older, he may start pestering other random people he meets for treats, which can be annoying.

DO NOT PRESSURISE OR FUSS

Should your puppy ever show nervousness about meeting someone, as before, totally ignore him. Do not pressurise him to be sociable or keep saying the *"go see"* command, as you will just destroy the integrity of this command for the future. Also do not allow the person you meet to suddenly crowd your puppy's space and make a big, noisy fuss of him; this usually does far more harm than good. Ask the person to ignore your puppy, and just drop a treat near to him. Wait patiently until he finally goes towards the treat, then say *"go see!"* and praise him – *"good boy!"* – just before he eats it.

Next, wait until your puppy will take a treat from the person's hand. As before, say *"go see!"* and praise him – *"good boy!"* – just before he eats it. Then end this encounter on a good note until you see the person again.

The more you patiently repeat this exercise with someone your puppy was originally worried about, without pressurising him in any way, the sooner he should overcome his fears. Also, the more people you encourage your puppy to meet when out – of all ages, sizes and sexes – twinning it in his mind with a highly rewarding experience, the greater social confidence he will gain around people over time, including those he has not met before.

SOCIALISING YOUR PUPPY WITH OTHER DOGS

When it comes to socialising your collie puppy with other dogs when out, it is very important you choose these other dogs very carefully, as a frightening encounter with another dog at a formative stage in your puppy's social development could really set him back, in terms of confidence. As today's

SOCIALISATION CLASSES

As the owner of a young collie puppy, you may be advised to take him to a specially run socialisation group for puppies. Puppy socialisation classes – where young dogs of all ages and breeds are allowed to freely interact together – can be fun. But how beneficial they may be to your puppy, in terms of teaching him the right canine social lessons and skills, can depend greatly on his individual personality and how well individual classes are run.

Some of these classes can just be too chaotic, with the sense that the organisers are simply presiding over a canine free-for-all, instead of more consciously taking control of what individual puppies are learning from the experience. This means your puppy could just as easily learn a bad social lesson as a good one. If, for instance, you have puppies of very different ages, sizes and confidence levels and an older confident puppy from a larger breed suddenly lands on your younger and more nervous little collie puppy, this could terrify him. It could also make him far more fearful, or defensive towards, other dogs in the future.

If you have any doubts about the benefits of a socialisation group for your puppy, follow instead the advice I have laid out in this chapter on social training and stage managing your puppy's early social encounters yourself.

EARLIEST SOCIAL LESSONS

Collie puppies vary greatly in terms of how well they manage their earliest social encounters with new dogs. Some will have a greater natural confidence, others will be more shy. Often this behaviour will have a genetic component, but it will also be influenced by the quality of the interactions puppies had with their littermates and other adult dogs in their earliest weeks of life. Puppies who were bullied by more dominant littermates may have lower levels of confidence around other dogs as a result.

Puppies, by contrast, who came from a litter where they were the only puppy may sometimes have unnaturally high levels of confidence; having never been suitably challenged by their peers. The same can happen with a litter of two puppies, where one was far more dominant over the other. The more dominant puppy may then try to take his over-confident view of his own status into his interactions with adult dogs later on, sometimes with unpleasant results.

The best early social background your puppy can come from is one where he had sufficient littermates to learn the joys of playful canine interaction, but also adult dogs who would quickly put him in his place, in a firm, but essentially benign, manner should he show disrespect.

I never like a puppy to leave my home without first learning how to show submissive behaviour towards an adult or superior dog, such as lowering his head and body posture, or rolling over on to his back. It is a behaviour that can prevent so much conflict with other dogs he may meet later. If your young puppy shows similar respectful, submissive behaviour towards adult dogs when you go out, it is always a good sign, in that he already has some basic canine social expertise. Once the respect has been shown, most adult dogs may then be far happier about playing with him.

CHOOSING THE RIGHT DOGS

The kind of adult dogs you should first introduce your puppy to will depend on his own character and behaviour. If he is a very confident dog, begin with telling him to *"go see!"* dogs who are essentially very friendly and benign, and happy to play with him – but who will also make it clear to him when he is being annoying or disrespectful. This is the best way to keep honing your puppy's social skills while, at the same time, making him aware that there will be limits set on the way he can behave with older or more superior dogs.

If you know the dogs you are introducing your puppy to are essentially good-natured, and would never really harm him, do not interfere too much when they are correcting your puppy or putting him in his place. There are many social lessons dogs can only learn from other dogs and through interfering you are preventing them learning them.

If you have a less confident puppy, you will need to begin differently. Start with getting him to *"go see!"* very gentle older dogs who put no social pressure on your puppy whatsoever,

fear in a puppy can so often become tomorrow's aggression, you do not want this to happen.

Not all adult dogs will be as tolerant with puppies as others. At the same time, if puppies behave in a rude or disrespectful way to adult dogs it will often trigger an aggressive reprimand. Disrespectful behaviour in puppies includes approaching in an over-boisterous manner and trying to climb over another dog's neck or shoulders. Owners can often get upset when an adult dog reacts in a hostile way to a disrespectful puppy, but it is pretty normal canine behaviour, unless the aggression used to correct a puppy is more extreme.

and just potter along doing their own thing. Allow your puppy to walk out regularly with them to gain a bit of confidence.

Next, do you know anyone who also has a puppy about the same age as yours? Start taking your puppy out with him so that they can play together. Your puppy's confidence with other dogs needs to build up very gradually – just adding two or three new playful or placid dogs to his repertoire of friends every week with the *"go see!"* command.

Never, ever, let a shy puppy interact with a dog who could intimidate, bully or frighten him. He will need to be far older, and much more socially confident, before he could take an experience like this in his stride.

At the same time, however, it is important not to be too over-protective of a shy puppy, in a way that reinforces his sense of being a natural victim, as opposed to a viable and successful social operator in the world of dogs. The quickest way to make a dog feel a victim in this way is to keep avoiding other dogs, for fear of your dog's reaction, and constantly reinforcing his anxious or nervous behaviour towards other dogs by giving it attention. Always ignore a dog who behaves in an anxious or fearful way around other dogs, and only give him attention and praise when he shows more confidence in his interactions with them.

SOCIALLY RETREATING
A lot of people leave too long a gap between a puppy's fright and his positive reintroduction to other dogs. In this time, his fear will only have grown. If he is older, it may even turn into defensive aggression when reencountering other dogs – particularly those he doesn't already know, or who remind him of the dog who previously attacked him.

This is the point where so many people start retreating from the canine social stage with their puppy. Their own body language when out becomes increasingly tense and anxious, which the puppy picks up on, and they may also begin avoiding other dogs for fear of how he will react towards them. In so doing, they are not only further ingraining their puppy's wrong attitudes towards other dogs, but also allowing him to dictate the terms of future social encounters he shares with you. This is something only *you* should do.

Sometimes, even without an attack of the kind I have described, collie puppies can just suddenly lose their social confidence. Typically this can happen just prior to or during adolescence, as covered in more detail in Chapter Nine. Whatever the reason for your collie suddenly losing social confidence around other dogs, be aware of how quickly this can subsequently develop into some form of more fearful or defensive behaviour. So the quicker you spot this, the easier it will be to turn around with the right help.

Some collie puppies may start off having social relationships with other dogs and then later start directing their working instincts on to them – i.e. eyeing, stalking, herding – once

these instincts start to develop in earnest. This can be incredibly annoying for both owners and other dogs and your collie has to be trained out of it, via getting his focus retuned into you. How you teach your dog to better focus on you was covered in the last chapter.

AN ONGOING PROCESS
The whole point of your collie puppy's earliest social education is to instil right lessons and habits into him before he has had a chance to learn less desirable ones, and to make him feel most at ease with the environment and life he shares with you. Do be aware, however, that reinforcing a dog's social confidence and responsiveness to you, and your commands in training, are things that should not stop in puppyhood. Dogs can so easily forget what we don't keep reminding them to remember, so these are processes that should be continued with throughout their lives.

HOW AND WHY IT CAN ALL GO WRONG
The part of your collie puppy's social education where you make him feel at ease with other dogs is incredibly important because, as previously outlined, this will allow him to be a balanced and socially bi-lingual individual throughout his life, instead of being able to relate mostly to people.

Anyone who has tried to learn, or re-learn, a foreign language later in life, as opposed to when they were young, knows how much harder this will always be. Dogs have the same developmental windows of opportunity; stages in early life where certain skills and lessons will always be that much easier for them to absorb and retain.

Having said all this, things can still go wrong in your puppy's early socialisation with other dogs. He could, for instance, be suddenly attacked by another dog who rushed up from nowhere. Sadly, such incidents now seem to be all too common, given the ever-growing number of irresponsible people around today with aggressive, out of control dogs. Such an experience, however, will shake you up and frighten your puppy as well.

If your puppy shows obvious submission to another dog and gets attacked, this can be all the more frightening for him. Moreover, through discovering that submission doesn't work as a strategy to prevent an attack, many dogs can later become over-defensive/aggressive in their approach towards other dogs instead, in the hope that this will better protect them from another assault.

It is crucial, however, not to allow any bad early fright like this linger in your puppy's brain. As soon as you possibly can, you must get him back out socialising with other dogs, beginning with known canine friends and then working up again to a bigger circle of canine social companions. The quicker you do this after a fright, the more likely it is that your puppy will recover from it, and gradually build his confidence back up again.

Chapter Seven

ANALYSING AND ADAPTING YOUR TRAINING

Why training goes wrong; tuning training to your dog's individual personality

As your collie puppy grows, the extent of his natural personality and abilities will become ever clearer to you. Collies with inherently kind, biddable and more outgoing personalities – and with a high level of responsiveness to any form of training – can often flatter their owners, making them believe it is primarily their own talents, rather than the innate qualities of their dog, that has made him turn out so well.

Conversely there will be people who work much harder with their dogs and feel a sense of frustration or failure when he turns out less well, or responds less enthusiastically to their training. But it could just be that they have got a naturally more challenging collie who needs an extra level of expertise and insight to get the best out of him.

As stressed before, some collies can seem lazy, others can be over-energetic, super-sensitive or powered by excessively high working instincts and drives, but this is generally down to the dynamics of their individual genetic character or brain function.

Some collies live to please their owners, others are far more independently minded and thus more resistant to an owner's attempts to control their behaviour. Whatever the essential nature of your own collie, you will need to tailor and adapt your training to this at all times, in order to maximise his potential.

This begins with a better understanding of why some collies can appear harder than others to train, as now outlined.

WHERE DOES A COLLIE'S 'WORKING DRIVE' COME FROM?

When looking for a good sheep dog, or one destined to be most successful at different types of competition work, you will often hear people say they want a collie with sufficient "working drive".

Specific levels of working drive (i.e. levels of eagerness, energy and responsiveness) usually run in collie families, and are rooted in the way individual dogs' brains and metabolisms are genetically programmed to work.

A massive array of behaviours and attitudes in dogs are governed by how their brains and metabolisms react to external stimuli. More energetic and excitable dogs, for instance, will be those who readily fire arousal hormones, like adrenaline and cortisol, into their systems, and keep the effects of these sustained. They can also be highly motivated dogs in training, because they register strong pleasure responses in the brain from specific physical actions, or the rewards given for them.

The mood chemical behind these pleasure responses is dopamine, which also lies at the heart of most forms of addictive behaviour in animals. Collies whose arousal and pleasure/addiction responses are too highly tuned often become quite manic and over-obsessive dogs, whose brains are hard to discipline and control.

In contrast, dogs in whom a heightened mental/physical state is less easy to arouse or sustain by the brain, often tend to be regarded as lazy. Similarly, they may be less prone to getting strong dopamine responses from specific actions or rewards, which can make them seem less enthused or motivated when it comes to training.

Of course, the way collies like these are trained will still also be critical because a good or clever trainer will find a way to elicit some dopamine response from a dog, and connect it to a particular behaviour. Many of the seemingly 'lazier' collies can make far less challenging pet dogs. Work or competition wise, however, their potential will always be lower.

Ideally in a competition collie you want a dog whose working enthusiasm is not gained at the expense of his controllability. The ability of a collie to immediately self-calm or slam the brakes on his own excitement, when commanded, usually calls for some degree of more specialised or selective breeding. So when you say you are looking for a collie with exactly the right level of "working drive", what you really mean is a dog with exactly the right kind of genetic brain function and metabolism.

WHEN TRAINING FAILS

So often, in training, when a collie shuts off or fails to comply with a command, an owner will get upset and frustrated because they think their dog is rejecting them personally. In fact, he is just rejecting their technique or approach.

It is critical to understand how much your own use of body

language, energy and commands in training will govern the way your dog responds to you in return.

When, for instance, your dog is too excited, anxious or distracted to concentrate on you and a particular command, you need to completely calm your own body energy down; i.e. keep still or make very slow movements and also keep your voice very, very low. All too often, an owner will respond to a seemingly un-co-operative, or mentally agitated/over-aroused dog, by becoming highly animated themselves in movement, voice tone and body energy.

In shouting more loudly at their dog, or repeatedly nagging him to comply with a specific command, they may think they are 'encouraging' him to respond better. But they are actually, instead, just putting intense additional pressure on him, which makes him less able to concentrate and more likely to switch off by avoiding eye contact.

If you want your dog's focus in a distracting or stressful environment, you must keep very calm and project very little energy yourself. It is also important to understand that authority is always a very quiet quality. The quieter and calmer you are in pressurised situations, the more your dog will always respond to you.

ACTIVE RESISTANCE TO TRAINING AND COMMANDS

What some may call a "disobedient" collie, I call a dog who is either more actively or passively resistant to the process of being trained, or responding to specific commands.

Sometimes, as already outlined, this is simply down to an owner's approach or to inherent differences in the brain function/genetic personality of individual dogs. But over and above these considerations, there can be other reasons why a collie's responses to training are less enthusiastic.

It can be common for adolescent dogs, for example, to suddenly become more forgetful or defiant about commands they previously responded well to as puppies. As outlined in Chapter Nine, in most cases this is a transient problem that can be resolved over time, with the right handling and level of persistence.

With collies that owners have always found more difficult to train, however, the problem can sometimes date back to their earliest background as puppies.

PUPPIES WHO DID NOT BOND EARLY ENOUGH WITH PEOPLE

If your collie spent most of his earliest weeks and months of life with other dogs, this could hamper his ability, when older, to make strong social bonds with human beings.

Puppies like this do not always come from the grimmest of surroundings. Some can come from the smartest of breeders, who just happened to let their puppies spend too much of their early life with other dogs in kennel runs or indoor crates. This can impair their ability to socially attach to people later on.

A dog who has not made a strong social attachment to one or more people during early puppyhood will always be harder to train. This is because he will not have been conditioned, at a most formative stage of life, to find interactions with human beings highly rewarding, which is the essential starting point for the training of any dog. Puppies who have been ill treated by people early on in their lives can have similar reservations about interacting with them later on.

If you think any of the above could apply to your young collie, rest assured that you can still do much to turn him around. To do this you must put a lot more effort into heightening his levels of owner focus and building that all important one to one bond with him (as outlined in Chapter Five) before trying to teach him further commands. It can also help if you feed your young dog entirely by hand, as opposed to giving him meals in a bowl, so that he has to earn every morsel by responding to you in some way – e.g. coming to you, focusing on you, or complying with a basic command. Also see, *Rebuilding a bond* in Part Two, page 181.

The strength and nature of the social bond between dog and owner always has great impact on the quality of a dog's responses in training. Things like treats and toys help to reinforce this bond still further, but will never be sufficient substitutes if the bond is not already there. Similarly, praise is of little value to a dog as a reward if it does not matter greatly to him whether he pleases you or not.

THE RISKS OF TRAINING DIFFERENT DOGS TOGETHER

As already highlighted, the character of individual collies always has to be taken into account when establishing the best training approach for each dog. This may be fine when you are working one to one with a dog, but problems can arise when you try to train collies with different types of personality together.

Let us imagine, for instance, that you are working on an exercise with a highly sensitive dog, and meanwhile another of your dogs, with a much more forceful and pushy nature, keeps whining in the background, or trying to muscle in on the other dog's work (as can so often happen). Your constant correction of this pushy dog, for his undesirable behaviour, can start to psychologically crush your sensitive collie and give him progressively more negative vibes about the exercise you are working on, or the whole training process itself.

The same can be true when you train with other people, and their harsher or louder approach towards their dogs deeply upsets your own sensitive dog. So do be mindful of these risks and wherever possible train sensitive dogs either one-on-one, or in situations free of the kind of external pressures I have just described.

INSUFFICIENTLY MOTIVATED

Some collie puppies may build positive attachments with people – and with their owners – but become progressively less responsive to training commands as they get a bit older. This is not just to do with adolescence. It is very common for an owner, without realising it, to encourage or even *train* their dog to behave in a more disobedient way.

Dwindling responsiveness to commands also happens when owners over train dogs, with endless repetitions of the same exercise, or do not make training and co-operating with commands a continually enjoyable and rewarding experience. I like to see my own dogs bursting with enthusiasm and excitement at the prospect of doing some work with me and if this did not happen, I would immediately know that I was doing something wrong that quickly needed changing.

Collies can become harder to motivate in training if they already get tons of attention and praise from owners for doing relatively little for them. This is much like paying builders before they have done a job; where is the incentive then to work any harder, faster or better for you? If you refuse to give dogs like this access to anything like treats, toys and praise – or even food – other than in return for complying with one of your commands, you may find their levels of motivation and responsiveness in training improve no end.

HOW TO TRAIN A COLLIE TO BE DISOBEDIENT
It is just as easy to train a collie to be disobedient as it is to train one to be responsive and co-operative. You just have to do a lot of wrong things without realising it, as follows:

- Keep applying verbal commands to wrong behaviours, so that they become disconnected from the right response in a dog's head. For example, you keep calling your dog to come to you while he is ignoring you, as opposed to running back to you. This is how you progressively teach a dog to ignore any recall sound you make – and particularly the calling of his name
- Keep mistiming rewards; e.g. you reward your dog as he is moving forward or getting up when you asked him to "stay" or reward him for barking when you asked him to be "quiet!"
- Give your dog a lot of fuss and attention for not complying with a command – even if this is just pleading, wheedling or simple exasperation – and, by contrast, take much of his good behaviour for granted. This just makes non-compliance more rewarding for him. Good behaviour or co-operation must always pay for your dog.
- Fail to attach negative consequences to non-co-operation – though this does not involve verbal or physical punishment. A negative consequence can range from keeping your dog on a long line so that he cannot defy a recall command, banishing him to his own quarters, or making him lie down and stay down if he is behaving in an undesirable way. This also underlines your authority.
- Not appreciating that both your own authority and your

dog's responsiveness to your commands become progressively undermined if you do not persistently follow through every command you give him until he complies with it. The quicker and more often you give up on asking your dog to do something, the more he will resist your commands in the future.

Please note: there are some exceptions to the above approach, depending on the type of command or exercise in question, and the kind of dog you are trying to apply it to. Also see, *Remotivating super-sensitive dogs*, page 73 and *Battles of will*, page 74.

PASSIVE RESISTANCE TO TRAINING AND COMMANDS
Passive kinds of resistance to training in collies usually have very different roots to the more active examples just outlined.

The first results directly from an owner losing control of their dog's working focus and instincts.

In other words, in order to exert maximum control over any collie's behaviour you have to teach him, from day one, that your commands always take precedence over his urge to pursue his working instincts. This requires, in turn, good early focus training, of a kind previously outlined in this book, plus consistently conditioning your dog to find any co-operation with your commands intensely rewarding.

Without such persistent early training/conditioning, all too easily a reverse situation will arise, where the dog decides that pursuing his working instincts is a far higher priority in his life than you.

This problem usually begins with a young dog's focus being allowed to escape on to all the wrong targets – e.g. other dogs, birds, traffic, cyclists – and chase them. The more he chases and works these things, the more of a buzz he gets from it and the less you, running along behind, will even register on his mental radar.

Once a collie totally disconnects from an owner in this way, and becomes an animal driven totally by his own immediate instincts and desires, he not only becomes very hard to control but also potentially a danger to himself or others.

Collies like these are not disobedient as such; they have just been allowed to develop the wrong mental priorities in life. Once this happens it can take a lot of work to turn them around, depending on how early you spot the problem or how serious it has become. (Also see *Anti-chase training* in the next chapter and *Chase Behaviour* in Part Two).

HIGHLY SENSITIVE DOGS
The second kind of more passive resistance to training is generally seen in highly sensitive collies – frequently bitches – and invariably it results from a training style or approach that is too harsh for the dog to cope with.

Most collies are sensitive dogs, but some will always be more sensitive than others and how well you recognise this will determine how successfully or not you will train them.

Super-sensitive collies are always very obvious to me. Typically they will be quite submissive in nature and respond very readily to any owner instruction that calls for the inhibition of their movement – e.g. *wait, down* or *stay*. This is why, unlike stronger-willed dogs (outlined in *Battles of will*, page 74), you will rarely have to persist to get them to comply with such commands. They also tend to have highly mobile ears that twitch and flick back or forwards at the slightest sounds, including any perceived verbal command from an owner.

I have also found that dogs like these often display a higher degree of learned helplessness (the psychological syndrome I outlined in Chapter Five), which diminishes their confidence in being able to solve problems by themselves. As a result, they may often need far more feedback and encouragement from owners during the training of exercises that require them to display greater initiative or self-confidence.

CHANGING YOUR APPROACH

The submissive nature and sound super-sensitivity present in these dogs should alert you to the need to train them with calmness, kindness, quietness and the lightest of touches. You must do everything possible to hide any outward show of disapproval or impatience, while at the same time boosting the dog's confidence in his own abilities

In fact, when handled correctly these dogs are a total dream to train because they are essentially so willing and eager to please. Unfortunately, however, owners can so often ruin them by being too loud, pressurising or hostile in their training approach.

Problems arise most commonly when the dog is asked to do an exercise that requires confidence and the use of his own initiative – e.g. *retrieve*, or a *scent* task, or the *send away* exercise.

If, in the teaching or undertaking of these exercises, an owner has been in any way harsh, pressurising or disapproving in their approach, the dog can quickly form negative associations with them.

He may then noticeably shut down (e.g. freeze, avoid eye contact, cower and tuck up his body and show reluctance to come close to you) or panic (e.g. become very restless, agitated, whiney) whenever he is asked to do one of these exercises again; not just because he has lost confidence but also because his mind is principally preoccupied with the fear of facing his owner's disapproval if he gets it wrong. Because this worry also disrupts his ability to think clearly, it makes it more likely that he *will* get the exercise wrong. At which point his owner may get even madder or more frustrated because he thinks his dog is wilfully disobeying him. So the dog gets to fear the exercises more and more and, thus, becomes increasingly more reluctant to do them. It is a vicious circle.

SPIRITUALLY BROKEN

It breaks my heart how many potentially brilliant collies have had the willingness and talent crushed out of them by ignorant handling, of a kind so woefully out of tune with the psychological sensitivities of the dogs concerned.

The tell-tale signs of collies who have been spiritually broken by such heavy-handed training are everywhere to see, particularly in the way they persistently avoid eye contact with their owners or always return so slowly and apprehensively to them when called, with their heads submissively lowered and tails between their legs.

There is no sense of joy about anything they do – no sparkle in the eye or that eager, bouncing, ebullient sense of self-belief I so adore seeing in this breed. It is a truly pitiful sight. Never let this be you and your dog.

Always try to understand the differences between a genuinely defiant collie who needs you to show more resolve, one who is confused and in need of clearer guidance from you, and one who is merely freezing in panic as a result of your hostile manner. Then adapt your future training approach accordingly.

REMOTIVATING SUPER-SENSITIVE DOGS

If you have a highly sensitive collie who has developed hang-ups about one or more training exercises due to an over-pressurising approach, do *not* keep forcing him to do them. You will only make matters worse. Instead, abandon these exercises for a while and go back to basics, rebuilding a happier relationship with your dog.

Concentrate on lots of enjoyable shared walks together and play with him. Then work on some exercises you know he responds well to and go overboard with praise each and every time he complies. Make him feel really good about himself every time he co-operates with you. *Never* correct him when he gets anything wrong.

Next, completely dismantle the original exercise that was giving you problems and work out at which part of it your dog started to get worried or apprehensive. If, for example, it was retrieve, your dog may have started to get anxious right at the beginning of the exercise, at the moment where you first picked up something in your hand to throw – typically a dumbbell – and asked him to sit next to you.

If this is the case, put one of his favourite toys in your hand instead and sit on the floor with it. This will immediately make your body language far less intimidating. Ask your dog to come to you while you are sitting on the floor with the toy. Make your voice really light, happy and inviting.

When your dog responds to this, praise him really well and give him a tasty treat. Do this several times. Once this is going well, call your dog, praise him and give him a treat, then put the toy on the floor in front of him. As he goes and picks it up, say something like "hold!" or "go get it!". Whatever command you use *must be different* from the original one you used for retrieve, as this may prompt his old fears.

Once your dog picks up the toy, ask him to "give" it to you, then immediately praise him and reward him with some more treats. Do this about twice and no more, ending on a good note.

Over the next few days, do the same exercise; call your dog to you while you are on the floor, holding his toy, and praise and reward him for coming. Then praise and reward him for getting the toy, holding it, and giving it to you on command. Each time throw the toy a little further away for him to get and bring to you.

Then begin throwing it for him while you are kneeling on the floor, as opposed to sitting down. Thereafter ask him to "wait" next to you while you throw the toy, and before you send him off to get it, and then "give" it to you.

When this is going really well, try throwing another item for him to get. If he responds just as well, you have just about mended this exercise. The final step will be getting him to respond just as well while you are standing next to him as opposed to sitting on the floor. If he goes back to being apprehensive at any time keep rebuilding the exercise again, as before, until he finally regains his confidence.

Whenever you are trying to rebuild confidence in a dog about an exercise, it is vital to always keep your mood as happy and light as possible. Never correct your dog for wrong actions, or show any shred of impatience, frustration or disapproval; all of which will only reverse any progress you make.

BATTLES OF WILL

There is no doubt that some collies will always find it harder than others to accept an owner's authority, and this will come out most commonly in their response to commands like *down* and *wait* or *stay*; particularly in contexts which are outside their normal training environment, or where there are increased levels of surrounding distraction.

Very often owners visit me with collies they reckon are "pretty obedient", so I take them to a local park or exercise area and ask them to command their dogs to lie down and stay down for two to three minutes, without previously showing them or offering them any kind of physical reward – i.e. a treat or a toy. Frequently, the dogs will not do this and will keep moving or resisting or focusing on other things and their owners are horrified.

The explanation for this, however, is pretty simple. The owners have generally trained *down* and *stay* for a specific period, such as 30 seconds, and in a limited amount of contexts – such as at home or in training class – and always associated the exercise's beginning and completion with a physical reward they hold in their hand. This means the dog has become conditioned to stay down on an owner's command only in a specific place, for a specific time, and in

return for a reward he has already seen in an owner's possession.

If you then take the dog to a different place he has not already connected with the command and the reward, you are left with only the strength of your own authority to make him stay put amid an array of less familiar distractions. The more he resists the less likely it is that your authority, alone, is sufficient to make him stay still for a sustained length of time when you command him to.

To overcome this problem you must keep practising these kinds of *down/wait/stay* control exercises with your dog everywhere you go – including walks out every day – and for varying lengths of time, ranging from one to three minutes, or even longer if you are intending to train your collie up to Obedience competition level. If your dog will not initially comply, keep him on a long line and do not get frustrated or upset or try to bribe him by showing him a toy or treat.

There may be future occasions where you really need your dog to obey a control command instantly, for his own safety, and you do not have any toys or treats to hand. So instead, stay calm, patient and quietly determined until you finally get what you want from your dog, however long it takes. Understand that these battles of will must always be won by you in order to safeguard your dog's ongoing compliance, safety and respect for you.

If you fail to keep calm, or give up on seeing a command through with your dog, this will only encourage him to keep resisting your authority more often, and for longer periods of time. Depending on the individual dog, and how often you have given up enforcing a command on him in the past, these tests can sometimes last a long time. But the more often you do them and the more consistently you see them through, the less resistance your dog will eventually display.

Do ensure, however, that as soon as your dog complies with a command, after a lengthy battle of will, you *immediately* reinforce this right response with much praise. Only then get a toy out and let him have a really fun game with you. You always need to make your dog feel immensely pleased with himself for making the right choice in these kinds of situation (i.e. co-operation), as opposed to feeling browbeaten into submission by you. Collies can be very proud dogs. It is not necessary to demoralise or humiliate them to get your own way. Respect that, and they will respect you all the more in return.

DIFFERENT TYPES OF TRAINING EXERCISE AND APPROACH

It is also helpful to understand that the training of collies, be this for competition purposes, or just optimum management in everyday life, usually calls for two basic types of exercise and approach.

First there are the control exercises, such as *Sit* or *Down* and *Wait* or *Stay* or *Watch me*, which allow you to control or inhibit your dog's movement and behaviour. To be most reliably and consistently complied with, however, they also revolve around your dog's willingness to accept your authority. This, in turn, requires calm but strong body language and energy from you.

The second kind of exercise is where you ask your collie to perpetuate otherwise quite unnatural behaviours (e.g. Obedience-style heelwork) or act independently of your immediate control and use his own initiative; e.g. retrieve or scent tasks. These are *motivation exercises*; i.e. they call for high levels of reward-based training (using praise, toys, and treats) in order to make the dog enjoy them. There would, after all, otherwise be nothing very exciting or rewarding for a dog about clamping himself to an owner's leg or picking up a dumbbell or a piece of cloth.

Some collies will like the *motivation exercises* that bring them high and continual levels of reward, but may be more resistant to the control ones involving the assertion of your authority. Other dogs may happily comply with your authority but need ever higher levels of praise, reward and confidence-boosting to do the motivation/initiative tasks well on a consistent basis.

As previously outlined, this can all depend on the nature of the individual collie, but it can also depend on the owner, too. Some people can be good at asserting their authority over their collies but less good at knowing how to free up their dog's confidence in tasks requiring a lighter and more encouraging/inspiring approach. Other people can be brilliant at motivational types of training but less good at asserting their authority over their dogs, particularly in situations where an immediate response to a control command is critical.

Sometimes a higher resistance to an owner's authority, and a hypersensitivity to any harsher form of handling, can co-exist in one and the same dog. To be the best kind of collie trainer, you not only need to master the different training approaches I have outlined with equal success, but also know which approach to use on which dog and when – not just for competition purposes but in everyday life. Only then will your training style be totally in tune with your dog.

FASHIONS IN TRAINING

I have long been fascinated by the different ways people train collies; why they favour one particular method over another and why they will persist with techniques which, to me at least, seem outdated or unnecessarily unkind.

I was recently reading a book, for instance, where a sheepdog trainer explained how you teach a collie to lie down in the following way: pull the dog's head to the ground by his collar, while simultaneously pushing down his back and shoulders. And I thought, *why?* Why do this when, with a far more enlightened and respectful approach, you can teach a collie to lie down quite willingly for you, without

touching him or physically abusing him in any way (as outlined in Chapter Five).

In recent decades, harsher and more coercive methods of dog training have been increasingly discredited and proven to be not just cruel and mentally damaging to dogs but also, for the most part, less effective than techniques that are primarily reward-based.

At the same time, however, I do not necessarily agree that positive reinforcement methods alone (with their entire emphasis on rewarding, if not bribing, dogs for good behaviour – usually with food) are the answer to all training and behaviour issues in dogs, anymore than more liberal modern parenting techniques have proved to be the solution to less desirable behaviour in children.

This is because experience has taught me that dogs and children are just the same; they will keep pushing the boundaries of what they can get away with until someone stops them. Thus with both, there will always be times when you just have to show some authority and put your foot down, in order to evolve behaviour in them that is most socially acceptable.

Today I see many owners who are so scared of seeming harsh, or upsetting their dogs in any way, that they are unable to enforce any meaningful sense of control or discipline upon them. As a result, their dogs just become increasingly more neurotic and badly behaved. For the benefit of such owners, and as I hope is illustrated throughout this book, if you go about it the right way, it is always possible to exert authority over dogs without ever frightening them, harming them or losing their affection.

BEING OPEN TO CHANGE

The way I train and interact with dogs has emerged through experience and, probably like any other trainer, through a fair degree of trial and error. I think it essential, however, that all of us involved in training dogs keep our methods and approaches under constant review.

We must use our imaginations and knowledge of dogs' different personalities to tailor training to their individual needs, rather than just keep blindly doing what we have always done, or copying what we have seen other people do, regardless of how appropriate it is, or how well it is working, for a particular dog.

Similarly, we should always keep our minds open to the prospect of doing something in a better or kinder way. Show me a person who never has any doubts about the way he or she handles dogs, and I will show you a bad trainer.

Over years of living and working with collies, they have always told me themselves, through their reactions, when I am getting things wrong – when I am too harsh, or too soft, or too vague or just downright confusing and useless – and I thank them for it. It has been, and continues to be, an education with much, I am sure, I still have to learn.

Chapter Eight

MORE ADVANCED TRAINING

Working with your dog's natural abilities and instincts; anti-chase training; scent work; stretching your dog's mind

In the last chapter, I looked at common reasons why training goes wrong with some collies, and outlined the need to continually adapt your training approach to the nature of individual dogs. Now let us look at the extent to which you can stretch your own dog's natural abilities, and keep his working drives under optimum control.

Many collie owners lose control of their dogs' chase and other working instincts simply through not knowing how to prevent this with the right early training. Other owners wildly underestimate what their collies are capable of learning and doing and, as a result, leave their minds continually under occupied. This is not only a waste of a brilliant canine brain but also increases the likelihood that their dogs will develop a range of more negative behaviours or neurotic habits, for want of something better to do.

The collie's mind is programmed to stay busy, with some dogs more demanding of stimulation on this front than others. But, generally, if you do not find sufficient positive outlets for your collie's mental energy, you will end up with one chronically frustrated dog, and all the behavioural fallout that so often accompanies it.

GETTING THE BASICS RIGHT

In order to stretch your dog's abilities to the limit, you will first need to have completed all the early training groundwork outlined in earlier chapters. In other words, you will need to have done the following:

• Taught your collie to respect your authority and commands.
• Built a bond with him that ensures he is totally focused

Getting the basics right includes teaching your collie to focus on you. Note how this collie bitch is eyeing and circling her toy-wielding owner much as she would otherwise work livestock.

on you, even in distracting surroundings.

- Conditioned him to believe that cooperating with you will always bring high rewards.
- Taught him basic control and co-operation exercises (i.e., everything from *down* and *wait* and *stay* to *recall* and *retrieve*) and reinforced these in a multitude of different contexts and environments

If you have neglected this essential foundation work, attempting more ambitious training goals will always be harder for you, because you will basically be trying to run before you can walk – and the same applies to your dog.

So, if you are finding it difficult to do more advanced training with your collie, including some of the exercises laid out in this chapter, go back to basics. Restudy the vital early training groundwork laid out in previous chapters of this book, which puts your dog in the best frame of mind for learning and responding to you. There may be one or more elements that need more work before trying to progress further with his training. This would especially be the case if you had a rescue collie, as opposed to a dog you had owned from early puppyhood, or a puppy you only began trying to train when he was considerably older.

Let us now move on to some more advanced and all-important exercises to teach your collie.

ANTI-CHASE TRAINING
Beyond the basic early focus, control and co-operation exercises laid out in previous chapters, the next priority for you to master will be *anti-chase training* – or exercises that will allow you to keep optimum control of your dog when he is on the move.

You can begin seeing the strength of an individual collie's chase instinct when he is only two to three months old. The earlier this instinct starts and the stronger it appears, the more vital it is that you begin the following training with him as soon as possible. Typically, I will start this training with my own dogs around 14-16 weeks of age.
Note: it is advisable to begin teaching all the following anti-chase or movement control exercises with your dog on a long line, beginning with *down on the move*.

DOWN ON THE MOVE
The *down on the move* or *emergency down* exercise basically represents the brakes on your dog. If you do not teach it, and relentlessly reinforce it, your dog becomes the equivalent of an unguided missile when you let him off the lead and he sees a chase target. Whether he is moving towards you or away from you, an instant response when you ask him to drop into the *down* position and *wait*, could one day save your dog's life.

Imagine, for instance, that your dog has run across a busy road and is then trying to get back to you. By telling him to

drop *"down"* on the other side of this road and *"wait"* until you cross over to get him, you have possibly saved his life.

The same applies when your dog is running away from you to chase something into the road or over a cliff; getting him to stop, drop *down* and *wait* will immediately prevent any further danger or injury. I often wonder how many collies would still be alive today if their owners had only taught them to stop and drop on command.

To train your collie to drop when he is moving *towards* you, or *away* from you, he should already have very reliable responses to both the *down* and *wait* commands (covered in Chapter Five), to the point where he is able to respond to just the *verbal* commands for these exercises, without the hand signals as well. Let us start with your dog running *towards* you.

TRAINING YOUR DOG TO DROP DOWN WHEN HE IS RUNNING TOWARDS YOU
To prepare for this exercise, try getting your dog to drop into a *down* position when you are standing right in front of him. Then ask him to *"wait"*. As soon as he does this, praise him well – *"good boy!"* – but he must *not* move again until you give him a verbal release command – *"okay!"* – that tells him he can move again. As soon as he has gone *down* and *waited* and then not moved until you released him, praise him really well – *"good boy!"* – and then i*nstantly* give him a toy or treat as a reward.

Whether you are trying to stop your dog running towards or away from you, this verbal release command after a *down-then-wait* is incredibly important, because it conditions your dog not to move again, after dropping *down*, until you tell him to.

WHY DO YOU USE "WAIT" AND NOT "STAY" AFTER DROPPING YOUR DOG?
Strictly speaking (and as outlined in Chapter Five), a release command should be used to end a *stay* exercise. I prefer, however, to use a *wait* verbal command after I have dropped a dog to preserve the integrity of my *stay* command. The *stay* has to begin with me standing in front of a dog and giving him a specific hand signal, and ends with me going back to the dog, and touching him when I release him – *"okay!"*.

I cannot do these things if a dog is moving away from me and has his back to me, or has dropped some distance away from me. After my dog has dropped *down* some distance away and I have asked him to *wait*, I may then want to *recall* him back to me and you never recall a dog back to you out of a *stay* command. You always go back to him and release him instead.

INCREASING THE DROPPING DISTANCE
Once you have got your dog to go *down* on command and then *wait* while a short distance away from you on the line,

then start trying this while you are further and further away from him. If your dog moves forward at any time, instantly correct him by making him walk back to where you originally asked him to drop, and say *"Down"* and then *"Wait"* again.

Do not be over-harsh when you do this; you simply need to signify an error to your dog, not scare him out of his wits. By contrast, go overboard with praise every time your dog does drop *Down* on command for you when some distance away and then *Waits* until you release him – *"Okay!"*. Also remember to keep praising and rewarding him – e.g. with a toy – for his co-operation.

DROPPING YOUR DOG WHEN HE IS MOVING

From this step, try asking your dog to go *down* and *wait* while he is actually *moving* towards you. Begin by asking him to *"wait"* while you walk away from him, to the point where he is at the end of his line, and keep one of his favourite toys in your hand.

Then start reeling your dog gently towards you on the line – do *not* give a *recall* command as this will only confuse him at this stage. As soon as your dog has come forward a few steps, ask him suddenly to go *down* and *wait*. The *instant* he does this, give him a release command – *"okay!"* – then praise him – *"good boy!"* – and throw him his toy.

If your dog keeps coming forward when you ask him to drop *down*, again, immediately correct him by making him walk back to where you originally asked him to drop. Ask him to go *down* and *wait* again. When he complies, instantly release him – *"okay!"*– and praise him then reward him with his toy.

When first teaching and reinforcing this exercise, you have to make the rewards of co-operation *instantaneous* and feel brilliant for your dog, because the speed with which your dog responds to a *down on the move* command is initially determined by how quickly you reward him for doing it. Thus, your own timing in this exercise will also be critical.

If, early on, you make the right connection in your dog's head between a rapid *down* response, on the move, and an immediate reward, your dog's *down* response should remain just as fast later, even if you then ask him to *wait* for a while before rewarding him.

HOW AND WHEN TO USE YOUR DOWN ON THE MOVE EXERCISES

It is very important to make down on the move exercises part of an everyday fun game for your dog, and not to overdo them, otherwise his responses to them could get slower and slower. A maximum of one or two good responses each day, when out on a walk, is enough – and do not keep doing them in the same places. You always want to keep that element of surprise; suddenly asking your dog to drop down and wait when he is least expecting it and

running pretty fast, as opposed to just ambling along.

How well he responds in these circumstances will give you a better idea of how quickly you could stop your dog in a real chase situation or some other crisis, if you really had to.

MAINTAINING GOOD RESPONSES

If your dog's responses to down on the move exercises are often poor, you must keep improving his training again on the long line.

Please also remember not to keep saying *"Down"* or *"Wait"* to your dog if he is not actually doing these things at the time. Otherwise, you will never be able to reinforce the right responses to these commands. If your dog ignores the first or second *Down* command, be patient. Go back to him and ask him to *Sit* instead and praise him. Then try getting him to go *Down* from the *Sit* and praise him when he does. This is often easier for dogs. Do this until your dog correctly responds to *Down* first time and add *Wait* only while he is not moving.

When his response is very good you can then recall your dog from a *Down* and *Wait* and then get him to drop and wait again while he is coming towards you. These exercises teach your collie ever greater self-control and focus on you.

ONGOING PRACTISE

On top of the instant and ongoing reward factor, you will need to practise down on the move and wait exercises in as many different contexts and locations as possible to make them really reliable in your dog, and only then should you try them with him off the line.

Incorporate down on the move and wait, when your dog is coming towards you, into daily walks, and as a preamble to a game.

DROPPING YOUR DOG WHEN HE IS RUNNING AWAY FROM YOU

To train your collie to drop *down* and *wait* when he is running *away* from you, do the following. First, make him *sit* next to you while he is on a long line and throw one of his favourite toys a few metres ahead of you. Make sure the length of line you keep your dog on is shorter than the distance between him and the toy.

As soon as your dog runs to get the toy, the line will stop him just before he gets to it. At this point, ask him to drop *down* and *wait*. If he does this, immediately release him – *"okay!"* – then praise him and let him get his toy and play with it. If he will not drop *down* and *wait*, walk ahead in front of him and pick up the toy. Then begin the exercise again. Your dog has to learn that he will not get his toy until he first drops *down* and *waits* on your command.

As soon as he has learnt this, try throwing the toy further and further ahead of him so that each time you have to stop him and make him drop *down* and *wait* when he is moving

TEACHING THE MID-CHASE RECALL

The thrown toy triggers the chasing impulse in your dog.

Before he reaches the toy you must command your collie to stop and drop down.

He should then look back to you, awaiting his next command.

Instead of allowing your dog to get his toy, recall him to you.

Praise him well for coming back to you, then let him get his toy as a further reward for his co-operation.

Note: A long training line should be used on your collie until you have perfected this exercise.

faster and further away from you. Any time he does not respond to your commands, as before, keep picking up the toy and start the exercise again.

Then, as with the previous exercise, start making the whole *down* and *wait* response, while your dog is running away from you or towards something, part of a regular game when you are out. Get into the habit of throwing a toy ahead of your dog, and then suddenly making him drop *down* and *wait* before he can get it. Also lengthen the time you make him *wait* before releasing him – *"okay"*! – then praise him well as he goes to get his toy.

MAINTAINING GOOD RESPONSES

Any time your dog fails to comply with your commands, remove the toy you have thrown for him and begin the exercise again. Only try this exercise with your dog off the line once his responses are really reliable. To make this exercise even more reliable in my own dogs, I regularly add a bit of competition between them. For example, I will throw out a toy for one dog and if he does not drop down quickly enough, on command, when running towards it, I let another one of my dogs go and get his toy instead. It's incredible how much quicker he will drop down the next time he is asked.

THE MID-CHASE RECALL

Another excellent exercise to teach and keep practising with your collie is the *mid-chase recall*. In this exercise you drop your dog into a *down* on the move, as before, and ask him to *wait,* but instead of releasing him to get his toy you *recall* him back to you, so that he has to leave the toy behind.

Initially your collie may keep running forward to get his toy when you recall him, because he has become programmed to do this. In which case, keep him on the long line. If he tries to move forward after you recall him, put your foot on the line to stop him and recall him back to you again, using the line to bring him back to you if necessary. As soon as he comes back to you, ask him to *sit* and *wait.* Only once he has done this, praise him well – *"good boy"* – then release him – *"okay!"* – to go and get his toy.

As with the other *down on the move* exercises, keep practising this one in a variety of different contexts, as part of a regular game. Then keep switching which exercise you do on a frequent basis – i.e. sometimes you release your dog forward to get his toy, after he has gone *down* and *waited* on command, at other times you *recall* him back to you, ask him to *sit* and *wait,* and then release him to get his toy.

Such training conditions your dog to have far more mental discipline over his actions, and remain highly responsive to your commands, even while he is in chase mode, or moving some distance away from you. I also find the *mid-chase recall* exercise encourages your collie to turn and look back at you

after he has dropped *down on the move*, rather than just keep focused on his toy ahead, and this further improves your control of him.

If you have ambitions to work your dog in pursuits such as Competitive Obedience or Agility, good control over your dog when he is on the move will also be vital.

'WAIT' WHILE YOUR DOG IS AHEAD OF YOU OR BEHIND YOU

Once your dog understands the principle that 'wait', while he is moving towards you or away from you, means he must stop and stay still until you give him a release command – *"okay!"* – then you can also use this command to halt his movement without dropping him.

If, for instance, your dog has moved some way ahead of you on a walk and you want to stop him, say *"wait"* as before to halt his movement. Once he has stopped and waited you can then either *recall* him to you or give him a release command – *"okay!"* – to continue moving. Each time he complies, praise him really well.

Ideally you want to work towards a situation where each time you stop your dog on a walk in this way, and ask him to *wait,* he immediately looks back to you for the next command. This shows supreme focus on you, and makes it more likely he will stop focusing on anything else he might otherwise have approached or chased.

If you experience trouble stopping your dog in this way when he is off lead, keep putting him back on the long line and work much harder on the exercise until it is more reliable.

PUT TO THE TEST

There is no doubt that the kind of training I have just outlined will test all the following things:

- Your dog's level of respect for you and your commands.
- His level of focus on you
- The true reliability of any previous control/co-operation exercises you have taught him.

How well – or not – you manage the timing of commands and rewards to get the right responses will also test your own skills as a trainer. However, the longer and harder you work on these exercises, the better the focus and response levels you should get from your dog, especially if you always make co-operation extremely rewarding for him. But if you continue to struggle and cannot understand what is going wrong, do seek professional help. An outside view of a problem between dog and owner in training – especially an expert one – can often work wonders. Also see, *How good is your dog?* page 82 and *Finding the right 'expert' help*, page 199.

STRETCHING YOUR CONTROL DISTANCE

Between every owner and collie, there is a specific distance wherein the owner has the highest chance of controlling their dog's movement. The more authority the owner has – and the better trained the dog – the longer this distance is likely to be. In other words, the owner can maintain the same level of control over their dog, with relevant commands, even when he is 20 metres or more away from them. This, after all, is what shepherds have to do when working their dogs with livestock.

Conversely, the less authority the owner has and/or the less well trained the dog – particularly in terms of owner focus levels – the shorter the distance will be. This means, in turn, that the owner will rapidly lose control of their dog's behaviour once he moves just a metre or two away from them.

As a collie owner, your goal should be to stretch the control distance between you and your dog all the time, with the kind of training I have outlined in this chapter. The aim is to reach a point where you can stop and drop him and then make him wait or recall him, even when he has taken off after something at speed or is some way away from you. Then, like any good shepherd, you truly are in control of your dog's working drives.

ANTICIPATION

All the anti-chase and movement control training in the world, however, is not going to be much good to you if you do not know exactly when to use it with your dog. Anticipation with collies is everything; your dog's mind moves at rapid speed and you have to learn how to keep up with it.

Too many owners are not able to read, or anticipate, the earliest signs of a collie about to chase something, and therefore aren't able to abort their dog's chase activity in time with a suitably checking/restraining command.

The best chance you will ever have of stopping a collie chasing something – with appropriate *down/wait* commands – is while the chase is still a *thought* in his mind. This thought will typically be signalled by a sudden sense of alertness in your dog. His ears will be pricked and his eyes intensely focused on a distant chase target. *Before* he even progresses on to the next movement, such as crouch or stalking mode, *this* is the time to stop him.

If you do not do this, and your dog moves on to a full-blown chase, then the further and faster he moves away from you towards his chase target, the less chance you have of stopping him, unless you have created an exceptionally lengthy control distance.

LEAVE AND COME!

Another handy exercise to teach your dog is *leave and come*! This conditions your dog to leave a particular object and immediately return to you. It can be used just as effectively when you want your dog to stop approaching another person, dog, animal, etc. and return to you.

Once again it is best to begin training this exercise with your dog on a long line. Put some really tasty treats in your pocket and get your dog's empty food bowl. Put the bowl some way ahead of him and let him see you do this. Do not then send him to the food bowl; let him start approaching it of his own accord. Also make sure the length of line you have your dog on is just shorter than the distance between him and the food bowl.

As soon as your dog is almost at the food bowl, start reeling him back to you on the line. The *instant* he turns to leave the bowl say *"leave!"*. Then *recall* him to you in your usual way (e.g. *"come!"*), using the line if necessary. As soon as he returns to you, praise him really well – *"good boy!"* – and give him two or more tasty treats.

INCREASING TEMPTATION

The next step is to put some moderately exciting food in your dog's bowl, like grated carrots. Let him see you do this, then repeat the exercise. Progressively try to put more tempting food in your dog's bowl for him to *"leave"* on command. But bear in mind, for this exercise to work the treats you have in your hand must *always* be tastier and more alluring than what you put in his bowl.

Be aware that dogs, by nature, are programmed to be scavengers and competitive eaters and thus can find it hard to leave behind an obvious food opportunity without adequate incentives to do so. But the more you practise this exercise, the more your dog will become conditioned to believe that whatever he is *leaving,* in response to your command, will never be as good as what you are offering him instead.

Needless to say, if your dog ever eats what is in his bowl, despite your *"leave and come!"* command, and then trots after you still expecting an additional treat, *do not* give one to him. Always use the line, for as long as necessary, to prevent your dog eating what is in the bowl, because if he is ever able to eat what is in the bowl while you are telling him to *leave* it you have completely ruined this whole command.

Ideally, with sufficient practise, you want to be able to get to the point where you can get your dog to *"leave and come!"* before he has even got to the bowl to see what is in it, whether or not he is on a line. But do not let your dog off the line for this exercise until you really feel you have it cracked.

LEAVING TOYS

You can also train this same exercise using *toys,* instead of food. Again, start this at home with your dog on a line. Put out a toy for your dog to see, and go up to, but the moment he gets really near it, turn him on the line and say *"leave!"* as you do this, then *recall* him to you. Make sure that you have one or two special toys your dog loves but rarely has access to, other than as a reward for learning something new or doing something special. Praise him – *"good boy!"* – then immediately reward him with a favourite toy when he comes back to you, after *leaving* the original toy on command.

LEAVING THINGS ON A WALK

A good way to test out how well you are doing with this exercise is to use it, every so often, when you see your dog sniffing something on a walk. Ask him to *"leave and come!"* in return for praise and an alternative reward be this food or a special toy – whichever he values most.

If he comes immediately, congratulations! If not, the exercise needs a bit more work. Do not, however, ask your dog to *"leave and come!"* too often on a walk or he may eventually find this tedious and stop responding. As with the earlier *emergency down* control exercises, this is a command that always has to retain a sense of sudden urgency and surprise.

Wherever or whenever you ask your dog to *"leave and come!"*, do remember to make your voice really encouraging and inviting, and to always praise/reward your dog fulsomely for co-operating. As before, do *not* keep saying *"leave and come!"* to your dog if he is intent on neither leaving something nor coming to you when you ask him, or you will quickly destroy the whole validity of this command.

TEACHING LEAVE! USING TRAINING DISCS

An alternative way to teach your dog to *leave!* things is with the use of training discs, available from pet stores or suppliers of training aids.

For readers unfamiliar with discs, their purpose is to interrupt a dog's course of action and to also connect this course of action with failure. To practise the following *leave!* exercise using discs you will need another person to help you. Then proceed as follows.

First, get some tasty treats in your hand and have your dog sitting next to you. Your helper should sit about three metres away from you and your dog. Begin by throwing one treat at a time ahead of you, and instruct your dog to get one each time. Once he is reliably doing this, then suddenly throw a treat out but do *not* tell your dog he can get it. The chances are he will still move to get the treat. As he does so, throw down the training discs. Your helper must also remove the treat from the floor at exactly the same time as you throw the discs down – before your dog can eat it. At the same time, say *"leave!"*

Keep doing this exercise until your dog stops going for the treat the moment the training discs are thrown and/or he hears the word *"leave!"*. Timing, however, remains critical in this exercise. If your dog is still able to get the treat while you are saying *"leave"*, you are, again, completely

undermining the future efficacy of this command. Also be careful not to *hit* your dog with the discs when you throw them, as you may frighten him.

Once your dog has learned from this exercise to give up on what he is approaching when the discs are thrown and/or he hears the word *"leave!"*, you can practise this command on walks, as before, to test how reliable it is, and detect whether or not you need to give it more work.

HOW GOOD IS YOUR DOG?

When trying to teach your collie exercises and commands laid out in this chapter, you might at times feel demoralised or frustrated. Progress might not be going as fast as you would like, and you may start to wonder how much of this is down to you and the quality of your training, and how much is simply down to the limitations of your own particular dog.

There is no doubt that collies vary greatly when it comes to how fast they learn new things and how responsive they are to an owner's commands, which makes the original selection of your own dog so important if your goals are more ambitious on the training front.

Sometimes potentially brilliant dogs are wasted on uninspiring and unambitious owners, who barely scratch the surface of their dogs' capabilities. At other times diligent owners have to put ten times the work into their less amenable collies to get the same results other collie owners achieve easily in weeks or days.

The most important thing, however, is not to give up when things are not going well initially, or to take failure too personally. Keep remembering that everybody has bad days in training. Everybody has days when they think their dog will never master a particular exercise, and they want to rip their hair out with frustration or despair. With patience and persistent application, however, they usually get there in the end.

It may well be that your style or method of training is stopping you from getting better results from your collie. The only way to test this is to take him to a more expert trainer. He or she should soon be able to tell you whether or not you are right and – even more importantly – what you could do to get far better results.

See *Further Information* in Part Two of this book for more advice on seeking expert help.

SCENT AND SEARCH WORK

Scent and search tasks are a great way to keep your collie's brain positively occupied. More buzzy or hyper collies will benefit particularly from such exercises, carried out regularly, as it will help to keep their minds more balanced. The more you ask a collie to use and stretch his brain, the calmer he becomes.

Conversely, a mentally over-excited/over-aroused collie can

never think straight, leading owners, erroneously, to believe he is stupid. Trust me, although I have met countless collies whose normal brain function has been severely impaired by stress, anxiety, persistent over-arousal, or intense inhibition caused by over-heavy handling, I have met far fewer, if any, who were actually stupid.

Like most dogs, collies have a fantastic sense of smell, infinitely more powerful than our own, and if you link this superior sense to their brainpower, you can see why they are so popular for Search and Rescue work. But how many collie owners will regularly make good use of these superior instincts and skills?

UNDERUSED INSTINCTS

In the wild, a great part of a dog's life is spent searching for food – be this in the form of hunting or scavenging. Modern life for the domestic dog makes this whole process unnecessary. His food usually comes in the form of one or two meals a day put in a bowl, by owners, and is quickly consumed; it is just a further way in which we encourage the aforementioned learned helplessness mental state in dogs.

The less a dog has to use his natural instincts and intelligence to survive, the more he will stop trying to solve problems for himself and will increasingly look to his owner, instead, to provide him with everything he needs.

I am a great believer in encouraging dogs to use their superior skills to solve problems for themselves. This is not just to keep these skills in good order, but to also restore in them a sense of belief in their own initiative/brainpower and ability to exert some control over their own lives. The easiest way to begin this process is by searching for food. You can do the same with your collie, as follows.

FINDING FOOD

Every day, or every other day, do not give your collie one of his meals in a bowl. Hide it all around the garden instead, in small pieces, for him to find.

If your collie is new to scent work, you will have to begin with him actually watching you put food in different places, piece by piece. Each time you put down a piece, invite him to go and get it. As he goes to get it, say words like: *"food – find it!"*. Do and say the same with every new piece you put down.

Once your dog has got the hang of this process, and understands exactly what *"food – find it!"* means, try hiding one or two pieces of food somewhere while he is not watching you. Repeat your command. If he searches out the hidden pieces of food, praise him really well. Now you can keep hiding food without him watching you, making the food progressively harder for your dog to find.

At this point you can also leave your dog indoors while you hide his food in the garden, then invite him out to *"find it!"*.

GOLDEN RULES FOR SCENT AND SEARCH TASKS

If you are keen to train your collie to do a variety of different scent and search tasks, please keep these golden rules in mind:

- Always make sure your dog understands what object you are asking him to find.
- Initially, keep saying an object's name as you show it to your dog and let him smell it. Then repeat the object's name, together with "find it!", as your dog is actually getting the object, so that he can make the connection in his mind with your command and what he is doing when you say it.
- Always praise your dog fulsomely for finding something on command, before rewarding him.
- Always make sure every search ends in success for your dog to maintain his motivation to pursue searches. Dogs with lower self-confidence or a higher dependency on owners to solve problems for them can easily give up on searches if they feel they will fail. If your dog is clearly struggling to find something, hide it again while he is not watching you. Make it easier for him to find this time, and when he does find it, praise him fulsomely as usual.
- At the same time, do not unwittingly reinforce your dog's sense of helplessness by continually interfering (e.g. pointing to where he should go), or giving him umpteen additional commands, when he is still actively searching. If your dog stops for a while to think, or to consider where he should search next, let him do this without you saying or doing anything. The more you interfere, the more he may lose confidence in what he is doing or give up.

FINDING USEFUL OBJECTS

1. Start by teaching your dog to recognise an object, such as these car keys, and then give it a name.
2. Drop the keys nearby and encourage your collie to "Find".
3. Using his nose to find the keys.
4. Returning the keys to hand.

The smaller the pieces of food you use, and the better you hide them, the more of a challenge you will be giving your dog. If you use dried food, you can also hide this round the house for your dog to find.

FINDING TOYS

Next, you can invite your dog to find toys. Be aware, however, that if you want your collie to find any object and bring it to you, he will first need to have learned the *retrieve* exercise, as outlined in Chapter Five.

Again, to begin with, let our collie see you put a toy somewhere, like behind the sofa, and as he goes to get it say: "*toy – find it!*" Always praise him really well each time he finds a toy, and then have a game with him and the toy. Once he understands what "*toy – find it!*" means, you can hide a toy for him to find without him seeing you do this.

If you want to stretch your collie's brain still further, move on to identifying different toys by a different name and sound – e.g. *ball*, or *tuggy*, or *squeaky toy*. Remember to make each toy name sound very different, and to first repeatedly show your dog each toy, accompanied by the name for it, until he fully understands which name/sound means which toy. You can also let him smell each toy while you attach the name to it.

Only when you are sure your dog knows which name means which toy, ask him to go and find different toys by name – e.g. "*tuggy - find it!*", "*ball - find it!*". A lot of collies can become incredibly clever at this task, to the point where they can easily distinguish between ten or more different toys that owners ask them to find on command.

But if you want an example of a collie with mind-blowing expertise on this front, look no further than a bitch called Chaser from South Carolina, USA. As part of an ongoing animal behaviour research programme, she has proved able to identify over 1000 toys by name and retrieve them. My own toy-mad bitch, Lara, would probably kill to get on a research programme like this!

FINDING USEFUL OBJECTS

Once your collie understands how to search for different things, on command, why not make even better use of this skill? I train my own dogs to find things like my car keys, mobile phone or their leads – all things you could lose some day on a walk.

The principle is the same with each item; i.e. you initially hold an object up for your dog to see and smell and attach a specific name to it. Then you regularly ask your dog to find the object at home, or in your garden. Always praise your dog – "*good boy!*" – and reward him with a treat or toy when he brings the item to you.

Only when you are sure your dog understands the different items you want him to find can you test this when you are out. Because dogs track things more by scent than by sight, this means my dogs are often far better than me at finding lost objects, particularly if they have dropped into deeper undergrowth or sand or piles of leaves. Each time they find the object because it has my scent on it.

Watching my dogs use their superior sense in this way continually fills me with admiration and awe. It is also a skill that has got me out of some otherwise pretty dire predicaments. Thank you, dogs.

WHICH AIDS SHOULD YOU USE IN TRAINING AND WHEN?

When I am training a new dog, I constantly review and revise which aids or rewards I should use – and when I should use them – to get the best out of him. Every collie can be different in this respect, and it is important to appreciate this and use a lot of initial trial and error to see what works best with your own dog.

PRAISE

Let us begin with *praise*. Praise, to me, is the most vital first cue to a dog that he has just done something not only correct but also rewarding – two notions that should always go together in his head. Many collies adore praise, others can take it or leave it. But these differences may be just as much to do with earlier associations (if any) a dog has made with the concept of human praise as the kind of bond he has with his owner.

As stated earlier, praise in training should always come just *before* a physical reward, like a treat or toy. Over time, this conditions your dog to find your praise, in itself, rewarding because he views it as the precursor to something really pleasant.

If, however, you give your dog a physical reward *first*, then praise him afterwards, your praise becomes a less important afterthought for him. It also means he may not co-operate with you in future, until he first sees you holding a treat or toy.

TOYS

Next, *toys*. If you have a collie who is very energetic, and who quickly becomes obsessed with toy rewards, then you may develop two problems if you are not careful.

The first is that it may prove harder to keep your dog in a calmer state for exercises that require precision or clearer thinking, as his mind becomes totally preoccupied with the excitement of getting his toy. The second is that your praise could become far less significant to him; i.e. just a distraction he has to endure en route to what he really wants – his toy! This means that later on praise, in itself, without a toy, may not be a big enough reward for him. To get round these problems, get into the habit of only ever praising your dog, and then rewarding him with his toy, for being in a *calm* mental state, prior to and during exercises which require clear thinking.

In other words, if he whines, fidgets, or bounces about when you are trying to train him, immediately make him go *down* and *wait* and walk away from him. Do this every time he gets over-excited. Once he has quietened down, begin training again and thereafter make it clear to your dog that your praise, and his toy, only ever come after he has shown calmer behaviour. This also teaches a dog far greater mental self discipline. Also, do not always give your dog a toy after praise in training.

Over time you can work out how often you should give your dog his toy after praise, and not give it to him, in order to keep him in the most ideal mental state for training. Greater unpredictability as to when your dog will get his toy after your praise will also make him concentrate that much harder on you.

TREATS

Treats can be a highly valuable aid in training, particularly when used with a clicker – a device I will cover in a moment. The plus with food treats, as with toys, is that they instantly build a connection in a dog's mind between a specific action and a reward. The dog will then want to repeat the action that triggered the reward.

The downside with treats, however, is that owners can become over-reliant on them, using them each and every time they want their dog to do something. This is how you train (or should I say, *bribe*) a dog to only co-operate with you in return for food, and to not co-operate with you if he does not see the food in your hand.

If your dog is always more preoccupied with the food you have in your hand or pocket, or which he imagines to always be there, he will not be focusing quite so hard on you, or the exercise you are asking him to do.

To overcome these kinds of problems remember, as ever, to always praise your dog *before* giving him any food reward. Then gradually decrease the amount of times you give him food after praise. But make these occurrences highly random; i.e. sometimes your dog will get six or seven treats in training, at other times two or just one. By making the occurrence of treats after praise that much more unpredictable for your dog, he should concentrate that much harder on what you are asking him to do.

Having begun the process of praising and then rewarding your dog with food or toys or both, you can then gradually reduce the amount of times you use these extra aids, and use praise alone far more often. Never, however, abandon them suddenly or for good, or you will progressively sap your dog's motivation. Continue to use toys and treats every so often, in return for a really good response either in training, or when out on a walk. As long as your dog believes a toy or treat could come his way any time, in return for co-operation, he will continue to work well for you.

RESIDENTIAL TRAINING COURSES

Today, you will see many residential training courses or workshops advertised, offering the chance for you to get expert help with your dog. Some of these, inevitably, will always be better than others.

If you are looking for courses to help train your dog for a particular competitive discipline, such as Obedience or Agility, then always research first the instructors running them – either by word of mouth or the Internet. I would always look for people who are kind, sympathetic and inspiring, towards both owners and their dogs. By contrast, people who take a more hyper-critical and bullying approach are putting the needs of their own egos above those of their clients.

You pay good money to a trainer for them to help you, not to watch them show off. Avoid people like this at all costs, unless you want to keep coming home feeling demoralised and inadequate.

The one thing I definitely would not recommend is sending your dog away somewhere, without you, for some form of training or re-training. Owners so often view this as a quick fix for an untrained or problem dog, but it is also extremely risky. If a trainer uses a wrong or harsher approach on your dog, and damages him psychologically as a result, it is you who will have to live with the consequences of this, not the trainer.

Similarly, if you are not around to see what a person is doing to train, or retrain, your dog, you will not be able to replicate the same results when you bring him home.

CLICKERS

A clicker device can be an absolute boon in training if you know how to use it correctly. However, it can be a complete waste of time – if not a disaster – if you use it incorrectly, in terms of how quickly and effectively it allows you to attach rewards to wrong behaviours.

People's misuses of clickers usually stem from a basic lack of understanding as to exactly how they work. A clicker works in the following way:

First, you have to undergo an initial conditioning process with your dog, whereby he learns to associate the sound of a clicker with a food reward.

To do this, repeatedly click the clicker in front of your dog and after every click, immediately give him a treat. With a dog as bright as a collie, this connection is often made pretty quickly.

Once your dog understands that the 'click' sound means an imminent reward, you can then attach a click, followed by a treat, to any particular 'snapshot' of behaviour that you would like him to repeat. Later, you can then substitute the click with a verbal command for the same behaviour.

Let us assume, for instance, that you want to use a clicker to teach your dog to *sit*. In your left hand hold the clicker

Precision timing is required for successful clicker training.

and in your right hand hold a treat over his head, which will prompt him to sit. As your dog sits, quickly click the clicker and give your dog a treat. Once he has done this several times, substitute the click with a verbal command – "*sit!*" – as he sits and then praise and reward him.

Really, a clicker initially takes the place of an owner's verbal praise in cueing to a dog that he has just done something both right and ultimately rewarding. A clicker is a brilliant device to use in more advanced training, such as Canine Freestyle or Competitive Obedience, where you need to teach and reinforce very precise actions in your dog. By freezing in his memory, via a click and reward, only utterly perfect actions, you make these actions more and more likely to be repeated by him.

Another plus is their utter simplicity; in using just one consistent sound to signal right behaviour to a dog, you can remove all the obstacles caused by human verbal ambiguity or inconsistency in the training process, especially when it comes to teaching something new.

CLICKER DOWNSIDES

The downside of clickers revolves around timing. Owners cannot always click and reward with the split second precision required to freeze only one specific action or behaviour in their dog's mind. As a result they end up freezing the wrong behaviour instead, and associating it with a reward.

To test your own reactions on this front, make a small mark on a wall around shoulder height and continually throw up a ball. Click your clicker every time the ball is level with your wall mark on the way down. Get someone else to watch you, to see how consistently accurate, or not, you are with your timing. If you are persistently inaccurate, you need to practise until you get a lot better at your timing. If you are still consistently failing to be spot on after that,

clicker training may not be for you.

The point at which you substitute a click with a verbal command for an action, or later use praise, instead of a click, to herald a reward for that action, can also get many folk in a pickle. You cannot, after all, spend your whole life walking around with clickers and treats every time you want your dog to do something.

If you have a highly sensitive collie, he might not like the sound of a clicker. Either way, clicker training has to be very much a one-on-one activity. I am horrified to see group dog training classes where everybody is using clickers and treats at the same time. How confusing that must be for any dog, trying to establish which click is coming from where and for what? If you have any doubts about how to use clicker training to best effect with your own dog, do seek further expert help, preferably on the aforementioned one-on-one basis.

Clicker training can also be very useful in many forms of behaviour modification.

Within this chapter I have, hopefully, shown you how to take your collie's training up to another level, using the right approach and techniques. The more you train your dog to do different things, the more you stretch his superb brain and the more disciplined his whole mind becomes. He is then the working, thinking, fiercely intelligent animal he was always born to be, forever focused on you for the next instruction, instead of a furry maniac who buzzes and ricochets around your home and life like a demented wasp.

However, the last thing you should ever be when training any dog is complacent. Just when everything appears to be going swimmingly with your collie, a sudden challenge can come along and change the whole way he behaves – the first and biggest of which tends to be adolescence. The next chapter outlines what you can expect from this phase of your collie's life, and how to survive it.

Chapter Nine

THE ADOLESCENT COLLIE

Common changes and problems in teenage dogs; to neuter or not to neuter; to breed or not to breed

In the first six to seven months of life, your collie puppy will be growing fast and his mind will be like a sponge, soaking up a vast range of new sights, sounds, experiences and social encounters, as well as any training you may have worked on with him.

He will have begun to develop noticeable idiosyncrasies and quirks of character, including how intrinsically confident, or not, he happens to be as a dog. He may have begun to show some, or all, of the classic collie working traits – i.e. eyeing, stalking, chasing, herding and nipping when aroused – which so often comes as quite a shock for those with less experience of the breed.

All in all, you will think you have got to know your young dog pretty well. Then suddenly adolescence hits, and if anything is going to go wrong with his training or behaviour, this is when it is most likely to happen. It is not an easy time for dogs, but neither is it an easy time for owners, as their dogs shed their puppy dependency and become increasingly more wilful or challenging in their behaviour.

GREATER AND LESSER EFFECTS

The complicating factor with adolescence in collies, as in most dogs, is that every dog can be affected by it differently – in terms of when it begins, how long it lasts, and how dramatic, or not, its impact is on their behaviour. Even two dogs of the same sex and from the same litter can have very varying responses to this period of physical and psychological upheaval, which roughly ranges from six months to two years of age, although it can sometimes begin earlier or last longer.

Parents often agonise as to why they can have three children, two of whom have a problem-free passage through adolescence, while the third becomes a drug addict who attracts trouble like a magnet and fritters his life away in a crack den. These days, scientists would claim the answer lies in a range of individual genetic variations and mutations in brain function, which predisposes all animals towards certain types of behaviours. Not that that helps much, mind.

A SHAKE-UP PERIOD

The way I see adolescence in collies is that it is a shake up

period, exposing any underlying faults in a dog's inherent character, as well as the nature of the relationship he shares with you. Further, any genetic tendency towards traits like fear, aggression or more obsessive chasing can become magnified once adolescence strikes.

It is, therefore, not surprising that this is the stage in life where so many people begin to despair of their collies, and hand them over to rescue centres, because they cannot see any light at the end of the tunnel.

In a handful of cases, the dogs in question may well have turned into dangerous liabilities. Far more often than not, however, they just needed better understanding and handling through an undeniably testing, but also essentially transient, period in their lives.

You cannot condemn a teenage dog for not behaving the same way he did as a puppy, because psychologically and emotionally he is no longer capable of doing so. Similarly, if you did not teach your collie to respect you when he was a puppy, or relentlessly train and encourage him to focus on you when he was very young, such processes can only get harder the older he gets.

Let us now look at some of the most common physical and behavioural symptoms you might find in your adolescent collie.

THE SIGNS AND EFFECTS OF ADOLESCENCE

The early signs of a dog entering puberty, or adolescence – i.e. male dogs beginning to cock their legs or scent-mark, and bitches having their first heats – may seem obvious. But other changes to behaviour, as a result of hormonal upheaval, can build up more slowly or subtly.

Many adolescent collies (see *Don't panic!*) can seem more distracted in training, or may appear to have forgotten exercises and commands they previously responded to well. This is because the growing process has turned their brains into the equivalent of overloaded power stations, straining to develop new connections to all the physical expansions occurring in their bodies. In time, with good ongoing training and once the growing process is complete, your dog's concentration levels should improve again.

MORE CHALLENGING ENCOUNTERS WITH OTHER DOGS

Adolescent collies can also become far more interested in other dogs. But while as puppies they were viewing them as potential playmates, this time they will be regarding them more in the sense of potential breeding partners or sexual and territorial rivals.

Some fellow canine encounters involving teenage male collies, in particular, can get a bit tricky. This is because the dogs in question have a hormonally fuelled confidence which is not matched by their level of social experience. As a result, they can have a tendency to overplay their hands with other dogs and get into trouble.

Testosterone, the hormone responsible for so much reckless and risk-taking behaviour in male dogs, is coursing through their bodies at extremely high levels. It is also what prompts them into behaviours like the inappropriate mounting of other dogs, male or female, or more hostile challenges towards other male dogs, typified by the dog stiffening his body and putting his head over another dog's neck.

BETTER HANDLING YOUR DOG'S TEENAGE ENCOUNTERS

Teenage male collies may often initiate tense stand offs with other male dogs which they then cannot exit gracefully as, in moving away at the wrong moment, they risk showing weakness and thus increase their chances of being attacked.

If your teenage collie gets stuck in an encounter like this, he will not respond to you when you try to call him back as he just cannot afford to make the wrong move at the wrong moment for fear of the consequences. Similarly, if you try shouting at your dog and grabbing him, you are more likely to up the general hostility level and trigger a fight.

By far the best strategy is to walk *calmly* between the two dogs and instruct your own dog to back away using either the '*off!*' or '*leave!*' command. Then stand in front of your dog to break the eye contact between the two dogs and stop the other dog approaching him. Also try to back the other dog off by moving forward and giving him a correction – "*hey!*". If all this is done in a really calm but resolute way it usually defuses the situation. Your dog may also be greatly relieved by your intervention, which has given him an escape route out of the confrontation.

AVOIDING ESCALATIONS IN HOSTILITY

You never want things to escalate to the point where your collie attacks another dog or gets attacked himself, as this can so often be the starting point for a collie's future aggression with other dogs. Always try to use, the aforementioned conflict defusing strategy instead, should a strange male dog come running up to your collie with seemingly hostile or challenging intent.

You should also never allow your collie to run up to

DON'T PANIC!

Time and again, I see collie owners panic at the behavioural changes brought about by adolescence in their dogs. It is incredibly important to keep remembering that much of this new behaviour will still be at an experimental stage – i.e. not yet set in stone. This means you can still immediately correct it – "hey!" – to deter your dog from repeating it until it becomes ingrained. Similarly, you can continue to invite preferable behaviour from your dog, and richly reward this instead. Both actions will limit the chances of him persisting with less desirable habits.

The onset of adolescence can also affect dogs' responses to training, or their performance in the competition environment. Whether your adolescent collie is male or female, again, do not panic or give up if he or she suddenly seems to lose concentration, forgets previously well-taught commands or makes a hash of a competition round.

Such events are incredibly common at this phase in your dog's development and will pass with time, as long as you continue to make training as enjoyable and rewarding as possible, and keep practising it in many different environments and contexts. You will also need to teach your collie to get better and better at working and focusing on you through distraction, particularly when surrounded by many other dogs.

Also appreciate that some adolescent collies can be experiencing a certain amount of pain or discomfort resulting from the physical effects of the growing process; see Growing pains page 93.

anybody else's dog in a challenging way and follow instead the social encounter guidelines covered in Chapter Six, where you train your dog to keep "*close!*" whenever other people or dogs approach, and then tell him which ones he may or should not "*go see!*".

Also see, *Challenges to the* close *command*, page 90.

THE SECOND FEAR PERIOD

On reaching adolescence, collies of either sex can start to become increasingly more territorial, wary, fearful or reactive in their behaviour towards less familiar people or dogs. They can also become more fearful of stranger sights or louder noises. This is not just to do with a poorer earlier socialisation – although undoubtedly this will play a part. It is also to do with the second fear period dogs commonly go through around eight to ten months of age.

Typically it is a phase where dogs have a sudden slump in social confidence. A dog seemingly re-evaluates his past reactions to previous experiences, and may then view more negatively things he formerly trusted as safe or okay. It is important to see this period as a critical watershed in your young dog's development; the moment where, with the wrong approach or handling he could so easily go on to develop longer-lasting fear-based problems.

REWARDING FEAR

Some collies go through their second fear period with only the most minor of 'wobbles', like suddenly barking at something or someone whose appearance momentarily unsettles them. Always make light of these events and encourage your dog to "*go see!*" what he was scared of, using the guidelines for this exercise laid out in Chapter Six. Such incidents usually get fewer and fewer as the dog regains his confidence as he matures.

Other dogs can have more violent reactions, and this is where so often owners handle things the wrong way. If a dog starts growling or barking at another person or dog, for instance, out of fear, instead of immediately and calmly correcting the dog – "*hey!*" – then giving him a moment to regroup and behave differently, the owner panics. Their cute and cuddly little pup has suddenly become *an aggressive dog.* Oh no!

So either the owner shouts at his dog, which usually makes things worse, or immediately takes him away from the person or dog he was being aggressive towards; thus instantly rewarding his fearful reaction by removing the problem for him.

You cannot teach dogs to be more socially confident or tolerant through constantly removing them from social encounters the moment they show fear or hostility.

INCREASING SOCIAL TOLERANCE

Some collies will always find it much harder to be sociable with stranger dogs and people beyond adolescence. Often this behaviour has a genetic root, although it can be severely worsened by a poor early socialisation period where the dog was not positively exposed to a very wide range of other people and dogs while still well under 16 weeks of age.

If a dog has not got the genetic and psychological tools to be a sociable individual by adolescence, he will never be that

way. Neither does it do any good to try and force him to be that way if he is not up to it. The most you can hope for with dogs like these is that you teach them to be socially *tolerant*; i.e. able to accept the presence of other people and dogs without excessive fear or the use of aggression. In Chapter Six, I outlined how you do this with puppies, but you can teach or reinforce the same lessons in dogs of any age. Please note: The whole issue of *fear* and *aggression* in collies is covered in Part Two (pages 152 and 170).

CHALLENGES TO THE CLOSE! COMMAND

If a dog is going to challenge you over your right to stop him approaching other dogs – which is usually also a test of how much, or little, authority you still hold in his eyes – he is going to do it as a teenager. Typically he may stay *Close!* on command for a little while, and then suddenly make a dash ahead of you to get to another dog before you can stop him. The more he can get away with this, the more your *Close!* commands, and whole authority, become undermined.

Should this keep happening, you will have to go back to basics, putting your dog on the long line again and making your training of the *Close!* command more reliable. Similarly, work a lot harder to hold his attention when other dogs pass, by getting out toys for him to fixate on, or throwing treats up in the air for him to catch in his mouth.

Dogs can get into the habit of breaking a *Close!* command the moment you have passed another person or dog, because they over-anticipate the customary verbal release command – like "*Okay!*" – you usually give them at this point. For this reason always keep your dog *Close!* until you have gone some way beyond another person or dog.

TRAINING REVISITED FOR TEENAGE DOGS

If your training starts to go pear-shaped once your collie reaches adolescence, over and above the common loss of concentration and increased forgetfulness caused by growth and hormonal upheaval, it may be that the kind of training that worked for your dog as a puppy no longer works for him now he is older.

The older a collie gets, the more his adult character becomes apparent. If he is a particularly strong-minded dog, he is more likely to challenge you over control commands like down, wait or stay. To know how to deal with this, *see Battles of will,* page 74.

Your dog's response to the *Recall* command may also get poorer, particularly when he sees other dogs, or if his working focus escapes on to the wrong targets. Do not get into a situation where you continually find yourself calling a dog who is blatantly ignoring you. This undermines your authority and allows your dog to discover that he can do what he likes when off lead, and there is nothing you can do to stop him.

It may well be that you did not teach *Recall* adequately to your dog when he was a puppy (as outlined in Chapter Five), or have allowed the command to become corrupted through your dog continually ignoring it. To solve the problem see *Recall failures* in Part Two, page 182.

Also understand that as a dog gets older, you may have to make more effort to motivate him for some tasks. This is because you are continually competing with other surrounding distractions in his mind. Dogs, just like us, can become bored with doing the same things over and over again. So mix up your exercises, and vary your rewards; keep exercises requiring high motivation fun and do not over-train.

This is what puts more teenage dogs off the training process than anything else. Remember it is the quality of your dog's response in training that matters most, not the quantity of responses he gives you. As soon as you get that good response – stop! Praise your dog, reward him, have a break and maybe a game and then move on. Leave it some time, if not until the next day, before repeating the same exercise.

In making teenage collies do the same exercise again and again, you can also undermine their confidence. You may think you are striving for perfection, but your dog may start to think, instead, that he is continually doing something wrong. In trying to guess what you really want, he may become stressed and thus make even bigger mistakes – or simply give up trying.

OBSESSIVE AND PHOBIC BEHAVIOURS

As previously highlighted in this chapter, adolescence in dogs is an upheaval period that not only exposes any basic faults in a dog's character or temperament; it is also a time when any other particular neuroses or behavioural quirks can become more intense or ingrained.

Many of the more annoying, or disturbing, obsessions and phobias found in collies can hit their heights around adolescence and beyond – unless you do more to prevent this happening. Once again these important subjects will be covered in greater detail in Part Two.

SEXUAL MATURITY

Take it for granted that as your collie gets older and sexually matures, he will become progressively more distracted not just by the presence of other dogs, but also their scent. If he is a male collie, he will do that revolting thing of licking other dog's urine and sampling its overtones and undertones in the manner of a master sommelier. Bitches, however, can do this as well, especially at the height of their heat cycles.

It is not ideal behaviour in a social companion, but it is perfectly normal behaviour for dogs. In fact, there is much about the behaviour of sexually mature dogs that owners don't seem to like, which leads them to consider whether neutering or spaying might be the answer. But is it the right solution for your own particular collie?

Neutering and spaying operations have become so routine for dogs these days that owners do not always appreciate that there can be potential downsides, as well as benefits, attached to them. Let us now look at the pros and cons of these procedures.

HEALTH BENEFITS

The most obvious benefit of spaying or neutering dogs is the prevention of unwanted litters of puppies. Spaying bitches also prevents them developing a womb infection called *pyometra* (see Chapter Twelve, page 146). If done early enough, it is also thought to minimise their chances of developing mammary tumours in later life. Similarly, castrated male dogs are considered to be at lower risk of developing prostate problems when they are older.

DOWNSIDES

Potential downsides of neutering or spaying, on the other hand, can include a fuzzier or woollier coat quality, urinary incontinence, which can require a dog to be on long-term medication, and weight gain, unless the dog's diet and exercise regime are adjusted accordingly. Many neutered male dogs may also attract more unwelcome attention – be this aggressive or sexual in nature – from entire male dogs.

Over and above these more well-documented side-effects, however, recent studies undertaken in the USA now suggest there could be other downsides to neutering and spaying which affect both health and behaviour.

These include a higher risk in later life of developing bone and cardiac cancers, hypothyroidism (i.e. an under-active thyroid gland), cruciate ligament ruptures and other joint problems. The latter are thought to be more prevalent in dogs neutered prior to puberty, or full physical maturity, as sex hormones have a specific effect on both the growth and density of bones.

EFFECTS ON BEHAVIOUR

The same US studies also include one by the American Kennel Club Canine Health Foundation, which reported significantly more behavioural problems in spayed/neutered bitches and dogs; fearful behaviour being the most common problem in spayed bitches, and aggression the commonest problem in neutered male dogs.

Clearly, we have no way of knowing how much better, or not, the health record and behaviour of these dogs would have been if they had remained entire. But what does come across – and has also been borne out by my own experiences/observations as a behaviourist for many years – is how wrong it is to imagine that neutering and spaying are magic-wand procedures that can only ever make any dog's behaviour better.

In fact, sex hormones can frequently have a beneficial influence on a dog's behaviour. A higher level of female hormones in entire bitches, for instance, is often what gives a calmer, gentler and more biddable edge to their demeanour. Thus, when you greatly reduce such hormonal influences in bitches, you can run the risk of them becoming more fearful, or even aggressive, in their behaviour.

In male dogs, testosterone can not only give them extra confidence, as individuals, but also often inspires that special spark, sharpness and enthusiasm so vitally important in any working or competition dog. Additionally, if a male dog's aggression is primarily fear-based, removing more confidence-boosting levels of testosterone can actually make his aggression worse.

MALE DOGS

There are some situations where castration really seems the best option for a male dog; in cases, for instance, where his status-related aggression towards other males, scent-marking round the home, humping of people or objects, or escaping and roaming after bitches have all become intolerable.

It is also advisable in cases where one or both of the dog's testicles have not fully descended by the age of ten months – conditions known as *monorchidism* and *cryptorchidism* respectively. Such retained testicles have a high chance of turning cancerous if not surgically removed. As both *monorchidism* and *cryptorchidism* tend to be hereditary conditions, dogs with either of them should also never be used for breeding.

Sometimes owners of entire male dogs will be offered hormone treatment (or 'chemical castration') which aims to replicate the effects of surgical neutering, just to see what changes to behaviour, if any, may result. This is certainly worth trying if you have doubts about the operation itself. Be aware, however, that how a dog behaves on such hormone treatment is no foolproof guarantee of how he may behave after he has actually been surgically castrated, and also that the effects of castration, on behaviour, can take up to six months or more to be fully evident.

BITCHES

If you have a bitch who suffers dreadfully during her heats, and/or the pseudo pregnancy phase that follows eight to 12 weeks afterwards, and you have no intention of breeding from her, then spaying is usually the kindest option. If you cannot guarantee 100-per-cent vigilance of your entire bitch during her heat cycles, it is also best to get her spayed, rather than run the risk of unplanned and unwanted pregnancies should any male dog mate with her.

If, having weighed up all the aforementioned considerations, you think you would prefer to keep your bitch entire, then you must know how to manage her heats correctly, what to expect from the pseudo pregnancy phase of her cycle, and how to be alert to the previously mentioned and potentially life-threatening condition of *pyometra,* which entire bitches can suffer post-heat, especially if they have

never been bred from. *All these subjects will be covered more fully in Chapter Twelve.*

The behaviour of entire bitches can fluctuate tremendously, according to which stage they happen to be in their heat cycle. To get the best idea of how your bitch might behave, if spayed, study her behaviour exactly midway between one heat and the next. This is when her reproductive hormone levels should be at their lowest.

MAKING A DECISION

So where does all this debate leave you, when it comes to making a decision about neutering or spaying your own dog? It is important to understand that a dog's body, just like a human one, contains an incredibly complex balance of different hormonal systems interacting together, and it can take just a subtle deficit or surplus of one particular hormone to have a significant impact on his health or behaviour.

Appreciate that neutering, or not neutering, can always have a potential downside. You thus have to weigh up all the risks and benefits of each option before deciding which one is best for your own particular dog or bitch.

Bear in mind that once the neutering or spaying procedures have been performed on your dog, the effects will be irreversible. If you are going ahead with the operation purely, or predominantly, for health reasons, that is one thing. But if you are neutering or spaying to try to change some less desirable behaviour in your dog, you need to be pretty sure beforehand that the behaviour in question is primarily related to higher levels of sex hormones. If the cause is principally genetic or learned behaviour, instead, it is unlikely to be cured by neutering, and the behaviour could even get worse as a result of having the operation.

My own view is that it is best to wait until a collie has developed his or her full adult character and completed his or her full adult growth before deciding whether to neuter or spay. In bitches this also means waiting until after they have had their first heat. Thereafter, seek some sound professional advice as to how the neutering or spaying procedure may affect the behaviour of your own particular dog – although be aware that not all post spaying/neutering behaviours in individual dogs will be easy to predict in advance.

A good vet should be able to suggest advice and explore the issue in depth with you, to help you make the best decision, rather than just rush your dog on to the operation table before any such deeper discussion has been made.

Please note, there is additional information on how hormones affect behaviour in Part Two, see *Hormonally fuelled behaviour, page 177.*

RESCUED DOGS

A high proportion of rescued collies may have been neutered or spayed before you get them. This is in line with the policies of different rescue organisations, which should be respected. Nobody knows better than these organisations how much suffering results from the over breeding of dogs, and thus this is an understandable measure they take to reduce the incidence of this kind of problem.

GROWING PAINS

Not all of the upheaval in the minds and bodies of teenage collies is related purely to sex hormones. It is also related to a process that is happening at exactly the same time: growth. Growing uses a lot of energy and you may need to adapt your dog's diet accordingly, especially if he is one of those high-powered lean collies who burn calories at a rapid rate. But do proceed with caution.

In recent years, research by veterinary experts has come to the conclusion that diets promoting excessive growth in young dogs, over a short period of time, can have an adverse impact on developing skeletons, potentially exacerbating joint conditions such as *hip dysplasia* and another disorder called OCD (*osteochondritis dissicans*) which commonly affects elbows and shoulders (*see Chapter Twelve for more information*).

Also avoid the feeding of any dietary supplements that have not previously been approved by your vet.

LIMITING EXERCISE

Signs of HD and OCD are usually first seen in adolescent collies, although in more severe cases they can be apparent in even earlier puppyhood.

Classic symptoms are a noticeable lameness, stiffness or distinct discomfort in either back legs or hips (HD) or front legs (OCD), particularly after demanding exercise. Both conditions are thought to have a strong hereditary factor and, diet apart, can be worsened by trauma or too much exercise when the dog is still young and his bones are not yet properly formed.

For this reason, it is wise to restrict your puppy's exercise until he is at least six months old, and do not allow him to over-stress his joints by too much jumping – e.g. off furniture or out of cars, or running up and down stairs. I personally prefer to lift, or gently support puppies in and out of cars until they are at least nine or ten months old. Excessive trauma to a young dog's joints can often store up bigger problems for later life, including arthritis

ONGOING MANAGEMENT OF THE TEENAGE COLLIE AS A FAMILY DOG

Around the teenage period and beyond, many collies can begin the process of evaluating who the stronger and weaker members of a household are and then reacting to them accordingly.

Quite commonly, a maturing dog will develop a desire to only obey one household member he views as strongest, or of most value to him, and become increasingly less

TO BREED OR NOT TO BREED?

If the only reason you are keeping your female or male collie entire is out of an intention to breed from them in the future, please consider the following questions first:

- Do you own a pedigree collie?

- Does he/she have an exceptionally sound temperament – honestly?

- Has he/she shown particular talent/success in the show or competition ring?

- Has your dog been tested for all known health faults in the breed – e.g. hip scored, eye and hearing tested – and got good results?

- Does he/she descend from similarly screened dogs with fabulous temperaments/no health faults?

- Do you have up to eight or nine excellent homes lined up for a future litter that is produced?

- Are you prepared to keep any puppy you cannot find a good home for, or rehome/keep any puppy who is returned to you? When you breed dogs, you have a lifelong commitment to their welfare.

If the answer is no to any or most of the above questions, why bother? As I hope was extensively highlighted in Chapter Three, breeding collies well takes a tremendous amount of skill, effort, expense and dedication. It is not something to do on a sentimental whim. As outlined in the next chapter, the rescued dog world is already awash with unwanted collies and collie crosses, too many of whom were only bred because someone saw this as a cash opportunity, or because an owner thought it was a nice idea at the time.

Obsessive behaviour may escalate during adolescence, such as 'catching water'.

responsive towards any other member he deems as weak, or he may attempt to manipulate or bully them in different ways.

Such behaviour can begin suddenly or build up gradually beyond puppyhood. Much of it is to do with the dog developing his adult identity, and establishing the limits of his own power, in terms of how much he can influence or inhibit the actions of others with his own behaviour. You must see this process for what it is and deal with it correctly. If not, your collie could become a highly divisive force within your household or, in rare cases, a physical threat to some members within it.

INSTINCTIVE RESPONSES TO WEAKNESS

A great deal of the angst caused by controlling or bullying teenage dogs derives from an owner's belief that their dog's level of emotional attachment, respect and responsiveness, should be the same towards all household members, regardless of how differently those members might present themselves to him.

They do not understand how instinctive and exploitative dogs' responses can be towards weakness in other animals, including the people they share their lives with; their minds completely free of any of the emotional or moral inhibitions that feature in most human relationships.

For more advice on this issue, see *Aggression* (page 152) and *Manipulative behaviour* (page 177) in Part Two.

SURVIVING ADOLESCENCE

As mentioned at the beginning of this chapter, you may be lucky enough to own a teenage collie who navigates the transition from puppyhood to adulthood with scarcely a moment's bother or concern. But if not, at least you now have a better idea of the most common problems that can develop or arise, and why, and also know that you are most certainly not alone in facing them.

Overall, you should see adolescence as a period when your earlier puppy relationship with your collie is now changing to something different. You cannot rely on his infant dependency anymore to retain his co-operation and generally be the centre of his world. You must forge a more adult bond with him, instead, based on mutual trust and respect.

There may be tantrums and much exasperation, and the odd tearful moment of frustration or despair along the way. We have all been there! But in the end, as long as you stick to your guns and your training, and show patience, calmness and iron determination in the face of all challenges, you should emerge from this phase with a dog who is a pleasure to own again. A good sense of humour is also pretty vital to preserve your own sanity.

An adolescent dog may be worried by situations that he previously took in his stride.

By keeping the encounter low-key, the dog is able to overcome his initial concern so that he can investigate.

A productive meeting as the collie has learnt that there was nothing to fear

95

Chapter Ten
THE RESCUED COLLIE

Acquiring, rehoming and rehabilitating rescued dogs; Common issues and problems found in collies with a past

Many collies find themselves in rescue through no fault of their own.

Border Collies and collie crosses are now one of the most common dogs found in rescue centres. In the UK, one specialist rescue organisation alone, The Border Collie Trust GB, rehomes around 500 dogs a year. But worldwide, collies seem to be all-too-often dogs that people cannot, or will not, keep. (*Note*: Border Collie rescue organisations in the UK, USA, Canada, Australia and New Zealand feature in the *Further Information* section in Part Two of this book).

It is a massive canine welfare problem, and a monument to our failure to both breed and own these highly special dogs with consideration for the quality of their future lives.

A DISPOSABLE AGE

Among the many collies up for rehoming today, you will get dogs who have only been relinquished with great reluctance. You will get others who have developed problems that can range from the minor to the major, and dogs who have been hideously neglected, abused and then abandoned. Countless more dogs will have been discarded purely because they have suddenly found themselves superfluous to an owner's requirements.

The ease with which people will now offload or recycle their unwanted dogs is frequently attributed to a modern disposable age, wherein human beings will view family pets just like any other commodity to be thrown away when they tire of it, or the fancy takes them. Sometimes dogs will be discarded simply for the crime of being old or sick.

But was there ever a golden age where everybody showed far greater care and commitment towards their dogs? Just as there has always been a faction of human society who has treated dogs in a responsible and caring way, there has always been another who has treated dogs badly, or regarded their welfare with cavalier indifference. It is part and parcel of the essentially schizophrenic nature of the human race and attitudes that arise from people's individual upbringings.

Much of the suffering inflicted on dogs by people, be it physical or psychological, is also down to plain ignorance, rather than deliberate cruelty, and the answer to this is said to be 'better education'. But given that ignorance, and bloody-minded reluctance to change one's attitudes or ways, are so often qualities that go hand in hand in people, it can be a lot harder to re-educate them than you might think.

A SAFETY NET

What the canine rescue industry does is provide a safety net for dogs who might otherwise have been disposed of by owners in far more brutal ways. It also, of course, provides a safety net for people who just want to offload the responsibility of their dog on to someone else.

There is an argument that the easier you make it for people to get rid of their dogs in this way, the more they will do it. But equally there is an argument that if you did not provide this easier way, dogs would be subjected to far more suffering. Ultimately I think that dogs will always be better off with people who want them, as opposed to those who do not, and that they all deserve the chance of a happier and more successful life than the one they may have had before.

WHY COLLIES END UP IN RESCUE

Some of the most common reasons given for the rehoming of collies are owners emigrating, or moving to accommodation where dogs are not allowed, or a new baby arriving or a child becoming allergic to the dog. The cynic in me would suggest that often these are less reasons than excuses, to make owners feel better about abandoning their dogs or to disguise any more potentially serious problems they may have.

The notion, for instance, that when getting a collie puppy a couple would not also consider the future prospect of them having a baby is to me quite incomprehensible. Similarly, it is weird how often children only become allergic to their dogs once they have moved beyond cute puppyhood and into the more challenging phase of adolescence.

Either way, such economy with the truth can make life that much harder for rescue organisations, and would-be rehomers, who can only derive a more realistic picture of a dog's true character and behaviour over time.

Many rescued collies, particularly those whose owners have died, or are sound family dogs who have been the victims of a relationship split, may give you no problems whatsoever once rehomed. Others can be trickier, with issues ranging from aggression and destructiveness to working instincts and behaviours that have spiralled out of

control. Many can also be quite timid or fearful in their behaviour towards strangers or dogs, particularly if they have come from a more socially isolated background.

THE UNWANTED

Over the years I have visited umpteen canine rescue organisations and shelters, including those specialising in the collie breed, and understand completely what people's initial reactions to these places can be.

They always remind me poignantly of the utter helplessness of dogs; creatures devoid of any voice, or rights, other than those human beings choose to give them. The beauty or horror of a dog's life so often revolves entirely around chance; that one, early, fateful throw of the dice which determines the nature of the person who breeds him or buys him and takes him home.

Any person can own a dog, no matter how mad, bad, ignorant or cruel they happen to be; similarly anyone can get rid of one when they feel like it. In all my years of dealing with dogs I have never got over this essential injustice and betrayal inflicted on them, courtesy of the human race.

When you visit any rescue centre, you are likely to feel tremendous distress and sadness when looking at the faces of all those unwanted dogs. Then you may feel enormous anger towards previous owners who have abandoned them and then removed themselves from the consequences of their actions. You can see this as an act of intense moral cowardice and betrayal on their part. Many people who work in rescue feel exactly the same way to begin with.

With greater time and experience, however, you slowly realise how little difference your emotional reactions and sympathy make to the lives of homeless dogs. What they need most is good, ongoing care, practical assessments regarding their futures, and people who can move them on to new and better lives as soon as possible.

ARE YOU THE RIGHT PERSON FOR A RESCUED COLLIE?

When seeking to acquire a rescued collie it is important to be realistic, in terms of your own expectations, and what level of rehabilitation may be involved. Be aware that just because you feel sorry for a dog does not necessarily mean you will be the right new owner for him.

As a rule, it's never a good idea to begin the quest for a rescue collie with a 'perfect' dog in mind. Most rescued collies will need some degree of behaviour modification and training once you bring them home.

Many people seeking older rescued collies may imagine that, unlike puppies, they will already be fully toilet trained and capable of being left alone for hours on end. Never take this for granted. Some rescued collies may still have toilet training issues, due to poor earlier rearing and guidance.

Others may come with existing separation issues. Frequently these problems only become apparent once the dog has left the rescue kennel environment and moved back into a domestic home.

SAVIOUR SYNDROME
Also be aware of 'saviour syndrome', where people are in love with the idea of rescuing an unwanted dog from a horrendous background, but are less enchanted with the reality of living with the baggage he brings with him. There can also be a hidden expectation, among new owners, that the rescued dog should show his gratitude to them via suitably compliant and desirable behaviour – "… after all we have done for him…" etc.

Unfortunately dogs, and especially damaged ones, have no ability to think like this when newly rehomed. Many of them will have developed ingrained bad habits. Others are likely to be carrying high levels of pre-existing stress and insecurity which programmes them to operate in pure survival mode; acting instinctively from moment to moment rather than seeing any bigger picture in terms of their new life with you. It can take a lot of time and patience to steadily evolve them into new routines and different ways of thinking and behaving.

TRYING TO REPLACE WHAT YOU PREVIOUSLY HAD
If you have had a rescued collie in the past, which turned out to be your ideal dog, there is the temptation to think that any next rescued collie you get – especially one who looks similar – will be just the same. Given how much collies can vary, as a result of their individual breeding and backgrounds, this is most unlikely.

A lot of totally unreasonable frustration and resentment can be targeted at rescued collies by new owners, purely for the crime of not being like the previous dogs they have loved and lost and are probably still mourning.

Only when you are truly ready to accept that a new rescued collie you get may be totally unlike your last dog are you in the right frame of mind to take one on. Keep remembering how much time it took for your last rescued dog to adapt to your everyday routines and become so special to you, and give your next dog the opportunity and time to steadily grow into your life and heart in much the same way.

CHOOSING A RESCUE SOURCE
When looking for a collie to rescue or rehome you have several options. The first most obvious option is to take on a dog direct from another owner. It is possible that you have already got to know this dog and his owner fairly well, and therefore feel this is a fairly safe bet.

Still be careful, however, as a dog you visit or see out periodically does not necessarily give you a true picture of

what he might be like to live with 24/7. Also, the need for owners to rehome a dog can sometimes make them gloss over, or omit to mention, any more annoying habits or deeper rooted problems he may have, for fear that it will put you off. Come to think of it, why *is* an owner getting rid of their collie? Does the reason seem truly genuine?

Unless you are really sure about the nature of a dog you are seeking to rehome and feel that his owner has been totally honest with you, be aware of the pitfalls of these kinds of arrangement, essentially built on trust.

The first is that unlike official rescue organisations, which make professional and objective assessments of the dogs in their care – including any problems they may have – you are only going on an owner's word and personal opinion about their dog, which is likely to be somewhat less expert or objective. Good rescue organisations will also always offer back-up behaviour support and advice for your rehomed dog, or offer to take him back should this prove necessary.

GUARANTEES
Would the owner you have taken a dog from, directly, give you the same kind of guarantee? Even if they did, would they stick to it when pushed? This is a second potential pitfall.

I have heard countless horror stories of collies being taken on directly from former owners, often via the Internet or other types of advertisement and sometimes for quite considerable amounts of money. The dogs in question then proved to have serious problems, like aggression, but the former owners, having taken their money and offloaded their responsibility, then refused outright to have their dogs back, despite promising they would beforehand.

As a general rule, *never get a rescue dog via the Internet*, from people you do not know and a background you have not seen, and without any expert professional assessment being made of the dog's overall character and behaviour before you get him.

MAKING AN OFFICIAL AGREEMENT
If your mind is set on taking on a collie direct from another home, it would be wise to draw up some kind of written and signed agreement between yourself and his former owner; including his or her guarantee that they would take their dog back from you should this ever prove necessary.

Make sure you pay a former owner some kind of fee for their dog – even if this is minimal – and get a receipt. This makes the dog legally yours; for sadly, in the eyes of the law, dogs are merely viewed as chattels, as opposed to creatures with which we share meaningful relationships. By making the dog legally yours, this also makes it much harder for a former owner to try to claim him back at a later date.

The kennel environment can often exacerbate a collie's problems.

Specialist rescue centres will often start work on retraining.

The best rescue centres will provide activity and mental stimulation for the dogs while they wait to be rehomed.

SPECIALIST RESCUE ORGANISATIONS

Aside from direct owner-to-owner rehomings, you could also try the wealth of collie-specific rescue organisations. The previously mentioned Border Collie Trust GB is one of the oldest, biggest and most well-known in the UK, but worldwide there are now similar breed-specific rescue organisations (listed in the *Further Information* section, in Part Two).

You may decide on a collie rescue organisation that is nearest to where you live. Many smaller rescue organisations may not have dedicated centres, or kennels, where you can visit and see all the dogs they have available. They may have a foster set-up instead, whereby volunteers look after individual collies in their own homes until they can be placed in new ones.

This can have advantages, in terms of sparing dogs any additional stress from the kennel environment, and also providing an early warning of any problems a dog may have within a domestic home. Still note, however, that how a collie behaves with a foster carer is no guarantee of how he may behave when he comes to live with you, as certain problems in rescued dogs can take time, or specific triggers, to re-emerge.

Kennels are often an unavoidable option for organisations with bigger numbers of dogs to rehome. However comfortable many rescue kennel environments can now be, it can still inhibit or mask the true character of a dog to some degree, and similarly not accurately tell you how he may behave once returned to a domestic home. Most experienced rescue staff appreciate this reality, and thus will do what they can to make additional assessments of dogs outside of the kennel environment, whenever possible, and give would-be owners the chance to do the same.

MAINSTREAM RESCUE ORGANISATIONS

Another option for a rescued collie would be through one of the mainstream animal rehoming charities; such as, in the UK, The Dogs Trust, The Blue Cross or Battersea Dogs' Home (contact details, as before, listed in the *Further Information* section).

These bigger organisations often have collies needing new homes, and usually offer good support and back up once you have taken on one of their dogs.

WHAT SHOULD YOU LOOK FOR IN A GOOD RESCUE ORGANISATION?

To me, the biggest priorities in dog rescue organisations are not just how well they care for their animals – in terms of ensuring optimum physical and psychological health – but also how good they are at assessing individual dogs.

Predicting how individual rescued collies may behave with particular people in new homes is not the easiest of missions, and takes considerable skill and experience. But it is still the factor that will be most crucial to you, as a would-be new owner. Thus, the more effort that appears to have gone into these individual assessments of dogs, the better.

It is very rare that a rescued collie goes straight into a new home without any existing behaviour issues that need to be both predicted and addressed. The act of rehoming can, in itself, be highly traumatic for many dogs, as can the whole kennel environment for dogs that are not used to it. So a rescue organisation that glosses over any potential faults or issues in their dogs should be treated with more suspicion.

Similarly, while many would-be owners can get annoyed or put off by the amount of grilling a rescue organisation will give them before allowing them to have one of their dogs, it is, in fact, a very good sign. A rescue organisation, by comparison, who will let dogs go to anyone, is not making the future welfare of their animals the highest priority. Rescued dogs who are allowed to go to anyone are often the dogs who keep being returned. Unfortunately, the more homes a dog has, the more his problems tend to escalate.

Finally, be prepared to make some kind of donation to a rescue organisation for your dog. The exact amount tends to be governed by the kind of dog up for rehoming and the policies of different rescue bodies.

IMPORTANT THINGS TO FIND OUT ABOUT A RESCUE COLLIE

Here are some of the most important points to establish about a rescued collie:

- How old is the dog?
- Does he have any existing medical problems?
- Is he on any ongoing medication?
- Is he neutered and microchipped?
- What is known about his background?
- Why did his previous owners not want him?
- What behavioural issues is he known to have?
- Is the problem chase behaviour/other misdirected working instinct?
- Is the problem aggression – with people or other dogs or both?
- Is the problem destructiveness and/or separation issues?
- Is the dog extremely nervous?
- Can the dog be left alone for up to three hours?
- Is the dog okay with children?
- Is the dog okay with other pets, such as cats?
- Does the dog behave differently out of the kennel environment? In which case, can you see this for yourself?

You may not be able to get answers to all your questions but the more you can find out in advance, the better.

TAKING A CHANCE

Even the best behavioural assessors in the world cannot know everything about a dog prior to him going to a new home. This is because so much behaviour in dogs is context-specific; i.e. the dog has to be placed in a specific context or scenario, which he associates with a past behaviour, for this behaviour to re-occur.

Sometimes this specific context or scenario will never arise when the dog is within a rescue environment, but will when he goes to a new home. This is why the early settling-in period with any rescue dog should always be handled with care and caution (for more advice on this and all aspects of successfully rehoming rescue collies, see, *Rehabilitating rescued collies,* page 183).

Taking on a rescued collie will always involve some element of chance, but the same can be said when you get a puppy. Many of the general rules and principles that apply to settling in new puppies – as covered in Chapters Four and Five – can equally apply to rescued dogs, but with a greater emphasis on identifying and dealing with a range of pre-existing issues or problems that may stem from their past lives. Naturally the longer a dog has lived, and the more homes he has had, the more baggage he is capable of accumulating.

THE RIGHT DOGS AND OWNERS

When we say that certain dogs and people are made for each other, we mean that they have an ability to understand and fulfil each other's needs without conflict. This often happens with rescued collies and new owners and when it does it is a total joy to see.

Some people, however, no matter how well-meaning, are definitely not made for some collies and if so, it is important to be guided in this matter by judgements more experienced than your own, in order that neither owner nor dog later fall short of each other's needs or expectations.

If a rescue organisation says that you, or your circumstances, are not right for one of their collies you may be disappointed, but also be aware that they are potentially saving you and the dog in question from living an unhappy life together. It may also be the case that there is another rescued collie on offer far more suited to your personality and circumstances, which you may have previously overlooked.

THE VALUE OF A DOG

In the rescue world it is so common for people to evaluate and pick dogs primarily on the basis of what they look like – pretty, cute, sympathy inducing, younger rather than older. But ultimately the most important thing about any rescued collie – or any dog, for that matter – is his fundamental nature and what is going on in his head.

Some rescued collies may not have the flashiest of looks, but they have the kindest of hearts. Sometimes their essential goodness lies initially hidden; buried under the weight of all the fear, worry, insecurity and hurt they may have experienced in their past lives. But with time and perseverance and kindness you can still find it again.

I rescued a collie bitch when she was 13 years old. Physically and psychologically she was in an appalling shape, due to a long history of mistreatment and neglect. I had her for three joyous years, wherein she underwent a quite incredible transformation, proving that it is never too late to turn a collie around.

Her name was Kim. What Kim essentially taught me was to have the patience to allow a troubled dog to heal, and slowly reassemble a sense of trust out of the ashes of a past life. She also taught me about the true value of a dog, which you only sufficiently appreciate over time.

With dogs, as with people, we can all be so easily dazzled by the superficial things, like speed and youth and beauty, while overlooking all the quieter, deeper qualities that ultimately make any individual so special; things like courage, intelligence, patience, kindness and a generous and forgiving heart.

The qualities, in fact, which we so easily take for granted in dogs, while they are with us, are the very same things we always miss the most when they are gone.

Chapter Eleven

THE COMPETITIVE COLLIE

Training your dog for different competitive pursuits

A large number of Border Collies and their owners get involved in competitive pursuits of some kind, such as Showing, Obedience, Agility, Flyball, or Working Trials.

Sometimes the idea of competing in a particular event grows slowly on owners after they have got their dog. At other times, collies will be acquired chiefly for their competition-winning potential, because they descend from dogs who excel at a particular pursuit.

Such has become the popularity of the collie breed for competition work worldwide, that there are now probably far more dogs involved in these pursuits than in their traditional role of managing sheep. However, the option to try out your dog's working skills with sheep is still open to you (see *Sheep work, page 131*).

If you want to get involved in the world of competition, a Border Collie is the breed of choice.

THE PROS AND CONS OF COMPETING

On the face of it, competition training and participation has much to offer a breed as notoriously energetic, intelligent and mentally responsive as the Border Collie. And it is certainly always better for these dogs to be doing something that stimulates and stretches their minds than have them go slowly off their rockers through under activity and boredom.

Similarly, competition work and participation invariably requires owners to up their level of training with their dog, and expand his social tolerance in order to cope with the show environment; factors which can also only be beneficial.

Like many other readers, I am sure, some of my happiest moments with dogs have come via competition training or participation. As with so much else in life, however, there can be some less well-considered downsides to competing with collies in different pursuits; most of these are stress-related and covered later in this chapter.

Those wanting greater technical detail on different kinds of competition for collies, other than what is outlined here, can find them in a wealth of specialist publications and Internet websites now dedicated to individual pursuits, or via the websites of their national Kennel Clubs or Associations.

My chief interest in this chapter on competition, as throughout this whole book, remains with the mind of the Border Collie; explaining how it can be adapted to different types of training and competing, but also how things can go wrong when you fail to sufficiently respect the nature and limitations of your dog.

Wherever possible, I also hope to explain how to best avoid these problems, or put them right.

REALISTIC CONSIDERATIONS

There are two basic essentials for doing well in any competition with a collie. The first is the right dog – i.e. one most genetically suited to the pursuit you have in mind.

For some reason, a notion can exist among many owners that all collies should be good at everything competition-wise when they simply cannot be, anymore than we can all be good at maths or pole-vaulting or growing tropical orchids. Some collies are just not genetically (i.e. mentally/physically) suited to some competitive pursuits full stop, and the earlier an owner accepts this reality, the more grief can be spared for both owner and dog.

Being the versatile breed they are, however, collies who are not suited to one particular pursuit can so often prove good, or even exceptional, at another. So this is something to bear in mind.

THE RIGHT RELATIONSHIP

The second competition-essential is the right relationship. If you have not taught your collie to be totally tuned in to you,

ideally from as early an age as possible, then you will struggle to attain the higher levels of training required for competition work. It will also be a tremendous challenge keeping his concentration on you amid the myriad distractions of a typical show environment.

A dog who is not concentrating on you cannot respond to any of your commands. So improving your dog's all-round focus training, of a kind laid out in Chapter Five, may be a good idea prior to any kind of competition work. It is also wise to keep working on this all the time.

Keep remembering that what is possible of any dog in competition is dictated by the quality of his genes and the quality of his training and handling. People whose dogs consistently win at the highest level of competition usually do so because they have got all these factors exactly right.

SHOWING

A classic example of needing a dog with exactly the right genes to succeed is pedigree or breed showing. Not only do Border Collies need to be Kennel Club registered, in order to take part in higher levels of show competition – i.e. Open and Championship Shows – but they will also need to conform, as closely as possible, to the Breed Standard for Border Collies as laid out by their national Kennel Club.

The Breed Standard is a list of ideal features desired in a type of pedigree dog. These Standards are drawn up by the Kennel Clubs (or equivalent governing associations) of different countries, following consultation with breed experts and then used as a guide for judges. Different countries' Kennel Clubs (e.g. USA, Australia, New Zealand) may have slight differences in their Breed Standards for the Border Collie. For instance, the American Kennel Club's Breed Standard is far more detailed in description than the UK version.

THEORY, PERSONAL OPINION AND THE X FACTOR

In pedigree showing, the Breed Standard may well be the basic theoretical guide a judge should keep in their head when choosing winning dogs but, over and above this, there will still always be personal preference and opinion. It is a fact of life that judges can all have very differing views when it comes to selecting a dog which, for them, is the best in the ring.

As well as the distinct personal preferences held by judges, there is also the undeniable X factor. Some dogs will just move and stand superbly well in the show ring – often as a result of expert handling – or have a noticeable charisma which keeps holding the judge's eye, and these are factors that so often make one particular show collie stand out from the rest, and eventually progresses him to become a Show Champion.

Systems of judging vary, depending on the national Kennel Club, but in the UK a dog attains the title Show

You need to start off with a puppy that has the potential to win in the show ring.

Showing can be stressful for some collies.

Champion once he has won three Kennel Club Challenge Certificates (CCs) at Championship shows. The awarding of a CC to a dog at a Championship show means he has beaten all other rivals in his breed – although there is generally both a bitch and dog CC up for grabs at these shows.

It is estimated that only around five per cent of dogs in any pedigree breed ever attain top success in the show ring – and the greater number of dogs there are in any breed, the greater the competition for top placings is likely to be.

GETTING STARTED

If you are interested in beginning a show career with your pedigree Border Collie, here are things to bear in mind. First, be prepared for this activity, like most competitive events, to involve a fair amount of time, travelling and expense – in terms of entry fees and petrol.

Second, be realistic. We all think our dogs are the best in the world, but does your pedigree collie really have show-winning potential? Some dogs may be of a type which is favoured by some judges but not others. Other dogs may have less desirable aspects of conformation, anatomy, pigmentation or coat type which will bar them from any type of showing success, even if these do not affect their

health or quality of life and companionship one jot.

However you may feel about the rights or wrongs of it, pedigree showing involves your dog being judged not just for his superior anatomical construction and soundness, and aesthetic appeal, but also how well, or not, he happens to conform to a breed look or type that is most fashionable in the show ring at a certain time. How well you handle your dog, and get him to stand and move in the ring, can additionally make a considerable difference to where he eventually gets placed.

DIFFERENT SHOW EVENTS

Most people's first experience of showing their dog will occur at a less formal event such as (in the UK) a Companion Dog Show. These are locally held shows you can enter on the day. Although your dog will need to look like a purebred Border Collie (as opposed to a collie cross) in order to take part in a Companion show breed class, he does not have to be Kennel Club registered.

Companion show breed classes can vary in the way they are classified. If there is a pastoral breed class listed, this is the one your collie should be entered in. If there is not a pastoral breed class listed, and instead there are show categories like sporting and non-sporting, your collie should be entered in the non-sporting class. He can also, of course, take part in general breed classes like the Open category, and any others which may apply to him, such as puppy, yearling or veteran.

In contrast to Companion Dog shows, entries for more formal Open and Championship shows will need to be made some time in advance of the relevant competition, and your dog will need to be Kennel Club registered.

EARLY EXPERIENCE
Companion shows may be informal, but you may find some fairly experienced show exhibitors and handlers competing. Watching them, in turn, should give you an idea of how you should show your own dog properly – in terms of the way you should stand him and move him in front of the judge. The higher up the showing ladder you go, the more expertise you will need to display in the handling of your dog, in order for him to do well.

Apart from watching others with greater experience, you can gain such expertise with your dog by taking him to special ringcraft classes. These are generally run by local canine associations, or breed clubs and societies.

For the more ambitious novice competitor, one of the downsides of Companion shows is that the judge will rarely be a Border Collie breed specialist. This means he/she may not recognise your dog's outstanding quality, as a specimen of his breed, or spot his less desirable breed faults. Alternatively, of course, when picking a winning dog, they may just prefer many other breeds to Border Collies! Either way, it can make it harder for you to gain a true picture of your dog's suitability for showing at a higher level.

If you have any doubts about your collie's true potential, ask more experienced collie show folk to give you an honest opinion. You can meet people like this at a local Open show. An experienced Border Collie judge could also give you a frank appraisal of your dog's show assets, or lack of them. Such frank appraisals given early on – however hard to take – could save you an awful lot of disappointment further down the line.

TEMPERAMENT
I have yet to dwell on the temperament desired in a show collie. The UK Kennel Club Breed Standard states that the Border Collie's temperament should be: "keen, alert, responsive and intelligent", and "neither nervous nor aggressive".

The American Kennel Club Standard states that: "any tendencies toward viciousness, nervousness or shyness are very serious faults".

You could not put it much clearer than that. Such considerations are vital, because a collie with a fundamentally unsound temperament – i.e. nervous, aggressive, easily spooked – can be as big a liability as a

working sheepdog as he can as a social companion.

Ostensibly, a show collie acts as an ambassador for his breed, reflecting qualities that are most desirable in the dogs he represents. Thus if he has an intrinsically unsound or aggressive temperament then, regardless of what else he might have going for him physically, he remains a deeply flawed dog and, as such, discredits his breed.

I would like to think that most good and experienced judges of show collies are well aware of this important issue; that they are smart enough to know when a dog's dodgier temperament is being masked by clever handling and show zero tolerance towards any form of overt aggression from a dog in the ring.

SHOW-STRESSED DOGS
The ring temperament issue, however, can be complicated by the presence of what I call show-stressed dogs. These are collies who are generally good natured but come under intense mental pressure from all the cumulative stresses of the showing pursuit; i.e. the lengthy travelling, intrusive grooming, prolonged confinement in the car and/or benching area, restriction of normal activity and behaviour, disruption to normal routine – not to mention the relentless noise and movement of other people and dogs, which can cause sensory overload in collies' brains.

While many collies might cope with just two or three of these stress factors for a limited period of time, the steady addition of all the others may push the psychological pressure in some dogs to breaking point, whereupon stress-relieving behaviour of some kind occurs – e.g. whining, barking, lunging, growling, snapping, or intense restlessness.

If you are unlucky this will happen in the show ring, where all the standing and waiting around is the last straw for your dog. If you are even more unlucky, your dog will take his frustration out on the judge, who comes straight into his space to give him a hearty all-over inspection just as his head is about to blow.

YOUR RESPONSIBILITY
Whatever may be the mitigating cause of your dog's aggressive or less desirable behaviour in the ring, please understand that a judge is still entirely within his or her rights to assess it at face value and take whatever steps they deem necessary to deal with it.

It is your job, not the judge's, to contemplate the state of mind that may have lead to your dog's behaviour. Similarly, it is your responsibility to ensure that it does not happen again if you want to carry on showing your dog.

MINIMISING STRESS IN SHOW DOGS
Many of the stress problems seen in show collies originate from the fact that they have not been sufficiently socialised

or better equipped, psychologically, for the demands of the showing pursuit – or indeed, any competition environment – while still young puppies.

Let us imagine, for instance, that you have a Border Collie of six months of age who has previously spent much of his life in a relatively isolated social environment, such as kennels, or in a domestic setting where he had a minimal early social education (the necessity of which was outlined in earlier chapters). The mind of this dog is simply not geared up to cope with the pressures and stresses caused by his first show outing.

The equivalent of this scenario would be like taking a teenager who had lived in a tiny, sleepy village in the back of nowhere all his life, and then suddenly dumping him in the middle of London or New York at the peak of the rush hour.

Should you be surprised, therefore, if your woefully under-prepared dog reacts adversely during a first show outing? Most experienced show handlers are aware of the need to psychologically prepare their dogs for the showing experience from as young an age as possible.

Your dog, in essence, has to feel confident and relaxed about these following pictures in his head, and needs to be regularly exposed to them, in a highly positive way, from early puppyhood onwards:

- Noisy, bustling environments where there are lot of people and other dogs (note, if you take your collie puppy to a show before he has completed his vaccinations, be very careful to always carry him and not expose him to any risk of infection from other dogs).
- Encounters with strange people and dogs, both in and outside the home environment.
- Strange people and dogs suddenly coming into his 'head space'.
- Being handled/inspected by lots of different people – i.e. running their hands all over his body, lifting his tail, looking in his ears or mouth. Initially make these inspections very quick and short and then immediately follow them with praise and a treat/toy *before* your puppy has had a chance to become wary or anxious. You want him to connect such inspections in his brain with feelings of reward and confidence. Only when you have got to this stage can you extend the length of these inspections, but always keep making them rewarding
- *Note*, clicker training can be very helpful in making puppies feel more at ease with being handled/inspected in the above manner.

Show collies also have to develop a particularly high tolerance to the whole business of being shampooed and groomed and generally fussed around with, intimately, on a regular basis. Thus if you have a dog who is already persistently resistant or snappy when you try to undertake such procedures at home, you have to wonder how he will later cope with similar kinds of physical manhandling from total strangers (i.e. show judges).

WHY SHOW DOGS TURN SNAPPY

Most owners/exhibitors are shocked when their dog suddenly shows aggression in the show ring or growls, snaps or backs nervously away from the judge who has come to inspect him. But this initial moment of wariness can so often be inadvertently rewarded. Either the person doing the inspection immediately backs off – understandably! – in the face of hostility, or the handler reinforces the fearful behaviour in his dog with the wrong kind of attention, such as trying to verbally/physically reassure him or soothe him.

What the dog has found rewarding, behaviour-wise, in this one context may then be repeated whenever you try to get someone to inspect him again.

Also be aware that shouting at a dog who has behaved in a nervous/aggressive manner in the ring simply heightens his mental tension, and similarly his subsequent levels of defensive reactivity. As with all fear or panic based aggressive responses, it is always important to stay calm and suitably correct your dog for his behaviour instead, as outlined in Chapter Five (see *Giving a correction, page 47*).

People and dogs, particularly strangers, coming suddenly into their head space commonly sets off a defensive lung-nip reflex in some collies, which in turn often reflects their lower level of social tolerance or confidence. This is because the more socially confident a dog, the less mental pressure he feels when strangers approach him and, thus, the less likely he is to resort to the kind of defensive behaviour triggered by that pressure.

It is also the case that, whatever you do, some collies will always have lower social tolerances twinned with more readily activated lunge-nip reflexes (see *Aggression* in Part Two). This behaviour invariably has some genetic component. Often it can be resolved with the aid of expert help and retraining. If not, an owner may need to better consider how suitable their dog truly is for the pressures brought about by the showing pursuit.

GETTING HELP

I can fully understand how heartbreaking it can be to have an exquisitely beautiful pedigree collie whose behaviour lets you down in the show ring. Sometimes this problem is rooted in less scrupulous breeding practices –i.e. looks being favoured at the expense of temperament in some part of the dog's genetic past – but at other times it can just be sheer bad luck; the dog has a sudden moment of panic and then has his fearful behaviour rewarded in some way.

Either way, I cannot stress how vital it is to get expert help – preferably from a Border Collie specialist – the *instant* your dog first displays fear or hostility in the show ring. Do not imagine, as so many owners do, that these kinds of problems will just go away in a dog over time or prove to be one-offs. They won't.

It can also help to be far more mindful of other external pressures placed on collies by the whole competition experience, as outlined in *Reducing the Stresses of Competition*

THE PROS AND CONS OF COLLIES AS SHOW DOGS

Over the years I have found that people who breed and own Border Collies for more active or brain-stretching pastimes can often be a bit sniffy about show breeders and the show version of this dog they now produce.

It is often said that the modern show collie is now too "fat, fluffy and brainless" a specimen to fulfil the function for which this breed was originally designed. But I think this is a somewhat harsh over-generalisation.

Undoubtedly, like most breed purists, I do not like fat collies of any kind, nor those seemingly lacking the alertness, athleticism, responsiveness and drive I so prize in these dogs. There are also physical/temperamental characteristics in some modern show lines that are definitely not to my taste.

This said, however, I cannot see what is intrinsically wrong in wanting to breed beautiful looking Border Collies, as long as factors such as health, temperament and the essential working brain of the dog have not been adversely compromised along the way. There are show breeders talented and dedicated enough to achieve this goal, and I think they should be given the credit for it where it is due.

I have also found that the most enthusiastic promoters of, and subscribers to, genetic health screening and research in collies are often among the show breeding fraternity. They may not always get everything right, but then again, who does? Let us not forget that there are plenty of other folk, other than just show breeders, capable of breeding less than perfect dogs.

UNREGISTERED DOGS

UK residents please note; if your Border Collie is not already on the Kennel Club Breed register, he must be put on the KC Activity register instead, before being able to take part in competitive events such as Obedience, Agility, Flyball or Working Trials at Open level, or at any Kennel Club licensed event run strictly to KC regulations. Whatever country you live in, always check via your national Kennel Club, council or organisation what the rules are regarding your dog's eligibility for different competitions.

OBEDIENCE

Obedience training, to my mind, is one of the most beneficial pursuits you could get your collie involved in, regardless of how far or not you subsequently take him in competition.

The biggest benefits of the Obedience training pursuit for collies are:

- It constantly improves your bond with your dog and his level of responsiveness towards you and your commands. These are benefits you can then extend into your everyday life with him.
- It encourages your collie to maintain a healthy and balanced state of mind. This is because most Obedience exercises demand a high level of concentration and mental self-discipline in a dog. Once again, these benefits tend to persist beyond the actual Obedience training process.
- It lays down the essential training groundwork – such as good owner focus and response to basic commands – your dog will need if you intend to compete in other pursuits, such as Agility or Working Trials (which are both covered later in this chapter).
- It consistently tests and stretches your own abilities as a trainer – although to be fair, the same could be said for many other canine pursuits requiring supreme accuracy and control, as well as the forging of a virtually telepathic bond between dog and handler

Be aware that, as with Showing, your dog will need to display a *sound temperament* for this pursuit, passing a judge's temperament test at novice level. This test involves the judge approaching your dog from the front and running their hands down his back. Any sign of nervousness or aggression will be penalised.

OBEDIENCE IN EUROPE, AUSTRALIA AND NEW ZEALAND

In many countries throughout Europe – and elsewhere in the world – tests, grades and other rules for Obedience competition will be governed by the Fédération Cynologique Internationale (FCI). Australia and New Zealand are also members of the FCI. Contact details for this organisation appear in the *Further Information* section in Part Two of this book.

THE EXERCISES

Obedience exercises and grading systems can also vary in different countries – see, *Obedience in the USA and Canada* and *Obedience in Europe, Australia and New Zealand*. Your relevant national Kennel Club or organisation can inform you of the specific exercises required for competitive Obedience, at different levels, in your own country.

In the UK, depending on the type of show and the level you are competing at, here are the Obedience exercises in full that you may need to learn:

HEELWORK

At any level of competition you will be asked to do a heelwork round. This involves your dog staying as close to

OBEDIENCE IN THE USA AND CANADA

In the USA, the competitive Obedience pursuit was originally the brainchild of Mrs Helen Whitehouse Walker, a Standard Poodle breeder from New York, who devised specific canine skill tests in the 1930s to demonstrate the intelligence of her dogs.

The first American Kennel Club (AKC) licensed Obedience trial was held in 1936.

In American Obedience, many exercises may seem similar to those found in the UK version of the pursuit, but with variations such as directional retrieves/retrieves over a hurdle and 'silent signal' exercises.

There are also three main levels of competition – Novice, Open and Utility – which each require handlers and dogs to master and display specific skills. These tests also become more challenging, and demanding of total accuracy, as you advance up the competition ladder.

In the Novice Class, dogs earn an AKC Companion Dog (CD) title after receiving three qualifying scores under two different judges. The next Open Class is more challenging, with more exercises done off leash and retrieving and jumping tests are added. In the Open Class, dogs earn an AKC Companion Dog Excellent (CDX) title after receiving three qualifying scores under two different judges.

The top Utility Class, which includes scent discrimination, directed retrieves, jumping and silent signal exercises, is the most challenging. Dogs earn an AKC Utility Dog (UD) title after receiving three qualifying scores under two different judges.

The Obedience Trial Championship (OTCH) title is often referred to as the "PhD" for dogs, and is the highest Obedience honour a dog can receive in the USA. To obtain this a dog and handler must earn 100 points by placing first, second, third or fourth in the Open B or Utility B class. Three first places must also be awarded from the Open B and Utility B classes.

Note, as I write, optional Obedience titling classes – Graduate Novice, Graduate Open and Versatility – have just been developed by the AKC, as well as Wild Card classes and a new 'Master Program' for competing handlers and dogs. For details of these contact the AKC (listed in the Further Information section of this book, Part Two).

Obedience competition in Canada is run along very similar grading systems/exercises to the above.

you as possible on command while you walk a set course, which includes a series of turns and halts. When you halt, or stop, your dog must sit closely and straight by your side.

The judge devises the heelwork round, and his or her steward will then call this out for you once you enter the competition ring. The steward will also tell you which other exercises you must do in a specific class, while the judge marks you.

The heelwork rounds, as well as the number of turns and complexity of these turns (i.e. right turn, about turn, left turn, left about turn, double about turn, double left about turn, plus diagonal turns), get more testing as you progress upwards in competition. At the more advanced heelwork level you will also be asked to leave your dog waiting in set positions – down, sitting, standing – as you walk away from him, then later recall him back into the heelwork position when instructed to do so by the steward. You will also be required to perform heelwork at slow, normal and fast paces.

The higher you go in Obedience competition the more you will be penalised for any additional commands in heelwork, or any other exercise, other than those allowed in a particular class, or any additional body gestures/signals deemed by the judge to be extra training cues

NOVICE RECALL

A standard novice *recall* exercise in Obedience involves you asking your dog to *sit* or lie *down* and *wait* next to you, at the steward's request. The steward then tells you to walk a set distance away from your dog, then turn and halt facing him. The steward will tell you when to *recall* your dog, whereupon he must come straight towards you and also sit straight in front of you.

You may then be asked by the steward to *'finish'* your dog – i.e. the dog must finish the exercise by sitting next to you in the heelwork position. He may go behind you or in front of you to do this, as long as he ends up sitting close and straight next to you.

'A' RECALL

A more advanced *'A' recall* involves you making your dog *wait* while you walk away from him, as before, but when *recalled* this time your dog has to join you on the move, while you are walking a pattern (as in normal heelwork) instructed by the steward. Your dog must not only join you on command and immediately adopt the correct heelwork position, but also maintain this until the steward asks you to *halt* or formerly ends the exercise.

RETRIEVE

A formal retrieve begins with your dog sitting next to you and waiting. At the steward's request you then throw a training dumbbell out ahead of you. The steward will then tell you when to send your dog to get this dumbbell and bring it back to you in his mouth. Your dog should also sit neatly and straight in front of you when presenting this dumbbell to you. The steward then tells you when to take the dumbbell from your dog's mouth and also when to finish this exercise, with your dog sitting next to you.

As you progress in competition, the items your dog must retrieve will get more and more testing and/or unusual.

STAYS

Stay exercises involve your dog remaining in a set position – sit, down and, sometimes, stand – for a set time on command and not moving until you have been told by a steward to go back to him, and then release him to finish the exercise.

Stays are usually done separately from your main Obedience round. They are usually organised collectively in a specific ring, with all competing dogs in a class doing them together. If the class is particularly big the dogs may be broken up into smaller groups. The advantages of dogs all doing stays together are a) it is a more challenging test for the dog, and b) competition stewards can watch all the dogs together and penalise them accordingly should any move.

As you progress in competition, your dog may have to remain longer and longer in a commanded stay position, even when you leave him in the ring and go somewhere else out of sight.

SENDAWAY

The sendaway exercise involves you sending your dog, on command, to a fixed point or marker, devised by the judge, and then dropping him into the down position on command.

DISTANT CONTROL

Distant control requires your dog to adopt different positions (stand, down, sit) on your command, and as instructed by a steward, while he is some distance away from you. When changing positions your dog should not move more than a body length forwards, backwards or sideways.

SCENT DISCRIMINATION

Scent discrimination requires your dog to identify and retrieve a cloth with a specific person's scent on, amid an array of other dummy cloths left there to confuse him, or send him off track.

GETTING STARTED

Most people begin their involvement in Obedience training and competition via their local dog training club. Once shown and instructed in the basic Obedience exercises previously outlined, they may then begin competing with their dog at a more informal event; e.g. in a Limited Obedience competition run by a local training club, or in Obedience classes put on by a previously mentioned Companion Dog show.

Thereafter, they may then move on to more serious competitions at Open or even Championship level. In Open Obedience competition, the more you win and, thus, the further you progress up the competition ladder, the more will be required of you and your dog in terms of the skill and accuracy with which you complete different exercises. Similarly, you will be allowed to use fewer and fewer additional commands.

In the UK, owners and dogs who have never competed in Open Obedience before start at Pre-beginner level (whereas in the USA they will begin at Novice level).

Once they have won this class they will move on to Beginner classes, then Novice, Class A, Class B, and (Open) Class C. Finally, the very top class is Championship C or 'ticket'. At Championship shows this class is the one where Obedience Challenge Certificates are awarded to winners; three of these CCs (or tickets) making a dog an Obedience Champion.

Once a handler has won out of the Pre-beginner and Beginner classes with a dog, he or she cannot compete in these again, even with a different dog. They can only enter at Novice level and upwards at any show. As a result, Novice classes tend to be filled with many highly experienced trainers with new dogs which makes them so hard for less experienced handlers to win out of and thus progress.

GOLDEN RULES FOR GOOD OBEDIENCE TRAINING

- Whether Obedience training or competing, keep remembering that you and your dog are working together as a team.
- The more sensitive you are to your dog's needs and feelings, the more successful your training partnership will be.
- If your dog looks bored, stop training.
- If your dog looks stressed, stop training.
- If your dog looks hesitant/confused about an exercise, find a way to make it much more fun and easier for him to understand.
- Do not keep correcting your dog for mistakes in motivational exercises (e.g. retrieve, scent, sendaway) – you will steadily undermine his enthusiasm and confidence. Instead, simply go overboard with praise and rewards any time he gets something right.
- Always make your dog feel brilliantly clever and pleased with himself whenever he does an exercise well. Remember, the more confident you make your dog in his own abilities, the better he will always perform for you.
- Keep remembering that dogs think in pictures, not sequences like us. Thus, as outlined in the main text, you must break any Obedience exercise down into all the separate actions your dog needs to learn, individually, before he can string them all together in his mind as a sequence to follow on command.
- Keep filling your Obedience training with energy, fun, rewards and regular surprises. Otherwise, you will bore your dog to death.
- Keep mixing training exercises up, and doing short parts of them in different orders before stopping to praise and reward your dog. This way he will never know what you will ask him to do next, or when he will get his reward. This also avoids the problem of anticipation, for which you will lose marks in competition.
- Keep doing your Obedience training in a multitude of different contexts, including on daily walks and in busy places, so your dog learns to concentrate on you and respond to your commands wherever he happens to be.
- Always stop training an exercise while your dog is still keen. Never repeat the same exercise more than three times. You can always return to an exercise later, or the next day, if you want to further improve it.
- Always end a training session on a good note – i.e. with your dog doing something well, and you praising him and having a fun game with him.

UNDER TRAINING

As with any other pursuit, some collies will always be more genetically suited to the demands of Obedience work than others; a factor that usually becomes increasingly more apparent, in individual dogs, the higher up the competition ladder you go. This said, however, a lot of the problems found in Obedience training and competition can revolve more around owners than dogs.

Some owners, for instance, will under train their dogs and, thus, under prepare them for the demands of the Obedience competition ring. They will then blame their dogs, rather than themselves, for a less than stunning performance. Under training a dog includes not teaching him to sustain the same level of focus and response to different exercises, amid a multitude of different contexts and environments, well before you expose him to the additional pressures of competition, as outlined in *Golden rules for good Obedience training, page 110.*

OVER TRAINING

Other owners will relentlessly *over* train their dogs, making them do the same exercises again and again in the search for ever greater perfection, and to the point where the dog feels increasingly bored, demoralised or persecuted. This is the quickest possible way to put a collie off Obedience training for life. The same is true of harsher or more coercive forms of training, as previously mentioned in this book.

It is incredibly important to keep remembering that only *you* know the reason why you are making your dog do the same things again and again, and what the ultimate aim of all this is – i.e. competition success. Your dog does not, and cannot, know this. Thus, the only way you can inspire him to be as passionate about Obedience work as you is to continually make it as fun, exciting and rewarding for him as possible.

In many Obedience classes you will see some classic examples of over-trained collies. They will look bored, or become easily distracted by external events outside the ring, instead of sustaining intense focus on their owners. Some may also yawn (generally more a sign of stress than tiredness in this context) or show increasingly lethargic responses to their owner's commands.

In general, dogs who have been Obedience trained (or should I say drilled) coercively, excessively, or with very little imagination, fun or energy will exhibit the same dull body language and under-motivated look.

PROBLEMS WITH OBEDIENCE EXERCISES

Having outlined some general background to the Obedience pursuit, let us now look at what can most commonly go wrong with individual training exercises.

HEELWORK

As with many other Obedience exercises, where people most commonly go wrong with heelwork, is to see it and train it as one long sequence of activity. In other words, they will start off with their dog sitting close and straight (hopefully!) next to them, then move forward to walk a longish series of straight lines, turns and halts.

As they do this, they just expect their dog to know that he should be staying very close to them all the time, in a particular position, and that he should be looking and feeling very excited about it, because at the end of this sequence he will get a reward – i.e. a treat or a favourite toy.

But he's still not always very close, or looking very excited about this exercise – *why?*

As ever, such problems stem back to two vital

considerations about dogs that I have constantly outlined in this book. The first is that dogs think in pictures, not sequences like us. Once you understand this concept you can also appreciate the need to break each Obedience exercise down into separate pictures or actions for your dog. You then train these different pictures to him separately, and constantly reward him for each of them, before stringing them all together to complete the whole sequence of an exercise.

The second consideration to grasp is that dogs quickly learn to associate specific contexts with specific feelings or events. So if you have ever made an exercise boring for your dog, or negative due to constant correction, he will not forget it and it will dull his future enthusiasm for it. The same dullness can occur if you constantly make your dog wait too long for his reward when training an exercise, or always give him a reward at the same point of an exercise (i.e. commonly at the end of it). In both cases your dog may start to switch off during any part of an exercise where he has learned there will be no imminent reward.

Now let us look at how the above considerations may apply to Obedience training with your dog, beginning with a classic heelwork round and going through this, step by step or picture by picture, so you are better able to see what might be going wrong.

Step One: The start of heelwork
Step One in the heelwork exercise is where you ask your dog to sit next to you, and focus on you, prior to him moving forward with you. You might think this initial preparation/set off action for heelwork is just one training picture for your dog, when it actually involves three separate smaller exercises for him to learn, namely:

- Sit close and straight next to you (*close sit*).
- Keep his head on your side, in preparation for heelwork, and keep his focus on you (*watch me*).
- Move forward with you, sustaining this same closeness/focus, in the heelwork position (*with me*).

You must, therefore, teach these individual actions separately to your dog as follows. (*Note*, as most readers may already be aware, dogs in Obedience competition must always be worked on your *left* hand side).

First, *close sit*. Using either a favourite toy or a clicker and treats, keep inviting your dog to sit next to you, as close and straight as possible. Only when he is in *exactly* the right position, praise (or click) and reward him immediately. Then later add words to this action – "*close sit*" – just before you praise and reward him.

Second, *watch me*. Once you have taught your dog *close sit*, then move on to *close sit* and *watch me*. With your dog sitting next to you, keep inviting him (using a toy or clicker and treats as before) to put his head on your side and look

With training, your collie will be completely secure in the heelwork position, regardless of changes in direction or pace.

at you. As soon as he is doing this, immediately praise and reward him. Then later add words to this action – "*watch me*" – before praising and rewarding him.

Third, *with me*. From *close sit* and *watch me*, your dog then needs to learn that he must move forward with you in heelwork when you so command him ("*with me*"). So after *close sit* and *watch me*, encourage your dog to move forwards with you, and as he does so, immediately praise and reward him as before. Then add words to this action – "*with me*" – before praising and rewarding him.

Some trainers prefer to use a particular leg to set off in heelwork, to better cue their dogs for this activity. They will then set off with the other leg in exercises (such as *recall*) where their dog must wait as they move off.

Once you have taught your dog the *close sit*, plus *watch me* and *with me* commands/actions separately, and then continually run them together in training, one after the other, he should soon see these later as a predictable sequence of pictures in his head.

By making all these short and separate pre-heelwork actions continually rewarding for your dog, he should also

start any heelwork round with maximum focus and enthusiasm. This is because he has now learnt that in heelwork a reward can come any time, even right at the beginning.

Finishes

Teaching your dog what *close sit* means, as an exercise in itself, will also help when you do halts in heelwork and need your dog to sit close and straight, or when you are asked to "*finish*" an exercise and need him to sit close and straight next to you. You can *finish* an exercise by asking your dog to go closely round the back of you, then sit next to you, or go straight from sitting in front of you to sitting next to you.

Do remember, however, to always teach/practice *finish* as a *separate* exercise or picture for your dog in training, rather than always tag it on to the end of a *recall* or *retrieve* exercise. If you do the latter your dog is more likely to anticipate a finish at the end of these exercises in competition, for which you will lose marks.

Step Two: The heelwork position

In Step Two of heelwork we will focus on the next required picture for your dog; the actual *heelwork position* itself. To avoid common problems like a dog coming off your leg, trailing behind or moving too far ahead of you, it is extremely important to teach him from the outset that there is only one right position in heelwork – next to your side, and close.

The correct heelwork position, in other words, also has to be taught as a regular exercise or picture in itself, and consistently rewarded.

Moreover, if you do not establish for your dog, from the start, an optimum heelwork position, in which he trots next to you not just closely, but also neatly and in a straight line, it is all too easy for him to later get into habits like lagging or crabbing or generally swinging his bottom out, untidily, from side to side – which will throw him off your leg at the same time.

So when first teaching heelwork to your dog, always go for quality, rather than quantity, of response. It is always better to just walk three or four steps forward with your dog in the right position, and immediately reward him for this, than attempt 20 or 30 steps, during which he is sometimes in the right position, and sometimes not. This is how dogs get the chance to develop and perpetuate bad habits, for want of clearer guidance.

As well as immediately praising and rewarding your dog with a toy or click/treat, for being in the right heelwork position, also move on to attaching a word or command to this action – such as the aforementioned "*with me*".

If you start by teaching your dog a picture of four or five steps where he is in the ideal heelwork position, you can then gradually add on another picture of four or five perfect steps which are exactly the same, and another, until he is able to stay in the right position for a longer and longer distance.

Step Three: Turns

Step Three involves mastering the turns in heelwork. People can get into a real pickle with these for the same reason they do so with their heelwork position; they don't teach each turn as a separate exercise or picture for their dog to remember.

Mastering top quality Obedience heelwork, in general, usually calls for some additional training help/advice - see *Finding the Right Help, page 199* – as so much of what you or your dog are doing wrong won't be easy for you to see yourself.

All the turns in heelwork must not only be taught separately to your dog in training, but also be individually rewarded, to reinforce each of them as correct and desirable actions. You will also need to attach specific words to each turn as he does them – i.e. *"right turn"*, *"left turn"* etc. – before praising and rewarding him.

Only by working on the quality of these turns relentlessly, and likewise your dog's heelwork position in general, can you eventually get to the stage where he expertly follows your own movements round a heelwork course with few extra commands.

Footwork

The quality of your own footwork in heelwork is also critical. The more it sticks to the same predictable sequence, particularly on turns, the easier it will be for your dog to follow you and stay close to you. If you keep changing the way you approach heelwork turns or halts with your feet, you will confuse your dog – particularly one as movement sensitive as the Border Collie. This, in turn, can lead to hesitation or errors on his behalf.

Usually without realising it, many people fail to even walk a straight line in heelwork. Generally this is because they are too busy looking at their dog instead or, in competition, because of straightforward nerves. I am sure everybody can identify with this factor – see, *Nerves and errors*, page 114.

Ultimately, however, you have to get out of the habit of always looking at your dog during heelwork. This will not only mean you can walk straighter lines in a ring but also you will assume a much more preferable upright and confident body posture. If you train your dog properly, he should be looking at your hand, anyway, and not your face, when doing heelwork, in anticipation of his reward.

Hand position

Because your dog is constantly watching your left hand in heelwork, anticipating the toy or treat you may be holding in

it, how you place this hand is also key to keeping him in the right heelwork position.

In other words, the more you move this hand, the more your dog is likely to move out of position to follow it. Once you have mastered a hand position that keeps your dog in exactly the right heelwork position, stick with it and don't keep moving it. Such movements will be penalised, anyway, when you move into higher classes.

NOVICE RECALL AND 'A' RECALL

As previously outlined, the Novice *recall* exercise begins with a dog being told to *wait* while his owner walks away from him, on the steward's instruction, and then turns to face him. A common problem at the beginning of this exercise is a dog not *waiting* when his owner moves away; following after him or her instead.

The most likely cause of this is that the dog has got confused between the *sit* and *wait* exercise, after which you walk away and leave him, and the *close sit, watch me* and *with me* sequence before heelwork, after which you move off together. The body language of the owner could also have signalled the beginning of heelwork to the dog, in some way, without them realising it.

Keep remembering to teach *sit* and *wait* and *close sit, watch me* and *with me* as different sequences in training, so your dog always knows which is which.

When you prepare your dog to *"wait"* you should also display different body language to the *close sit/watch me/with me* sequence; i.e. a hand held out in front of your dog, while he is next to you, for *wait*, (as highlighted in Chapter Five) and a hand kept on your side (as if you were holding a toy or treat in it) for the *close sit* sequence before heelwork.

The same applies in *A recall*, where you ask your dog to *"wait"* before moving away from him on the steward's instruction. Put your hand out in front of your dog, while he is next to you, before you leave him, to signal the *wait* command.

Sometimes dogs move before their owners have called them, in both Novice and A recall, simply due to over-anticipation; a very common occurrence in dogs as exceptionally responsive as collies. To get round this problem, in training, regularly ask your dog to *"wait"*, and then go back to him *instead of recalling him*.

Do not, however, then give him a *release* command (*"okay!"*), as he will start to confuse this *wait* exercise with a *stay* one. Instead, do the following:

• Ask your dog to *wait*, move away from him and then turn and face him.
• Then return to your dog *while he is still waiting.*
• Repeat the *wait* command *while he is still waiting.*
• Move away from your dog again.
• This time *recall* him.

If you do this every time you train or practice Obedience *recalls* it is far less likely that that your dog will move once you've asked him to *wait*.

NERVES AND ERRORS

Canine competition – where the spotlight is very much on the quality of our own handling, as well as the performance of our dog – can understandably make a lot of people very nervous. This, in turn, can undermine the success of your round in many ways, which it might help to be better aware of.

The first problem is loss of consistency. In other words, in order to replicate, in the competition ring, the level of performance you normally get from your dog in training, you must do everything in the ring much as you would as if you were still just training him. Every subtlety of your movements, commands, body language and general 'upbeat' mood and energy should be kept as close as possible to what you normally do in training.

Under the pressure of competing, this may not always be easy, but the more you deviate from your normal training mood, cues, footwork etc. in the ring, the more you can confuse or unnerve your dog – especially one as movement and mood sensitive as the collie – which in turn will make errors more likely. More nervous, hesitant, pressurising or aggressive body language from a handler under pressure, when competing, can also heighten the risk of dogs becoming ring shy later.

The second problem can be loss of hander concentration. When preoccupied with nerves in the ring, it can also be easy to forget a course or not listen hard enough to what a steward or judge is telling you to do. In Agility, you may miss obstacles, do them in the wrong order, or start a round too soon. In Obedience, you may turn right when asked to turn left, or fail to hear a halt instruction in time – don't worry, everybody does these things at some stage!

To get your nerves under better control it can really help to get friends, or fellow training club members, to regularly set up mock competition rounds for you, in countless different places – particularly those with some level of surrounding noise/distraction – as if you were genuinely competing. This way focusing on a set course and/or following another person's instructions in more distracting environments will become second nature to you and your dog. It will also make it easier for you to maintain a more consistent working approach with your dog, no matter where you are.

Also remember to take some long, deep breaths when you first go in the ring. Do not rush into any exercise before you have sufficiently calmed yourself mentally and collected your thoughts. Then focus on your dog in an equally calm but also confident manner. The more you can then convince him that you are both having the most brilliant time in that ring, the more likely it is that this will happen.

Meanwhile, rest assured that even top handlers in any pursuit can suffer from nerves. We are all human beings first, and dog competitors second.

RETRIEVE

Retrieve can be one of the most commonly corrupted exercises in Obedience, due to the way owners often approach it. First, they do not break it down into all its different steps or pictures for the dog:

- First *Sit*.
- Then *Wait* while an item is thrown.
- Then *Go forward* on command to get the thrown item.
- Then *Hold* the item.
- Then *Recall* back with it.
- Then *Present* the item; i.e. sit straight and close in front of owner with held item in mouth.
- Then *Wait* again.
- Then *Give* the item to owner on command.

There will also be a *Finish* at the end of the exercise in competition but, as previously mentioned, you always teach this as a separate exercise in training.

Owners commonly see the *Retrieve* exercise as one whole sequence for their dog to complete at once, rather than a series of little steps/pictures that need to be taught separately to him, then strung together. As a result, their dog is less able to understand what he is doing wrong when an owner keeps asking him to repeat the whole *Retrieve* exercise, again and again. He can thus get progressively more demoralised or reluctant to do it.

The same happens if owners over-correct, or harshly correct, dogs for mistakes in some part of *Retrieve*.

Identifying the problem picture

In all cases, you have to try to identify which part of the whole *retrieve* sequence your dog is having most problems with, and work separately on this. If, for example, he is simply reluctant to retrieve anything you throw, just work on this.

You will need to make just getting and *holding* something you have thrown far more rewarding for your dog; e.g. actions he associates with something pleasant like a game.

For more detailed advice on dismantling the *retrieve* exercise and making it far more rewarding and enjoyable for your dog, see *Remotivating super-sensitive dogs* (Chapter Seven).

Problems with *hold*

A common problem owners can have with *retrieve* is getting a dog to keep hold of something in his mouth until they ask him to *give* it to them i.e., after he has brought a dumbbell or any other item back to them he quickly drops it on the floor.

This problem usually dates back to their earlier teaching of the *Give* command (Chapter Five, page 56), where they allowed their dog to get into the habit of quickly dropping any item he brought back to them, in anticipation of eating the treat to come.

To master any formal *retrieve* exercise, you have to teach your dog that he will only be rewarded for the *combined* actions of *getting* something, *Holding* it and then *giving* it to you *when commanded*, and not just getting it and then dumping it whenever or wherever he likes.

It may take some patience to break the above habit, but you have to keep waiting until your dog is actually holding something he's *Retrieved* in his mouth, if only for a second or two, so that you can then attach the right command to this action – "*Hold*". You can then say "*give*" as you take the item from him, followed by much praise and a reward.

Gradually, you then need to stretch the amount of time your dog will "*Hold*" something, on command, before you ask him to "*Give*" it to you, whereupon you can praise and reward him. Once your dog realises the key to his reward is now *Hold* then *give*, and not just *give*, you have this problem sorted.

Forcing the *Hold*

Countless *Retrieve* exercises get ruined through owners physically forcing a dog to *Hold* something in his mouth. As soon as you do this, once again, you have attached negative connotations to this whole exercise, of a kind that frequently compromises a dog's future willingness or confidence to do it. So be mindful of this. Keep remembering that patience employed at the start of teaching any exercise will always bring you better, and more longer lasting, results in a dog's future performance than any physical coercion used to force a dog into a specific action.

Once you have identified the one or more pictures of a *retrieve* exercise that were going wrong for your dog, and rectified them separately in training, you can then slot them back into the whole *Retrieve* sequence again.

Speed of response in *recall* and *retrieve* exercises

The speed with which a dog returns to you in the *recall* and

The Retrieve exercise must be broken down into its component parts.

retrieve exercises is generally dictated by how you originally trained them.

If your dog is not returning very fast, you have either made these exercises too boring in training, or you have been too critical of your dog when teaching some part of these exercises, or you have made your dog wait too long for rewards. Any of these things can dull the kind of response you later get.

Be aware of these risks, because if you do not address the problem of an unenthusiastic dog very early on, and put it right with more exciting, motivating and confidence-inspiring training, he will just get slower and slower.

STAYS

The commonest problem with *stays* are usually dogs breaking them, i.e. moving, or changing position when you have instructed them to remain still. Once again this problem tends to date back to your original, and ongoing, training of *Stay* and how reliable a picture of this exercise you have left in your dog's head.

As outlined in Chapter Five (*Wait and stay, page 54*) where many owners go wrong is in not, from the outset, making the *stay* exercise a very different picture in their dog's mind from *wait*.

"*Wait*" for a dog (as used before *Recall, Retrieve* etc.) should mean remain where you are until I ask you to so something else. "*Stay*", on the other hand, means remain where you are until I come back to release you from this command. Both exercises should not only have different verbal commands, but also different hand signals to suitably distinguish them from each other. If you do not do this, a dog gets confused, and may move in anticipation during a 'Stay' exercise out of a belief that you originally asked him to "*Wait*". Sometimes I have seen owners give their dog the hand gesture for 'Stay' while *verbally* asking him to "*Wait*", or vice versa, which can be equally confusing.

Training Obedience *stays*

The most important thing about Obedience level *stays* are

that you practise these exercises in a wealth of different locations/contexts with your dog – not just at home or in a training class. Every time you do the *stay* exercise with your dog, you must also go through all its different steps in the same order, and in the same way, as follows:

• Ask your dog to *"Sit"* or lie *"Down"*.
• Go in front of your dog and give him your specific hand signal and verbal command for *"Stay"*.
• Move away from your dog for a set amount of time
• Return to your dog and stand next to him. *Do not look at your dog or touch him initially*. Not only may this encourage him to move, but touching a dog in an Obedience *stay* before a steward has told you to release him will be penalised. Whenever I am training *Stay*, I always leave at least 10 seconds between returning to a dog and releasing him. This teaches a dog that when you return to him in a *stay* there will always be a delay before he is released, and during this delay he must remain still.
• Release your dog with your set release command/gesture – e.g. *"Okay!"* and/or touch your dog's shoulder.
• Praise your dog really well for his co-operation, then have a really rewarding game with him

If you always follow these same identical steps every time you do a *stay* exercise, no matter where you are when you do it, your dog will get a much more reliable picture of *Stay* in his head.

Moving from sit to down in *Stay*

In *stays,* if dogs move position it is usually from a *Sitting* position to a *Down* position. It is rarer for them to move from a *down* position to a *Sitting* one – though I'm sure there will always be those who do!

For this reason I tend to always train *stays* with my dogs in the *sitting* position, not the *Down* position. I find this strengthens the connection in a dog's head between the *stay* exercise and the need to remain in a sitting position. By contrast, I would do *Down* stays only when required in competition, or as a pure safety exercise at any other time.

If, in competition, your dog continually drops from a *sit* to a *down* position in a stay, as soon as you walk away from him, be aware that you need to repair this exercise *from scratch* in training.

Begin by walking just *one step* away from him, after asking him to *Stay* (using your customary verbal and hand *stay* signals) then immediately go back to him. Then move on to two steps, then three etc., only stretching the distance you walk away from him as he gets more and more reliable at remaining in a *sit* once you have asked him to *"Stay"*.

Breaking *stays*, full stop

While some dogs may break *Stays* out of a sheer lack of respect for both you and your commands, the vast majority

break them through confusion (of a kind already outlined) or a genuine inability to sustain concentration.

Stays, after all, are exercises requiring a fairly high level of mental self-discipline and focus in a dog, and the higher up in Obedience you go, the longer the *Stays* will get and the more superior these qualities will need to be. So if you have not taught, and constantly reinforced, the skills of mental focus and self-discipline in your collie from puppyhood onwards – as outlined in Chapter Five – do not expect him to suddenly find them at an Obedience competition.

When training *Stays*, it is also incredibly important to never let a wrong response go uncorrected, or prove rewarding. In other words, always put a dog who has moved from *Sit* to *Down* immediately back into *Sit* before continuing and finishing the exercise as usual. If your dog keeps moving forwards or towards you in a *Stay,* keep putting him back in a place further away from you than where you originally left him.

Note: Only do this in training. Owners moving dogs back to original or other positions during stays in competition is usually frowned upon, due to the distraction it can cause other dogs.

Do not be harsh when you correct your dog in *Stays*. This will only cause him stress or upset and thus make future errors more likely because anxiety always has an adverse effect on a dog's concentration.

With *stays*, quality rather than quantity of response remains the key again. It is better to start off with lots of short *stays* that your dog always does reliably, and very gradually stretch the time he does these faultlessly, than give him stays that are too long, too soon, making it more likely he will break them, which could become a habit.

SENDAWAY

The Sendaway exercise is something we can all make a hash of through imagining a dog can see the task as we do. In other words, we think: "why doesn't he understand I want him to run to the middle of that box/go through those two front markers instead of round them?", or "why is he running off in a completely different direction to where I asked him to go?".

The answer, as ever, lies in the picture of this exercise we left in our dog's head when originally training it. The thing about *sendaway* is that while the target we ask our dog to run towards can vary a lot in competition – i.e. it can be a triangle of cones, or a box, or a set of markers that are more unusual objects, or are more unusually arranged – the principle remains the same; namely, our dog has to run ahead in a straight line to these targets, on our command, and then drop into a *down* at a fixed point when we ask him to.

Things usually go wrong in *sendaway* when we start to confuse our dog as to whether we want him to run ahead in a straight line until stopped, or whether we want him to approach a specific object, like a marker, instead. At which point, why shouldn't one marker be just as good to

TEACHING THE SENDAWAY

The Collie must focus on the sendaway target.

He should then have the confidence to run out straight to it when commanded.

Once dropped in the right spot, the dog must then wait until he is recalled by the handler.

approach as any other?

So the most important thing is simply to concentrate on teaching your dog to run ahead of you in a straight line, when commanded, until you stop him. In order for your dog to do this, he needs to think you are sending him forward to get a particular object – such as a toy – otherwise this exercise will not make sense to him.

Running to toys

When out on walks and elsewhere, get into the habit of putting a toy straight ahead of your dog, and then asking him to run to it and get it with a specific command – e.g., "*Go!*". Do not always ask him to drop *down* once he has got to the toy, as constantly anticipating this command from you will make his *Sendaways* ever-slower.

The same is true if you constantly correct your dog for going off in the wrong direction. In fact, this can make some dogs freeze and be reluctant to move at all when given a later *Sendaway* command.

It is always best to ignore a dog going in the wrong direction. Simply pick up the toy you wanted him to get, wait for him to return to you, then set up the exercise again – maybe this time putting the toy a little nearer to your dog so he can better see it. When he runs straight to it this time, praise him really well.

Increasing distance and using markers

Only when your dog is really confident about running away from you, in a straight line, towards a toy, start putting his toy a little further away from him when you send him off. Then use toys that are harder for him to see from a distance; i.e. he will only see the toy once he has run up to it in a straight line. This will encourage a dog to still run off fast and straight, even when he cannot see the toy he is running to.

When this is going well, the next step is to put out two markers, e.g. cones, about a metre ahead of your dog before you send him off. Space these on either side of your dog about two or three metres apart. He needs to learn to run through these en route to his toy. Gradually you can put these markers a little further ahead of him, but he should still run through them to get to his toy.

Using markers in different formations

Now add more and more markers for him to run through to get to his toy. Sometimes arrange these in a tapering triangle formation with your dog's toy placed at the cone that marks the tip of this triangle. At other times put your dog's toy at the tip of this triangle instead of a cone. Also regularly arrange the cones into a box, with your dog's toy just beyond this box.

All that matters each time is that your dog continues to run in a straight line ahead of you, on command, to get his

toy. It is then up to you how well you position your dog for *sendaway* so that he always takes off in a line that takes him straight through the centre of all your markers.

Only at this point move on to occasionally dropping your dog *down on the move* (to teach this, see Chapter Eight, page 77) after you have given him the *sendaway* command.

I prefer to do this when I have not put a toy out ahead for my dog, as I do not want him to keep running to find the toy is not there, which could undermine his faith in this exercise. Having dropped my dog, I then recall him to me instead for his toy and a game. This is, essentially, the *mid-chase recall* exercise, as outlined in Chapter Eight, page 80.

This way, a dog learns that running straight to a toy, or dropping en route to a toy then coming back to me, are equally rewarding actions or pictures.

Different trainers have different ways of teaching *sendaway*; some of which might suit you and your dog better than others. So if this exercise is going wrong for you, shop around until you find a trainer and method that is most effective in putting it right.

This apart, please note that many Border Collies may find it hard to run in a direct straight line towards distant objects (such as an arrangement of cones) because their natural instinct, as herding dogs, is to run *round* them. This is classic outrun behaviour, and the way sheepdogs are programmed to approach livestock ahead of them. So do take this factor into account during your training.

Begin by training your dog to run only a short distance ahead, in a straight line, to a toy. Then gradually increase the distance he runs in a straight line ahead to the toy. Only then add the distractions he must run through/past while he still runs ahead in a straight line to the toy.

DISTANT CONTROL

The commonest problems in *distant control* are the dog moving too far forwards, backwards or sideways, or the dog adopting the wrong position on command as a result of confusion or over-anticipation.

This again goes back to early training. It is very important to get your dog's position changes absolutely right when he is first in front of you and close to you. Only then try commanding your dog to adopt different positions – i.e. *sit, down, stand* - at progressively further distances away from you while they remain correct.

Wrong forwards/backwards/sideways movement

When a dog goes from a sit to a down position, he inevitably moves forward. To counteract this forward movement during *sit to down*, it is a good idea to make your dog walk a step or two backwards when you ask him to *stand*.

Many people teach this through placing a foot between their dog's front legs, while he is sitting or lying down, and then moving forward, which makes him both stand up and

A collie is on his own when it comes to the scent test.

A confident decision.

step back. If you do this too forcefully or fast, however, your dog will leap back sideways into a *stand* instead, which will set the pattern for how he does this exercise at a distance in the future. Alternatively, he may move too far backwards when standing, and get into this habit instead. So only use gentle, minimum forward movement when initially teaching *stand,* so the dog moves back only a couple of steps in a straighter line.

Anticipation can be a big problem in *distant control*. It is usually caused by owners making their dogs move too quickly from one position to the other on command in training, and/or inadvertently using additional body movements/gestures in-between position commands without realising it. It is vital to keep absolutely still between position commands. Similarly, get into the habit of establishing good pauses between one position command to the next in training.

In training, I personally like to end *distant control* sequences with a *stand* command, and a pause in this position of at least 10 seconds, before releasing my dogs from the exercise and praising and rewarding them. This in because I have found that my dogs are most likely to anticipate moving from *stand* to *sit* than any other position change.

If your dog has a position he most commonly moves from at distance before being commanded, this is the one I recommend you always end your training with – with a good pause tagged on, as previously outlined, before formally releasing him from the exercise and praising him.

SCENT DISCRIMINATION

One of the biggest problems with scent discrimination tasks is owners pushing their dogs too far and too fast, before they are ready. Owners can also be far too critical of any failure on their dog's behalf in scent tests - conveniently forgetting how rubbish they would be, themselves, at pinpointing the correct cloth, out of umpteen others, on the basis of a few shed skin flakes and sweat molecules.

Scent exercises, perhaps more than any other, require supreme confidence in a dog; a constant feeling that every time he sets off on a scent mission he will always succeed. You only gain this kind of confidence over time, as a result of consistently sympathetic training and a steady history of past success.

Scent is also one of those exercises where so many more coercively trained dogs can hit the buffers, because you cannot expect them to work freely and confidently while simultaneously worrying about the consequences of getting things wrong.

Starting scent

The first thing I would recommend, before going any further in scent training, is to just teach a dog to pick up a scent cloth correctly. Do this as a separate picture or exercise in itself.

Regularly put a cloth down for your dog to pick up, initially while he is right next to you, and praise and reward him fulsomely every time he does this *neatly*. Do *not* get impatient, frustrated or keep correcting your dog if he picks the cloth up sloppily, or you could ruin his confidence about approaching such cloths in the future. Always praise him for bringing the cloth to you, however he does it. Just go far more overboard with praise and rewards each time he does it cleanly, without mouthing it or shaking it.

Similarly, only ask him to bring the cloth to you from further and further away once he is picking it up cleanly on a reliable basis..

Note, whenever I am asking a dog to retrieve a scent cloth, I always use the specific command *"find it!"* as he goes to get it, as this is the command I would use later in a proper scent exercise.

Many owners try to teach a neat cloth pick up while doing the whole scent discrimination exercise, but I feel this just muddies the waters. If a dog brings back the right cloth to you and you *still* correct him, for the *way* he brought it back, he could just as easily think you are correcting him for bringing back the wrong cloth and rapidly start losing confidence in his ability to do this exercise.

Extending scent skills

Once you have got your dog nicely retrieving a scent cloth for you, next start putting this cloth in different places – not just at home – and ask him to *"find it"* and bring it back to you, then praise and reward him. This gets your dog into the habit of viewing the cloth, your scent and the command *"find it!"* as one picture in his head.

Only when this step is really reliable should you move on to asking your dog to pick up your cloth (*"find it!"*) amid a collection of other objects. These can be any objects, though none of them should have your scent on, and your dog should not be able to lift them easily – e.g. a brick, or a tin of beans.

When your dog is happily finding and returning your scent cloth, amid a range of other objects and scents, you can start more serious scent discrimination; i.e. start putting your scent cloth next to dummy cloths that look exactly the same, but do not have your scent on them. You will need serving tongs to do this.

It is incredibly important at this stage, and throughout training, to make the dummy cloths consistently unappealing to your dog if he tries to pick them up by mistake. You can either nail them deeply into the ground, or make each dummy scent cloth into an envelope, which contains something flat and heavy like a ceramic tile. When doing this, do remember not to transfer any of your scent on to the dummy cloths.

Making incorrect cloths more unappealing gives your dog the highest chance of consistent success in training, which, in turn, will boost his confidence.

It is, however, important to understand that some dogs will always be more consistently successful in scent discrimination exercises than others. This is not just because

of excellent training (which certainly makes a big difference), or a good sense of smell, but because of their particular personality; i.e., the dog is exceptionally focused, and approaches any task asked of him with a superior sense of purpose and commitment. In Obedience, you strike gold when you get a collie like this.

When dogs fail scent, by contrast, owners need to put this in the right context. If human beings had a better understanding of the sheer scale of scent traffic hitting the average dog's nose and brain every day, they would also realise why screening all this out, in order to pinpoint one particular set of scent molecules, on command, can be such a big ask for many of them, before you even add the additional pressures of the competition environment.

OVER CONTROL

Much as I, like many others, may enjoy Obedience training, I can also recognise that this pursuit can have some dangers and downsides that are worth considering.

I totally agree with top Working Trials trainer Wendy Beasley, who says that Obedience folk, in their constant pursuit of accuracy/precision at all times, can sometimes become too 'over-controlling' of their dogs; forever seeking to rule their every thought and action, be this in training, competition - or sometimes, also, just everyday life.

Psychologically, this can become highly oppressive and stifling for dogs and also intensify a 'learned helplessness' mindset (for more on this syndrome see Chapter Five). The dog starts to believe he can't do anything by himself, without the immediate say so or close supervision of his handler. This in turn undermines his confidence to perform any task where higher degrees of initiative/self-belief are required – e.g. scent, sendaway.

In Obedience there will always be a fine line to tread between teaching a dog to do exercises with reliable accuracy, and totally shutting down the initiative/self-belief centres of his brain through excessive interference and correction. To me it is always better to let a dog initially make mistakes, en route to accuracy, yet retain his confidence, than try to crush all errors out of him from day one, and sacrifice his confidence as a result.

EXPERT HELP

If you are serious about the pursuit of Obedience, and feel you have a potentially very talented dog, I would urge you to seek the help of a top Obedience competitor and trainer for more extensive help and advice. He or she can show you how to polish your performance in all the exercises, and prevent you and your dog learning, or perpetuating, any bad habits.

In Obedience it is always the little things – e.g. gappy heelwork, crooked sits, messy turns, over-anticipation – that lose you so many marks, and these can be eradicated, or

WINDING UP COLLIES IN COMPETITION – WHY DO OWNERS DO IT?

I have long been puzzled as to why some owners insist on winding their collies up into a frenzy, prior to a competition round, with a lot of screaming, bouncing about and other half demented-looking forms of intense mental provocation.

How did this habit get established, why do owners feel it is necessary, and how can pushing a naturally excitable dog to hysteria levels help him perform any better than he otherwise might? Do you see top Olympic athletes jumping around hysterically just before a race, or shepherds' dogs wound up into yapping lunacy just prior to working sheep? Or do you see them in a state of supreme mental focus instead?

The obvious downside to winding up collies, as described, is that their brains become adrenaline flooded. As a result, they can lose focus and are more likely to make errors. They may start barking or spinning around in the ring, or may miss turns in Obedience or jumps in Agility. They also waste an awful lot of energy.

If your dog has sufficient natural drive, and you have trained him to find a particular pursuit highly rewarding, that is all you should need to get him to perform well in competition. If neither of the above apply, it is unlikely that any amount of screaming and shouting or swinging him off toys will make much difference. Indeed, it is more likely to unnerve your dog out of a belief that you have suddenly gone quite mad!

Also be aware that when training your dog for competition, teaching him the right 'head' you want him to be in for a particular pursuit (i.e. eager, but focused) is also just as important as teaching him the relative competition exercises themselves.

THE DANGERS OF TUGGER TOYS

Along with the previously mentioned 'winding up' process for collies, owners should also be mindful of the dangers of making their dogs attack tugger toys or leads as a source of reward or mental 'boost' in competition training.

Leaving aside the physical damage that can be done to collies via these violent tugging, bouncing or swinging games (i.e. strains/injuries to their jaws, teeth, neck vertebrae, shoulders and spines), the activity can spiral some dogs into an incredibly aggressive and more hyper-reactive frame of mind.

There are obviously risks attached to deliberately encouraging a dog to be aggressive, and then making him view this behaviour as a reward, and similarly to associating an aggressive/hyper-reactive mental state with a specific pursuit, or pursuit environment.

Additionally, even if not intentionally, collies can often bite owners' hands or fingers during the excitement of frantic tugging sessions, and it is unwise to allow such behaviour to then become a part of a reward process in their minds. It could also progressively lower their future level of bite inhibition, both towards you, as an owner, and other people.

All dogs need to be taught, and reminded from puppyhood onwards, that touching – let alone biting – a person's hands/fingers with their teeth is strictly taboo.

The worst kinds of dogs to use tugger toys with are those who will not instantly let go of them when commanded to do so. There are other toys you can use as training rewards – e.g. balls, Frisbees – which are less likely to trigger more undesirable behavioural side effects.

Speed and focus are vital for the
agility competitor.

much improved, with better knowledge and training. A good trainer can also go through static exercises with you - i.e. show you how to do things such as perfect sits or turns as separate exercises or pictures – and tell you when your dog is in the ideal heelwork position, or sitting straight/crooked when viewed from the back, which you cannot easily see for yourself when training a dog.

If it is any consolation, nobody ever gets everything right in Obedience. Just as top handlers can get as nervous as anyone else in competition, their dogs can also mess up exercises sometimes. This is just part and parcel of the everyday unpredictability of animals, people and life events. It is not, and never should be seen as, the end of the world.

Meanwhile, for more help in tracking down a good Obedience trainer, see *Finding the right expert* in the *Further Information* section, page 199.

AGILITY

Any coverage of collie competition has to address Agility; a pursuit first introduced at Crufts in l978 and which is now attracting greater and greater numbers of enthusiasts worldwide. In the UK alone there are now around 300 licensed Agility shows annually, as well as many other specially organised events. It is yet another pastime in which collies excel and dominate, and where their unique combination of athleticism and supreme mental responsiveness sets them apart from the rest of the field.

I am sure there are many readers who adore Agility training and competition with their dogs, and I totally respect this. I can also completely understand the appeal of pursuits like Agility and Flyball for both owners and dogs alike.

In common with other competitive pursuits, however, I do also have some sincere concerns about the level of stress that can be caused to collies via Agility and Flyball training/competition - especially when handled by less experienced or breed-knowledgeable owners – and these will be covered later in this section (see, *Agility, Flyball and stress, page 127*).

WHAT AGILITY INVOLVES

Agility involves dogs negotiating a set course of obstacles (explained in more detail later) in the fastest possible time. To the more novice onlooker, Agility appears to be much like show jumping for dogs – which, in many ways, it is. You can also get the impression that it is an event primarily to do with speed when, in fact, the most vital overriding element is *control.*

There is no point, after all, in having the fastest dog in the ring if you cannot get him to do obstacles in the right order, or control where he goes or when he stops. Thus, on top of having the right dog – and certainly some collies are better designed physically and mentally for this pursuit than others – doing well in Agility also requires a high level of training.

It is the only way to consistently combine speed with accuracy in your dog.

As with Obedience, you progress to higher classes in Agility competition the more you win. Similarly, in different countries, grades or rules governing the Agility pursuit may differ to some degree, and this can easily be investigated by contacting your relevant national Kennel club, council or organisation (see *National Kennel Clubs and Border collie breed and working dog organisations* in the *Further Information* section, Part Two).

In the UK, Agility competition classes progress up from Grades 1-7. At the very top are Agility Championship Classes, offering handlers the chance to win the Agility Certificates that will lead to their dogs becoming Agility Champions.

Due to the physical demands of Agility, both handlers and their dogs also have to be pretty fit. For the same reason, dogs are not allowed to compete in Agility until they are 18 months old. Additionally, dogs must be measured by official Agility measurers before they compete at their first show, in order that they compete in their relevant size category.

Most people get involved in Agility with their collies via a local training club; these clubs, in turn, should be listed with your national Kennel Club, council or organisation.

THE OBSTACLES

There are minor differences in Agility competitions/equipment specifications, depending on which country you are competing in, but the format is broadly the same; an increasingly vital factor with the growth of international competitions.

Basically, there is a combination of 16 obstacles that can be used on an Agility course:

Hurdles
These are a maximum of 650mm (2.2ft) in height and 1.2m (4ft) in width, and competing dogs must jump them without knocking them over. The top part of the hurdle must always be easily displaced, to prevent dogs hurting themselves.

Rising spread jump
This jump comprises two hurdles positioned closely together, with the first hurdle set lower than the second.

Brush fence
Another sort of hurdle, again with an easily displaced top unit.

Hoop (Tyre)
Dogs must jump through a hoop or tyre suspended from a frame at a fixed height.

Table

Dogs must lie down on this table for a time set by the judge. The table itself should be a minimum of 940mm (3ft) square and must be of stable construction with a non-slip surface.

Long jump

This requires a dog to leap a maximum length of 1.5m (5ft), clearing a series of low jumps.

Water jump

This usually features a low hurdle placed in front of a long jump of shallow water.

Wishing well or Lych Gate

This hurdle must have a roof to it and, again, features a displaceable top bar

Collapsible tunnel

This tunnel has a rigid round entrance. Non-slip cloth thereafter forms the body of the tunnel, which can be up to 13m (10ft) long. The dog must make his way through this and the exit at the other end.

Pipe tunnel

This is a fixed tunnel, a minimum of 610mm (2ft) wide and up to 3m (10ft) long.

Weaving poles

These are a series of up to 12 upright poles, set in a line. A dog has to weave in and out of the complete series of poles without missing any of them. As I write a standard distance of 600m between the poles is about to be introduced by the UK Kennel Club.

Pause box

An area 1.2m (4ft) by 1.2m (4ft) on the ground of the ring where the dog has to pause for a period specified by the judge.

'A' Frame

Dogs must negotiate this 'A' shaped structure comprising 2 ramps with non-slip surfaces. There are 'contact points' at the base of each ramp, coloured differently to the rest of the obstacle.

A dog's paws must come into contact with these when climbing and leaving the obstacle, in order to avoid penalty points.

See-Saw

This is a pivoted plank, minimum length of 3.5m (12ft), which the dog must negotiate, again touching the relevant contact points.

Dog walk

This is a plank approximately 1.3m (4.5ft) high, with firmly fixed ramps at either end. The dog must walk over this, ensuring again that his paws touch relevant contact points.

Cross over

Note, there was formerly another obstacle, the *Cross over*, comprising a raised square table with ramps leading up all four sides. Approval for this obstacle was withdrawn with effect from January 1st 2009 in the UK.

AGILITY TRAINING

There are quite a few training dilemmas for collie owners wishing to do well in Agility. Chief among these is that the dogs with the most natural talent for this sport – i.e. high level of drive, speed, reactivity and responsiveness – are also so often those most vulnerable to the effects of mental overload and stress, of which more later.

Owners, additionally, can routinely underestimate how much training their collies will need to prepare them adequately for Agility competition. The dogs not only have to be acquainted with all the different obstacles as separate pictures in their heads, they must also be taught to associate the negotiation of these with feelings of confidence and reward.

Initially dogs may be consistently rewarded – i.e. with praise, plus toys and food - for negotiating Agility obstacles, until eventually the physical/mental excitement generated by, and associated with, the activity becomes a reward in itself.

It is also essential that you teach your dog different words/commands for different obstacles, distinct signals to tell him which way you want him to go round a course or obstacle, and that you regularly work your dog on both sides of your body, left and right. You do not want your dog to always expect you to be in one place, in relation to an obstacle. You want him to learn you could be anywhere, and similarly he may need to turn or move in any direction, any time, on your command.

CHALLENGES AND PROBLEMS IN AGILITY TRAINING

When beginning Agility work with collies, you can come across the following different types of dog who may give you more challenges in training.

The first is what I call, the *bull in a china shop*. This is the dog with tons of drive, energy and confidence, but who can rapidly lose focus and handler responsiveness once he gets too excited.

The second is the *speedy but spooky* type. This dog usually combines speed with greater handler responsiveness, but is more easily distracted/unnerved by things like louder external noises or less familiar pictures; i.e. obstacles positioned in a more unusual or less expected sequence.

Finally there is the *safe but slow* model. This dog may have consistent accuracy when negotiating an obstacle course, but lacks sufficient physical drive or speed. Over and above never winning any prizes, this lack of speed can cause additional physical problems for the dog; depriving him of the forward momentum/propulsion that makes jumping any object that much easier for a four-legged animal and thus far less stressful for the body.

WHY PROBLEMS OCCUR OR PERSIST

Many of the Agility problems seen in collies develop – or become exacerbated – by less experienced early training. It is incredibly important to understand how quickly collies develop, and then stubbornly retain, their attitudes to different things as a result of the way they were first exposed to them.

If, for instance, your collie has initial reservations about a particular Agility obstacle, such as the dog walk, or the collapsible tunnel, and you keep forcing him to negotiate it, you may not only give him lasting hang-ups about this one particular obstacle, you could also put him off the whole Agility pursuit for life.

Walking along a plank at height (*dog walk*), or having an object tip and move when you step on it (*see-saw)*, or entering a dark hole (*collapsible tunnel*) are instinctively worrying experiences for most dogs until you can progressively condition them to believe otherwise.

So patience, as ever, is the key. Your dog has to decide for himself when he feels ready to negotiate a particular obstacle, whereupon you can amply reward him. But until that point arrives, do not coerce or physically force him, and similarly do not cajole or make a big fuss when he shows concern or resistance towards an obstacle, as you may inadvertently reinforce this negative state of mind.

On-going, but low-key, encouragement is usually best for obstacle-phobic dogs as well as artfully targeted clicker training.

A problem can also arise when a dog gets to like one particular obstacle – such as the pipe tunnel – *too* much, with the result that he makes a bee-line for it the moment his round starts, and ignores a handler's alternative commands through over-excitement.

The key to solving this problem lies in better all round training; teaching your dog to leave or avoid obstacles on command, and also working on gaining far better control of your dog's movement, especially at speed.

LOSING SPEED AND FOCUS

Having familiarised their dogs with the pictures of different Agility obstacles, many owners can then find problems when they string these obstacles into a sequence or course.

Their concern for accuracy, for instance, may lead them to initially over-check their dog as he moves from one obstacle to the next. This can result in a dog going ever-slower round Agility equipment, in constant anticipation of the next correction.

Making your dog too excited about doing Agility, on the other hand, can lead to a different problem; i.e. a progressive loss of focus and control. You can end up with a dog who not only makes more errors, but also starts taking his own favoured course round Agility equipment (as highlighted earlier) while blinkered to any instructions from you.

If you look at this problem from the perspective of you being a shepherd, and the Agility obstacles being the sheep, your dog's storming and anarchic approach would have your flock scattered to the four winds in panic, or shooting over a cliff!

OVER-EXCITEMENT

In Chapter Five, page 51, *The obsession target and the handler*, I explained the principle that the obsession target in a collie's head is the thing he has past – and usually repeatedly – connected with a pleasure/excitement response; i.e. anything from sheep to chasing toys to Agility obstacles – and of course, *you,* acting as the chief gateway to such things.

Having forged the connection in your collie's head between Agility obstacles and pleasure, and allowed these to then become obsession targets for him, the handler's skill then lies in how well they can train their dog to approach/negotiate these obsession targets without him over-exciting himself into error. Shepherds face exactly the same kind of challenge with their dogs every day, in terms of controlling the manner and speed at which they approach livestock.

If, however, you do not understand this continual need to discipline your dog's approach to obsession targets, while still maintaining sufficient working drive and enthusiasm, things can escalate out of control pretty fast. In other words, your dog can rapidly get to the point where he does not have to actually *do* Agility to get excessively agitated/excited. He only has to *see* Agility equipment for his brain to go *yahoo! – pleasure coming!*

FIDGETING, SPINNING AND YAPPING

Depending on the level of mental arousal that then erupts, you may have trouble getting your dog to *wait* on the start line, he may yap and whine and spin around between obstacles, or you may get your hand or thigh bitten. These are all symptoms of a dog unable to contain the mental pressure caused by intense over arousal.

When collies feel intense mental pressure they resort to default physical actions that are most instinctive to them as a breed – i.e. running, circling, lunging, nipping – whereas activities like barking and whining are usually outlets for the frustration they feel at not being able to do whatever they want to do quickly enough.

For all these reasons, as an Agility enthusiast, you will need to know far more about how and why this pursuit can stress your dog, and what you can do to reduce it (see, *Agility, Flyball and stress*, page 127 and *Reducing stress at competitions, page 130*).

FLYBALL

Flyball, as a pursuit, originated in the USA about 20 years ago, since when it has attracted an ever bigger following. Many people who take up Flyball have a previous background in Agility as this sport demands similar things of their dogs – i.e. a high level of speed and responsiveness, but also control. This is again why Border Collies, and other collie types are so successful at it.

Flyball events are basically knockout contests. Two teams of four dogs run next to each other down parallel racing lanes. As the dogs run down the lanes they must clear four hurdles, ending at the flyball box. Here they must push a pedal to release a ball. They then catch the ball and race back over the hurdles to the finishing point, where they started.

The dogs with the fastest times progressively knock out their rivals, in each flyball round, until there is an eventual winner. In the meantime dogs missing hurdles or dropping the ball will be penalised.

SPEED VERSUS ACCURACY

Flyball can present some similar training dilemmas to Agility; namely how to get a dog consistently negotiating hurdles and retrieving balls accurately without losing speed.

Different dogs, inevitably, will also be more naturally suited, genetically, to this pursuit than others. Some collies are not particularly natural or keen retrievers, for instance. Others, especially when over-excited, may persistently see hurdles as an illogical impediment to their main goal or obsession target – i.e. the ball in the flyball box when running away from an owner, or the owner's reward once they are running back to the finish line. Thus they may consistently run round them or past them.

A lot of Flyball dogs originate from an Agility background. As with Agility, there is far more training involved in Flyball than many a casual spectator may imagine. There is also the same need to train separate pictures to a dog – i.e. jumping hurdles, releasing the ball from the flyball box, turning sharply to maintain speed and a good line back over the hurdles, etc. These then get strung together later as a sequence.

The fast and furious sport of flyball.

AGILITY, FLYBALL AND STRESS

As mentioned earlier in this chapter, some pursuits and competition environments will always be more stressful for collies, because their whole design has the capacity to cause either intense frustration (i.e. prolonged restriction of normal movement/behaviour), or extreme mental over-arousal, or both, in participating dogs.

Agility and Flyball are two more potentially stressful pastimes for collies. This is not just because of the physical demands of the pursuits themselves but also the kind of highly charged environments in which they tend to take place, with much surrounding noise and excitement generated by other people and dogs. This can act like a constant over-stimulatory tsunami washing over a dog's head.

Moreover, one of the biggest problems for enthusiasts of these more physically active/exciting pursuits is that the collies destined to be most successful at them – i.e. exceptionally fast, agile and mentally responsive – can also be those most vulnerable to any form of stress, and its mental and physical side-effects.

Much of this increased vulnerability to stress in collies may derive from the fact that they are highly sensitive to both noise and movement. They also traditionally existed in environments of relatively low external sensory input; i.e. remote rural hillsides, where the main focus for their finely tuned senses were the animals they worked. So if you put them in environments of excessive sensory input, in terms of noise, crowding and movement, their mental arousal mechanisms can hit maximum thrust, if not overload, very quickly.

HOW STRESS WORKS

There are many caring handlers in Agility today who not only acknowledge the issue of stress in their collies but also constantly strive to better understand it and keep it to a minimum.

Conversely, when owners flatly deny that their dogs suffer any stress at all from a particular pursuit, or pursuit environment, I do wonder if they really understand enough about the science of stress in animals, or the way it works.

They may link stress in their dogs, for example, only to more obvious outward symptoms, such as shaking/shivering, persistent whining, barking or spinning, extreme restlessness and agitation, hyper-reactivity and increased aggression.

Many dogs without these visible symptoms can still be undergoing intense stress, however. This is because a high amount of stress in animals is absorbed *sub consciously*; i.e. the senses send stress signals directly to the sub conscious mind, without an individual consciously being aware of it.

Thus, how stressed a dog looks or seems is never a reliable guide of how stressed he really is. The only way to know for sure would be to measure his cortisol – i.e. stress hormone – levels.

Note: There will be far more on the whole science of stress in dogs in Part Two under *Stress and stress related problems*, including fuller explanations of the physical/mental damage stress can do to dogs in both the shorter and longer term.

WHY COMPETITION STRESS CAN BE HARD TO PREVENT

Limiting dogs' stress levels at competitions, through giving them different self-calming/focus exercises to do, is often a desired goal by considerate handlers, and can certainly help to some degree.

The reason this is not always effective enough, however, as a stress-reducing strategy, goes back to the reality that how much stress any dog registers and absorbs from his external environment is not always something *he* can consciously control – let alone you.

In other words, a dog's effort of concentration on a handler's commands may make him *seem* calmer, but you are just engaging/distracting his *conscious* mind. You still cannot stop his senses sending environment-related stress information to his *sub-conscious* mind, and his body then processing all this on some deeper level.

Again, this is a subject covered in far greater depth in Part Two under *Stress and stress related problems*

EXCITEMENT

There can be a common misconception among many owners that 'excitement' is a 'good' or even 'healthy' thing for their dog to experience. But in fact it is just another form of stress, with no less harmful impact on him, physically and mentally - especially if sustained -than any other form of extreme mental/emotional arousal, such as terror, anxiety or panic.

Stress-wise, it is the intensity and duration of a dog's aroused mental state that are always the most critical factors; i.e. the greater your dog's excitement, and the longer he sustains the excited state, the greater stress his mind and body are placed under.

The more excited a collie gets, the more serious the risk can also be of triggering a condition called *Border Collie Collapse* (see Chapter Twelve, page 137), in dogs prone to this particular disorder.

INJURY

Another concern I have with collies and pursuits like Agility and Flyball is the risk of shorter or longer term physical injury. Because collies are often very driven dogs, producing high levels of adrenaline, they can have a tendency to readily work on through pain. I have seen collies try to keep working when they have a broken leg, or a major bowel bleed or have just fallen off a cliff, purely due to the influence of adrenaline.

This can make it harder for owners to realise when they may be pushing their dogs too far physically in training or competition. Of course, as ever, some handlers will always be far more considerate and mindful of these risks than others. Also see, *Reducing stress and injuries during competition*, page 196.

BEHAVIOUR CHANGES CAUSED BY PERPETUAL OVER-STIMULATION

The whole personality and behaviour of collies can sometimes change due to the persistent adrenaline flooding they get via Agility or Flyball training/competition. The dogs, for example, can become excessively excitable, reactive and lunge-nippy, and can generally find it far harder to mentally wind down.

This can particularly be the case with collies who are consistently over-competed/over trained. Veering from one activity-stimulated 'high' to another, the dogs can end up stuck in more permanently or longer term aroused state, unless much effort is made to wind them down again between training/competition sessions or events. Just as importantly, you must also stop them *self*-winding, between training/competition sessions, simply to keep the adrenaline 'buzz' alive (see *Self-stimulators*, Page 189.

If you do not let your collie's adrenaline levels adequately subside, from one highly exciting experience to the next, he will find it harder and harder to return, longer-term, to a truly balanced state, even when you are not working or competing him.

Also keep remembering that the Border Collie is designed to be a calm, focused, thinking dog 90 per cent of the time and an explosive athlete 10 per cent of the time, if not less.

So if your dog is continually a hyped up, yappy, over-excitable nutter, forever charging around like a deflating balloon, then something somewhere is definitely going wrong.

Some collies will always be more genetically prone than others to sustained or self-sustaining over-stimulation. These will always take more effort to keep in, or return to, a state of optimum mental balance. For more advice on this, see *Stress and stress-related problems*, Part Two, page 194.

MORE ENLIGHTENED THINKING

It really heartens me that today Agility handlers are taking training/competition stress exposure in their dogs far more seriously, and the issue is regularly discussed on the forums of popular websites such as *Agilitynet*.

There will always be a compromise to be made between stimulation – physical and mental – which is positively beneficial for collies, and that which is so excessive that it begins to do them harm. Anyone who loves both competitions, and their dogs, needs to be aware of these risks.

See *Reducing stress and injuries during competition*, page 196.

THE RIGHT TRAINER

In both Agility and Flyball, it is also essential to get help from a trainer who makes consideration for the physical and psychological welfare of dogs their highest priority. Finding exactly the right role model, training wise, for these kinds of pursuit can always make such a difference. For more advice on this, see *Finding the right expert help* in the *Further information section, page 199*.

WORKING TRIALS

Working Trials tends to be one of those activities that many collie owners have heard of, but never got round to trying; usually because of the relatively fewer number of WT events held in the UK compared to other canine pursuits. In other countries, WT events can be even harder to find, but it may be they will eventually get the Working Trials bug, in the same way they have embraced other competitive pursuits for dogs which originated elsewhere.

The easiest way to describe the sport of Working Trials is as a ladder of progressively more challenging stakes, each comprising groups of set exercises. These exercises, in turn, test the following skills in dogs (and likewise the skill of their handlers' training): agility, control and nosework.

The exercises in question were originally devised to test the qualities desired in German Shepherd Dogs. It was assumed that if a dog was able to carry out all of the working trials tests, he would be of sound temperament, have sufficient intelligence and be fit and healthy. Such dogs were also viewed as having the best potential in terms of future breeding stock. This same testing concept then spread in appeal to breeders of other breeds.

Today Working Trials are carried out under test conditions and open to all, providing competing dogs are over 18 months of age and entered on either the KC breed or Activity register. In the USA, there is a small following for the pursuit of Working Trials, but Tracking (nosework) is categorised as a separate activity under American Kennel Club rules and is popular among a wide variety of breeds, as well as collies.

There is a graduated progression through the WT stakes, and each stake comprises groups of exercises as follows:

COMPANION DOG (CD)

Group 1: *Control* exercises. These comprise basic heelwork, on and off lead, recall to handler, sendaway, and sit and down stays. The down stays are for ten minutes, with the dog out of sight of the handler.

Group 2. *Agility* exercises. There are three elements to this section. A clear jump (usually 3 ft/0.9m high), a long jump (usually 9 ft/2.7 metres long) and a 6 ft/1.8m scale.

Group 3: *Nosework:* This requires the location and retrieval of three articles bearing human scent from a marked out area 15 yards/14m square. The retrieval of a dumbbell is also included in this group in CD only.

Power, agility and focus – the Border Collie is the ultimate competition dog.

Note: Scent articles to recover in WT vary greatly but some examples are: a wooden clothes peg, plastic tie wrap, plastic bottle top, a door key, small piece of carpet or cloth and a piece of scouring pad. There is also a time limit set for the location of these items.

UTILITY DOG (UD) AND WORKING DOG (WD)

Control and Agility groups are basically the same as above; i.e. heel free, sendaway, retrieve a 10 minute down stay and steadiness to gunshot. Sometimes the gunshot test is carried out with the handler standing next to their dog, and sometimes whilst you are walking away from the judge with your dog. At other times you have to leave your dog some 10-15 paces away while the gun is fired.

Nosework consists of following the track of a human scent trail which is approximately half a mile long and the recovery of two articles placed on the line of the track, plus a search for and retrieval of four articles from a 25 yard square area. The UD track is half an hour old and the WD track is one and a half hours old.

TRACKING DOG (TD) AND PATROL DOG (PD)

In these, the nosework varies from the other stakes. The PD track has two articles to recover and is two hours old, and the TD track has three articles to recover and is three hours old.

The Control sections in these stakes vary as well. Both stakes have a 'speak on command' test in place of the retrieve, and the sendaway includes redirection(s) of the dog. The Patrol Dog stake also includes a patrol group, which tests the dog's ability to search for and locate people, plus test of courage exercises.

MARKS, QUALIFICATIONS AND ULTIMATE GOALS

In Working Trials dogs do not 'win out' of stakes in the way they might in other kinds of competition, like Obedience. They simply qualify in them.

You need 80 per cent of the total marks in each stake to gain either a Certificate of Merit at an Open Trial or a Certificate of Excellence at a Championship Trial. The latter allow the 'ex' suffix to be gained and placed against a dog's name – i.e. CDex through to TDex and PDex. This 'ex' in WT simply means 'achieving excellent'.

The ultimate goal for any trialist is to gain their dog(s) the coveted Working Trials Champion title. This is achieved by winning two Challenge Certificates at Championship Tracking Dog and/or Patrol Dog stakes.

THE REWARDS OF WORKING TRIALS

For most WT enthusiasts, the rewards of this pastime include the incredibly pleasant rural venues typically selected for trials, and the exceptional bond they build with their dogs through the training involved. Working trials take place in open country and can be completed over a day or several days. They also go ahead regardless of weather conditions, so you could find yourself tracking in glorious sunshine or in thick fog, wind and rain.

Working Trials also offer owners the chance to both test and stretch the limits of their dogs' capabilities; i.e. brain power, scent tracking skills, obedience skills and all round agility, athleticism and fitness. It is a pursuit for those who favour the collie as the calm, thinking dog of its original roots. In similar vein, levels of stress exhibited by collies attending WT events are virtually non-existent, compared to those evident in dogs undertaking some other competitive activities.

Because the emphasis in Working Trials – until the very highest level – is placed on people all qualifying their dogs in different stakes, as opposed to openly competing with each other, it can lead to a greater sense of camaraderie and mutual support among trialists.

COLLIES AND WORKING TRIALS

Anyone interested in training their collie for Working Trials would be well advised, from the outset, to get help from expert instructors who know both the collie breed, and the

REDUCING STRESS AND INJURIES DURING COMPETITIONS

The level of stress an individual collie will experience at a competition will be down to many different factors, beginning with his own genetic temperament and how much psychological preparation he has had or not, since puppyhood, to cope with the demands of the competition environment (as highlighted earlier in this chapter).

Dogs with inadequate early socialisation will always react more adversely to show environments, as will those on whom intense extra pressure is placed by handlers. Either of these factors can inflict the stress responsible for dogs doing things such as running out of a competition ring, or shutting down from handlers and avoiding eye contact with them during a competition round.

The general atmosphere of a competition venue can also be very relevant; i.e. how much noise/stress-related behaviour is being exhibited by other dogs. Much of the barking/whining heard from collies at shows derives from simple frustration. They get wound up by the pressures of their immediate environment, and then have nowhere for this built-up tension to go, other than in animated vocalisation.

To reduce such tension, it is incredibly important to present competitions to your dog as part of an overall fun day out for him, as opposed to tedious ordeals to be survived rather than enjoyed.

Rather than leaving your dog in a car for lengthy periods, or just aimlessly standing around, keep your dog as mentally and physically occupied as possible, in between performance rounds or sessions. Give him lots of short, but fun, training tasks to keep his concentration high and play games with him. When possible, keep removing him from the show venue so he can wind down again. Let him explore the surrounding countryside; this will be new and exciting for him and do much to disperse built up inner stress.

All in all, be aware that how positive, or negative, you render the whole competition experience to your collie, from day one, will greatly influence his attitude to all subsequent events – as well as his prevailing levels of stress when attending them.

Also see *Overactivity and the risks for collies*, page 138.

It is to be hoped that any owner involving their dog in more active pursuits, such as Agility or Flyball, will have first ensured he is sufficiently fit, and thus well able to cope with the physical demands of such sports.

Less fit, or overweight dogs, on the other hand, carry a far higher risk of getting injured. Dogs who are consistently over-trained in such demanding pursuits, prior to competition, can also carry a higher risk of injury. With all canine athletes there can be a fine line between optimum fitness and a dog's muscles, tendons, joints, spine and immune system being put under excessive strain.

Dogs who are injured do not always appear so until their adrenaline levels subside. Similarly, initial strains or sprains in dogs that could progress on to more serious injuries will not always be immediately apparent. So get into the habit of regularly feeling your dog all over during both training and competition. Feel particularly for tender spots that your dog reacts to when you touch them, or areas around joints or the neck and spine that are noticeably warmer than other parts of the body, suggesting inflammation. Stop any training immediately if this happens, and seek veterinary advice.

Also be aware that today's unresolved, or inadequately addressed, injury in a dog can be a source of more chronic and painful arthritis in older age.

Physical injury/discomfort issues do not just exist in Agility or Flyball dogs. It's very common, for instance, for Obedience collies to suffer aches and strains in their necks and spines as a result of the more unnatural 'head up and back' position they have to sustain in heelwork. Anyone who has ever painted a ceiling knows exactly what this feels like. Thus, it is a good idea to thoroughly massage your dog's neck, shoulders and back after any heelwork session, to relieve any built-up tension.

relevant WT exercises, inside out. One of the best-known trainers of this kind, in the UK, is Wendy Beasley.

Wendy has owned, worked and bred Border Collies for 35 years. During that time she has won 10 WT Challenge Certificates (or tickets), 10 Reserve CCs with her dog, WT Ch. Bridgalpine Libra of Stardell, now retired, who is the highest winning PD bitch of all time, and has won six WT Challenge Certificates, and six Reserve CCs with her current dog WT CH Glenalpine Phoebe of Stardell. She is also the author of *A Beginner's Guide to Working Trials* (TFH books).

GETTING INVOLVED

Hopefully readers will gain some incredibly valuable insights into Working Trials training with collies, via Wendy's expertise. There are a number of WT clubs throughout the country that not only host trials, but also hold training sessions. For more inforamtion on this, see *Finding the Right Help*, page 199 and and *Useful Addresses*, page 202.

SHEEP WORK

Finally, as a choice of alternative activity for your collie, why not take him back to his working roots? Giving a companion collie the chance to test his working ability with sheep is now becoming an increasingly popular pastime among owners. Many shepherds and sheepdog trainers now run special courses with this aim in mind. Via their guidance you should be able to discover how much natural ability your dog has, or not, for livestock work as well as training techniques shepherds use to get the best out of their dogs.

Many people find these courses a highly enjoyable and educational experience for themselves and their dogs alike. As shepherds and farmers have been breeding, working and living with these dogs for eons longer than anybody else,

they can also often offer a particularly profound understanding of the breed.

For more details on these courses see pages 199 and 200.

COMPETITIONS AND US

Throughout this chapter I have looked at what can be involved in training collies for different pursuits while, hopefully, also making owners think harder about the potential downsides, as well as benefits, attached to different competitive pastimes.

Amid the pleasure of our own enjoyment, it can be easy to overlook the reality that dog competitions, of any kind, are a purely human invention, designed mainly for the benefit of humans, which we consciously choose to do. We do not give our dogs the same choices in this matter and, similarly, the prizes we may strive so hungrily or obsessively to obtain in competition, are totally meaningless to them.

Over the years I have seen brilliant dogs handled by equally brilliant, caring trainers in competitions. But I have also seen many dogs treated appallingly by owners, purely as a result of their own need to win things, and feel better about themselves. It is important to understand how the pressures of competition and ambition can change us all – sometimes making us that little bit blinder to the best interests of our dogs.

It is always possible to train for, and compete in, different pursuits while never losing respect for your dog and his physical/psychological wellbeing. In fact, the more respect you have for your dog, the better his performance can only be. The moment, by contrast, you think his overall welfare or happiness is ever less important than a piece of red ribbon and tin on your mantelpiece, is the moment, competition-wise, where you have definitely lost the plot.

Sheepdog trials allow a collie to use his natural talents.

Chapter Twelve

BORDER COLLIE HEALTH

Breed specific health problems and health screening; optimum diet and exercise to keep your dog's mind and body in perfect shape

Border Collies, certainly compared to many other pedigree breeds today, are pretty healthy dogs. Much of this is to do with them descending from a relatively large and diverse gene base. It is also to do with their long historical background as working dogs.

Our modern collies' ancestors were bred with a somewhat Darwinian ruthlessness, in the sense that only the genes of the fittest, fastest and smartest dogs survived. Farmers and shepherds could not afford to keep collies with anything other than the physical and mental ability to be good sheepdogs. Anything that was less up to the grade, on this front, was likely to be culled.

This said, collies today can still suffer a range of inherited health disorders. Sometimes these are purely the result of less scrupulous breeding practices, as outlined in Chapter Three. At other times – and certainly where disorders have a far more complex, or erratic, mode of inheritance – they can be more the result of sheer bad luck. In other words, a breeder could not know, or predict, that a specific fault would be passed on by two

dogs prior to mating them.

The advent of DNA testing to better identify genetic faults carried in dogs has been incredibly useful in this respect. Later on in this chapter (see, *Can you help?*, page 138), I will also be highlighting how readers can help ongoing research into collie health disorders through taking part in DNA testing programmes themselves.

Now let us look at these disorders in greater detail. As they can be life quality diminishing, if not life-threatening, to your dog, you need to be aware of them, as well as what steps – if any – can be taken to prevent them.

TRAPPED NEUTROPHIL SYNDROME (TNS)

TNS is an inherited disorder of the immune system. Puppies are born with it and then their health progressively deteriorates. Symptoms, which can be seen in puppies who are only weeks' old, include poor growth, lack of appetite, vomiting and lameness. The disorder essentially revolves around a very poor immune response and is invariably fatal, with few puppies making it much beyond six or seven months of age.

CAN DNA TESTING GIVE US FAULT-FREE COLLIES?

Due to the often complex nature of genetic inheritance, it has always been possible in the past to put two seemingly highly sound dogs together and have them produce puppies which are less sound, as any breeder knows. But today we now have the added advantage of DNA testing to reduce such risks.

Even as I write, new DNA tests are being devised to establish whether or not dogs are carriers of different disorders, even if they do not suffer from these disorders themselves. DNA testing can even predict what coat length or colour dogs' offspring are likely to have.

In theory, you might imagine that DNA testing could eventually lead us to future generations of collies in whom all faults have been eradicated, through more intensely selective breeding. In reality, this is a nigh impossible goal to achieve.

First, because most, if not all, pedigree dogs carry a mixture of both good and less good genetic traits. So if you exclude from breeding any dog who carries a known genetic fault, you also lose all his or her good traits from the overall breed gene pool.

Second, because genes keep changing all the time, over successive generations. In other words, every time two dogs have puppies these puppies will develop and carry on new genetic mutations that their parents did not have. This is all part of the natural evolutionary process.

Finally, in narrowing your breeding of collies down to those who do not carry specific identified faults you eventually encounter another problem; i.e., a higher level of inbreeding which, in turn, could lead to the development of new genetic faults or defects.

The skill of breeding good dogs has always been in choosing dams and sires who cancel out each other's genetic faults as successfully as possible, i.e. they do not both carry, or pass on, the same genetic faults to their offspring. DNA testing, therefore, should be viewed as a fantastically helpful tool in the perpetuation of this process, but never as the ultimate solution to all genetic faults in dogs.

Meanwhile, genetic conditions in collies for which DNA tests are now available are outlined in this chapter.

WHERE CAN YOU GET A DNA TEST DONE?

Your vet can normally arrange a DNA test for your dog, for a range of different conditions. Such tests are also often organised by different collie breed clubs or societies.

A lot of canine DNA testing will be done by private laboratories or firms who advertise their services on the Internet. Whatever DNA test you are interested in having done, do first check that both the results and the firm undertaking the testing are recognised and accepted by your governing national Kennel Club or authority.

Having a puppy with TNS can be devastating for owners. The best way to prevent this happening to you is to ensure that parents of your puppy have been screened TNS clear through DNA testing which is now available.

EYE CONDITIONS

Eye conditions in dogs can often have a quite complex mode of inheritance – i.e. skip generations and then recur – or not become apparent in some dogs until later life. These possibilities mean that dogs may carry eye problems, despite being tested unaffected by them via physical (i.e. ophthalmoscope) examination. Similarly, some seemingly normal dogs may have been bred from before their eye problems developed or became more obviously apparent.

With the advent of DNA research, it is now becoming clear that health problems which were previously thought to have the same causes and symptoms in all breeds, are also somewhat more complicated.

In other words, not only will different breeds have their own specific form of a certain defect, but it may also be caused by different factors in different breeds – be these genetic, environmental (e.g. diet-related) or a complex combination of both. Moreover, in different breeds different genes may be responsible for conditions with similar symptoms.

Clearly DNA research still has some way to go before it more fully unravels all these mysteries relating to canine health. When it comes to eye conditions in collies, without doubt better physical screening practices in past years have done much to reduce their incidence. But the future way forward for eliminating them even further may lie more in DNA testing than the ophthalmoscope.

Let us now look at inherited eye conditions in Border Collies in more detail.

COLLIE EYE ANOMALY (CEA)

This is an inherited congenital disease of both eyes, whose inner structures improperly develop. In more severe cases it can lead to blindness. Traditionally, good breeders would screen their litters for this condition at around six to seven weeks of age when it is most readily seen. The inspection is done by a veterinary eye specialist. This physical test can tell you which puppies are unaffected by CEA, but not those who may be carriers of the condition.

Nowadays a DNA test is also available to tell you which dogs are CEA clear – i.e. neither affected by, nor carriers of, the condition. If you get a puppy that has been physically eye-tested for CEA (as opposed to DNA tested) and passed 'unaffected', make sure his whole litter has also been passed as unaffected. This lowers the chance of your puppy being a carrier of CEA, though it still cannot completely rule it out.

If both your puppy's parents have been DNA tested CEA clear, he will neither have nor carry the condition.

CENTRAL PROGRESSIVE RETINAL ATROPHY (CPRA)/RETINAL PIGMENT EPITHELIAL DYSTROPHY (RPED)

Central Progressive Retinal Atrophy is an inherited eye disorder that usually becomes apparent when dogs are around two to six years old. It is caused by defects in retinal structure and, because of its typical later onset cannot, unlike CEA, be tested for in puppies. The condition is typically characterised by a dog being unable to see stationary objects well, and also by his seeming ability to see better in dimmer light conditions. As its name suggests, the disorder causes progressive deterioration in a dog's eyesight and in some cases can lead to blindness.

Note: Veterinary eye specialists have just reclassified CPRA in collies as a condition known instead as Retinal Pigment Epithelial Dystrophy (RPED). As I write there is no DNA test for CPRA/RPED in collies, although it is, hopefully, in the pipeline. Currently the best way to minimise its occurrence in future dogs is to have all breeding stock regularly screened for it via expert ophthalmic examination. As dogs can develop CPRA/RPED at any age between 18 months and nine years, most reputable breeders will test their breeding stock annually.

PRIMARY LENS LUXATION (PLL)

This is a condition in collies caused by a weakening in the ligament holding the lens in the centre of the eye. This results in the lens subsequently slipping or displacing, causing light sensitivity, excessive tear production and eyelid spasms caused by acute pain.

PLL symptoms are first usually seen in dogs when they are around three to seven years of age. Without surgical intervention to remove the lens from the eye, the dog may be in persistent pain and go on to develop secondary glaucoma or blindness.

Sometimes PLL affects both eyes in a dog, one in advance of the other. As with CPRA, dogs can be routinely screened for this condition via physical examination before being bred from. A DNA test for this condition is also available.

GLAUCOMA

Primary glaucoma – as opposed to the secondary kind, which can be caused by factors including trauma, injury, infections or Primary Lens Luxation (previously mentioned) – is a condition that can be seen in Border Collies, albeit relatively rarely, from puppyhood onwards. Collies can now by tested (Gonioscopy) for a predisposition to glaucoma, which appears more prevalent in NZ/Australian breeding lines. It is wise to get a puppy only from screened 'clear' parents.

The more strongly disposed a dog is towards glaucoma, genetically, the earlier on in life he may develop it.

What causes it?
Glaucoma basically results from pressure building up in an

eyeball – or both eyeballs – as a result of a fluid imbalance. The fluid in question is called aqueous humour, which is essential to retain the eye's shape. The body is constantly adding to, and draining away, this fluid inside the eyeball in order to keep its internal pressure at an optimum level.

In some individuals, however, the pressure within the eyeball gets too high, usually as a result of some fault in the draining procedure. If not immediately addressed, this pressure build-up can then start damaging the eye's internal structures – such as the retina and optic nerve – and culminate in permanent vision loss or blindness. Glaucoma can also be an incredibly painful condition for dogs.

Because so many owners consider glaucoma to be an older dog's problem, they might not be alert to its earliest symptoms in a younger dog or even a puppy. Yet the earlier you spot the first signs of glaucoma in a dog of any age, the faster you can halt its progress with appropriate veterinary treatment, and also save your dog's sight. Similarly, you will spare him considerable pain.

Signs and symptoms

Earliest signs of glaucoma in dogs can be similar to those of PLL and include the dog constantly squinting or rubbing his eye with a paw due to pain and excessive tear production. This apart, the dog may have a dilated pupil in the affected eye, and specifically red and pronounced blood vessels running across the white of his eye – not to be confused with the more extensive redness of entire eye whites caused by problems like conjunctivitis. As soon as you see any of these symptoms get your dog to a vet immediately for treatment. Once glaucoma becomes far more noticeable – i.e. there is a marked bulging out and cloudiness of the eye – the damage to the dog's sight has usually already been done.

Also note that once a dog has had glaucoma in one eye, he may well get it in the other – even if this is months or even years later. As I write, no DNA test is yet available for glaucoma in collies. Many experts also believe the condition can have a highly complex mode of inheritance, with potentially more than one gene being involved.

CONGENITAL DEAFNESS

Collies, in common with other breeds featuring larger amounts of white coat pigment, can be prone to congenital deafness; there is a recognised genetic link between these two things. Generally the more white there is in a collie's coat, the higher the risk of deafness can be, but this rule is not hard and fast.

Deafness is one of those faults that can pop up intermittently in lines of collies, even from parents who are sound of hearing. This is why many good breeders hearing-test their puppies, before selling them, to be on the safe side. If you have any concerns about the hearing of your puppy before getting him, make sure he has undergone an

official BAER (Brainstem auditory evoked response) test, run by specialists, to rule out deafness in one or both ears.

LATER ONSET DEAFNESS

Over and above congenital deafness, there now seems to be another form of later onset deafness in collies, which appears to affect their hearing around four to six years of age – not to be confused with the normal hearing loss that affects dogs in older age.

The deafness in question appears to be hereditary and can affect one or both ears and results in a varying degree of hearing loss. Research is currently underway to establish a DNA test for this particular hearing loss condition in collies. Once again see, *Can you help?* p138, if you are interested in taking part in this research with your own dog.

MANAGING COLLIES WITH POORER SIGHT OR HEARING

If you are unlucky enough to acquire a dog with impaired sight or hearing, keep remembering how often nature compensates when one faculty is compromised. In other words, if your dog's sight is bad his hearing may well have become sharper. This means you will have to put far more emphasis on verbal commands in training.

With blind, or visually impaired, dogs it is also very important to keep the layout of your home, or your dog's living environment, exactly the same. This is because, over time, dogs who cannot see well make a mental map in their heads of where different objects are – such as furniture, water/food bowls or doorways – which enables them to navigate them.

If, by contrast, your dog's hearing is poor or non-existent, his sight can still be good. This means you will need to put far more emphasis on physical body signals in training. Many deaf dogs can also get very good at lip reading, if you shape words for commands in your mouth very clearly. Some of the verbal and body signal cues you can use for training visually or hearing limited dogs are outlined in Chapter Five, but you can also adapt these to best suit your own collie, as many owners do.

Some deaf/visually impaired collies become so clever at compensating for their disability that it takes owners some time to realise the full extent of their problem. Your dog's safety, however, remains important if he cannot see or hear well. So it is sensible to keep him on a long line when you go out, particularly in an area where he could easily get lost or find his way into danger.

HIP DYSPLASIA

Hip Dysplasia is one of the commonest inherited diseases in dogs. Basically the structure of one, or both, hips are malconstructed, causing significant pain, discomfort and reduced movement as the dog grows older.

In a normal, healthy dog the ball at the top of the femur (thigh) bone is well rounded and fits smoothly and snugly into the pelvic socket, allowing ease and comfort of movement. In a dog with Hip Dysplasia, the pelvic socket it too shallow and the head of the femur distorted, leading to slack surrounding ligaments and excessive movement within the joint. This is what causes the pain and leads to subsequent arthritis.

Early signs of HD can be seen in puppies of around five months onwards. They may show discomfort jumping or getting up from a sitting position. When running they may also adopt a bunny hop with their back legs. In less extreme cases, owners may not even realise their collies have HD because this breed can be so good at masking the condition, or adapting to it. In more extreme cases, the dog may have difficultly even walking. A veterinary X-ray usually confirms the diagnosis.

Dogs with HD will need very careful management throughout their lives, particularly in terms of keeping their weight down, and arranging the most beneficial type of exercise programme for them. Hydrotherapy can also be very useful.

The best way to minimise the chances of your collie having HD is to ensure that both his parents had good hip scores.

HIP SCORING

In a bid to limit Hip Dysplasia in pedigree breeding stock, the British Veterinary Association and UK Kennel Club run a special hip scoring scheme. A vet will submit an X-ray of a dog's hips to a special BVA panel, which then grades the quality of each hip's construction on a points basis ranging from 0 to 53; the lower the score the better. A perfect hip is '0'. The points for both hips are then added together for a final score.

Perfect hips, therefore, will score 0:0 – or a total of 0. The worst hips will score 53:53 – or a total of 106. Each pedigree breed will also have an 'average' score which dogs should either be around or ideally well below. In Border Collies this is a total of 13 for both hips. When choosing a puppy, ideally look for scores of below 13 in both his parents.

Note: In the UK, Ireland, Australia and New Zealand, scoring for canine HD/OCD is undertaken via the above KC/BVA scheme. Throughout most of Europe it will be run by the FCI (Federation Cynologique Internationale) and in the USA and Canada, by the Orthopedic (note•US spelling) Foundation for Animals (OFA). Different schemes will also grade the quality of hips/elbows in different ways.

OSTEOCHONDRITIS DESSICANS (OCD)

Osteochondritis Dessicans is another developmental disorder that most commonly affects the shoulders and elbows of growing dogs of about four to nine months of age. Although it has a hereditary factor, it can be greatly worsened by a wrong diet (i.e. one that promotes over-rapid growth or has inappropriate additional mineral supplements, like calcium) and excessive exercise in late puppyhood.

In growing dogs, cartilage plates on the joint surfaces of limb bones eventually convert and harden into bone. When a dog has OCD, instead of converting into bone, this cartilage just grows thicker and thicker and then cracks when the joint is under stress. Eventually a piece of cartilage can break free from underlying bone, then lie loose within a joint capsule and cause pain and lameness. A surgical operation is usually required to remove this.

OCD is less common in collies than HD, but prior to being bred from, adult dogs can be elbow-scored – much as with hip scoring – to test their predisposition towards this problem. Bodies governing OCD scoring are the same as those mentioned under Hip Scoring.

CEROID LIPOFUSCINOSIS (CL OR BATTEN'S DISEASE)

CL is a relatively rare disease in Border Collies. Similar to Batten's disease in humans, it usually develops in dogs of around 16 to 24 months of age and involves a progressive degeneration of brain and eye cells. Symptoms include muscle weakness, seizures and cognitive dysfunction. Affected dogs rarely live much beyond two years of age, depending on how old the dog is when symptoms first appear.

There is no cure as yet for the disease, but a DNA test is now available in several countries to detect the gene responsible for it. Many breeders are now DNA testing their dogs for CL before breeding from them.

EPILEPSY

There can be many different triggers for epilepsy in all dogs, ranging from an underactive thyroid and the distemper virus to poisoning and a brain injury or tumour. Additionally, however, there is an inherited form of the condition, usually referred to as primary epilepsy. Border Collies, like many other dog breeds, can be affected by this.

Primary epilepsy commonly starts to manifest itself in collies between one and four years of age, although later onsets, and very varying symptoms, can occur. As I write (see, *Can you help?, page 138*), research is underway to pinpoint the gene, or genetic mutation, responsible for primary epilepsy in Border Collies. Should they be able to isolate it, and then form a DNA test to screen for it in individual dogs, this would be a massive breakthrough.

Until that day comes, far more responsible breeding practices are the key. Dogs who either have primary epilepsy, or have immediate relatives with the condition,

MANAGEMENT OF THE EPILEPTIC DOG

For owners with no previous knowledge of epilepsy in dogs, a first fit can be a very alarming experience, depending on its severity. As with humans, there can be *petit mal* attacks, localised to just one part of the brain. Less severe, they manifest themselves in a host of symptoms ranging from a noted mental absence, leg twitching or a sudden personality change and bouts of uncontrollable barking.

Grand mal fits, affecting the whole brain, will be more dramatic and unmistakable, most often happening when the dog is at rest – though they should not be confused with a dog who is simply twitching normally and flickering his eyes as a result of dreaming in his sleep.

Symptoms include loss of bladder and bowel control. The dog may chomp his jaws and salivate profusely while his lips are drawn back. There may also be an open but unseeing look in his eyes and rigid, paddling movements made with his legs.

Fits can be highly unpredictable in frequency and severity, but owners will need to learn to keep a cool head while such attacks are going on (usually for two to five minutes). Any excess noise (e.g. music, T.V.) and light in the surrounding environment should be reduced and care should be taken to ensure that the dog cannot damage himself on any nearby hard or sharp objects. Do not try to sit your dog up or pull his tongue out of his mouth, as this could result in you being bitten.

Medication today can do much to improve the life quality of epileptic dogs. There is also much more advice available to owners of epileptic dogs; see the Further information section in Part Two, page 201, for more details.

should never be bred from, regardless of what else they might have going for them. Just this one step, in itself, could have saved so many dogs and owners an awful lot of suffering.

SHADOW CHASING

Shadow chasing – where a dog obsessively fixates on light beams or shadows – is often classed as a behavioural issue stemming from factors such as boredom or under-stimulation, whereas I tend to think of it more as an inherited psychological disorder.

As highlighted in Chapter Two, there is no doubt the habit runs in certain lines of dogs, so is likely to have a genetic root. The level of compulsiveness involved in this behaviour also puts it more on a par with other forms of OCD (Obsessive Compulsive Disorder). Humans with OCD are not readily deemed to be suffering from boredom or under stimulation, but psychological urges and impulses which they find highly difficult to control. Why shouldn't dogs be the same?

My personal instinct is not to want to own, or breed from, a dog who shadow chases or who features dogs with this

habit in his immediate lines. Meanwhile, advice on how to tackle more obsessive behaviour patterns in Collies appears in Part Two, page 180.

MALIGNANT HYPERTHERMIA (MH)

Malignant hyperthermia, also often termed 'canine stress syndrome', is a disorder that's genetically predisposed in certain dogs – Labrador Retrievers being a particularly common example. MH is rooted in a fault in the gene governing the release of calcium into a dog's metabolism. This, in turn, makes the metabolism work abnormally when challenged by specific stresses or triggers – e.g. over-exercise, sudden excitement, certain drugs, eating or fasting.

Typically, the dog overheats, may pant heavily and also display a range of other symptoms such as stiffness of the muscles, muscle tremors, eye pupil dilation, irregular heartbeat and seizures or collapse. Dogs with MH are also a very high anaesthetic risk, and the condition can be fatal.

Traditionally, Border Collies have also been thought to suffer from MH. But there is now some scientific opinion that many collies previously diagnosed with MH, or thought to suffer it,

CAN YOU HELP?

Research is currently underway in the UK and USA to establish the gene mutation responsible for the following conditions in collies: primary epilepsy, Border Collie Collapse (BCC) and later onset deafness. Research into the genetic link with epilepsy is being carried out by the Animal Health Trust in the UK; the link with BCC is being investigated by the University of Minnesota in the USA, and the link with later onset deafness by the University of California-Davis in the USA. In all cases researchers will need DNA samples from dogs affected by the relevant conditions. Details on how you can submit samples, and find out more about the research, are listed in the Further information section in Part Two, page 199.

are actually affected by a different condition that is much more breed specific – Border Collie Collapse (BCC).

A diagnosis of MH is usually made by testing a dog's response to substances such as caffeine or halothane (anaesthetic gas) – both of which are known to trigger MH symptoms. If your dog has the condition, he will need very careful management. Stress and exercise levels must be strictly controlled, and similarly his feeding regime. Your vet can best advise you on what other treatment options are available.

BORDER COLLIE COLLAPSE (BCC)

As previously stated, many collies may be diagnosed with the relatively rare condition of MH when, in fact, they are suffering from Border Collie Collapse; a more breed-specific condition recently identified by the College of Veterinary Medicine at the University of Minnesota in the USA.

BCC, in the past, was also thought to be the same as Exercise Induced Collapse (EIC), a disorder commonly found in Labradors and other retriever breeds, as the symptoms appear so similar; i.e., after a relatively short period of strenuous or excitement-inducing activity, the dog collapses, appears over-heated and loses normal muscle function.

It has since been discovered that the genetic fault responsible for EIC in other breeds was not present in Border Collies suffering similar symptoms. Thus, research is

currently ongoing to isolate a different genetic trigger for the problem in this breed.

Collies affected by BCC may also suddenly collapse after 5-15 minutes of strenuous/exciting activity, in an over-heated state, and develop a stiff, stilted gait. They may also seem dazed or confused and wobble as if drunk. Some dogs are even unable to walk. The symptoms can worsen around five minutes *after* a dog has ceased exercise and, typically, they will last for up to 30 minutes, after which the dog seems perfectly normal again.

The problem seems most common in more excitable, driven collies, and those training for Agility and Flyball competitions. It is also more likely to occur in warmer weather. Treatment for BCC, other than minimising physical and mental stress in affected dogs, is currently limited until its exact cause is better established. *Also see Can you help?*

OVERACTIVITY AND THE RISKS FOR COLLIES

Due to the essentially keen nature of many collies, there can be a tendency for owners not to realise when they are over-taxing their dogs, both physically and mentally. This can particularly be the case in pursuits like Agility and Flyball, or when owners make their dogs run back and forth non-stop after a ball. The dogs become excessively excited and, as a result, may often work through pain.

As highlighted in the last chapter, dogs who are perpetually aroused in this way can also become highly stressed. This, in turn, makes their immune systems more vulnerable and increases the chance of developing illnesses and skin and digestive problems.

The body and mind of the Border Collie combine to form a highly sensitive machine. It is not a machine designed to work flat out for prolonged periods, with the body working at full throttle and the brain in virtual meltdown It is designed, instead, to glide smoothly from calm thinking to limited and calculated athletic activity, and then back to calm thinking again. The more you mess up this ideal balance, the more problems can arise in your dog.

Also be alert to some of the more serious disorders that can affect collies when stressed. If your dog shows any symptoms of Border Collie Collapse (see page 137), it is imperative that you immediately cease all strenuous or exciting exercise and get him checked out by a vet. Failure to do so may have fatal consequences.

THE MDR GENE DEFECT

Some collies can be born with a defective gene which makes them more vulnerable to the effects of certain drugs, toxins or parasitical treatments. The gene in question is the Multi Drug Resistant (MDR) one. Normally this gene is responsible for pumping toxins away from the brain, but a fault in it makes the brain membrane more permeable, allowing these substances to get through.

Ivermectin, a strong parasitical treatment, can have a particularly harmful effect on dogs with a faulty MDR gene. In some cases it can lead to them entering a coma, or even dying. Other medications, including those used to treat diarrhoea in humans, can have a similarly adverse effect.

The trouble with the faulty MDR gene in collies, to date, has been that its existence would always be discovered too late – i.e. *after* the dog has had an adverse reaction to a particular drug or toxin. There is now a DNA test to screen for it. It is particularly wise to screen dogs who come from lines in which this problem has previously been seen. Also see, *Additives, medications and the collie brain, page 140.*

SKIN AND DIGESTIVE PROBLEMS

It is often said that collies, as a breed, are prone to skin and digestive problems. But the same can be said for most of dogdom these days. In fact, the number of dogs from all breeds who are beset by some level of skin irritation or digestive dysfunction seems to have hit epidemic proportions.

My feeling about collies is that, just like other breeds, there are some dogs whose skin or digestive problems have a major genetic factor, over and above what external trigger exacerbates them. In other dogs the genetic factor may be less significant than the environmental trigger.

IMMUNE MALFUNCTION

Skin and digestive problems can be most severe in dogs who have some fundamental immune system malfunction. This usually has a genetic root, and is of a kind that causes the body to over-react to different environmental stimuli, or simply start attacking itself, as is the case with most auto-immune conditions.

Problems like these will be typified by persistent symptoms; e.g. in skin conditions, constant scratching until the skin becomes raw. Some auto-immune-related skin conditions, like pemphigus, can also cause an eruption of sores around the eyes, nose and mouth.

Auto-immune digestive disorders often result in chronic loose motions and/or diarrhoea. The symptoms of auto-immune-related skin conditions tend to continue even when a range of common irritants such as fleas or mange mites have been excluded. Auto-immune digestive problems can similarly persist even when the dog is placed on a very bland diet.

All in all, owners can often drive themselves mad trying to isolate the one environmental or dietary factor that is giving their dog so much skin or digestive trouble when, in fact, the most relevant factor of all is usually the abnormal functioning of their dog's immune system.

It is likely that dogs with such immune response problems will be put on courses of steroids at some time in their lives,

if only to give them some respite from symptoms. In the future the genetic fault responsible for more severe skin and digestive problems in dogs may well be isolated. If so, it would have a major beneficial effect on the life quality of later generations.

EXTERNAL TRIGGERS FOR SKIN PROBLEMS

Collies whose skin/digestive problems are related more to specific external triggers than an inherently malfunctioning immune response are easier to treat, providing you are able to isolate and eliminate the triggers in question.

Fleas remain one of the commonest sources of excessive itching in dogs. This is because most domestic dogs these days are infested by cat fleas – dog fleas now being that much rarer. As dogs are not naturally evolved hosts for these fleas, they can have a higher tendency to react adversely to their saliva, when bitten.

It is not always easy to know if your dog is infested with fleas, as only a small number of these minute parasites will remain on his body; the majority will be hiding in carpets, soft furnishing, bedding or cracks between walls and floors.

A sure test is to go over your dog with a fine flea comb, and tip all the coat debris you accumulate onto a damp piece of kitchen towel. You may see small brown specs that turn a rusty red when they land on the damp paper. These are flea droppings which mean, in short, that your dog has fleas.

MITES

Mange mites can also cause intense itching in dogs. Vets can test for the presence of these via skin scrapings and provide relevant treatment. Mites which cause mange in dogs are the *sarcoptic* and *demodex* varieties. Sarcoptic mites are generally picked up by dogs from the external environment – foxes being common carriers. Demodex mites, by contrast, are something dogs are usually born with, having picked them up from their mothers. With demodectic mange, the problem is less the mite itself but the dog's inability to mount a suitably strong immune response to eradicate it.

If you are going to treat your dog for fleas or mange mites then *please do be mindful of the risks some stronger parasitical remedies can pose to collies,* particularly if they are affected by the previously outlined faulty MDR gene. It may be something worth discussing with your vet prior to treatment.

HOUSEHOLD AND OTHER ENVIRONMENTAL IRRITANTS

If your dog continues to itch even after parasites have been investigated and, where necessary, treated, you should next consider whether some household product – such as air freshener or washing powder – could be the cause. If your dog only started itching after you introduced a new product of this kind, stop using it.

Like us, dogs can also have an adverse reaction to dust mites, or develop seasonal allergies to things like pollen or

ADDITIVES, MEDICATIONS AND THE COLLIE BRAIN

Readers should now be well aware of how the collie's highly responsive/reactive brain processes drive his character and behaviour. But the sensitive neurochemistry and metabolism of the collie can also react adversely to a wide number of environmental or ingested substances, ranging from insecticides and food additives to common medications.

Over the years I have seen many collies react badly – either psychologically or physically – to the ingestion of specific food colourings or other artificial additives; the symptoms stopping each time the causative ingredient was no longer given to the dog. This is why it is a good idea never to give your collie food – including treats – which contains such additives.

Some collies can also have adverse, or unexpected, reactions to different kinds of veterinary medication, including those that are commonly prescribed. The same is true of different food or mineral supplements. The dogs in question are not necessarily those who have a faulty MDR gene (see page 138). Sometimes it is the added colouring in, or even coating of, a drug or food/vitamin supplement that is causing more of a problem than the main substance itself.

Either way, do employ caution when introducing your collie to new medication or a supplement, and cease giving it the moment you see any adverse effects in him – be these behavioural (e.g. dog increasingly listless, disorientated or hyper), or physical (e.g. dog vomiting or hunched up with abdominal pain).

Please also be aware of how dangerous it can be to give dogs – and the collie breed in particular – medication designed for human consumption. Never give your dog any kind of medication without first clearing it with your vet.

moulds. Vets can now do allergy screening tests to tell you which substances are most likely to make your dog scratch and nibble his skin. Sometimes it can be hard, if not impossible, to totally exclude from your dog's life all the things that might make him itch and scratch. The option of antihistamine or steroid drugs are available to help treat this problem, but I would only go down this route if symptoms are particularly severe, which is a good general rule when it comes to collies and medication. .

LICK GRANULOMA
Lick granuloma – or lick dermatitis – is a condition seen in many breeds, but one I have also witnessed in a number of collies.

Basically the dog starts licking one, or both, forelegs continually until the hair is removed and the skin underneath becomes red, shiny and raw. In more extreme cases, further mutilation occurs and/or a serious infection sets in.

This problem is quite complex, because it tends to have both physical and psychological components. Typically, it will begin with some allergy or trauma related irritation to a leg or paw, which the dog licks. Because paw or leg licking then releases dopamine, the feel-good chemical, into his brain, a dog can rapidly find this activity highly addictive. Paw or leg licking can also become a comfort strategy a dog resorts to whenever he feels bored, anxious or frustrated.

In older dogs, constant paw licking can be a way to displace feelings of pain caused by chronic arthritis or other ailments. Like human nail-biting or thumb-sucking, once started, paw licking/chewing can become hideously compulsive for a dog – to the extent that he will not even stop when he has caused himself significant injury.

Treatment
Over the years, I have found the best way to deal with this problem is as follows:
- *First:* Spot more compulsive paw licking/chewing in your dog as early as possible. It is staggering how much mutilation a dog can inflict on a leg or paw before some

owners notice it. Additionally, the more damage your dog does to his paws, or legs, through this habit, the harder it can be to remedy; especially in situations where subsequent infection permeates through all layers of skin and down to the bone.

• *Second:* Stop your dog from being able to repeat the habit. The trouble with anti-lick strips or bandaging on paws is that they are often not a sufficient deterrent or barrier for dogs with an A grade licking compulsion, and will simply be ripped off. The only really reliable way to stop your dog paw licking, alas, is to place a buster collar on him; one of those plastic lampshade-like devices vets will give you after your dog has had an operation.

• *Third:* To avoid any additional distress, try to identify when your dog is most likely to indulge in his paw or leg licking habit, and only put the collar on him during these times/occasions.

• *Fourth:* Try to establish what is most likely to be the trigger for your dog's compulsive paw licking problem. The cause could be physical – i.e. an allergic reaction to some environmental substance or parasite. Alternatively the behaviour could be a displacement activity to take your dog's mind off another source of pain elsewhere. Either way, try to get these things better investigated and treated.

If you think the problem could be more psychological in origin, be aware that many collies can develop or escalate a paw licking habit in response to stressful factors like under-stimulation (i.e. boredom), separation from owners, a new dog/person introduced to a household or some similar disruption to the dog's normal living environment/routine. There may well be some changes you can make that will help your dog's state of mind no end.

The combination of physically stopping a dog from repeating this damaging habit, while simultaneously tackling its likely cause, usually gives you the best chance of curing it. Once dogs have shown a tendency towards this behaviour, however, you must always be alert to the prospect of them starting it again, even after a long period of being seemingly 'cured'. Also be aware that the entire subject of *Stress and stress-related problems* will be covered in Part Two of this book, page 194.

DIGESTIVE PROBLEMS
Sometimes an inappropriate diet can cause, or exacerbate, itchy skin in collies and sometimes it can also cause them digestive problems. In many collies, as in many dogs, skin and digestive problems often go together.

Colitis can be a problem in collies. A typical pattern of this complaint is that the dog's first motion of the day, after the gut has rested overnight, will usually be his firmest. Throughout the day his motions will then become looser and eventually develop a mucousy or jelly-like appearance, often with flecks of blood in it; symptoms which all denote distinct gut irritation.

While the dog may still seem fairly well in himself, continuing intestinal discomfort can greatly diminish his life quality and his appetite may also decline.

There are many who believe that stress, of some kind, can greatly increase the chance of a colitis episode in collies, which is something owners of affected dogs may want to consider. Over the years, however, I have found that digestive problems in collies – and most notably colitis – can frequently be improved, and sometimes cured altogether, by a change of diet. This is because the problem in question is mostly being caused by intolerance to a specific food substance or additive.

FINDING THE RIGHT DIET
Although dogs can develop food intolerances and digestive disturbances at any age, in my view these can often stem back to puppyhood. Some people think that first vaccinations can be a trigger, but it could also be early diet.

When puppies are being weaned, they are often put exclusively on a commercial puppy food that contains only one specific protein source, such as chicken. By being fed the same identical food ingredients day in and day out, without variety, sometimes the young developing gut can eventually acquire a sensitivity to one or more of them.

Making a collie puppy's early diet much more varied, on the other hand, gives the developing gut more of a challenge. It also gradually gets it used to many different types of food ingredient from an early age.

Once weaned, I introduce my own puppies to a wide range of different foods, initially in small amounts, including different kinds of vegetable and meat/poultry/fish protein – e.g. lamb, beef, tripe, turkey, offal, salmon, trout, pilchards, coley, tuna. Much of this will be raw - except poultry, which I always prefer to cook. Certainly in my own dogs, I have found that a constantly varied diet – with plenty of fresh food from day one – has limited the development of future gut problems.

In every collie, of course, digestive problems can have a different cause, or combination of causes. However, it does seem to be the case that many commercial canine diets do not suit a lot of collies, and they often thrive better on hypoallergenic ones instead, or those with minimum amounts of additives. Sometimes it can be a matter of trial and error to pinpoint the commercial diet that suits your collie best, or it may well be that a natural raw food diet will suit him even better.

Modern raw food diets, primarily comprising raw meat, bones and vegetables, are growing increasingly popular

DON'T LET YOUR COLLIE GET FAT!

Obesity in dogs is actually an owner-inflicted disease. Dogs rely totally on us to keep them healthy. By allowing a dog to become overweight we afford him a far poorer life quality and a much higher risk of illnesses such as arthritis, heart disease, diabetes and liver problems. Even a small amount of extra weight on a dog increases the strain on his entire body, over the years, and often leads to a much shorter lifespan, or far more unpleasant old age.

To their credit, many owners, when made more aware of their dog's weight problem, will do their best to rectify it as soon as possible. Other owners, however, will persist with a childishly stubborn attitude of denial; insisting their dog is "fine" or "perfectly happy", even when he can barely walk.

In this respect, they are putting themselves first and their dog's welfare second while so often, at the same time, claiming to "love" him. I never understand how anyone who genuinely loves a dog could inflict on him the intense suffering and shortened lifespan caused by obesity.

Because they are natural scavengers, most dogs will eat what you allow them to; it has nothing to do with their actual physical need. Fat dogs are also becoming so common these days that many owners have lost sight of what a healthy, normal weight for a dog should be.

It is hard to give ideal weights for all collies, as they can vary so much in terms of size and build. A rough guide for good collie weights is around 17-18 kg (37-40 lb) for adult bitches and 20-21 kg (44-46 lb) for adult males. If you have any doubts about your own dog's weight, do check with your vet. If the vet says your dog is overweight, accept that they will always be a better judge than you.

These days, there is also plenty of advice available from vets, in the form of exercise and dietary programmes, to help you restore your dog to a healthy weight.

among dog owners today. Many feel that a return to this more natural way of eating has a wide range of benefits for their dogs' health. To find out more about these kinds of diet, see *Finding the Right Help,* page 199.

FEEDING REGIMES

Once a collie reaches adulthood, owners usually make a decision as to whether they should feed their dog once or twice a day. I am never quite sure how this feeding tradition for dogs arose, given how happily most people will put away three meals a day themselves.

I have also heard some canine gurus say that it is good for dogs to regularly go a day or two without food. It may also be good for people, including dog gurus, to do the same, but I am not convinced that that many do.

My feeling is that dogs need predictable routines in their lives, and this includes regular daily mealtimes. As soon as you start messing with a dog's routines, you start to foster elements of insecurity in his head.

This apart, dogs have incredibly strong concentrations of hydrochloric acid in their stomachs. Thus the longer you leave their stomachs empty, the less this has to work on and the more discomfort some dogs can feel as a result. It can also lead to them eating grass and/or throwing up yellowy bile.

I have known many collies throw up bile in this way when their stomachs were lengthily empty, because they were only fed one meal a day. The problem was immediately cured when they were given two meals a day instead; a smaller one in the morning and a slightly bigger one in the evening. This is, therefore, the feeding regime I adopt for my dogs.

WEIGHING YOUR DOG

The amount of food I give my dogs will be tailored to factors such as their exercise levels, and how cold the weather is. I also weigh my dogs about every two months, to see who needs more food, or a bit less, in order to maintain their ideal weight.

Weighing your dog regularly is always a good idea. A sudden drop in weight, for instance, could point to a possible illness, or worm infestation. Similarly, weight gains that arise when you are giving your dog the same amount of food and exercise as normal can sometimes indicate a hormone-related illness – although do note that dogs who have been spayed or neutered may need their food intake cut back by around a quarter to prevent them gaining weight.

Be aware, too, that the scales will always be a more reliable guide to your dog's weight than your eyes. If you weigh your dog regularly, and cut his food back by just a little as soon as you see he is gaining weight, you can nip any obesity problem in the bud. By contrast, the more weight your dog gains, the harder it can be for you to get it off again.

EXERCISE

The amount of physical exercise collies should be given can be a subject attracting very varying views. At one end of the scale, you will get owners who say it's a myth that collies need lots of exercise. Given that collies are one of the most driven and active breeds on the planet, this is, of course, total nonsense. I really do not know many true collie folk who believe this, other than those who simply need to justify the under-exercising of their own dogs.

At the other end of the scale, there are owners who run their collies flat out for miles and miles, sometimes forcing them to follow them while they are on a bike or, seemingly, training for a marathon. They will say that sheepdogs, in their working role, routinely run 10-20 miles a day, or 20-40 miles a day or, at the loonier level of calculation, 40-60 miles a day. It keeps changing, depending on who you talk to.

What I would like to say about this is:
Firstly, have you seen most working collies, by the time they are eight or nine years old, after having run even 10-20 miles a day? A large number are riddled from head to foot with arthritis or other chronic back or joint complaints.
Secondly, do you want your own dog to end up like this if it could be avoided with better consideration of his longer-term physical health?
Finally, when you are running long distances, you can stop when you like. You are also making a conscious choice to subject your body to this level of physical stress. Your dog, on the other hand, has not been given either of these choices – you have simply imposed your own choices on him, regardless of the potential impact on his health.

AVOIDING LONGER TERM TRAUMA

It is vital to keep remembering how much shorter a dog's most active period of life can be, compared to our own. You should also be aware that the physical injuries, traumas or general over-wear collies' bodies sustain when younger so often come back to haunt them, in the form of arthritis, when older. Moreover, collies will often work or run through pain, making an existing injury or weakness worse. This is because of the effects of adrenaline and because dogs live totally in the moment. They cannot possibly see the link between today's physically reckless behaviour, and tomorrow's more painful old age. But you can.

Collies are much like thoroughbred horses; they will not necessarily stop when they feel tired or out of breath. They will just keep going to the point of collapse, especially if forced to do so – i.e. through being made to endlessly chase balls, or run behind owners on bicycles.

Establishing optimum exercise levels for collies can, of course, often be complicated by the fact that they vary so much as individuals. Some lighter built dogs can tolerate far more exercise than heavier built ones, as a result of far less stress being placed on their heart and joints, especially longer-term.

GETTING THE BALANCE RIGHT

With most collies, the key is to establish sufficient physical exercise to maintain a dog's physical fitness and stamina while, at the same time, keeping him as injury free as possible. Regular, steady, low-impact distance work, of a kind the dog's body was originally designed for, is usually best.

I typically aim for around two to three hours a day of this type of exercise with my own adult dogs, broken up into two separate daily outings, morning and afternoon. I have had dogs who are still happily doing this kind of distance work regularly at 12 or even 13 years of age. Although, as outlined in the next chapter, you would not expect older dogs with more severe arthritis, or other exercise-intolerance problems, to do the same.

In younger, but physically mature, dogs you can intersperse distance work with shorter bouts of more strenuous activity (e.g. ball catching or jumping) once their joints have fully warmed up. Before such strenuous activity, however, the dogs in question should already be pretty fit physically from prior distance work and gradient work (i.e. walking or running up steeper terrains). Otherwise they are more likely to sustain injuries.

Swimming can also be an excellent activity for collies of all ages, to keep all-round joint and muscular suppleness. It is always a good idea to punctuate your distance work with regular training exercises to keep your dog tuned in to you, and mentally sharp, and his responses good, no matter where you are.

OTHER BENEFITS OF EXERCISE

Physical exercise improves a dog's circulation, digestive function, joint and muscular function and all-round health. Exercise in the form of trips away from home also promotes psychological health in a dog, through the provision of ample mental stimulation.

Additionally, the social skills of dogs who regularly go out and meet other people and dogs will always be superior to those who go out less often.

It is not always easy to give your collie, or collies, the right amount of physical exercise daily, as I well understand. It often calls for us making sacrifices and pushing ourselves when we feel tired or unwell, or the weather is particularly uninviting. However, to my mind, this is part and parcel of the responsibility of owning dogs, and a breed as naturally active as the Border Collie in particular. If we do not want this responsibility, we do not have to own them. Let us not forget, also, that walking miles with dogs daily is pretty good for owners, too.

These factors apart, a vast number of the behavioural problems I see in dogs today are related in some way to their getting insufficient physical exercise and mental stimulation. Sustained deprivation like this turns a dog's mind into a pressure cooker, and the more naturally active the dog in question, the more likely it is to eventually blow, in some shape or form.

TEETH

I am continually astounded by how many otherwise good owners never clean their dogs' teeth or regularly inspect their mouths. Living with the foul breath of a dog whose teeth are never cleaned would be motivation enough, you would think, to do something about it. A dog's mouth and teeth, however, can also be sources of considerable discomfort for him, if not regularly checked and looked after.

Anyone who has had a sore mouth, or throat, or toothache will know that the pain can sometimes drive you half mad. But while we have recourse to a doctor or dentist the moment we get such pain, dogs only have us. They just have to hope we notice when they are suffering, and do something about it.

Sources of acute oral pain in dogs can include gum disease and abscesses, loose teeth, broken or fractured teeth and splinters in the throat, gums or roof of the mouth. Only by checking your dog's mouth and throat regularly, as part of an everyday health check, will you notice these things and be able to seek earliest possible treatment from your vet.

Cleaning your dog's teeth regularly – i.e. just once a week – will also make a massive difference to his oral health and minimise his chances of getting gum disease. For more advice on this, see *How to clean your dog's teeth*.

Studies reveal that 80 per cent of dogs over the age of three are now affected by gum disease. This is greatly down, in turn, to neglect on an owner's part of their oral hygiene. Also be aware that gum disease, from its earliest signs or symptoms, can lead on to far more serious health problems in dogs, such as heart disease, kidney disease and septicaemia (blood poisoning). I know of several collies who have died as a result of the latter condition, caused by dental abscesses that went unnoticed and untreated.

HOW TO CLEAN YOUR DOG'S TEETH

Cleaning your dog's teeth, at least once a week, will keep plaque and gum disease at bay, and also make a difference to his longer-term health. It will also save you the trauma and expense of your dog having to go to the vet to have his teeth cleaned under an anaesthetic, or have his teeth removed due to gum disease.

During a weekly dental clean you can also check for chipped or broken teeth, and any splinters or abnormalities

in your dog's mouth or throat. You should consult your vet if you detect any problems.

To clean your dog's teeth you do not need fancy dog toothpaste. Just use a baby's toothbrush and a solution comprising half a teaspoon of bicarbonate of soda dissolved in half a mug of boiling water. Put the bicarbonate of soda into the mug first, then put the toothbrush in it. Keep your toothbrush in the mug while you pour the boiling water on to the bicarbonate of soda, then stir the brush around in the solution to sterilise it. Wait for the solution to cool before using it.

Teeth-cleaning often proves traumatic because owners do not begin this process early enough – i.e. when their dog is a puppy. Many owners will also give up the moment their dog struggles or makes a fuss about having his teeth cleaned. This sets the pattern for how the dog will then behave later every time you try to clean his teeth.

It is better to start teeth-cleaning with your dog when he is in a more submissive/subdued position – i.e. turn him gently on to his back and hold him between your legs. This position also makes it far easier for you to clean all your dog's teeth and see right into his mouth.

If your dog panics or makes a fuss when you put him into this position, do not say anything; just keep calmly holding him still until he quietens down again. Initially this may take a little while, and may involve using considerable strength, to keep him still. But remain calm, patient and kind, as any aggression or impatience on your part will only frighten him and make him less likely to relax.

Begin by brushing just three or four teeth – not just the front sides of these teeth, but also behind and between them. Do this very gently and ensure your dog does not choke on the solution, or swallow too much of it. If your dog remains calm while you do this, praise him really well and then immediately release him. If he struggles and protests, keep holding him still, without saying anything, until he quietens down again and relaxes. Do this continually until you have finally been able to clean three or four of your dog's teeth while he remains relaxed – at which point, praise him well and release him.

It is important to only release your dog from teeth-cleaning and praise him once he has shown relaxed behaviour. By doing this you can gradually build up the number of your dog's teeth you can clean in one session, without him panicking. You will also progressively stretch his tolerance of this whole regular procedure.

Note: Nails are also much easier to trim with your dog held in this same subdued position, between your legs.

NAILS

Collies have oval-shaped paws. This means that the middle two claws on each foot often get less wear than the side two claws, which take most of the dog's weight.

It is important to keep all your dog's claws roughly the same length, and also ensure that none actually touch or scrape the ground. Uneven or overgrown claws could eventually alter your dog's posture, and ability to move efficiently, through forcing him to redistribute his weight to his feet in a more unnatural way.

If your dog's dew claws (which are positioned inside his front legs) become overgrown, and dig into his leg, they will cause him pain, so try to keep these regularly trimmed.

If you are uneasy about cutting your dog's claws, or are not sure if they are the right length, do consult your vet.

EARS

Ears can be a source of much discomfort to your dog if you do not strive to keep them healthy. Collies are not as prone as many other dogs to ear infections, but their ears should still be checked regularly to rule this out. Healthy ears should look clean and have a slightly earthy smell. If there is a redder look to them, and thick brown wax, or they are giving off a more putrid smell, these can be signs of inflammation, infection or ear mite infestation – all of which will require veterinary treatment.

Dogs with ear pain or discomfort will generally shake their heads a lot, and also continually scratch their ears. If previously mentioned sources of discomfort have been ruled out, check for foreign bodies, such as grass seeds, entering your dog's ears. Often these things will not be easy to find or remove, and thus, again, veterinary treatment will be required to extricate them.

HEALTH EMERGENCIES

Life threatening conditions or events can arise for your dog in a relatively short period of time, and I will now list the most common of these. They will all need emergency veterinary attention, and the sooner you recognise and address their earliest symptoms the better the outcome for your dog should be.

GASTRIC BLOAT / TORSION

Although more commonly seen in larger and deeper-chested dog breeds, gastric bloat/torsion can also occur in collies. The bloating in question results from excess gas from fermenting food, or air swallowed when eating, building up in a dog's stomach. The pressure from this expansion can then cause a twisting (or torsion) of the dog's stomach, with a restricting impact on circulation that can be fatal. The more the gut bloats and/or twists, impeding breathing and circulation and causing harm to other organs, the worse the prognosis for the affected dog.

Signs of bloat to watch out for include a fairly sudden onset of excessive panting and restlessness, plus the dog frequently looking round to his sides. Gastric discomfort is making the dog unable to settle, and he may continually retch, stretch, or eat grass in an effort to vomit up the cause of his woes. Any of these signs – especially with a noticeable, growing tightness or distension of a dog's abdomen – means that you should be out of the door as fast as possible, and on your way to the vet, having telephoned him or her in advance to warn of this emergency.

Such prompt action ideally gives the vet time to pump gas or air from your dog's stomach before it has the chance to twist - and this can, literally, be life saving. Once the stomach twists, and the longer it is twisted for, the bleaker the prognosis can often be.

Suggested causes of bloat include the eating of dried food followed by copious amounts of water, bolting food and thereby swallowing excessive amounts of air, and exercising too soon before or after a meal. Dogs can also swallow excess air when rapidly drinking water.

To prevent attacks of bloat, feeding a dog smaller amounts of food at a time, or even completely changing his diet – e.g. switching from dried to canned food, or even a natural food diet – may help.

Dogs feeding collectively, rather than singly, often have a far greater tendency to bolt down meals, due to the level of surrounding competition. Thus if you have a dog who more excessively bolts his food it may be wise to feed him separately.

A small portion of live yoghurt fed to your dog just after a meal may also be beneficial in dispersing stomach gasses. Finally, and as a rule, you should always allow a good hour to elapse between exercising your dog and feeding him.

HEATSTROKE

Heatstroke is a condition that no sensible owner should ever allow to occur. Classically, it happens when dogs are left in cars that soon turn into ovens, despite being well ventilated or initially left in the shade. Because the sun inevitably moves round, and metal intensifies heat, a dog should never be left unsupervised in a car on a hot day, even with seemingly adequate ventilation or initial shade. Neither should he be excessively exercised, or exposed to heat, during particularly hot weather.

However, accidents and oversights can and do still happen in this respect. If, as a result, a dog appears to be frantically panting and near to collapse with heatstroke (not to be confused with Border Collie Collapse, see page 137), you will need to bring his temperature down as quickly as possible. Hose or douse the dog with cool – but not icy cold – water. Cover the dog with a wet towel or blanket and remove him to a cool area immediately. Also add salt to the initial water he drinks, at the ratio of one teaspoonful of salt per half-litre.

Even if your dog seems to be recovering well from heatstroke, still take him to a vet for a check over, as he could still be suffering from shock.

ROAD ACCIDENT

Every year too many collies get run over, either because they have escaped to chase traffic, or because they have bolted in fright from loud bangs or other frightening stimuli.

When dogs get hit by cars, they are not just suffering possible wounds, but also shock, which can be an even greater killer. Signs of shock due to extensive bleeding, trauma or pain are: pale gums, weakness, loss of consciousness, cold skin and rapid, shallow breathing.

If your dog has been hit by a car, first keep him as warm and quiet as possible, ensuring that his airways are kept clear. If he appears to stop breathing, try mouth-to-nose resuscitation. Cup your dog's muzzle in your hands and gently blow down his nostrils roughly 20 times a minute.

If you suspect your dog has incurred a neck or spinal injury, get help from someone else to slip him on to a flat board, or other sturdy supportive structure. Otherwise move him flat on to a blanket, again getting help if you can to do this.

Next, ring ahead to your vet to explain what has happened, and that you will be on your way with a probable shock victim. If the accident has not happened near your home, take your dog to the nearest possible vet. Either way, the quicker you get to a vet, the quicker life-saving treatment for shock and lost blood can be administered to your dog. The first 12-24 hours after a road accident can be critical for a victim, allowing external and internal wounds (particularly haemorrhaging) to be fully assessed and addressed, as well as the possible complications of shock.

If your dog is bleeding profusely from an external wound, try tying a pressure bandage, or clean cloth or scarf, directly above the wound to stem the blood flow. A clean cloth pushed into the wound and held there tightly, then secured in place with a bandage, will also help.

It is wise to always carry a prepared first aid box for dogs in your car, containing items such as sterile bandages and dressings, tweezers, scissors, animal antiseptic and a roll of gauze tape. Likewise, always carry a blanket in the back of the car.

POISONING

Poisoning in dogs can often be complicated by the wide range of possible toxins they might consume, all of which may show different, or non-specific, symptoms requiring different antidotes and treatments. These are some of the commonest toxins for dogs; some of which may be given to them by owners, who do not realise they are poisonous to dogs:

- Human medicines
- Veterinary medicines (excess dose)
- Insecticides
- Weed killer
- Slug bait
- Garden plants, bulbs and house plants
- Rodent poisons
- Household cleaners
- Raisins and grapes
- Chewing gum
- Onions
- Chocolate
- Chemicals – e.g. alcohols, WD-40 and sewing machine oils
- Anti-freeze
- Home decoration/repair items – i.e. paint, solvents, glues Potpourris

A rapid way of dealing with a dog you suspect has eaten something poisonous is to make him sick. Do this by placing a teaspoonful of salt at the back of the tongue and then give him plenty of water. An exception to this treatment would be the possible intake of something caustic or corrosive, such as bleach or battery acid. Substances like these could further damage your dog's oesophagus and throat if they were brought back up.

Symptoms of poisoning in dogs range from salivation, excitability, weakness and lack of co-ordination to vomiting, diarrhoea, convulsions and collapse. In all cases, emergency treatment should be sought from your vet.

Obviously, owners should also do their best to keep all harmful substances away from their dog at all times.

PYOMETRA

Pyometra is a potentially life-threatening womb infection seen in unspayed bitches, particularly those who have not had pups. Generally it occurs during the days, weeks or even months that follow a bitch's heat. The cause is hormonally induced; mucous producing cells in the uterus, designed to prepare the womb for the carriage of puppy embryos, attract bacteria, which then result in progressively more serious infection.

Early signs of pyometra in bitches include excessive thirst, loss of appetite, general dullness and bloodshot eyes, due to toxins filtering into the bloodstream. Cases of open pyometra, where pus drains out through the bitch's vulva, are more easily recognised than closed kinds that do not have such an obvious symptom. Both mean prompt veterinary attention to prevent death from blood poisoning, dehydration and shock.

The most effective and permanent solution to the problem is an ovarohysterectomy (i.e. removal of the uterus and ovaries), plus fluid therapy and antibiotic treatment. Many bitches recover extremely well from such an operation.

Note: For more information on the physical and psychological changes bitches may experience, as a result of heat-cycle related hormonal activity, see *Hormonally fuelled behaviour* in Part Two, page 177.

SLOWING THE AGEING PROCESS: PHYSICAL AND MENTAL ACTIVITY

Keeping your ageing collie physically active, for as long as possible, is very important, even if this means reducing longer walks to three far shorter ones daily. If your dog regularly starts to lag some way behind you on a walk, seems in discomfort or shows other signs of exercise intolerance, then you will need to cut back on the distance you walk him in one go.

Mobility, however, is essential to keep a dog's heart, lungs, circulation and digestive system working well, and for him to retain muscle strength. The less a dog uses his muscles, the more these will diminish in power. Similarly, joints that are not regularly used will stiffen up and become more painful. Exercise for dogs, as for humans, is also known to be a natural anti-depressant.

A dog lacking mental stimulation will always age faster. So continually take your older dog to different places to experience new sights and smells, even if he cannot walk as far as before. Also take him out with you in the car for errands and continue giving him scent tasks to find toys and food. The more you stimulate an older dog's brain, the sharper it will stay for longer.

OTHER DANGER SIGNS

Aforementioned conditions apart, here are some general symptoms in dogs that can be warning signs of more serious conditions, and should therefore be promptly investigated by a vet:

- Sudden loss of appetite; sudden weight loss or gain
- Excessive thirst
- Persistent diarrhoea with or without vomiting
- Continual coughing and/or exercise intolerance
- Dullness and lethargy (most abnormal Collie traits!)
- Heavy or abnormal breathing
- Any new lumps, bumps or swellings
- Any purulent or bloody discharges from any orifice.

HEALTHY BODY, HEALTHY MIND

Throughout this chapter, I have focused on how you can keep your collie as physically healthy as possible. This is not just because this is a desired goal for any owner, but also because a dog who is in any kind of pain or discomfort can also become mentally affected by his suffering, in a way that can alter both his behaviour and entire quality of life.

Dogs in discomfort or pain generally become more irritable, distracted, defensive or depressed. This is why an underlying pain source, or medical problem, in your collie is always something that should first be considered, and then checked out, should his normal behaviour, or personality, suddenly change.

When a collie is physically fit, free from any ongoing source of stress or pain, has order and routine in his life, a healthy diet and ample physical and mental exercise to suit his needs, he becomes a totally balanced dog. As such, he will also be far less likely to give you many problems.

Chapter Thirteen

THE OLDER COLLIE

Understanding mental and physical changes occurring in the ageing dog

Middle age, and then old age, may often seem to creep up very stealthily on your collie, and how they affect him as an individual will be greatly down to two basic factors; namely, how fit and healthy you have kept him throughout his life, and how good his genes are.

A clear reflection of this is that, while some collies may seem old when only eight or nine years of age, others can still be leading highly active lives when aged 12 or beyond.

You cannot change your collie's genes but you can be aware that factors such as obesity, stress and insufficient physical exercise and mental stimulation will always make your dog age faster, and lead a generally poorer quality of life when older, as outlined in *Slowing the ageing process*.

THE ASSET OF LONGEVITY

It has long struck me as strange that the asset of longevity in dogs is not more greatly considered or prized by breeders. In a dog's pedigree, much emphasis may be put on the different health screens his ancestors have had, and the results, but no record of the age at which they died – or what illness, as opposed to trauma, denied them of a longer life. Yet what could be a more significant indicator of a dog's genetic health than the lifespans of his immediate relations?

We know that, in people, longevity runs in families, and the same goes for dogs. The rate at which they age will be greatly governed by genes. As I write, the Texas A & M University College of Veterinary Medicine, in the USA, is undertaking research into how genes affect the canine ageing process, with the ultimate aim of increasing both the lifespan and later life quality of dogs of all breeds. Thus recording the longevity potential of any dog, through a simple genetic test, may one day become the norm.

For the present, however, we just have to hope that the dog we get will live as long and active a life as possible, and do our best to bring this outcome about.

THE AGEING PROCESS

What we think of as simple ageing in dogs is really an ongoing process of cell deterioration and destruction, of a kind that happens in all animals over a period of time. The average lifespan for a Border Collie is considered to be around 13 years, but age-related changes in the dog – e.g. greying muzzle, hearing loss – will usually be seen some time before this. Indeed, these are usually the commonest first signs of a dog getting older.

During the ageing process in your dog, however, a lot else will be happening. His muscle, joint, heart, lung and other organ functions will gradually decline and his hearing and eyesight will also slowly lose their former sharpness.

EXTERNAL FACTORS

Over and above genetic pre-programming, governing the rate at which individual dogs may age, other external factors are thought to accelerate this process.

Among these are obesity, insufficient physical exercise, a poorer diet, and a lengthy exposure to a wide range of environmental toxins (including insecticides and flea, tick and worming treatments). Additionally, there are many who believe that the over frequent vaccinating of dogs can damage their immune systems.

STRESS

Psychological stress, of some kind or another, is also known to accelerate not just the ageing process in dogs, but also the development of more serious illnesses like diabetes or cancer. This is down to the impact the stressed mental state can have – especially longer term – on all parts of the body, including the immune system.

Many owners are not aware that the effect of stress in dogs is often cumulative. In other words, it can take a while, if not some years, for its full impact to be displayed in physical or mental health problems.

As previously stated, collies can be particularly vulnerable to stress related health and behavioural problems because they are dogs whose neurochemistry and metabolism are programmed to readily trigger and sustain a state of high arousal. This mentally aroused state causes stress chemicals and hormones to be produced which can then place severe strain on the body elsewhere, particularly the immune and digestive systems and the brain.

It is important to understand, however, that the consistently *under*-aroused mental state (i.e. depression) can be just as stressful for dogs, longer term, as the over-aroused one. Persistent under-arousal can be a particular problem in older dogs, as their bodies' arousal responses become weaker. It is also why they are more likely to seem, or become, depressed.

See *Depression (page 165)* and *Stress and stress related problems* (page 194) in Part Two.

BRAIN FUNCTION

A dog's brain function slowly deteriorates throughout his life. This is because brain neural cells, which govern so much of what happens in an animal's body, including motor and sensory functions, cannot divide or replicate. Thus, the neural cells a puppy is born with are the same ones that he later dies with, minus the ones lost along the way through trauma and the normal ageing process.

The loss of sensory function in a dog as his brain ages – including sight and hearing – correlates directly with the loss of his neural cells.

SENILE BEHAVIOUR

As age reduces the brain's effectiveness in older dogs they, just like older humans, can face the prospect of senile dementia. Interestingly, dogs and rats are the only non-primates known in old age to develop protein plaques in their brains similar to those found in humans with Alzheimer's disease.

When these protein plaques surround nerve cells in the brain they cause them to malfunction. This, in turn, may bring about changes in behaviour termed as cognitive dysfunction. Around 62 per cent of dogs aged 10 years and older are thought to experience at least some of the symptoms of canine cognitive dysfunction. These include confusion or disorientation, restlessness at night, loss of house training abilities, decreased activity levels, decreased attentiveness, and not recognising friends or family members.

Senile behaviour in dogs, additionally, includes the development, or intensification, of separation anxiety and noise phobias, plus increased shyness and vocalisation – particularly the tendency to seemingly bark at nothing. Senile

SLOWING THE AGEING PROCESS: WEIGHT AND DIET

Although genes may greatly govern the rate at which your collie ages, there is still much you can do to keep him healthier and more active for longer.

Most importantly, as stressed in the last chapter, do not let your dog get overweight. Consistent studies have shown that keeping a dog at a healthy weight, or even slightly underweight, makes more difference to his longevity than almost any other external factor. As dogs age, their metabolisms can also slow down, meaning they require up to 20 per cent less food to maintain a healthy weight.

Additionally, feed your older dog as much fresh food as possible, including oily fish like pilchards two or three times a week, which will benefit his coat, skin, joints and mental processes and plenty of leafy green vegetables like spinach which will benefit his eyesight. Either steam these vegetables or serve them raw. If you serve raw vegetables to dogs, you should semi-liquidise them in a blender. This is because dogs lack the digestive enzyme which breaks down cell walls in vegetables and plants.

Also limit your older dog's intake of wheat based carbohydrates, including biscuit-based treats. Carbohydrate sources like brown rice, oats or potatoes (with their skins left on to provide extra roughage/vitamins) will be far more beneficial and healthy for him. Slivers of raw carrot can be substitutes as treats, as can modern treats made entirely from dried fish skin. Older dogs with liver or kidney problems may need special tailormade diets available from vets. If you are not sure which diet would best suit your ageing or older dog, also consult your vet.

Show kindness and consideration to your ageing collie.

dogs can also become aggressive in a way that is unlike their normal character, and, as previously outlined, most old dogs cope far less well with stress than younger dogs.

Today medication is available to treat cognitive dysfunction in older dogs, and you may wish to discuss the possible pros and cons of this with your vet.

EYESIGHT

As dogs age, the lenses in their eyes lose elasticity, which makes it harder for them to focus on nearby objects. They may also see less well in the dark, or in very bright light.

Over a dog's lifetime, ultraviolet light can damage the lenses of his eyes, giving them a cloudier appearance. Older dogs often have hazy-looking eyes; a condition known as nuclear sclerosis, which does not, unlike cataracts, appear to greatly affect their vision.

Cataract development in collies, on the other hand, often has a genetic origin, depending on what age the problem begins. In some cases, and particularly in younger dogs, an

operation to cure these might be worth considering.

Some collies can also have a genetic tendency towards the development of glaucoma – a painful swelling of the eye – of a kind which develops in older age. For much more on this condition, see Chapter Twelve, page 132 and for more help on dealing with visually impaired collies, see *Managing collies with poorer sight or hearing, page 135.*

HEARING

As outlined in the last chapter, some collies can be born deaf, others will develop deafness relatively early on in their lives – i.e. between four and six years of age – and others will just lose their hearing as a natural part of getting older.

Because dogs – and collies in particular – can be so clever at reading human body language, and may often also lip-read some commands, the extent of an ageing dog's deafness may not always be apparent to an owner. This, in turn, is what so often leads them to imagine that their dog is becoming more wilful or disobedient in older age when he is simply unable to hear what they are saying.

An easy way to test how deaf your older dog is to wait until he is not looking at you, e.g. when he is in another room or in the garden, or walking ahead of you on the lead. Begin calling his name softly and then progressively increase the volume; the louder you have to call to just get his attention the deafer he is likely to be. You will need to do these sorts of tests a number of times until you are sure.

Sometimes people will drop objects on the floor suddenly to test an older dog's hearing, but as deaf dogs can still sense vibration, this is a less efficient guide. As your older dog loses some or all of his hearing, it is vital to keep reinforcing your training commands – especially *recall* – with physical gestures that he can respond to instead, as outlined in Chapter Five. Also, see, *Managing collies with poorer sight or hearing, page 135.*

VESTIBULAR SYNDROME

Vestibular Syndrome (VS) is a condition usually seen around middle-age and beyond in dogs - and collies, like most other breeds, can be affected by it.

VS symptoms can appear suddenly and be quite terrifying for both owner and dog alike. Typically, the dog will appear to have lost his balance. He might start reeling, staggering around in circles or keep falling over. There may also be a noticeable flickering of his eyes from side to side, which is known as nystagmus, and he may vomit.

Such symptoms can lead owners to imagine that their dog has suffered a stroke when, in fact, this is a far rarer occurrence in dogs than in people. Or they may think he has been poisoned – which, of course, may be something that needs ruling out. But the trigger for VS and its collective symptoms is, in fact, an inflammation of the dog's inner ear. This, in turn, affects his balance and spatial orientation mechanisms and the vomiting is caused by an accompanying motion sickness.

Sometimes an inner ear infection is the source of this inflammation but more commonly its cause remains unknown. It could, however, have some relation to the general ageing process in dogs.

The symptoms can last from a few days to around three weeks, but the good news is that most dogs make an incredibly good recovery, although many are left with a distinct head tilt. Sometimes a dog will have more than one VS attack in later life, and sometimes the condition can presage a more serious decline in a dog's overall health and faculties.

TREATMENT

If the above-mentioned VS symptoms change, escalate, or persist in your dog beyond three weeks, consult your vet as they may be linked to a more serious underlying condition. Your vet can also tell you what treatment, if any, should be given to your dog following a VS attack.

While suffering from VS, your dog must be looked after with great care. He may need hand feeding in regular small amounts to regain his appetite. He may also need you to carry or support him when he goes to the toilet outside, due to his loss of balance. The fright of a VS attack can also cause many dogs to lose confidence, and become more reluctant to leave the safety of the home environment.

Thus, as soon as feasible, once your dog is making a recovery, begin taking him out again, if only for short trips at first in the car. The longer you leave the gap between a VS attack and taking your dog out again, the scarier this is likely to be for him.

HEAT REGULATION

Older dogs, just like older people, can find it harder to regulate their body temperature when faced with extremes of heat or cold. Thus, when the weather is colder it might be a good idea to give your older collie an extra blanket and/or move his bed nearer to a heat source. Also keep his bed away from draughts.

When bathing an older dog, or hosing him down after a walk, also be sure to vigorously towel him down and get him warm and dry again as soon as possible.

Be careful how you exercise your older dog in hot weather, and install a fan near his bed when the temperature is particularly high.

COMING TO TERMS WITH AGEING AND LOSS

Throughout this chapter I have outlined the changes that are likely to happen in your collie as he ages, and how these may affect him both physically and mentally.

I would also like to stress, however, how difficult it can be for all of us to come to terms with a beloved dog getting old,

HEALTH CHECKS AND SCREENS

As your collie gets older, it is a good idea to get his health checked by the vet every six months. Your vet can check his heart, lungs and general wellbeing, and also give him a blood screen to highlight any developing problems, including those affecting the liver or kidneys. The earlier you spot these, the better they will respond to treatment. Conversely, by the time more obvious symptoms of liver or kidney disease are seen, considerable damage will already have been done to these organs.

About 80 per cent of entire male dogs over the age of eight can suffer from an enlarged prostate which, in turn, can lead to urinary problems and constipation, so ask your vet to keep an eye on this for you. Similarly unspayed bitches, in particular, can develop mammary tumours as they age. So regularly check your bitch's mammary glands and teats each time you groom her. If you find a new lump, however small, your vet may well recommend removing it. Most of these lumps/tumours are benign. If malignant, however, the earlier you spot it, and get it removed, the better the prognosis should be for your bitch.

and thus ever nearer to not being with us anymore. Inevitably, it fills us with a lingering sense of grief, which it does no harm to acknowledge and accept.

Ultimately, however, the love we feel for our dogs is best translated into doing our best by them in old age; showing them compassion, kindness and patience and understanding the limitations that have been placed on them by the passing years.

During their all too short lives, Border Collies may drive you crazy with their energy, pushiness, neuroses and assorted loony ways. They can be obsessive and challenging, ferociously proud and side-splittingly funny. They are also dogs with indefatigable loyalty, heart, willingness and spirit, whose intelligence continually takes your breath away.

It is because they bring so much to us that the pain is always that much sharper when they go.

HELP! THE A-Z ADVICE SECTION

Throughout the first part of this book, I attempted to better explain the roots and nature of the Border Collie, as well as ways of acquiring, raising, managing and training these dogs that can make future problems with them less likely.

It could be, however, that you already have problems with your collie, and would like to know far more about a particular psychological or behavioural issue your dog has presented you with; in which case, I hope this second part of the book proves of much additional help to you.

APPROACHING PROBLEMS

It is always best to seek professional advice the instant a problem starts. Do not wait until the behaviour becomes progressively more ingrained, or made worse by the wrong approach to remedying it. You will rarely get a better chance to solve problem behaviour in a dog, other than when it first manifests itself.

Additionally, be aware that it is the underlying cause of a problem, rather than its mere external symptoms, which always has to be addressed. Similarly, the desire to find quick fix solutions to complex psychological issues, via the incorrect use of deterrent devices, such as spray collars, can often do more harm than good, as outlined in *Deterrents: Use and abuse,* page 167.

FINDING HELP

Throughout the following A-Z Problem Guide, I have looked at a wide range of more troubling or challenging behaviours that can be found in Border Collies, and outlined some of my own professional approaches to them. Other behaviourists/trainers may favour different approaches. The most important considerations in this regard are that they know collies well, as a breed, and that their methods are not only effective and long-lasting, but also essentially *kind.*

This guide is exactly what I have termed it – a *guide*. As such, it should not be viewed as a substitute for getting the appropriate professional assessment, supervision and guidance I have previously suggested, when trying to diagnose and solve any problem in your dog. This is particularly the case with problems such as aggression and fear, because the wrong approach to such problems can not only make dogs worse, but also more dangerous.

Very many people tell me they have trouble finding the right professional help for their dogs' problems. Depending on where you live, the level of expertise you require may not be easily available locally, or the trainer or behaviourist you approach may not have sufficient experience of Border Collies. Given how many problems in collies are either highly breed specific, or greatly aggravated by breed related quirks of character or psychology, such experience in any expert you choose can be very important.

It is always worth doing extensive research, and travelling a significant distance, to secure the help of a person you feel is best able to assess and address your dog's problems. For far more advice on this, see *Finding the right expert help* in the *Further information* section, page 199.

AGGRESSION

Aggressive behaviour in a collie tends to be an issue of most concern to owners, because of the impact it can have on both their own lives, and wider society. It is also a problem, however, that is routinely misunderstood, as people often struggle to see the world from their dog's point of view.

Modern life with people brings many stresses for dogs, which ultimately need some outlet. Thus a first aggressive outburst in them, which takes owners by surprise, is often just a final release of pressures that had steadily built up over time, on a deeper and less obvious level – much in the manner of an erupting volcano or earthquake.

In this section, I hope to better explain the different mental pressures and challenges that can push collies, like all dogs, into an aggressive state, and highlight ways to manage collies that will make aggression in them less of a problem.

SURVIVAL RESPONSES

The first most important point to understand about aggression in dogs is that – as in most animals, including ourselves – it is primarily a survival response. Animals, in short, who cannot defend themselves, their resources, their territory or their young from external threat, do not tend to live long in the wild. Similarly if you are a predator, without aggressive impulses, you are destined to starve.

So aggression, in itself, is a perfectly natural behaviour in dogs. It only becomes a problem when it is used inappropriately towards other animals or people.

There are basically two types of aggression response in dogs: the *offensive* response and the *defensive* response. The offensive response (as in predatory behaviour) can be a more calculated action, controlled by the conscious mind, and characterised by the dog actively pursuing a target with aggressive intent. The defensive response, on the other hand, is a more instinctive aggressive reaction to immediate threat and, as such, will often be controlled by the sub-conscious mind.

Anyone who has suddenly put their foot down hard on the brakes in their car to prevent an accident will know what it is like to react to threat in an instinctive knee-jerk way; i.e. you perform the defensive action without consciously thinking about it first. Animals have evolved these sub-conscious defence reactions in order to respond to threat as fast as possible.

Lunge-nipping in collies (of which more later), when people or dogs pass closely by at their eye level, can be a typical example of defence behaviour launched by the sub-conscious mind.

INDIVIDUAL RESPONSES

Each collie can be different, in terms of how readily or not he will resort to aggression of either an offensive or defensive kind. When breeding collies to work livestock, it can often be hard to get a dog's aggression balance just right; i.e. too little aggressive 'presence', under pressure, and livestock will not respect the dog, and may challenge or threaten him. Too much aggressive drive, on the other hand, and the dog can become more unmanageable and a danger to livestock.

The most prized sheepdogs are those who can display a suitably commanding and intimidating presence before livestock, when required, without ever physically attacking them. Indeed, among the sheep trialling fraternity, a dog biting livestock – be this through over-predatory intent, or just sheer frustration – is viewed as a cardinal sin punishable by instant disqualification from competition.

Many collies can have low offensive aggression responses but high defensive ones – i.e. they will rarely be aggressive unless, or until, something comes straight into their space at eye level and is perceived as an immediate threat.

Other dogs will have stronger offensive responses; i.e. they will stalk or deliberately hunt down a threat to attack it, or use aggression in a highly calculated way to intimidate or dominate others. Sometimes the same dogs can have equally high defensive responses.

In some very troubled dogs, it can, in fact, be hard to work out where defensive aggression ends and offensive aggression begins (and vice versa), because their threat response mechanisms become so overused and distorted. Similarly, when sub-conscious defence responses are used by a dog, and prove continually rewarding, they can later turn into conscious actions used by the dog instead.

The least troublesome collies of all, as social companions, are those whose offensive aggression responses are either negligible, or have been trained purely on to legitimate targets – like toys – by owners. Similarly, their defensive aggression responses may only be launched under extreme duress.

However, additional internal/external pressures in any dog's life will always heighten his general level of reactivity, aggression wise.

WHY AGGRESSION DEVELOPS AND PERSISTS

Aggression responses in individual collies usually begin with a basic genetic predisposition towards certain behaviour. But, thereafter, the lessons any individual dog learns from his use of aggression, during his earliest and later life, will also be critical.

Young puppies who initially experiment with aggression, and continually find the experience negative, or highly unrewarding, tend not to persist with this behaviour. So if dogs persist with aggressive behaviour beyond puppyhood, it is usually because the behaviour has become continually rewarding for them in some way – see, *The rewards dogs get from aggression.*

THE AGGRESSIVE STATE OF MIND

When seeking to understand their dog's aggression problem, owners often get hung up on specific targets the dog has chosen for his hostile behaviour; e.g. "he doesn't like big/little/black/brown dogs" or "he hates men in baseball caps/father-in-law/the postman" and so on.

But in fact the targets for a dog's aggression are usually far less relevant than the state of mind that gives him the need to be aggressive in the first place. Most aggressive dogs are under some form of mental pressure, which then seeks to find a release in physically hostile or defensive behaviour. So, in order to stop aggressive behaviour, you first have to deal with the sources of mental pressure that trigger it.

COMMON MENTAL PRESSURES

Over the years I have dealt with many aggressive dogs, and the one thing most of them have in common is that they are not in a suitably balanced state of mind. Typically, they are highly reactive, agitated and hyper-alert, or cowed, hesitant, withdrawn and depressed – both descriptions represent dogs at either extreme of the stress scale.

THE REWARDS DOGS GET FROM AGGRESSION

Aggression usually persists in dogs because the behaviour is being continually rewarded in some way. Common examples of the rewards dogs get from aggression are:

- Attention from an owner, of a kind that reinforces the behaviour.
- The pleasurable release of inner tension.
- Removal of a sense of threat by making another person or dog go away.
- Sensation of relief.
- The securing and/or retention of a resource (as in possessive aggression).
- The reinforcement of higher status through the intimidation/control of others.
- The adrenalin buzz derived from an aggressive reaction.

This is why a critical first step with any aggressive dog is to work out where the reward for his behaviour is coming from, and try to stop it being perpetuated.

In each case you have to identify the most likely causes of the dog's inner state of psychological imbalance as these, in turn, are usually at the heart of his aggressive behaviour (also see *Stress and stress related problems, page 184*).

Pressure factors behind fear aggression, for example, tend to build up as follows:
- The dog perceives any new person or dog as a potential threat, due to inadequate early socialisation. *This in turn leads to*
- The dog lacking all social confidence, *which leads in turn to* Feelings of great anxiety/stress in the face of new social encounters, *which is released in*
- Offensive/defensive aggression towards other dogs/people.

Much extreme 'fear of the new' behaviour will have some genetic component at the heart of it, but it can then be seriously exacerbated by an owner's handling of early social anxiety experiences – e.g. inadvertently rewarding the dog for his negative reaction.

Before moving on to specific kinds of aggression in collies, and how each might best be tackled, I first want to better explain the previously mentioned lunge-nip reflex, as so often this instinctive response, rooted in the Border Collie's working past, is misunderstood, or confused with more serious types of aggression in these dogs.

UNDERSTANDING THE LUNGE-NIP REFLEX

The lunge-nip reflex is a response in sheepdogs to protect themselves from the threat of an attack, or challenge, from animals they are trying to herd, move or otherwise control.

Much of the skill of a sheepdog lies in using lunge-nip behaviour much in the manner of a shadow boxer; i.e. lunging, but then 'air snapping'; showing what a threat he can pose, without ever resorting to actual physical contact.

Sheepdogs who cannot muster a suitably fast defensive or counter-challenging response of this kind quickly lose the respect of livestock and are also far more likely to get attacked by them.

Because a sheepdog's reaction to another animal's challenge has to be exceptionally fast, the lunge-nip reflex is predominantly launched by the dog's sub-conscious mind; much like the previous example I described where you rapidly activate the brakes in your car, to avoid a crash, without consciously thinking about it first.

It is vital to understand the genetically pre-programmed, and sub-conscious, element of this defensive behaviour in collies, rather than always reading it as a sign of a dog consciously choosing to be hostile towards someone or something.

WHAT GOES WRONG

The lunge-nip reflex in collies only becomes a much bigger

problem, aggression-wise, when owners do not sufficiently understand the behaviour in their dog, or learn how to keep it under better control. As a result, what begins as a purely sub-conscious reflex in their dog then escalates into far more serious, and conscious, forms of aggression – as outlined on page 153.

The best way to see the lunge-nip reflex in collies is as an instinctive defence response to any sudden form of mental pressure, or perceived threat. When a dog is working sheep the pressure or threat in question is most likely to come from other animals suddenly moving towards him, ahead of him, or round him, at eye level.

In non livestock-working dogs, however, the same instinct can so easily get misdirected on to less appropriate targets like traffic, other people, other dogs, or even owners. Typically, it will be provoked by sudden movement and/or noise, which immediately arouses the dog's mental state (animated, screaming children, vacuum cleaners or motorbikes, being common examples). The more aroused a collie becomes, mentally, the more likely it is that lunge-nip behaviour will occur.

Sometimes the chief mental arousal trigger for lunge-nip behaviour in collies will be fear and anxiety – i.e. the dog feels constantly uneasy in the face of any new person/dog/experience due to poor early socialisation, and/or some deeper flaw in his genetic character.

At other times it will be pure excitement – as is often the case with dogs playing highly exciting games with other dogs, or undertaking certain competitive pursuits, or being trained for these with rewards like frantic tugger toy games, which further exacerbate aggressive drives.

It is incredibly important to always see the link between the level of excitement/arousal you expose your dog to, and the level of lunge-nipping that is likely to occur as a result.

VARYING LUNGE-NIP DRIVE
Individual collies, however, can still be programmed very differently, in terms of how and when they will use the lunge-nip reflex.

Some dogs may rarely, if ever, show any lunge-nip impulses at all. Others may need very little provocation/mental pressure to launch lunge-nip responses, but – as previously outlined - will not actually bite when they do so. They will just bare their teeth and air snap at a lunge target, instead, or use a form of gentler mouthing when they make contact.

This goes back to the earlier point I made (in *Individual responses, page 153* and *Understanding the lunge-nip reflex*) about good sheepdogs needing to have some innate reluctance to actually bite/attack livestock; a trait which may well have some deliberately bred-in genetic component.

However, how willing or not any collie may be to physically attack lunge-nip targets can also be greatly down to the general level of bite inhibition he has been taught by owners; not just when young but throughout his life. (See Part One; Chapter Four, *Giving a correction*, page 47 and *Please never do this!*, page 50 and also Chapter Eleven, *The Dangers of tugger toys*, page 121).

The most potentially dangerous dogs of all are those who not only lunge very readily but also bite hard when they do so. Such a lack of bite inhibition in any dog is always a bad sign.

BETTER CONTROLLING LUNGE-NIP BEHAVIOUR
Collies with minimum lunge-nip drive often need relatively little training to keep the instinct under control or relinquish it altogether.

If you have a dog, however, with very strong lunge-nip/lunge-grab instincts, more intense re-directing of these instincts, and better overall control of the dog's mental state, will be critical to avoid more serious problems with this behaviour.

Trying to totally suppress all lunge-nip/grab behaviour in dogs like these often proves counter-productive, as the constant restriction of such powerful natural instincts can lead to intense frustration in them, which may then get directed into other forms of less desirable behaviour.

It is far better to teach such dogs that there is only one legitimate target, or outlet, for their lunge-grab drives – toys (such as balls or Frisbees, but not tugger toys). Any other outlet is forbidden. As you control the toys, you also control the opportunities for your dog to use his instincts. This, in turn, should keep him all the more focused on you, as opposed to any other surrounding lunge-nip targets.

When using toys with your dog, however, you must always keep suitable control over his mental state and not let him get too excited or aroused; i.e. whining, barking, highly agitated, trying to jump up on you. It can be a very short step from such mental arousal in a collie to him nipping you or directing such impulses on to other nearby people or dogs.

So as soon as you see such growing excitement in your dog, immediately tell him to lie down and wait and watch you (training outlined in Part One, Chapter Five), and do not give him a toy again until he has remained settled and quiet for at least 20 seconds, if not more. Do this same exercise, even without a toy, each and every time he gets too excited, in any situation, to keep him in a far calmer mental state.

LUNGE-NIPPING DIRECTED AT OTHER DOGS
Many collie puppies may begin directing lunge-nip behaviour on to other dogs; grabbing at their necks with their teeth when excited. While mostly this can be a form of play behaviour for the puppy, of a kind regularly indulged in by dogs who live together or know each other well, not all dogs will welcome this approach.

Some retaliatory attack on a puppy, for his disrespectful behaviour, could then ensue. This may frighten him and lead him to be more defensively aggressive towards other dogs in the future.

For this reason it is vital to teach your collie puppy both acceptable, and unacceptable, ways of interacting with a new dog he meets, as outlined in Part One, Chapter Six. Because as soon as you have a dog who thinks it is not only acceptable, but also rewarding, to launch lunge-nip drives on to other dogs, when suitably aroused or excited, you are on your way to a much bigger future problem.

Having highlighted the origins and typical triggers of the lunge-nip reflex in collies, and the greater problems this instinct can lead to if not better understood and controlled, let us now look at more specific forms of aggression problem in the breed.

FEARFUL OR NERVOUS AGGRESSION

Fearful aggression in collies tends to be one of those classic examples of a sub-conscious defence reflex (i.e. lunge-nipping) later transforming into a conscious behaviour, as a result of the reward the dog gets from it.

As more fully outlined in Part One (Chapter Six), owners seldom appreciate the significance of what their dog learns from his first fear-aggressive experience, if only because they, themselves, are usually so shaken up by it, and can think only of departing a scene of conflict.

What typically happens, however, is that the dog reacts aggressively, in a sudden moment of panic, towards another person or dog. Then either this other person or dog goes away, or the owner takes his/her dog away from the aggression target. Both outcomes are viewed as highly rewarding by the aggressive dog.

HOW THE PROBLEM ESCALATES

From this initial experiment with fear-triggered defensive aggression, which proves so rewarding for the dog concerned, things can then rapidly escalate. The dog's aggression moves on from one specific target which worried him to any other target which is similar (i.e. any other person or dog). The more he gets the same rewarding result, the more confident and obsessive he becomes about being aggressive towards others – to the point where it is all he thinks about from the moment he leaves home to go for a walk.

As stated earlier, there is nearly always a genetic component behind more extreme fear aggression in collies, because you constantly see the same behaviour repeated in specific lines or families of dogs.

BODY LANGUAGE OF THE FEAR-AGGRESSIVE DOG

Fear-aggressive dogs often have some telltale body language. Many will strain forward on the lead, in perpetual hyper-alert mode, because they are highly stressed and continually

scouring the horizon for new threats. Their bodies are very tense and they may also pant heavily, even when it is not particularly hot.

Alternatively, you will get dogs caught in a constant state of conflict as to how to approach the potential threat of another person or dog. They may initially begin to approach in an actively submissive manner and then suddenly panic and switch to defensive aggression as the person/dog comes closer to them. This behaviour can be particularly common in collie bitches and stems, as ever, from a fundamental lack of social confidence.

AGGRAVATING FACTORS

Fear aggression in individual dogs can also be aggravated by many other additional stress factors, ranging from domestic tensions within a dog's living environment to an impaired faculty or pain source which undermines his sense of confidence. Quite a few fear-aggressive dogs I have seen, for instance, have noticeably poor eyesight.

Fearful dogs often start being aggressive through a basic lack of confidence and then become increasingly lazy in their social approach; i.e. as long as aggression is working, and making people and dogs go away, there is no motivation for them to learn or develop better social skills.

REMEDIAL TRAINING

Remedial training with fear-aggressive dogs involves slowly building up their social confidence, with the help of the right people and mentor dogs, while simultaneously preventing them getting any future reward from aggressive behaviour. The latter may include the use of spray collars as well as vastly improved owner handling skills (see *Improving your handling skills*). If spray collars are to be introduced, however, they have to be expertly timed and used (see, *Deterrents: use and abuse*, page 167).

Only when a dog's faith in aggression as a rewarding strategy is completely undermined, will he be forced to consider other, and better, forms of human/canine social interaction. Thereafter, all future rewards will be attached solely to this better behaviour.

IMPROVING YOUR HANDLING SKILLS

Owners with fear-aggressive dogs generally need to improve both their handling skills and authority levels so that their dog feels better guided and protected by them. They also need to better anticipate hostility in their dog, so that they can block it at its earliest stage with the right kind of corrections, using body language and energy, eye contact and voice (see, *Giving a correction*, page 47).

The part an owner can play in enabling their dog's fear aggression becomes apparent the moment you separate the dog from him or her. So often you will see the dog completely deflate, as soon as his owner departs, and turn from a take-on-the-world aggressive beast to a sad little lost baby, with his tail between his legs.

Owners, without realising it, so frequently give fearful dogs the confidence they need to be aggressive. It is always vital to learn what you need to change about *you*, in order to better help your dog solve his problem.

DOMINANCE OR 'CONTROL' AGGRESSION

Most owners would prefer to think that their collie was fear-aggressive, as opposed to a bullying thug who intimidates others, because this way they can portray him as a victim, which, in turn, reflects better on them.

Aggression launched by collies on to other dogs, however, is sometimes motivated less by fear in its truest sense, and more by a desire to control. This is all the more likely if the collie in question does not immediately become aggressive when he meets another dog and waits, instead, for the other dog to show some sign of weakness before attacking him.

Every time a collie dominates another dog through the use of aggression, his sense of his own higher status is enhanced and his desire to use aggression again gets ever stronger. See *The psychology of a bully*, page 158.

This behaviour can arise in collies who had unsettling experiences with other dogs when they were younger but, more often than not, such past experiences are less relevant to the dog's later aggression than owners might imagine; i.e. the dog is just more genetically compelled to behave this way. For just as collies who have never been threatened or attacked by other dogs can still develop dominant-aggressive behaviour towards them later, countless collies who *do* get attacked never become dominant-aggressive as a result.

The level of overall stress a dog is under can also be a major factor in his use of more controlling behaviours or strategies.

The key to dealing with dominant-aggressive collies is to take far firmer control of all their encounters with other dogs, in ways already outlined in this book (Part One, Chapter Six). You have to make it clear to your dog that it is *you*, and not them, who will decide what behaviour is appropriate when they meet other dogs.

Very often collies may aggressively dominate/intimidate other dogs they live with, and this must also be dealt with in a similarly firm manner. It is the duty of the leader of a pack of dogs to ensure that any conflict within the pack in kept to a minimum. The stronger the leader, the more stable and harmonious the pack will always be.

Moreover, collies who are allowed to get away with controlling other dogs with aggression can so often progress to controlling people the same way, as now outlined.

KEY STEPS TO LIMITING AGGRESSION IN COLLIES

- Raise your dog to be a socially confident and secure individual.
- Teach your dog to respect you from day one, and set appropriate limits on his behaviour.
- Always make the calm mental state rewarding for your dog, and constantly teach him greater emotional self-control and mental discipline.
- Do not allow your dog to manipulate or dominate you in any way .
- Take charge of all your dog's social encounters. Do not let him bully or harass other people or dogs.
- Continually teach him the difference between acceptable, and unacceptable, social behaviour and reward and correct him appropriately. Similarly, never assume your dog will always know what to do in different social contexts. He won't – so you must always tell him.
- Give your dog an ongoing sense of leadership and protection so that he always looks to you for guidance in different situations. Inadequate leadership causes dogs to make wrong (i.e. aggressive) decisions for themselves out of doubt or panic.
- Do not allow any other dogs or people to harass or stress your dog – he will lose trust in your ability to protect him.
- Give your dog sufficient positive, and legitimate, outlets for his working drives and energies, to avoid frustration. This includes better control and use of his lunge-nip drives.
- Work on reducing as many other mental pressure sources for your dog as possible (as outlined in the main text).

THE PSYCHOLOGY OF A BULLY

When you have a collie with a strong psychological need to dominate and control others, and place him in a household where there are no adequate limits imposed on his behaviour, it is invariably a recipe for trouble. The more the dog is able to control others, via the use of aggression, the greater his confidence grows in this behaviour and the bigger the problem becomes.

Often dogs who behave in this way are considered and termed 'dominant', in the sense that they view themselves as naturally superior in status. In fact they are just inherently insecure and also, often, highly stressed.

Like all bullies, they can also be great cowards in any situation where they are less able to establish immediate control; i.e. they will shiver and shake like babies when faced with louder noises or more unusual external experiences. Most canine bullies also know exactly how to pick their victims; they will not challenge dogs or people whose body language and demeanour display no sign of weakness.

Many rescue collies can have control issues of a kind just highlighted. But how much of this insecurity-related behaviour is caused by damaging past life experiences, and extreme stress, as opposed to fundamental genetic character, can often take time, and the right level of rehabilitation training, to better establish. See *Rehabilitating rescue dogs*, page 183.

DOGS WHO BULLY HOUSEHOLDS OR TAKE OVER

I often see situations where collies have been allowed to rule, or take over, whole households, with the use of intimidatory aggression. The dog will typically be aggressive in the following circumstances:

- When people try to move him from a certain area (e.g., hallway, bedroom, top of the stairs).
- When people try to move him off a favoured piece of furniture (e.g. sofa, owner's bed).
- When people try to make him go inside/outside the house.
- When people try to make him go into an indoor kennel (though note, in this case, the aggression could also be inspired by fear – see, *Using and abusing the indoor kennel*, Part One, Chapter Four, page 39).
- When visitors call.
- When people try to go through the front or back door.
- When people approach his food bowl, or approach him when he has a toy or other food item.
- When people try to grab him by the collar.
- When people challenge him in any way – i.e. try to correct or chastise him for bad behaviour.
- Similarly, if the dog has one particularly favoured person in a household, he will be aggressive to any human rival who comes too near to him or her.

Situations like this never happen overnight. They are a direct result of insufficient limits being set on the dog's behaviour earlier in his life.

HOW THE BULLYING PROBLEM ESCALATES

Nobody sets out to have a collie who completely rules their lives, with the use of aggression, as just outlined; whether the aggression concerned is targeted towards household members, or people they invite to visit them. Either scenario can be highly stressful, if not also potentially very dangerous.

It generally happens because owners begin their lives with their collies with a woefully over-lenient regime, which they may equate with a loving or caring attitude, but their dog views as a green light to take charge.

In Part One (Chapters Four and Five), I stressed how important it was to raise your collie puppy with appropriate early rules and restrictions, and to rigidly enforce these to prevent him learning any wrong lessons from displays of weakness on your part. I also outlined how collie puppies must be taught to both respect and co-operate with other members of their household when asked to do so, and learn that any aggression towards people, or even just touching them with their teeth, is strictly taboo.

If your dog had a genetic tendency to become more bullying or exploitative of weakness in later life, this would better keep the problem in check. If he did not have this tendency, you could later relax your earlier rules, as desired, and as long as this did not cause a noticeable deterioration in his subsequent behaviour – as often happens.

FIRST BITES

Frequently owners will imagine their dog's dominant-aggressive behaviour began 'out of the blue' when, in fact, it derived from a slow build up of confidence.

As explained more fully under *Manipulative behaviour (page 177),* the way this confidence is usually amassed is from many successful past episodes where the dog was able to manipulate or bully people into giving him his own way. It may be that the bullying in question was, initially, more psychological than physical or just involved lower-levels of aggression, like growling or teeth-baring, whenever the dog was challenged or thwarted from fulfilling his desires.

It is usually only from such a successful history of past manipulation/intimidation that a dog moves on to more serious aggression – i.e. biting – that shocks everybody or takes them by surprise.

ESCALATION IN AGGRESSION

It is often said of serial killers that their first murder is always the hardest, because it marks the initial crossing of a forbidden line. But then the more people they kill without getting caught, or the sky falling in, the more confident they get and the easier killing becomes.

Much the same kind of psychology, I believe, can arise in dogs who actually bite people hard – including household members – for the first time. Having done it once, and got away with it, the easier it becomes for them to do again.

People often say their dog shows immediate "remorse" after such an attack, but it is just as likely he is anticipating the retaliation to come. Fear of retaliation can be for dogs, as with humans, one of the greatest inhibitory factors governing the use - or avoidance - of aggressive behaviour.

If there is no retaliation, the dog gains ever more confidence in his use of aggression towards an owner or other household member. If there *is* retaliation, however – such as someone shouting at the dog and/or striking him – you then run the risk of him becoming even more aggressive to defend himself.

This is what makes situations like these so potentially dangerous. As outlined more fully in a moment, it is always better to steadily undermine the status confidence of dominant aggressive dogs, in non-confrontational ways, than to openly challenge them while they are still sufficiently confident to attack others at will. The less a dog feels he has to lose through being aggressive, the easier aggressive behaviour will become for him.

TACKLING DOMINANCE AGGRESSION

'Dominance aggression', in its truest sense, can be routinely misdiagnosed. This is why it is always vital to get your dog's aggression expertly assessed. Sometimes the dog may not be displaying deliberate aggression towards people/owners/household members at all; he may just be redirecting lunge-nip instincts triggered by other pressures.

Alternatively he may well be in pain or unwell, or frightened by the way someone approaches him, which, in turn, makes him behave in a more defensive way.

If dominance aggression is tackled in its earliest stages – i.e. while the dog is, say, only tentatively growling, to test his ability to intimidate others – it can often be resolved with the right remedial training. More serious restrictions must be placed on the dog's future behaviour, such as limiting his access to certain parts of the home, and making him earn any privilege he gets from owners – including all food – via appropriate compliance with a command.

In short – and as just highlighted under *Escalation in aggression* – you have to steadily undermine a dog's confidence in his position in your household and 'pack', as it is his ongoing perception of his own superiority, in relation to others, which drives him to attack them with less and less provocation.

HEARTBREAK

Some dogs will always be harder to cure of their dominance-aggression problems than others. So often I see owners break their hearts over dogs like these, because when they are good (i.e. getting their own way, not being challenged or just generally in total control of their environment) they can be so pleasant. But when they are not, they become an ongoing source of stress and misery.

People may realise that they need to be stricter with dominant-aggressive dogs. However, it can still be very hard for all members of a household to stick to tougher regimes with dogs – especially family pets – on a consistent 24/7 basis. It can also be very hard to live with a dog you no longer trust, or even openly fear.

The question then arises as to when you should give up. It is never up to me to decide if people should give up on a dog, or euthanase him because he has become too dangerously aggressive. This is a very personal thing, and everyone has different limits, in terms of what they are prepared to tolerate in a dog they own. But, depending on how dangerous the dog's aggression has become, sometimes it can be the only viable solution.

So very many times I have seen the agony owners face when forced to euthanase a dog because of his aggressive behaviour. They are overwhelmed by feelings of guilt, betrayal, pain and self-torture. Because no matter how much you tell them that dogs with more serious/extreme dominance aggression are usually born with a predisposition towards this behaviour, as opposed to it being exclusively caused by owners, they will still always feel failures who try to blame themselves.

If readers think I am forever harping on about the bad breeding of collies, which includes the perpetuation of 'pet' dogs cursed with genetically less sound minds, this is why. It doesn't just take a massive toll on dogs, but also on the people who own, love and then lose them for reasons they could not foresee.

Of course, there is always the possibility of rehoming dominant-aggressive dogs but, more often than not, this just shifts the same problem on elsewhere.

POSSESSIVE AGGRESSION

The roots of possessive aggression in individual collies can be tricky to pin down, because, again, the behaviour can frequently have some genetic origin, but a lot of it can also be learned. Mostly it begins with possessive behaviour over food in early puppyhood.

Genetically my dogs are more programmed to be sharers than non-sharers. I know this because all my adult dogs happily stick their heads in each others bowls. I also know this because when watching any of my young puppies feeding together, from a collective bowl, there is rarely any trouble.

Sometimes one puppy may instinctively experiment with growling, in order to repel rivals and keep more food for himself. But the others will not do it. Even more interestingly, I have yet to see a non-growling puppy take any notice whatsoever of the growling puppy; instead he or she just carries on eating regardless.

Thus the puppies, themselves, teach the growling littermate that food aggression is unrewarding, the moment he first tries this behaviour. I do also make sure, however, that my puppies continually get used to my hands being in their food while they are eating. Similarly, I constantly put food straight from my hands into their bowls.

STRONGER AND MORE REWARDING REACTIONS

In different litters of collie puppies, however, different lessons can be learned because different dynamics can occur. A more naturally assertive puppy, for instance, may use stronger aggression when eating, and repel a less assertive rival from the food. This instantly rings the reward bell in the aggressor's head, which, in turn, sets the pattern for how he will behave again in the future when a rival comes near his food.

The less assertive puppy, who was repelled, may also learn something unhelpful from this experience; i.e. that aggression of his own, in the future, is the key to holding on to his food. Either way, you now have two puppies who could develop future food possession/aggression problems.

PREVENTING THE FOOD AGGRESSION PROBLEM

Greater supervision of puppies by breeders, when they are very young, could do a lot to prevent future food aggression problems. If you have a puppy, for instance, who repels another puppy from food with aggression, immediately remove him from the rest of the litter at

mealtimes so that he does not keep contaminating them with his hostile attitude and behaviour.

Thereafter feed him separately, but also in a particular way, i.e. put a bowl or plate down in front of him, and put one bit of food at a time into this from your hand, so he learns that another presence around his dish is only ever a positive experience, bringing him his food. Similarly, put one or two last bits of food on the floor in front of your puppy while simultaneously, taking away his bowl. This way, again, your puppy sees the removal of his bowl as a completely positive experience.

Because puppies who are aggressive to littermates around food can so often move on to behaving the same way towards humans later, you must take this issue seriously and deal with it as early as possible. By isolating and feeding a food possessive puppy separately, in the above way, you should nip the problem in the bud.

HOW THE PROBLEM ESCALATES

Food aggression problems in collie puppies tend to escalate if the behaviour is consistently rewarded, and immediate re-training by breeders does not occur (see, *Preventing the food aggression problem*). When the dog is older, for instance, and an owner or other household member suddenly moves near his food bowl it could trigger the same aggressive lunging/snapping he previously used towards his littermates.

If the person near the food then backs off when threatened in this way, the dog gets an immediate reward for his reaction; meaning he is likely to ingrain it into a habit later on.

REACTING WITH AGGRESSION

Some people can react very aggressively, themselves, when a dog first shows aggression towards them around his food. This is usually because they do not understand how instinctive, rather than pre-meditated, such behaviour tends to be. They will see it instead as a sign of the dog's conscious "ingratitude" or lack of respect for them, which, in turn, should be punished in some way.

Unfortunately, because the behaviour was originally defensive in origin, owners shouting at their dogs or hitting them for food aggression can make them even more defensive in their reactions later on. And if you keep challenging and threatening a dog who has gone into high level defensive mode, he may bite you.

After he has bitten you, what can you do? Keep threatening your dog and keep getting bitten, or retreat to the position where you cannot even stay in the same room as your dog while he is eating, for fear of an attack?

Neither solution is particularly ideal. In the former you get hurt; in the latter your dog loses all respect for you.

SOLVING THE PROBLEM

By far the best way to deal with food aggression in an older collie is much as you would with a puppy; i.e. reducing or removing any sense of threat your dog may have attached to owners, or household members, near his food bowl.

As laid out in *Preventing the food aggression problem*, you must train your dog to believe that an owner or other household member near his food bowl can only be a positive thing. If you have a dog, however, who becomes aggressive just at the sight of his food bowl being put down, do not use a food bowl for the exercises previously outlined. Begin instead by putting the food you give him, piece by piece, from your hand, on the floor.

Also make your dog *sit* and *wait*, and/or lie *down*, before giving him each piece of food, in order that he shows increased respect towards you, as the provider of this valuable resource. Get all household members to do the same exercise with your dog, in the same way, so that he shows equal respect for them.

Once this is going well and your dog continues to show no aggression when fed in this way, you can progress to putting each bit of food you give him, from your hand, directly into his bowl. But never return to putting a whole bowl of food down for him until all hint of aggression around his food bowl has completely gone.

Similarly, do not give your dog items such as bones, chews or other treats, if he becomes aggressive towards anyone while in possession of them. Keep making it clear to your dog that all food comes directly from you, and other household members, in return for him showing ample respect, as previously outlined.

OTHER FORMS OF POSSESSIVE AGGRESSION

Once a dog gets a taste for possessive aggression – due to the rewards it consistently brings – there can be no end to the things he will possessively guard, ranging from food and toys and favoured furniture items to cars (see *Guarding behaviour in the car, page 165*), individual owners themselves, and whole areas of the home. This is how a dog escalates to being the bully highlighted earlier in *Dominance aggression, page 157*.

So it is continually important to bear in mind that dogs can never guard what they never get access to, or only ever get access to on your terms.

TERRITORIAL AGGRESSION

How does a collie ever get to think that who comes into your home territory, and the manner in which they should be approached, is entirely his decision rather than yours?

It happens because owners let it happen, through never giving their dog any better or firmer guidance. In Part One (Chapters Four to Six), I outlined the social training collies need in order to better understand their role in your

household pack, including how you expect them to behave when visitors call. This begins with making it clear enough to your dog that all visitors to your home belong to *you*.

It is okay for collies to alert you, through barking, that a visitor is approaching your property. It is not okay for them to do anything else, other than what you tell them they can do. Otherwise your dog will think he is in charge of your whole domestic territory, and not you.

Moreover, if you constantly let your collie run amok round your property, practising and ingraining territorial patterns of aggression, without any better social guidance or control, why suddenly expect him to transform into Mr Nice Guy the moment the postman comes through the gate or Auntie Beryl storms through the front door?

Dogs who behave in this way have to be taught where their social responsibilities end; whereafter, *you* take over to rule the domestic roost (as outlined in Part One, Chapter Six).

CAN ALL AGGRESSION BE CURED?

The commonest question people ask me, with regard to their dog's aggression is: "can he be cured?". The answer depends entirely on the dog and the nature of the aggression problem concerned.

In my own experience, problems which have principally been learned by the dog can be relatively easy to resolve. They also tend to be the most common cases I see.

Problems, however, which have a much stronger genetic component – i.e. are rooted in some essential flaw in the dog's temperament, character or whole way of perceiving his surrounding world – can often be much harder to resolve. As previously outlined (see *Heartbreak*, page 159), the prognosis for dogs who seriously threaten or attack owners without any sense of inhibition – to the extent where owners become frightened of them – can also often be less optimistic.

Ultimately, the extent to which aggression can be eliminated from a dog's life depends as much on the workings of his individual mind as the quality of his rehabilitation training. Some dogs are willing to move on a lot faster than others in this respect, but the incentives we give them for changing are also critical.

When we ask a dog to surrender aggression – a behaviour he may have become so reliant on in his life, for different reasons – we must make sure that we replace it with ways of thinking and acting that prove just as rewarding for him in the future, if not more so. Otherwise his motivation to change, and let go of old behaviour, will be that that much weaker.

Frequently dogs, once suitably retrained, are never aggressive again in their lives, but this can never be taken for granted. Because once a dog has been aggressive, and consistently gained rewards from this behaviour, he will never forget the lesson he has learned. And all future handling of a formerly aggressive dog must take this reality into account.

ANXIETY

See *Stress and stress related problems, page 194*, and also *Separation Distress, page 189*.

ATTENTION-SEEKING BEHAVIOUR

A vast array of more undesirable behaviours and states of mind in collies only get perpetuated as a result of the attention owners give them. Typical examples of wrong attitudes or behaviour reinforced by an owner's attention include fear, anxiety, aggression, jumping up, whining, barking, over-excitable or manic activity, and stealing trophy items that a dog will then run off with, and/or guard.

All of these things are covered in greater detail under their relevant headings in this Advice section. Also see *Fussy eaters and abnormal appetites, page 175* and *Manipulative behaviour*, page 177.

BARKING

Collies can be a particularly vocal breed, but there are still lots of different reasons why they - much like all dogs - bark. The commonest reasons include:

- Because they are excited.
- Because they are frightened.
- Because they are anxious.
- Because they are frustrated.
- Because they want to alert you to a threat.
- Because they want to get your attention.
- Because they want to pressurise you into performing a specific action faster – e.g. feeding them, taking them out, giving them a toy.

In all these cases, to stop the barking you need to use the "*quiet!*" command outlined in Chapter Five, page 48. But you may also need to better address the exact cause of barking in your dog, particularly if it becomes a more persistent problem.

EXCITEMENT

Collies often bark excitedly as a reaction to sudden or ongoing movement and noise (e.g. other traffic passing while they are in the car, or on the street, or other dogs moving and barking). They may also bark in anticipation of rapid movement (i.e. an owner throwing a ball) or rapid movement after a specific sound – i.e. doorbell, telephone. The latter is because they quickly work out that when owners hear the doorbell/telephone ring they immediately rush to where the sound has come from.

Other common excitement barking targets include the lawnmower, vacuum cleaner and garden hose. Some of these things may trigger your dog's eye, stalk and lunge-nip instincts as well.

Some owners are more tolerant of their dog's excitement barking than others. Or maybe they just don't know how to stop it. Either way, it is important to understand that a collie who is persistently barking is rapidly losing mental stability. The more he barks, the more excited he will get and the harder it will be for you to get him to be quiet again. Persistent barking also significantly increases stress levels in your dog, and is a notorious ploy used by some collies to keep their adrenaline levels high (see *Self-stimulators*, page 188).

So as well as employing the *quiet!* command to stop your dog's barking as early as possible, you should immediately invite other behaviour from him to calm him down again – e.g. *down, wait, watch me*. It may also be the case that you need to work a lot harder on your collie's overall emotional self-control, and ability to better wind himself down again once aroused, as highlighted in Part One, Chapter Five, and also *Stress and stress related problems*, page 194.

BARKING THROUGH FEAR, FRUSTRATION AND ANXIETY

Fearful dogs often bark hysterically at other people or dogs, not just to look more frightening, but also to release inner tension. They may do the same to reduce anxiety when left alone at home, or when frustrated due to boredom and confinement, or when confronted by louder or stranger noises which frighten or unsettle them. Human beings cry or shout or scream to release intense emotional pressure. Dogs bark.

So in order to stop the barking in such cases, you have got to address the source of fear, frustration or anxiety which triggers it in the first place. See, *Fearful or nervous aggression* earlier (page 156) plus *Fear and Phobias, page 170, Separation distress, page 189* and *Stress and stress related problems*, page 194.

Very often owners try to stop persistent barking in their dog with a range of deterrent devices, designed to make the barking experience less pleasant or comfortable for him. But if the barking was prompted by fear, anxiety or frustration, this just further ramps up the emotional pressure for a dog, through denying him a ready way to release it. It also means he may then externalise the emotional pressure in other ways – e.g. in intense paw licking/chewing or increased destructiveness.

ALARM BARKING

To my mind there is no problem, whatsoever, with collies barking in the face of a perceived threat – i.e. a visitor or possible intruder near your territory. In fact, such alarm barking can be viewed as a positive asset in a dog. It only becomes a problem when the dog will not stop barking when you ask him to, or gets so carried away with his defensive responsibilities that he flies at windows, or the front door, whenever anyone passes in the street.

HOW OWNERS MAKE BARKING WORSE

The most common reaction for an owner, when a dog keeps barking, is to shout at him. Yet this is also why barking in dogs so often gets worse.

By giving an aroused response of your own to a dog when he barks, as opposed to a distinct, alternative and trained-in command, like "quiet!", you have already begun the process of reinforcing the behaviour. This means it is more likely to develop into an attention-seeking strategy later.

By shouting at your dog when he is barking – particularly if you are not making eye contact with him – he may also just think you are joining in with his noise. Always remember the need to give dogs properly understood corrections for wrong behaviour, followed by an instruction to undertake a more preferable behaviour instead.

Alternatively he may place himself on endless barking patrol round your garden, and thoroughly annoy your neighbours with his noise.

Collies must be taught not only when to be *quiet!* on command in such circumstances, but also – as highlighted earlier in *Territorial aggression* (page 161) – when their guarding/patrolling behaviour must stop. If your collie will not stop defensive or alarm barking in the home or garden, when you ask him to, keep him on a longish line. You can then use this to bring him into the house from the garden when desired, or away from the windows and front door and into another room.

What often happens with collies is that they begin defence/alarm barking for genuine reasons, but once they see what a gratifying reaction this gets from owners they then progress the behaviour into an ongoing attention-seeking ploy. Be wise to this, and similar collie controlling tactics outlined in *Manipulative behaviour*, page 177.

Persistent, monotonous barking can be a particular problem in older collies, and can herald the onset of senile, or pre-senile, brain function, as outlined in Part One, Chapter Thirteen. Often the best way to deal with this is to distract your older dog into more positive (and quieter!) forms of behaviour – e.g. finding food hidden around the garden, or giving him a few training exercises he still knows well.

CAR PROBLEMS

Many collies' car problems date back to puppyhood, and the negative associations they made with car travel through a less scrupulous early socialisation on a breeder's part.

As outlined in Part One, Chapter Three, too many collie puppies' first experience of car travel coincides with the trauma of leaving their initial home and, thereafter, various visits to the vet. These events also tend to happen about the time a puppy is in the throes of his early fear period – i.e. learning to react fearfully to any new or more psychologically challenging experience.

In order to avoid future hang ups about cars, it is vital for a breeder to introduce collie puppies to car travel as early on in their lives as possible, and in a totally positive way, before fear responses to this experience have a chance to kick in.

My own collie puppies are regularly exposed to car travel from around five weeks of age onwards, and none have ever had any later problems with this experience when older.

MOTION SICKNESS

Many young puppies suffer motion sickness when first travelling in a car, which can increase their unease about repeating the car travelling experience later on. Mostly they grow out of it, but car-sickness in puppies or older dogs can be greatly reduced by tying the dog down, so that he is below window level in the car. The more the dog moves around, by contrast, the more his visual input will be in conflict with his inner ear balance mechanisms, and the sicker he will feel.

Over time most dogs discover for themselves that the way to avoid feeling sick is to stay still, or lie down, in the car while travelling.

MENTAL PRESSURE CAUSED BY CAR TRAVEL

Once a collie becomes in any way anxious or unsettled by car journeys he comes under immediate mental pressure whenever the experience is next imposed on him. This pressure may then need an outlet in something like barking, whining or flying at the car windows – although some collies will just do this because they find it exciting.

Car travel provides the following mental challenges for collies: confinement, noise and vibration, unpredictable movement and loss of control over movement, plus sensory over-stimulation caused by other passing and approaching traffic. The only way a dog can completely switch off his defence responses to these challenges is to be exposed to them so young in life that his brain registers them as completely normal (i.e. carrying no level of threat whatsoever).

CAR ANXIETY

If you have a collie who becomes intensely noisy and agitated in the car, through anxiety, or excitement, it may be a good idea to get him a special travelling crate, and cover this with a sheet to avoid pressures caused purely by visual over-stimulation. Travelling crates can also be a good idea for dogs who become anxious when left in the car and, thereafter, resort to destructive behaviour. However, the longer you leave a dog alone in a car, the more you can expect anxiety of some kind to ensue, unless the dog feels particularly happy and secure in the car environment.

It can be incredibly tempting to shout at dogs who bark and whine in the car while you are driving, not least because the behaviour can be so annoying and dangerously distracting. But if the barking and whining is caused more by anxiety than pure excitement (see *Over-excitement*), you may fall into the trap of simply reinforcing your dog's anxious behaviour by giving it so much attention.

REDUCING ANXIETY

Some older puppies (i.e. six months plus) can show reluctance to jump into or out of cars by themselves, only because owners have previously always picked them up or carried them in and out of the car. This is simply a mental block; the dog does not think he is physically able to do what you have always done for him when, beyond six months or so of age, he clearly can.

By throwing a treat or toy into your car for your young dog before each journey, and giving him an encouraging push to go and get it, he should soon happily get into the car by himself. When you want him to get out of the car, throw a treat or toy on the ground for him instead.

In cases of greater anxiety, it can be helpful to work back to the point where your dog first becomes worried about a car journey.

For instance, does your dog show great reluctance to even go near your car? Does he always put up some resistance to avoid getting in it – i.e. you physically have to put him in there? Does he begin shaking or shivering or whining the moment the car door is shut?

These are all signs of high anxiety. Dogs like these really need training that will give them far more positive associations with the car. I have solved many problems like these with clicker training; i.e. gradually encouraging a dog to enter a car by himself with the constant use of rewards. Similarly, rewards keep being given to the dog each time he shows confidence in or around the car.

If you intend to undertake such clicker training however, your timing must be spot on, as it can be incredibly easy for owners to make dogs more neurotic or fearful about cars, simply through inadvertently rewarding/reinforcing anxious reactions instead.

Alternatively, you can turn your car into a play area for your dog. Open all the doors, and make him keep running into the car to get toys and then straight out the other side again. At the same time, never give him any attention when he shows anxiety of any kind. Just keep praising him instead when he shows confidence.

Also do these games with the car engine running. Then play a game when you send your dog into the car, then shut the door behind him, then somebody else opens the door on the other side for him to run out (you will need a friend to help you do this). Keep varying the doors you open and close for your dog, and the toys you throw for him to get, and make the whole thing exciting and fun.

A dog who chooses to enter a car of his own accord will always be a less anxious individual, later on, than one who has forcibly been shoved into one, against his will.

OVER-EXCITEMENT

As previously mentioned, many collies bark and whine in the car, simply through over-excitement, as they anticipate the enjoyable outing or walk to come. This is all the more likely if a dog does not bark or whine on the car journey *back* from a walk, or only begins tuning up as you get nearer a walking destination he is highly familiar with.

Because this behaviour, as with all in-car barking and whining, can be both annoying and dangerously distracting it should not be tolerated. The best way to deal with it is to stop your car the instant your dog starts whining/barking (or stop it as soon as it is safe to do so). Then give your dog the *quiet!* command and make him lie down. Refuse to carry on the journey until both commands have been complied with.

If you do this *each and every time* your dog whines or barks in the car, through excitement, the behaviour will eventually stop. If you only do it sometimes, and at other times let your dog bark and whine while the journey continues, it will not stop.

GUARDING BEHAVIOUR IN THE CAR

The relatively small, confined space of the car can bring out defensive instincts in some collies, making them fly at the car windows aggressively whenever people or dogs come near or pass by. Because the behaviour often happens when an owner is not in the car with their dog, and thus is not in a position to instantly correct him, sometimes the best solution for such aggression is the use of remote control spray collar. This should, however, be used with expert timing, and preferably by a suitably experienced behaviourist or dog trainer.

Some collies may become aggressive in the car when passengers (or other dogs) try to get into the car with them, or when owners try to remove them from the car. Both are instinctive responses triggered by the dog suddenly feeling threatened in a confined space.

The answer to the first problem is to always put the aggressive dog into the car *after* other people or dogs have got in, to lessen any sense of sudden threat. The answer to the second problem is to open the car door, each time you park, and then throw a treat or toy out on the ground for your dog to get. Make sure you keep a lead on him when you do this. As your dog gets the treat or toy, simply pick up his lead. You have now got him out of the car without any conflict.

CHASE BEHAVIOUR

Misdirected, or inappropriate, chase behaviour is one of the commonest sources of angst for collie owners. Can there be anything more exasperating – as well as potentially very dangerous – than a collie who tears off up the street after traffic, or one who disappears over the horizon in hot pursuit of a distant cyclist or train? There are also collies who see any walk as an opportunity to charge up and down, chasing anything that moves, to the point where their lungs seem set to explode or they are sick with eye-rolling, tongue dripping exhaustion. I have seen them all.

Somewhere, somehow, the owners of these dogs lost control of their working focus and behaviour, and when this happens the consequences can be grim. The owners become less and less important to their dogs, as they learn how to constantly reward themselves, with exhilarating and increasingly addictive patterns of behaviour.

A LESSON LEARNT TOO LATE

I cannot tell you how much sympathy I have for people who are relatively new to the Border collie breed and thus do not sufficiently understand the need to both secure and maintain their dog's focus, and keep the brakes on his working drives and impulses, from as early an age as possible.

So often this lesson is only appreciated too late, and the longer a collie is able to fixate on inappropriate targets and chase them, the harder it can be to get his focus back.

However, with the right level of effort, and commitment to retraining, on an owner's part, it can be done.

In Part One (Chapter Eight), I highlighted the kind of anti-chase training your collie will need to keep his working drives better control. In the same chapter, I also emphasised that you cannot begin this kind of training with your dog until you have first secured better overall focus and respect from him, because he will not be sufficiently motivated to respond to you.

For more advice on getting this focus and respect back, see *Rebuilding a Bond*, page 181. Persistent chasers may also need some deterrent, such as a remotely controlled spray collar, attached to their chasing of 'wrong' targets, before other retraining can begin in earnest. Such deterrents should only be used with expert guidance – see *Deterrents: use and abuse, page 167*. Also see, *Herding behaviour, page 176*.

CHEWING

Persistent chewing is an instinctive behaviour in puppyhood, in order for dogs to strengthen jaws and embed new adult teeth. Typically the behaviour will last for up to a year (see Part One, Chapters Four and Five).

Beyond puppyhood, dogs should have learned to target chewing on to appropriate items provided by an owner, e.g., bones and hide chews. So if, in adulthood, chewing is persistently targeted on to less appropriate items – such as owners' belongings, household fixtures and furniture, or carpets and flooring – then other possibilities for this behaviour arise. These include:

- The dog never being taught respect for an owner's belongings and/or
- The dog never being taught to only direct his chewing on to appropriate items (these first two possibilities can be commonly found in rescue dogs).
- The dog using chewing to displace feelings of anxiety when he is left confined somewhere and/or alone.
- The dog chewing doorframes/doors in order to escape the state of confinement.

In the case of the first two possibilities, the dog simply has to be taught the same lessons and manners – i.e., respect for an owner's territory/belongings and which items he can and can't chew - as outlined for puppies in Part One, Chapters Four and Five. Also see *Stealing, page 193*. In the case of the second two possibilities, see *Separation distress, page 189.*.

DEPRESSION

Very many owners do not understand that depression in dogs, as in people, is a form of stress. As covered more fully in *Stress and stress related problems* (page 194), it is just as stressful, and thus harmful, for a dog to be mentally/physiologically under-aroused, for a sustained period, as it is for him to be persistently over-aroused. Either extreme pushes the dog out of that ideal state of core balance he needs to be in, in order to remain in optimum health and at minimum risk of more serious mental or physical deterioration.

DEPRESSION IN OLDER DOGS

Older collies can be particularly vulnerable to depression, not just because they are often living with some ongoing pain source – such as arthritis – but because the older a dog becomes the weaker his arousal mechanisms become. He is mentally and physically less able, in other words, to flood his body with feel-good chemicals in the same way a young dog can. It may well be that the persistent barking – so often found in older dogs – is a way to self-arouse themselves mentally when they are unable to do this anymore through more active physical exertion.

In Part One (Chapter Thirteen), I outlined how crucial it was to keep older collies physically and mentally active, as much as possible and for as long as possible, in order to prolong both their physical and mental health. Otherwise the dog can become trapped in a downward spiral of decline.

DEPRESSION CAUSED BY CONFINEMENT

Keeping dogs confined for lengthy periods commonly results in them becoming depressed. The depressed state does not necessarily happen right away. Many collies placed in confinement may initially go through a period of high agitation, if not near manic anxiety, as they try to escape the kennel or other restricted space they have been placed in.

It is only when they realise that such resistance to their fate is futile that depression sets in. The longer they are confined, the less mental or physical resistance they make to the state of confinement. This, in turn, means their mental/physical arousal systems become less and less active, which results in a persistent state of depression.

Many owners can imagine that their dogs are "coping fine" with lengthy periods of confinement and under-activity, because they do not understand what the state of depression or 'internalised stress' looks like in a dog, and a collie in particular.

Unless particularly elderly, a collie who sleeps lengthily throughout the day and shows scant or only moderate enthusiasm for play, training tasks and social interaction is not, for instance, a normal collie.

Rescue collies can commonly suffer depression as a result of previously living in confined circumstances. The confined circumstances are not always just the rescue kennels they may have been placed in prior to rehoming. A lot of collies can have a long history of being confined in small spaces by past owners, before they even get to rescue kennels or shelters. For more advice on dealing with dogs like these, see *Rehabilitating rescue dogs,* page 183.

DEPRESSION CAUSED BY LIFE EVENTS AND LIFESTYLE

Dogs – much like people – can become depressed as a reaction to traumatic life events, such as:
- The loss of an owner, or close fellow canine companion.
- A serious illness, or operation.
- A serious attack by another dog.
- Intense domestic upheaval, e.g. arrival of a new baby, or rival dog.

Life event depression usually passes in time, given patience on an owner's part, and sufficient effort made to lift the dog's mood rather than constantly reinforce and encourage it with an excess of sympathy.

Plenty of daily exercise and regular outings to new places can also do much to alleviate depression in dogs. Dogs who have lost companions need to find enjoyment again in the company of other dogs.

Dogs worrying about the arrival of babies, new dogs or other new house members need to be reassured of their importance to you, via plenty of one-to-one interactions. They also need to be persuaded that these new pack additions can only bring benefits to their lives. Wherever possible, keep connecting the presence of a new dog, person or baby with something really positive or rewarding in your dog's head, such as food, treats, attention and games.

LIFESTYLE-INFLICTED DEPRESSION

At other times it is the dog's overall lifestyle itself, which perpetuates ongoing depression in him, usually because it features one or more of the following factors, over and above the previously mentioned highly stressful state of regular confinement:
- Ongoing ill treatment/abuse/hostility from an owner.
- Ongoing lack of sufficient daily exercise/mental stimulation.
- Over oppressive lifestyle; i.e. constant correction/disapproval from owner and endless restrictions placed on a dog's normal/natural canine behaviour.
- Living in households that are too noisy/emotionally volatile.
- Living in households without any sense of leadership, guidance or routine.

Lifestyle-inflicted depression in dogs cannot be resolved as long as the lifestyle element causing the depressed mental state remains unchanged. It is truly worrying how many owners today are rushing to put their dogs on anti-depressant medication, without first better exploring, and addressing, how much of their dog's 'illness' is simply down to the way they make him live. In this way, they are simply chemically suppressing a dog's perfectly normal and natural reaction to the circumstances he finds himself in.

It can be understandably hard, in many busy households, to always give your collie's mental state sufficient daily consideration. But it is also part and parcel of the responsibilities of owning a highly intelligent animal, who is unable to either dictate or escape the lifestyle you choose to impose on him.

The better the lifestyle a dog has, the better he will always feel and thus behave. It is as simple as that – and also a whole lot cheaper, and healthier, than endless packets of pills.

DESTRUCTIVENESS

Puppies can be highly destructive creatures who devote much of their early energies to chewing and trashing things. It is purely instinctive behaviour at this stage, as a young dog explores his surrounding environment and develops predatory impulses.

During puppyhood (as outlined in Part One, Chapters Four and Five) we have to teach dogs, through constant correction and training, only to chew and destroy things that we have given them specifically for this purpose, and to leave everything else alone, because it belongs to *us*. If we do not get this message across clearly enough or consistently enough, early on, then dogs may retain inappropriately destructive impulses when older, and also do that much more damage, due to the power of their adult jaws and teeth.

Bored dogs will always be more destructive, as well as those who have never been taught to use their mental and physical energies in more positive ways. In such dogs, digging in the garden can also be a bigger problem (see *Digging,* Page 168). It should also be constantly remembered that dogs can only destroy what you give them access to destroy.

The vast majority of more troublesome destructive episodes in adult collies tend to occur, however, when owners are not present and in response to some specific emotional trigger. In other words, destructiveness is simply a displacement strategy, used to relieve the discomfort caused by feelings of frustration and anxiety.

In this respect, the subject is covered under *Separation distress,* page 189.

DETERRENTS: USE AND ABUSE

Deterrent devices, such as training discs or remotely-activated spray collars, will always be valuable tools in the behaviour modification of dogs, providing they are both expertly and humanely used.

A highly experienced trainer or behaviourist will know what deterrent device, or measure, to use for a specific problem. They will also know when to use it, and when not to use it, in order that a dog only learns what you want him to from the deterrent experience.

Unfortunately, many less knowledgeable owners (and trainers!) will not sufficiently understand how dogs learn, or how fast they can make mental associations with specific events. This is particularly the case with Border Collies, who both think and react with exceptional speed. They may also be unable to adequately read the state of mind a dog is in when they administer a deterrent response – and for all these reasons, they end up using deterrent devices incorrectly. As a result they may fail to solve a particular problem in a dog, or even make it worse.

THE PURPOSE OF A DETERRENT

The purpose of any deterrent device is to quickly interrupt a wrong behaviour, or state of mind, in a dog, and also attach negative consequences to it. Only once you do this can the opportunity arise to invite better ways of behaving, or thinking, which you then consistently reward. This is how you steadily evolve different and preferred behaviour in a dog.

WHY DETERRENTS FAIL

Sometimes deterrent devices do not work because their negative effects do not sufficiently outweigh the rewards a dog is getting from a particular behaviour.

More commonly, deterrent devices fail because they are used incorrectly. Owners may persistently over-use them on their dog, for example, to the point where he becomes completely de-sensitised to their negative effects and, thereafter, just slips straight back into old and rewarding patterns of wrong behaviour.

Alternatively – or additionally – they may persistently get the timing of a deterrent device wrong and, as a result, punish their dog for 'right' thoughts and actions, by mistake. Or, again through wrong timing, they may make a dog develop negative associations with things – including other dogs and people – which he previously regarded positively.

It is crucial to be aware of the extra problems you could give yourself, and your dog, through the misuse of deterrent devices.

CORRECT USE

Because Border Collies tend to be such highly sensitive dogs, psychologically, I have found that it often takes less to inhibit their behaviour, deterrent wise, than is the case with some other breeds.

With many collies, for instance, just the right level of energy, eye contact and verbal correction can be enough to stop, or check, a range of undesirable behaviours in them, including persistent barking and aggression.

In cases where you cannot make such direct eye contact with a dog, and/or where you need to correct his behaviour when he is some distance away from you, remote control spray collars can be highly effective, but only if (as stressed previously) they are expertly used and timed.

When working with collies and spray collars, my aim is to use them as rarely as possible, to suitably maintain their impact. Moreover, each time I use them, it will be to correct a dog while he is *on the brink of turning a wrong thought into a wrong action*. This is because the earlier, and more often, you prevent dogs turning wrong thoughts into wrong actions, the sooner those wrong actions stop happening.

If, by contrast, you constantly allow a dog to undertake a wrong action, and get the rewards from it, *before* you spray him, the deterrent effect will have come too late and, thus, will have less and less impact on changing his behaviour.

Of course, the ability to know, or best judge, when a dog is thinking the 'wrong' thing, and needs to be immediately deterred, does take some level of experience, which simply reemphasises the need for expert guidance with this kind of remedial training.

THE 'BIG GUNS' APPROACH

As someone who believes that with collies – if not most dogs – you begin with the minimal level of deterrent to solve a problem and then work up to stronger measures, as necessary, it appals me how often the reverse happens. Owners, or less enlightened/knowledgeable trainers, storm straight in with the big guns first, without any real insight into the deeper roots of a problem in a dog's head.

When you use devices such as electric shock collars on dogs, for instance (now banned in some countries), the capacity for abuse is endless and, similarly, the possibilities for giving dogs even bigger problems than they started with. To my mind, the only possible justification for using shock collars on dogs is *after* all other options have been explored, training-wise, and in situations where the problem behaviour of the dog in question would otherwise have fatal consequences for him. Even then, the use of the collar should only be undertaken by an expert trainer.

Another problem with using deterrent big guns first, is that if an owner/trainer messes up their application on a dog – to the point where he becomes immune or oblivious to their effects – this leaves you with little where else to go, deterrent-wise, when trying to retrain him.

THE FIRE EXTINGUISHER EXPERIENCE

A while ago, I dealt with a rescued bitch who persistently attacked other dogs when out. The owner had previously taken her to a trainer who addressed her aggression around other dogs by launching a fire extinguisher at her.

As too often can happen, I suspect the main reason for this approach by the trainer was in order for him to look big and clever, in seeming to find such an instant solution to a persistent problem. Certainly, while the bitch remained in the context where the trainer and fire extinguisher were present, her aggression towards other dogs was somewhat inhibited.

Anywhere else, however, she just went on attacking other dogs as normal. This was because she only associated the fire extinguisher deterrent with one person (the trainer) and one context (his training hall). It was also because the psychological motivation behind her aggressive behaviour remained unaddressed and, thus, unresolved. There is also the not insignificant factor that most owners tend not to drag fire extinguishers around with them when taking their dogs out for walks.

The most effective way to stop a dog being aggressive, in all contexts, is to pinpoint the reason why the dog needs to be aggressive in the first place, and then make that reason go away. This takes considerably more skill, time and effort than is involved in aiming a fire extinguisher at a dog. But it is also the only approach that, in the longer term, consistently works. Just like it worked for the rescued bitch in this story. Her aggression problems were eventually resolved through giving her far greater social confidence around other dogs, while simultaneously correcting any hostile intent with the immediate use of a verbal correction.

So readers, please heed my warnings about deterrents and their risks, and never have your heads turned by trainers who operate in them in such self-glorifying and highly ignorant ways. Because ultimately it is you, and not them, who will have to live with the consequences of any deterrent experience they mess up with your dog.

DIGGING

Nature programmes dogs to find survival behaviours – e.g. eating, mating, predatory chasing – compulsive and rewarding, otherwise the species would not carry on.

Digging is just another one of these behaviours. The main original function of digging for dogs is to unearth smaller prey, like rodents, and to fashion dens or nests. The activity tends to begin in collies, like most dogs, during early puppyhood. How keen, or not, a digger a dog becomes will depend on factors such as his genetic make-up, how consistently rewarding or not he finds the behaviour, and what other outlets he gets for his mental and physical energies.

For most owners, digging becomes a problem in their collie when he persists in excavating great holes in their lawn or garden beds. Sometimes it is recommended that dogs are given their own special area in the garden, where digging is permitted. However, this can prove confusing and it also allows garden digging to become a continually more ingrained habit.

Some collies naturally grow out of digging behaviour in the garden as they get older. Others do not. Either way, I much prefer to deter the behaviour altogether in my dogs in puppyhood, as soon as it starts.

DETERRENT ACTION

The way I do this is to set up a hose in the garden, which I can activate from inside the house. As soon as a puppy begins digging, I turn on the hose so that the water shoots at him. It is vital, however, that the puppy *never sees you activating the hose*. He must always believe that it is his digging, and not *you*, which brought about the sudden soaking, and nasty surprise.

As a deterrent to stop puppies digging in my garden, I have never yet known it not to work.

If you are going to stop puppies digging in your garden, however, you must ensure that you give them plenty of other outlets for their energies, in the way of toys and games, as well as plenty of appropriate things to chew. Similarly, when they are older, they can release their energies in regular daily outings and walks. Many collies resort to digging through boredom, and a lack of anything better to do.

If my dogs want to dig on the beach, or in the fields, they are perfectly free to do so. I just teach them that digging in *my garden* can have unpleasant consequences.

OTHER REASONS FOR DIGGING

Sometimes entire bitches will engage in frantic digging behaviour in the home during the pseudo pregnancy phase of their reproduction cycle. It is a compulsive activity which some have linked to a nesting urge, and others believe is a way the bitch displaces feelings of discomfort caused by uterine spasms.

Digging or clawing/pawing the ground is a way dogs of either sex may try to relieve pain caused by conditions such as arthritis, or gastric discomfort. This is something to be aware of, and check out with a vet, if necessary.

More destructive digging/clawing activity in the home can be used to displace the intense frustration or anxiety many dogs feel when left alone and confined, as outlined in *Separation distress*, Page 189.

The above reasons apart, clawing and scratching at the ground, or their bedding, can also just be a perfectly natural part of nesting or settling down behaviour for dogs.

DISOBEDIENCE

Disobedience covers a wide range of unruly and non-cooperative behaviours in collies. Most have a specific cause, or combination of causes, rooted in the dog's earliest training and social education – although sometimes there can also be an aggravating genetic factor.

These problems have all been covered earlier in Part One. Disobedience with regards to specific types of training, or command, is covered extensively in Chapter Seven.

In general, to better understand disobedience in a dog, you first need to understand the factors that motivate a dog to be *obedient* instead, and far more eager to co-operate with your commands. See *Rebuilding a Bond,* Page 181.

EMOTIONAL INCONTINENCE/SELF-CONTROL

Emotional incontinence – i.e. an individual's inability to keep explosive emotions, like anger or frustration, under better control – is a phenomenon blighting our modern world. It is at the heart of so many social and educational problems in human society today, and is a 'disease' that is increasingly spreading to our dogs.

The blame for modern emotional incontinence in people is often attributed to more liberal methods of parenting and teaching, i.e. adults have become afraid or inhibited about setting tougher limits on children's behaviour; preferring instead to cast themselves in the weaker and more indulgent role of being their buddy, which carries far fewer demands or responsibilities.

Children, today, are also being persistently over-stimulated, mentally, by devices such as televisions, mobile phones, computers – and noise, noise and yet more noise – to the point where their brains and bodies rarely get a chance to reach and sustain a state of calm.

In much the same way, dogs raised with no consistently enforced rules or limits placed on their behaviour, who are continually over-stimulated and never taught to master more conscious control over emotions like frustration, excitement or rage, will always have more problems, and be more difficult to live with.

I see collies like this all the time.

DISCIPLINE

Over past decades, people seem to have lost sight of their need to exert discipline when raising dogs. They do not realise that by failing to persistently check and shape their dog's behaviour, to better fit the demands of the world he will be inhabiting, they are doing him a gross disservice, as well as making life ten times more stressful for themselves.

Dogs raised without any ability to discipline their minds or inhibit their emotional impulses tend to be neurotic, unruly, and pretty stressed most of the time. So if you really care about your dog, teach him the following (as outlined in Part One, Chapters Four and Five), as early as possible:

- Concentration.
- Commitment to a task or goal.
- Emotional self-control.
- Respect for authority.
- Compliance with authority.
- Basic social manners/skills.

Because without these skills in place, your dog can never be anything other than a lower league player in the game of life. It goes without saying that, in order to teach these skills to your dog, you have first got to be able to master them yourself.

EMOTIONAL OVER DEPENDENCY/ATTACHMENT

Collies can have a tendency to become highly attached to their owners. This is what often lies behind their extreme trainability as breed, as well as what we like to regard as their intense loyalty and willingness. They are also, however, qualities typically displayed in dogs with higher degrees of learned helplessness; a psychological reliance/dependency syndrome covered in Part One (Chapter Five, page 45).

It is important to understand that the more you encourage, or enable, a dog to become emotionally dependent on you and your presence, the greater his psychological suffering will be whenever he is left alone, or has to be parted from you – as outlined in *Separation distress*, page 189.

It is much, much kinder to teach collies greater emotional self-reliance from day one, in order to minimise any suffering they may feel later when parted from you. Such early training in greater emotional self-reliance has been covered in detail in Part One, (Chapter Four).

FEAR AND PHOBIAS

Fear in dogs, as in all animals, is a vital survival response, because it triggers the behaviours – i.e. fight or flight – necessary to overcome/evade different environmental threats and challenges.

The more efficiently, and economically, a dog uses his fear responses – i.e. only in situations where he is genuinely under threat – the healthier he will be. This is because every sustained fear response in a dog will take a toll on him, physically and mentally. His heart rate and blood pressure will soar, for instance, and his body will be flooded with stress hormones which alter his metabolism and suppress his immune system.

OVER-SENSITIVITY

A lot of dogs have fear responses that are too over-sensitive and over-active. In other words, not only will the dog react just as readily to *perceived* threat as genuine threat – because his brain cannot better distinguish between the two – but the response will be excessive, and more lengthily sustained.

Like many behaviours/responses in individual dogs, very often this trait will have a genetic root and can be particularly common in collies, due to the super-sensitivity of their brains and reactive processes as a whole.

How well you raise and socialise a collie from puppyhood however (as outlined in Part One, Chapters Four to Six) can also determine the level of his later fear responses.

When you have a collie with over-sensitive reactions to threat, it can lead to a host of subsequent problems ranging from fear aggression (covered earlier, under *Aggression*, page 152) to more extreme phobias centred on specific noises, places or experiences. See *Fear and Confidence*, opposite.

Moreover, fear can be an incredibly contagious emotion.

In other words, a dog may start off feeling fearful about a certain noise, and then move on to feeling just as fearful about any other noises that remind him of the original fright. Or he could associate a frightening experience with a specific place, and refuse later to go anywhere near this place again. At worst, he could generalise his fear to the whole environment outside your home and become, pretty much, agoraphobic.

LESSER AND GREATER FEAR

Fearfulness in collies can be one of the toughest problems to deal with, because every dog's perception of what is frightening, and why, can be so very different, and similarly his level of reaction to it.

Some collies, with the right remedial training, can get over fears about certain sounds/objects/experiences relatively quickly. Other dogs will spend the greater part of their lives being complete nervous wrecks; shaking, cowering, running, hiding or attacking the world from the end of a lead, because there is a stronger genetic element driving the whole way they react to their external environment.

The limits of what you can achieve in a collie, in overcoming his fear, do not just depend on the quality of your retraining but also the level of his own willingness, or reluctance, to leave feelings of uncertainty and doubt behind. This, again, can revolve around the way his brain is programmed to respond, genetically.

Undoubtedly there are many collies around today whose natural levels of fearfulness are so high that they should never be bred from. Similarly, the parent dog(s) who passed this trait on to them should never have been bred from.

A predisposition towards highly fearful behaviour (as well as more extreme phobic reactions) gets passed on from parent dog to puppy as readily as any other genetic trait. Yet people still breed from nervous/fearful dogs all the time. It is as if this characteristic – which is so often linked to more extreme aggression and a devastatingly low life quality for affected dogs and their owners alike – was an easily dismissed minor flaw, or one that will magically disappear in the next generation. It never does.

TACKLING FEAR

Any dog can suddenly take fright – but the first time he has this reaction is the best chance you will ever have to change his attitude. This is because the behaviour is still new, and will only become ingrained if it is sufficiently rewarded.

The most important thing, therefore, is to never reward your dog's first fearful reaction with sympathetic attention – i.e. try to soothe or reassure him – as invariably this will reinforce the behaviour. The same is true if you immediately take your dog away from a person/dog/object/place he is afraid of, because this way he has seemingly persuaded you to avoid it, too.

Once a dog realises he can dictate to you what should be avoided, he loses confidence in your ability to protect him and, thus, his fear can rapidly escalate.

SHOWING STRENGTH

To train a dog to be less afraid, you have first got to begin from a position of strength, as opposed to weakness. Your dog has to believe not only that you are stronger than him, but also that you know far more about his surrounding world than he does.

Strength is shown to dogs in the form of cool, calm, quiet authority. Not through indulgence, panic, frustration, impatience or any other form of emotional weakness or agitation on an owner's behalf. Unless you can always get your level of calm authority right when faced with a frightened dog, you cannot change him because you cannot make him feel safe, and guided by a judgement which is superior to his own.

RUNNING AWAY

When collies are frightened they either react defensively (the fight response, already covered under *Aggression*), or run away (the flight response) or they freeze.

Collies who run away from a frightening sound/experience will often become deaf to an owner's commands to stop, despite normally being very obedient dogs. This is down to the effects of stress hormones, such as adrenaline and cortisol, which power sub-conscious, instinctive reactions to external threat in animals. Once this happens, their conscious minds are less able to take in external information.

Most dogs, when fleeing something frightening, will try to get back to a perceived place of safety – such as home, or an owner's car. If neither refuge is easily accessible to the dog, he may run endlessly round and round in circles, constantly trying to burn off the adrenaline/nervous energy that has built up in his body. If there seems no logic to where he is running, this is because, again, he is mainly operating sub-consciously, in alarm mode, which makes logical conscious thought far harder. This is what we normally refer to in humans as blind panic.

THE REWARDS OF RUNNING

Every time a collie is able to run away from something that has scared him, there can be a positive consequence to this behaviour; i.e. the immediate sense of relief which follows.

The feeling of relief in animals is caused by self-calming chemicals which flood the body, once the mind perceives that a threat has passed (a process more fully explained under *Stress and stress related problems,* page 194). It can also be a very pleasurable experience for a dog, mentally and physically.

Thus, every time a dog runs away from something, his

FEAR AND CONFIDENCE

Not only will every dog have a specific fear setting - in terms of how readily and strongly he will react when faced with something new or more potentially unsettling – he will also have a specific confidence setting; i.e., some dogs can recover, or 'self-calm', much more rapidly after a fear response than others.

Thus, when we call dogs 'more confident' or 'more fearful' in nature, we are really referring to how easily, or not, they will mount a fear response, and how rapidly, or not, they can recover from it afterwards.

As ever, these differences tend to have some genetic component. Dogs, however, can actually be conditioned to react more confidently/fearfully in later life, depending on how their earliest socialisation and fear responses are managed.

With the right training, confidence can also become a more natural 'habit' for a dog than fear, even if he is genetically programmed to be a more fearful dog.

COMMON FEAR RELATED PROBLEMS IN DOGS

- Aggression/timid behaviour towards other dogs.
- Aggression/timid behaviour towards less familiar people.
- Aggression/timid behaviour towards visitors to the home.
- Destructiveness/indoor fouling due to anxiety felt by the dog when left home alone.
- Noise phobias, e.g. fireworks, thunder, traffic.
- Phobias about particular places/experiences/objects.
- Agoraphobia; a dog refuses to leave the home environment.

mind's instinctive desire to seek relief is what drives him; it is the emotional holy grail, if you like, at the end of the running experience. Once you appreciate this, you will also understand how impossible it can be to teach a dog that something is safe as long as he is still getting rewarded for running away from it.

REACTING IN THE WRONG WAY

As a typical fear example, we will imagine that you are out walking your collie, off lead, and there is a sudden loud noise which frightens him; e.g. someone using a mechanical saw/hedge trimmer, or slamming the rear door of a truck, or dropping scaffolding poles, or opening the metal shutters of a shop or café.

Let's face it, human beings live in an incredibly noisy world – and every day we seem to invent some new insult to the ears. If something sounds loud to you, however, you can pretty much assume that it will sound even louder to your dog.

So your dog hears a scary sound, panics and then runs off, deaf to any attempts you make to stop him. He may run home. He may run back to your car. He may just run round and round in circles. What do you do?

- Follow your dog home and then stay there with him?
- Follow your dog back to the car and then drive him home?
- Eventually catch your dog, put him on the lead, then take him home?

These would *all* actually be the wrong thing to do, because they all reward him for running away. Your dog gets the all-important sense of relief from his actions, and he has also persuaded you that fleeing the scene of fright is the right thing to do.

Unfortunately, what this also means is that the next time you take your dog to the place where his fright happened, he will react just as fearfully, in anticipation of the same noise happening, even if it does not.

From this stage he may also react excessively to any noise that reminds him of the first fright, or he may refuse to go anywhere in the direction of the place where the first noise happened. This is the manner in which fear, once appropriately rewarded and reinforced, rapidly escalates.

REACTING IN THE RIGHT WAY

If your dog reacts fearfully to something and runs away it is far better to:
- Follow him calmly home, or to wherever he ended up (i.e. no screaming or shouting).
- Put him on the lead.
- Immediately return him to the scene of his fright.

If your dog remains anxious, do not talk to him or give him any attention of any kind while walking back to the 'scare site'. If he shows reluctance to move forward with you, do not give in to this or give it attention. Keep calm but positive, striding purposefully on with your dog, in order to push him past his mental block (also see, *Getting past the mental block*).

When you get back to the scare site, keep absolutely still until your dog winds down again. Do not look at him or talk to him while he is still agitated. Sit on the ground, or on a bench, if you like. The key is that you give your dog no attention at all until he has wound down and/or shown much more confidence.

PATIENCE

This may take some time, as some collies will always take longer to come down from states of extreme mental arousal (i.e. fear/excitement) than others. You just need to be very patient, as patience at this stage will pay dividends later on.

Eventually your dog will calm down, as there is only so long his body can sustain an acute adrenaline response. Once he has wound down, try offering him a treat or a toy. If he reacts positively to either, this is generally a sign of growing confidence – though do be aware that some panicky dogs will still snatch at treats or toys. So does your dog, also, just *look* a lot calmer to you than he was before? If so, at this point you can take him home again, in a very calm and matter-of-fact way. If your dog has no interest in the treat or toy, and still seems just as agitated, wait longer. Only when he responds more positively to either, and looks a lot calmer, take him home again.

In this way you have only rewarded confidence, not fear. You have also ensured that chemicals causing the feeling of wind down/relief in your dog have kicked in *while he is still in the place where he was originally scared*, as opposed to kicking in only *after he has run from this place*.

CONTINUAL RE-EXPOSURE

Later on, try your best to keep re-exposing your dog to the same initial noise/object/experience that scared him, or get someone else to recreate it for you. Keep your dog on a line while they do this, so he cannot run away, and then always react in the same way I have outlined. Do not let your dog off the line again around a scare site until his fear, and accompanying desire to run away, has completely gone.

By following this alternative approach your dog's recovery from his initial fright should be much quicker. It is also less likely that his initial fear will spread to other similar sounds.

This approach is really much in line with the old saying that you should get straight back in the saddle, once you have fallen off a horse; i.e. you never give avoidance/escape from an initial fear the chance to become ingrained as a favoured response or habit. Having fallen off quite a few horses in my time, I can also vouch that it works – for people, and for dogs.

Note: Exceptions where I would *not* make a dog go straight back to a scare site is in the case of any experience that could be genuinely harmful, or exceptionally traumatic, for your dog. The latter includes events such as thunderstorms or firework displays, as these often inspire terror in collies of such a height that increasing exposure to them, unnecessarily, is both cruel and – ultimately – counter-productive. See *Fireworks and thunderstorms*.

FREEZING AND THE MENTAL BLOCK

So far I have looked at the fight (under *Aggression*) and flight response to fear in dogs, but there is also *freezing*. This most typically happens when a dog is on a lead and, thus, cannot immediately run from the thing that scares him.

He may, of course, first try to run away while on the lead, pulling you with him. If this does not work he will then freeze and refuse to move forwards with you towards the thing he fears. At this point, many owners may give in, and let their dog go home, or avoid going where he does not want to go – which, again, simply rewards fear and allows it to become ingrained.

This is also exactly how dogs end up being agoraphobic; refusing to leave the home environment at all.

The more often you let your dog get a reward from stalling and freezing on the lead, and refusing to move on, the stronger his resistance will get each time. In allowing your dog to suck you into his own victim mentality and dictate where you both go, you have also shown great weakness. If you want to inspire your dog to move on through his fear-triggered mental block, and out the other side, then he needs you to show far greater strength and confidence.

GETTING PAST THE MENTAL BLOCK

Let us imagine that your dog will only go so far down the road with you on the lead and then he suddenly freezes and will not move forward with you, because he has hit his fear-triggered mental block.

At this point, the more you try to verbally reassure/pressurise him to move, the more fearful and paralysed he will become. It is far better not to let your dog stop. Also increase, rather than decrease, your own walking speed as you get near the point where your dog normally freezes. Owners often slow down themselves, or show tension/hesitation in their own body language (often without realising it) when they get near a place where their dog usually stops. Dogs quickly pick up on this level of weak/uncertain energy.

Through walking quickly and purposefully on, you are aiming to provide enough physical momentum, energy and confidence to power your dog through his mental block and out the other side, before he has had more time to think about it. If done correctly, this is all it takes to unblock the frozen mental state. It is also incredibly important to totally ignore, rather than indulge, your dog when he is behaving in an anxious way. Only when he shows confidence again, on the other side of his 'block', return attention to him again and keep praising him really well.

I have used this technique on countless freezing dogs with much success. In the case of dogs who have become so fearful they will not leave the home environment, a much more gradual programme of confidence building and rewarding will need to be put in place.

FIREWORKS AND THUNDERSTORMS

Fireworks and thunderstorms are about the commonest causes of more extreme noise phobias in collies, as they are in many other breeds.

One of the biggest problems with fireworks and thunderstorms, alike, is their random pattern of occurrence – i.e. neither owner nor dog can predict where and when they are going to happen. This makes it much harder for the dog to become de-sensitised to the sounds of thunderstorms/fireworks over time.

It can also be hard, if not near impossible, for an owner to keep recreating thunderstorm/firework experiences for their dog with sufficient authenticity, in order for him to be gradually taught different and better ways of reacting to them.

Sometimes training CDs, featuring firework and thunderstorm noises (among others) can help. But unfortunately fireworks and thunderstorms are rarely just noise events for dogs. They are phenomena which also bring a host of other scary sensations in their wake; i.e. bright flashing light, strong vibrations, a massive sudden drop in atmospheric pressure (as is the case with thunderstorms).

Moreover, while owners always think it is the claps and rumbles of thunder, during a thunderstorm, that scares their dog the most, it could in fact be the accompanying lightening, or the frantic patter of raindrops on the conservatory roof, which he finds most terrifying.

Similarly, some dogs may dread the bright flashes caused by fireworks more than the bangs. But because so much fear in dogs runs in associative sequences – i.e. this means *that* is about to happen – it will always be hard to tell which part of any thunder or firework experience scares your dog the most.

SANCTUARY

Unlike other lower-level noise experiences referred to earlier (see *Running away*), where a dog's initial fear/flight response can be overcome with constant, controlled re-exposure to the same sound, while more positive attitudes are attached to it, I feel differently about fireworks and thunderstorms.

These experiences can be so terrifying for collies that they should not be deliberately exposed to them outside. Psychologically, this could do more harm than good. It could also damage their hearing.

KEY STEPS TO PREVENTING AND TACKLING FEAR IN YOUR DOG

- Raise your dog to be socially confident.
- Teach him the Go see! command (outlined in Part One, Chapter Six, page 63).
- Train your dog how to behave (i.e. calmly, confidently, politely) in different social situations and constantly reward and praise him for getting this right.
- Take charge of all his social encounters.
- Be a strong and inspirational leader to your dog, to sustain his confidence in both you and your judgement.
- Work out the rewards your dog is getting from fearful responses (e.g. owner attention, removal of threat, or sensation of relief after running away), and try to stop this happening.
- Thereafter, only attach rewards to more confident behaviour.
- Understand that fearful behaviour and more confident behaviour are both habits a dog can learn, according to how they are each rewarded/reinforced over time.

If a thunderstorm is imminent, or throughout the firework season in your country, it is best to keep your collie on a long line, so that he cannot bolt in fright and get into danger. Should a thunderstorm or fireworks begin while you are out, then just walk your collie home/back to the car as calmly as possible; do not let him pull you, and do not talk to him or give him any attention at all while he is looking afraid.

As soon as you are home, put him in a special place of sanctuary (see below) to wind down again.

If your dog is at home when thunder/fireworks begin, he still needs this special place of sanctuary. A common reason why dogs get so worked up at home when thunder/fireworks begin is because they cannot run anywhere to displace all the nervous energy created by fear. At the same time, they may not have anywhere suitable to go that will make them feel safer, whereupon their self-calming mechanisms could begin to kick in.

MAKING A SANCTUARY

You will need to construct a special sanctuary for your dog, where he can go whenever he is really frightened.

In Part One (Chapter Four), I described the special refuge zone that all collies need in order to mentally wind down and rest in peace. The sanctuary you create for your dog when he is really frightened, however, may need to be much smaller and more closed in.

You may have already noticed your dog seeking out a particular small space in your home – e.g. under a dresser, or behind a sofa, or under a coffee table – whenever he is worried, or just wants to get away from everyone and everything. You may adapt this spot by putting some comfy bedding in, and also making it even more enclosed, if necessary, with blankets or cushions or boards.

Getting into a small, and more tucked away, space is instinctive behaviour in dogs when they want to feel safe, and goes back to the original dens they would have equated with safety in the wild.

Sometimes a little trial and error may be required until you finally pinpoint a sanctuary spot your dog is really happy with. You will know this from his keenness to go there, when under pressure, and also his contentment to remain there when frightened by something, rather than tearing aimlessly and restlessly around.

MANAGING THE FEAR EXPERIENCE

Whenever your collie is frightened by thunder or fireworks, it is important not to give him any attention at all – especially not sympathy or reassurance. Do not hug your dog, or cuddle him, or soothe him; all these things just make the problem worse, not better.

Instead, just direct him to his sanctuary spot. Let him stay there as long as he likes. Do not try to encourage him out – to have a meal or go out to the toilet etc. – while he is still afraid. This will just put more pressure on him. Wait until he comes out by himself. If he looks more confident, praise him. If he is still shaking, shivering or panting and looking afraid, keep ignoring him as before.

While your dog is in his sanctuary spot, carry on life as normal in your home, because your dog will constantly be watching your own behaviour, to see how you are coping with the scary external events. By keeping your reactions to your dog's fear very low key, and giving him a place to go where he can feel safe and wind down, he should gradually cope far better with the whole thunder/firework experience.

CHANGING RESPONSES

Sometimes collies get better at handling fireworks, thunderstorms and other scarier noises/experiences as they get older, and more used to them. This can particularly be the case when they are more elderly, because both their hearing and threat response mechanisms will have declined in acuity.

Alternatively, collies can suddenly become frightened about noises/experiences at any age, when they were not frightened of them before. This is just down to their brains revising a previous attitude to a threat. It can happen a lot as dogs grow older. When dogs are spayed or neutered, hormonal changes can also sometimes make them more fearful about experiences or sounds that previously did not bother them.

In cases of more extreme anxiety, tranquiliser medication may be suggested or recommended for your dog. This may well reduce more overt symptoms of fear, but it can also compromise his ability to learn anything new (i.e. different or better ways or behaving).

FUSSY EATERS AND ABNORMAL APPETITES

Do you have a collie who is a terribly fussy eater, or one with a seemingly abnormally large appetite? The key to dealing with such problems has to begin with a much better understanding of why dogs eat what they do.

The purpose of the appetite mechanism in an animal is to ensure that enough energy is being consumed, in the form of food, to fuel the level of energy being expended by its body.

Because dogs are programmed to be gorgers and scavengers, it can be incredibly easy to overfeed them, because their appetites are geared towards both feasting (i.e. eating large amounts in one go, as with newly killed prey), and opportunistic consumption (i.e. grabbing any food opportunity that arises).

In the wild, a dog may expend as much energy hunting for food as he gets from the food he consumes, and as a result he maintains a healthy weight. At other times, however, he expends more energy searching for food than he gets from the food he finds, and as a result he becomes underweight.

It is very much rarer for a dog in the wild to consistently find and eat more food than his body needs in energy, to the point where he becomes obese – if only because this would be completely counter-productive; i.e. the fatter a dog got, the less efficient he would get at hunting and competing for food.

MODERN LIVING

Modern living with people has completely wiped out a dog's normal way of hunting and eating food. Dogs no longer have to find food through hunting; they get it given to them daily by owners. This means they are not using up the energy expended by hours of tracking, hunting and foraging, yet the gorger/scavenger instincts are still there.

This is what makes owners so often imagine their dogs are still hungry, after they have just eaten a massive bowl of food. It is also what can make them consistently overfeed them.

If your collie is a normal, healthy weight, the amount of food and exercise you are giving him daily is completely right. Some collies will always need more food than others to maintain a healthy weight, due to the speed of their individual metabolisms. Other collies will always need less food to maintain a healthy weight because they have naturally slower metabolisms.

Either way, the amount of food you give your collie should always be tailored to what he requires to stay at a healthy weight, as opposed to what you *think* he needs, or what he is trying to persuade you he needs.

Also let your vet determine what a healthy weight for your dog actually is, as owners are notoriously bad at judging this for themselves.

HOW TO MAKE A DOG A FUSSY EATER

Some collies have such healthy appetites that they will never consume more food than their body needs, or will not consume food – unlike so many dogs – just because it is *there*.

Yet, for some reason, owners will not accept this and believe that unless their dog eats one or two set meals every single day he is somehow going to starve and die, despite the fact that he is a perfectly healthy weight.

So they hover around their dog's bowl trying to persuade him to eat, or start hand feeding him when he declines a meal. The dog then works out that if he doesn't eat his food, he gets tons of attention from an owner, which simply reinforces food-declining behaviour. Alternatively he may just feel more pressurised and anxious and, thus, even more reluctant to eat the food.

So next the owner tries to tempt him by adding much tastier food items (e.g. cheese, meat, sausage, treats) in his food bowl. This is how you teach a dog to decline a first bowl of less appetising food and hold out, instead, for something far tastier. This is, in short, how you make your dog a fussy eater.

To avoid this, or solve it, whenever you feed your dog, only leave his food down for about two minutes. If your dog does not eat it, take it away very casually, without saying anything, and do not feed him again until the next scheduled mealtime. Eventually your dog will eat the food you give him but, in the meantime, he will not suffer unduly if he goes a day or two without food.

Fussy eating often tends to be the preserve of the 'only' dog. Whenever you have two or more dogs living together, you find that levels of fussiness about food declines in relation to the number of rivals there are competing for it. *Note:* If your dog is normally a healthy eater and has developed a poorer appetite, or if he is continually hungry in a way he was not before, it is worth asking your vet to check him out for any possible underlying, or developing, medical condition.

GENETICALLY MOTIVATED BEHAVIOUR

Throughout this book I have continually stressed how much behaviour in collies – as in any animal, including ourselves – will have some genetic origin or component. This does not just apply to classic forms of working instinct in the breed, but everything about the way an individual dog's brain is programmed to think and interact with his external environment.

The reason why I find this so important to keep emphasising is because so often people's expectations of their dogs do not take into account their genetic limitations. In terms of how they can behave or what they can achieve, they think that all dogs begin their lives on a level playing field, when this simply is not so.

Similarly, breeders can so often blame owners for temperamental or behavioural problems in dogs which are greatly genetic in origin.

AN AGE OF DISCOVERY

In terms of what is now known about the true origins of any animal's personality or behaviour, we could not live in more enlightening times.

In human neuroscience, for instance, it has been discovered that subtle changes in genetic brain structure and function predisposes people towards a wealth of different behavioural characteristics or disorders, ranging from shyness, aggression, hyperactivity and OCD (Obsessive Compulsive Disorder) to autism, acute anxiety and the potential to be a psychopathic serial killer. Moreover, these predispositions tend to get passed down from one generation to another.

There has always been a feeling that certain kinds of less sound behaviour is inherited in both people and dogs, but now we know exactly what it is about them, both mentally and physiologically, that makes them so different to others.

NATURE VERSUS NURTURE

There are some who believe that genes will always be the main if not whole story, as far as a dog's personality and behaviour are concerned. There are others who believe that a dog's early rearing and life circumstances have a greater shaping influence on his later conduct; the classic nature versus nurture debate.

But I think the reality is a lot more complex. I believe that some dogs have adverse genetic tendencies that can be greatly offset by the right early rearing and later management and training. In other dogs the genetic loading towards a certain type of behaviour is so strong, that trying to act or think any differently will always be much more of a struggle.

Some dogs have the right genes but just live the wrong lives. The longer we study the whole genetic make-up of dogs, the more likely it is that we will eventually isolate individual faults, or patterns in their DNA, which predispose them towards more challenging behaviour, and thus more difficult lives.

HERDING BEHAVIOUR

As discussed throughout this book, herding is a natural part of collie working instinct or behaviour. It only becomes a problem when the dog uses the behaviour inappropriately; i.e. rounding up children or visitors, or any other target he has previously stalked and chased.

Collies who chase and then herd inappropriate things have to be trained not to do this, as outlined in Part One, Chapter Eight. Also see *Chase behaviour*, page 165.

Anti-chase training usually begins with the dog's working focus being re-directed on to the owner. However, re-directing a dog's working focus back on to you does not necessarily solve herding behaviour, because he could just start herding you, instead. Some collies are fairly weak herders; i.e. they will occasionally run around you, and that's that. Others can become positively obsessive about this behaviour; endlessly circling both you, and any other companion, when you are out walking.

Alternatively, at home, a collie may try to charge ahead of you through doorways, then circle you, or cut across you – and it can all become quite tiresome.

If you were a shepherd, and wanted to stop your dog herding sheep, you would make him lie *down* and *wait,* or just *wait,* until you gave him a command to move again. So do exactly the same when he is herding you, or anyone else. But first you have got to train him to lie *down* and *wait* (see Part One, Chapter Five).

Collies who become a persistent nuisance rounding up children or visitors should have their access to these people denied, if only to stop them being perpetually rewarded by the behaviour and, thus, making it ever more ingrained.

HORMONALLY FUELLED BEHAVIOUR

In Part One (Chapter Nine), I covered some of the physical/behavioural changes that can occur in collies (male and female) due to the influence of sex hormones once they reach adolescence. The same chapter also explored the issue of whether or not you should spay/neuter your dog, and the benefits and drawbacks that can follow such procedures.

In lowering or increasing the level of any hormone in a dog's body there will always be some knock-on effect of a kind owners may not always appreciate or realise.

People often underestimate, in general, how powerfully hormones affect the way any animal physically functions and behaves. Different hormones from different glands (see *The endocrine system,* page 178) send different messages to the nervous system, which then tells the body what to do. Here are just some functions and behaviours in dogs (as in all animals) that will be influenced by hormonal activity:

- Growth rate.
- Sexual development.
- Pregnancy/maternal behaviour.
- Metabolism.
- Levels of alertness/activity.
- Mood.
- Sleep/wake cycles.
- Levels of excitability/mental arousal.
- Levels of aggression
- Levels of fear/anxiety.
- Responses to threat.
- Responses to stress.

EFFECTS ON BEHAVIOUR

The more we understand about the functions of different glands and hormones in an animal's body, the better we can appreciate how much behaviour in dogs will be driven by their actions and effects.

Lethargy, depression, excitability, nervousness, anxiety, aggression; these are all behaviours, for example, or emotional states, whose roots originate in some form of lowered or heightened hormonal activity.

Some dogs' behaviour can alter suddenly, as a result of hormonal changes caused by illness (e.g. hypothyroidism, diabetes, Addison's disease) or other physical/environmental challenges (e.g. adolescence, neutering/spaying, extreme trauma or stress).

If you think your collie's changed behaviour could have some hormonal cause or link, this is something worth investigating with your vet, with a view to discussing what medication or other therapy may be helpful or appropriate.

JUMPING UP

Jumping up is basically a puppy habit which, if consistently rewarded, can turn into a more dominating, controlling or attention-seeking activity as a dog grows.

A common way of stopping a dog jumping up is simply to block any reward from this behaviour by standing completely still, with your arms folded and your back to him until he stops.

Unfortunately, however, you may find that for every person who does this correctly, there will be another who insists on rewarding the dog, instead, by making a fuss of him. Hence, the habit persists. It is far better to teach your dog the *off!* command instead (as outlined on page 47).

MANIC BEHAVIOUR

See *Self-stimulators* and *Stress and Stress related problems*

MANIPULATIVE BEHAVIOUR

In Part One (Chapter Two), I explained what naturally controlling and manipulative dogs many collies can be and that this, in turn, was a genetic character trait rooted in their working past. They were dogs, in short, bred to physically/psychologically dominate other animals, in order to drive or herd them where a shepherd/farmer wanted them to go.

In a working collie's mind, you are either the controller of his actions (i.e. shepherd) or the animal he controls (i.e. sheep). If your dog cannot manipulate or control you in any way – and is happy to respond to any command you give him – you remain the controller/shepherd. If your collie can easily control you – and manipulate you into doing what he wants you to do, rather than the other way around – you are more like the sheep. It's as simple as that.

If you do not want your dog to keep treating you like an animal he can control at will, you will need to start thinking and acting a bit more cleverly yourself.

HOW YOU LOSE THE BATTLE FOR CONTROL

A collie usually begins his bid for owner control via discovering what behaviours are most likely to get attention from you. Typically these will include barking or whining, or nipping at your feet/ankles, or staring, or nudging/pawing at you when you are sitting down.

Once these behaviours prove consistently successful in getting your attention, he will then develop them into more pressurising and controlling ploys. He may use them to make you do something faster – e.g. feed him, take him for a walk, throw him a ball. He may use them to make you redirect attention to him when you are doing something else or talking to somebody else. He may use them to stop you talking on the phone, or watching the TV, or going somewhere he does not want you to go, such as upstairs or out of the front/back door.

This is how a collie slowly takes control of your life – often without owners even realising it. At best, this manipulative behaviour can become exasperating to live with, at the very worst it could progress to more aggressive forms of control

THE ENDOCRINE SYSTEM

Hormones in dogs originate from glands collectively known as the endocrine system. This is where the different glands are, and what their hormones are designed to do:

- The pituitary gland is often called the master gland as it governs the activities of others. It is located on the underside of the brain and produces a wide range of hormones that control growth rate, sexual behaviour, and functions surrounding pregnancy.

- The thyroid gland, which lies in front of the trachea, regulates metabolism. It also determines how thin/fat dogs are, plus their individual alertness and activity levels. It can also influence levels of calmness, irritability and aggression

- The parathyroid glands are located behind the thyroid, and control calcium levels in the blood as well as levels of excitability.

- The pineal gland is located in the centre of the brain. It controls an individual's biological clock, and the hormones that regulate sleep-wake cycles.

- The pancreas lies between the small intestine and the stomach and secretes insulin, which controls the amount of sugar in the blood stream. Problems with the pancreas/insulin levels cause different types of diabetes.

- The gonads are located in male testes and female ovaries. These glands help develop an individual's male and female orientation and also secrete testosterone in males and oestrogen in females. Both of these hormones have been linked to aggression.

- The adrenal glands are located next to the kidneys. They produce cortisol and adrenaline which govern a dog's fight or flight response, and his reaction to stress. They also produce glucocorticoids and mineralocorticoids, which help to regulate metabolism and reduce inflammation. An excess of either, however, can suppress the immune system. Excess adrenaline is also linked to increased agitation, anxiety, excitability and aggression.

outlined earlier under *Aggression* (see *Dominance aggression*, page 157).

Collies who can easily control you also tend not to be very obedient or responsive to commands, other than when a direct, visible reward (i.e. treat, toy) – or should I say *bribe* – is involved.

TAKING BACK CONTROL
The key to resolving this is to stop allowing yourself to be manipulated by your dog, in ways now explained.

MOVEMENTS ROUND THE HOME
If, for instance, your collie tries to control your movements round the home, banish him to more restricted quarters, with the use of a dog gate, as previously outlined in this book. Teach him that he comes into the rest of *your* home only via *your* invitation. Similarly, he can only stay in your part of the home as long as he shows acceptable behaviour. As soon as he shows less acceptable behaviour, immediately return him to his own quarters.

PRESSURE BEFORE A WALK
If your dog barks and whines when you put on your coat and/or get out his lead, to pressurise you to move on faster with his walk, immediately put the lead away again and sit down. Try using the *quiet!* command outlined earlier in Part One (Chapter Five, page 48). If this does not work the first time, do not keep trying or you will completely ruin the command's future effectiveness.

Instead, totally ignore your dog until he is quiet again – no matter how long this takes. Then try getting your coat and the lead again. If your dog remains quiet, reinforce this desired behaviour by saying "*quiet!*", then praise him and go for your walk. If he still barks/whines, keep repeating the exercise. Never go out for a walk until your dog is calm and quiet.

Do the same exercise every walk time; always remembering to say "*quiet!*" to your dog while he is quiet/calm, then praising him before going on your walk. If you stick to your guns, it will take less and less time each day to make your dog quiet before a walk.

PRESSURE BEFORE A MEAL

If your dog barks/whines to get you to feed him faster at mealtimes, try the *quiet!* command. If it does not work the first time, you can try these measures instead:

- Keep walking out of the kitchen and sitting down somewhere else, totally ignoring your dog while he barks/whines. Refuse to feed him until he is quiet. Only when he is quiet, reinforce this with "*quiet!*", then praise him and feed him.
- Make your dog lie *down* and *wait*. Each time he barks/whines, move him further and further out of the kitchen, and away from his expected food, making him lie *down* and *wait* each time. Only when he is quiet, call him to you to *sit* and *wait*. As long as he remains quiet, say "*quiet!*", then praise him and give him his food. If he is *not* quiet, after you call him to you, keep moving him further and further back out of the kitchen, as before, to lie *down* and *wait*.
- *Note:* Collies should always be made to *sit* and *wait* at least 10 seconds, before you allow them to eat their food. This perpetuates their ability to master emotional self-control, and also displays their respect for your authority.

BEGGING FOR FOOD

No dog should be allowed to manipulate you into giving him food from your plate/dinner table, or food you are eating in general, through tactics like staring and whining.

If you do not think this is a sign of weakness on your part, just ask yourself how readily your dog would offer or surrender food to *you,* from his own bowl, if you tried these tactics yourself.

Any food given to your collie should be placed in his bowl. You should then make him *wait,* as above, before giving him permission to eat it. Any other treats/extras you give him should only be used as rewards in training, or given to him only after he has first complied with a command.

PRESSURE FOR ATTENTION/PLAY

Never let a collie pester you for attention by barking/whining. If a *quiet!* command does not instantly work, ignore him totally until he is quiet again – going out the room if necessary, or immediately placing him in separate quarters. Collies who bark at the TV, or while you

are on the phone, should be immediately banished to separate quarters if they will not obey the *quiet!* command.

Similarly, do not let a collie pressurise you into playing with him, through nudging, pawing or dropping toys on your lap. This game can become endless and tiresome. Instead, make it clear to your dog that you initiate all games with toys, and also decide when they end. Once you have decided a game is ended, no amount of pressure on his behalf should make play start again.

PRESSURE WHEN YOU ARE OUT ON A WALK

If you stop on a walk for some reason – e.g. to talk to someone – and your collie tries to pressurise you to move on, or give him back attention, through barking/whining or nipping your feet/ankles, immediately make him lie *down* and *wait*. If he still barks/whines/pressurises, make him lie *down* and *wait* further and further away from you, each time, until he is finally quiet. Only call him back to you to carry on your walk when he is quiet.

If you take a toy out with you on a walk, do not allow your collie to pressurise you into throwing it for him with barking/whining etc. Make him *sit* or lie *down* and *wait;* only throw it for him when he is quiet. Similarly, do not allow your collie to dump a toy at your feet, then stare at it, or bark at you, to make you throw it again.

Instead, train your dog to bring a toy to you and place it in your hand, after you have thrown it. Then make your dog *sit* or lie *down* and *wait,* quietly, before you throw it again. Alternatively, put the toy in your pocket to signify the game is over. Once you have decided the game is over, totally ignore any barking/whining/pressurising from your dog to start it again. He has to learn that games will only ever begin when he is quiet.

THE CONSTANT TEST

The way to see manipulative behaviour in collies is as a form of constant test; i.e. your dog is continually testing the level of your own weakness which, in turn, will dictate the level of pressure he will use to try to control you. The more resistance he meets, and the more often he meets it, the less pressure he will try to apply.

This kind of testing may go on throughout your dog's life with you. Owners may notice, for instance, that when they are ill, or stressed, or highly distracted, their collies begin to play up or take more liberties. This is because an owner's energy has suddenly got weaker – and the dogs know it.

There is no point putting any kind of moral slant on this behaviour. To me, it is part and parcel of the price you pay for owning such a supremely intelligent dog. All intelligent animals are programmed to exploit weakness in some way – including us. It is just that some will always be much better at doing it than others.

MISUSE OF WORKING INSTINCT/BEHAVIOUR

Working instinct and behaviour in Border Collies covers a pretty broad spectrum of genetic traits, from basic repetitive motor sequences – i.e. eye, stalk, chase, herd, lunge-nip – to more complex psychological quirks and sensitivities rooted in their origins as livestock herding dogs.

Working instinct/behaviour traits in collies only become a problem when:

- They are misunderstood and mishandled, particularly during early rearing and training.
- The dog's working focus/drive gets directed on to wrong targets.
- The stress/arousal mechanisms in the dog are so hyper-sensitive/strong that he struggles to maintain mental balance.
- The hypersensitivity of the dog's brain - and his arousal mechanisms - makes him generally more fearful/reactive to threat or perceived threat.
- The obsessive leanings of the dog get magnified into more seriously compulsive/repetitive patterns of behaviour.
- The controlling nature of the dog gets directed on to other dogs/people/owners and household members.

Most of these behaviours/psychological quirks have already been covered elsewhere in this section. See: *Aggression; Chase behaviour; Fear and Phobias; Herding behaviour; Manipulative behaviour; Obsessive compulsive behaviour patterns; Self-stimulators* and *Self-mesmerisers*. They have also been covered in depth throughout Part One.

MOUNTING BEHAVIOUR

Mounting is not always a purely sexual behaviour in dogs. In either sex, mounting is also used to dominate other dogs, or people. Bitches, for instance, may mount their growing pups, or other canine rivals, to denote their status superiority.

Male dogs may use mounting behaviour on objects like cushions, to relieve not only sexual frustration but also feelings of high excitement, or anxiety. When owners make a significant fuss about it, it can then develop into a major attention-seeking ploy.

Because so much mounting behaviour in male dogs, in particular, can become learned, castration will not necessarily stop it. It will only stop the element of the behaviour fuelled by sex hormones.

Many male dogs, whether entire or neutered, can grow out of mounting behaviour as they get older, providing it is persistently deterred, rather than rewarded. To stop your dog mounting anything or anyone, simply use the *off!* command highlighted earlier in Part One (Chapter Five, page 47).

If, however, you are going to keep deterring a dog from performing a behaviour he has previously found highly

rewarding, you must ensure you offer him an alternative behaviour – e.g. tell him to go and get a toy – that he finds equally rewarding. Otherwise you will end up with a highly frustrated dog constantly looking for other ways to displace inner tension.

NEUROSIS

See *Obsessive compulsive behaviour patterns, Self-mesmerisers, Self-stimulators, Stress and stress related problems.*

NIPPING AND BITING

See *Aggression*

OBSESSIVE COMPULSIVE BEHAVIOUR PATTERNS

In Part One (Chapter Two), I explained the roots of more obsessive compulsive behaviour patterns in Border Collies, as well as the fact that levels of obsessive drive in individual dogs tend to be inherited.

The trouble with more obsessive drive in Border Collies is that while this is usually an asset in a working dog, it can often be a problem in a pet or companion dog. This is particularly true when the dog in question finds it very difficult to desist from certain patterns of obsessive activity, such as shadow chasing, or herding/circling inappropriate things, or making objects like leaves, earth or water move and then lunge-nipping at them. A collie of this type can also find it very hard to properly settle or wind down, unless much work is put into keeping him, longer term, in a calmer mental state.

An additional concern is that both pursuing an obsessive activity, and being physically prevented from pursuing it by you, can put 'high drive' dogs under a significant degree of stress. Many of them become so compelled to pursue an obsessive habit that they can actually become aggressive when you try to stop them doing it.

You can thus get stuck in an endless cycle where you cannot stop your dog stressing himself in some way, no matter what you do, within the confines and lifestyle of a typical domestic environment.

THE WORKING DRIVE/OBSESSIVE DRIVE BALANCE

If at all possible, you should try to avoid getting the above kinds of dog as social companions, because they can be so incredibly demanding and challenging to own.

It is also wrong to assume that a collie who is highly responsive to training also has to be manically obsessive in other ways. Nor should you consider levels of working drive/obsessive drive in collies to be one and the same thing, or two inevitable sides of the same dog.

The key to the working drive/obsessive drive balance lies in an individual dog's breeding. The best dogs to train and own are those with good working drive, but no additional elements of more obsessive neurosis.

Once you realise that levels of both obsessive drive and working drive in collies tend to be genetic, a good study of any dog's immediate relatives should tell you how obsessive his future behaviour is likely to be. In particular, look out for any more excessively obsessive habits in related dogs.

I, personally, prefer to avoid lines of dogs in whom habits like shadow chasing are relentlessly pursued, because I consider this mentally abnormal behaviour.

WHAT IS NORMAL AND LESS NORMAL OBSESSIVE DRIVE IN COLLIES?

Not every owner, alas, will realise that they have a more extreme obsessive compulsive collie until it is too late – especially if the behaviour takes a while to develop in earnest.

It is also important to understand the difference between a dog who consciously *chooses* to do something, because he has previously found it pleasant/rewarding, and one who feels *compelled* to act in a certain way due to some deeper seated form of psychological neurosis.

The compulsion element of obsessive activity is always the key, rather than the form in which it is displayed. It is also why, if you stop a truly obsessive compulsive dog obsessing about one particular activity or target, he will just go and redirect the same urge elsewhere.

The reason why overly obsessive behaviour in collies can be so hard to cure is because what you are basically trying to cure is the way an individual dog's brain is programmed to work. Some dogs' brains will always be more resistant than others to the process of being changed, or taught to think and act in different ways.

If you have a dog whose seemingly obsessive behaviour can easily be stopped when you give him an alternative command, or one who will happily settle and rest after exercise or training, without constantly seeking to resume an obsessive cycle of behaviour, you have a fairly normal collie.

If you think your dog is far more obsessive than this, there are ways of keeping the problem under better control.

BETTER MANAGING COLLIE OCD

Methods of better managing more obsessive compulsive behaviours in collies are as follows:

- First, understand the genetic element driving the behaviour, and do not encourage obsessive activity in any way. Many owners may deliberately shine torch beams for their collie puppies to chase, for instance, because they find this amusing – until the behaviour completely takes over their dog's life.
- Understand how rapidly certain working behaviours can become addictive for collies. Do not let your dog keep endlessly repeating cycles or sequences of working behaviour (i.e. eye, stalk, chase, herd, lunge-nip). Instead, constantly interrupt these sequences as early as possible

and give alternative commands to your dog (e.g. stop, down, wait).
- Teach your dog greater mental discipline and emotional self-control, as outlined in Part One (Chapter Five).
- Teach your dog to focus primarily on you, and your commands (again, see Part One, Chapter Five).
- Give your dog more positive outlets for his mental drives – e.g. scent and search tasks.
- Give him plenty of distance work for physical exercise, rather than endless ball chasing, which always encourages a more obsessive/neurotic mental state.
- Also see *Winding down a collie* under *Self-stimulators*, and *Self-mesmerisers*.

PULLING ON THE LEAD

Pulling on the lead is a habit that can be corrected in any dog, given sufficiently persistent training on an owner's part, as outlined in Part One (Chapter Five, page 58.),

Dogs only keep pulling on the lead as long as an owner allows this behaviour to remain rewarding for their dog.

REBUILDING A BOND

As persistently stressed throughout this book, the nature of the relationship you have with your collie – and his level of responsiveness to your commands – begins and ends with the quality of the bond you have built with him.

Your dog needs to see you as an inspirational leader, and the most important point of focus in his life. If you get this bonding process right with your collie, while he is a puppy (see Part One, Chapters Four and Five), he should become an incredibly rewarding dog to train and own.

If you do not get this right, then quite a few problems could ensue. Your dog, for instance, could become socially/emotionally attached to another dog, or other dogs, he lives with and, thus, become less focused on you. Typically, this can be seen with littermates who live together, or puppies who spent more quality time with other resident dogs than their owners when they were growing up.

Alternatively, collie puppies left too much to their own devices when young can develop highly independent patterns of behaviour, for want of better guidance, such as chasing and herding inappropriate things. Once they have done this enough times, and learned to find it incredibly rewarding, it can become harder and harder for an owner to impose the importance of their presence in their dog's head. It also becomes increasingly difficult to persuade the dog that training has more to offer, in the way of reward, than the 'bad behaviour' he is already getting such a buzz from.

INDEPENDENT AND DEPENDENT DOGS

Be aware, also, that how owner independent or dependent a collie happens to be can have a genetic component. Some dogs will always get more pleasure from acting on their own initiative, especially if they are allowed to learn this habit and then constantly reinforce it when they are fairly young.

Other dogs will naturally show a higher degree of dependency which, in turn, can be linked to the syndrome of learned helplessness (see Part One, Chapter Five, page 59). The skill with dogs like these is to build a bond with them that is sufficiently close to secure high training responsiveness, but not so close that the dog then becomes emotionally *over* dependent and, thus, is more likely to develop separation distress when you leave him somewhere alone.

Many rescued collies can come from backgrounds where they have made no important social/emotional bonds with people as puppies, and/or they were given very little meaningful training early in life, of a kind that continually linked cooperating with people with rewarding outcomes. Therefore, it should never be seen as surprising when these dogs have little early responsiveness to their new owners' commands.

THE RECALL TEST

If there is one command that really tests the strength of a collie's bond with his owner – and his accompanying level or responsiveness – it is the *Recall* when the dog is faced with competing distractions, e.g. other dogs, or things he likes to chase.

The truly owner-bonded dog will always come back pretty quickly when called, providing he has also been well trained in this exercise. The less bonded/responsive dog will not. If you have the latter dog, try not to despair. Think instead of ways in which you could make yourself much more important to your dog. This, in turn, will put you on a much better footing to improve his overall training. Also see, *Recall failures*.

STARTING AGAIN

There are several different techniques you can use to repair a failing bond with your collie, or build one where it did not exist before. These are highlighted in *Rehabilitating rescued dogs*, as the problem of a non-existent owner bond can be commonest in them. However, they should work just as well with any collie.

Whatever the background of the collie you own, the problems attached to a poor, or non-existent, owner bond remain the same.

RECALL FAILURES

In Part One (Chapter Five, page 54), I explained the basic principles of teaching *Recall* to a dog. I also highlighted that the biggest mistake, recall-wise, was to allow a dog off the lead before he had been sufficiently conditioned to come back when called, through the use of consistent rewards.

What you basically need to teach a dog is a *returning response*, which you later attach your recall command, or

sound, to. The more rewarding you make each of your dog's initial returns to you, when called, the faster and more reliable his returning responses should get.

Very often *Recall* fails in a dog because the training of this command has not been done correctly, or the dog has a less sound working bond/relationship with his owner – as previously highlighted under *Rebuilding a bond*.

The *Recall* command can also fail, or become less and less reliable in a dog, for the following reasons:

- You get into the habit of calling your dog's name, instead of giving him a proper, trained-in, *Recall* command.
- You forget to keep regularly reinforcing good *Recall* responses in your dog with high value rewards (i.e. treats and toys he only gets for coming back to you, on command, when you are out).
- You do not frequently make *Recall* an exciting thing for your dog to do – e.g., recall him, then run off fast, so your dog has to chase you. If recall is not an exciting activity for your dog, he will become less and less enthusiastic about it.
- You get into the habit of calling your dog, again and again, while he is not coming back. This just teaches your dog to ignore you to the sound of his name being called.
- Always wait until your dog's concentration is disengaged (i.e. he is not smelling something/locked into an encounter with another dog) before calling him back. The best time of all to call him back is when he is actually looking at you.
- When your dog does not come back quickly, you take out your frustration on him when he finally does return. This will make him even more reluctant to return next time.
- You always call your dog back to put him on the lead/take him home. Dogs quickly get wise to this chain of events. Get into the habit, during a walk, of regularly calling your dog to you, grabbing his collar for a few seconds, then giving him a treat or toy before immediately sending him off again. In this way, he will never know when you are really going to put him on the lead.
- Additionally, do not always put your dog's lead on him at the same place each time on a walk. Dogs catch on to this very quickly. Sometimes put a lead on your dog five minutes into a walk, then take it off again. Other times put it on 10 or 20 minutes into a walk, then take it off again. Similarly, sometimes put your dog's lead on five or 10 minutes before the end of a walk, and sometimes one minute before the end of a walk. At other times put it on right at the end of a walk. In general, keep him guessing.
- If your dog persists in ignoring *Recall* commands, you must place him back on a long line, and begin his training of the recall exercise all over again. It may be a good idea to devise a new recall word or sound this time, to replace the original one that has now become corrupted/rendered

useless. See Part One, (Chapter Five, page 54) for the correct way to teach *Recall* to your dog.

REHABILITATING RESCUED DOGS

As covered extensively in Part One (Chapter Ten), very many Border Collies end up in rescue centres or shelters, or are otherwise disposed of by original owners. There are a lot of different reasons why this happens.

Sometimes the dog is simply the victim of a relationship breakdown, or his original owner dies or experiences a sudden change in living or working circumstances. Sometimes the relentless energy and working instincts of the dog are too much for an owner to cope with and, similarly, the dog's more sensitive, reactive and driven personality. It is a sad reality that countless people are still acquiring Border Collies with little real understanding of the true nature and needs of these dogs.

Many collies will enter the rescue system as strays and, thus, with no previous history available to work on. Large numbers of people will also put their collies up for rehoming without being honest about the problems they have experienced with their behaviour – particularly in cases where the dogs have been aggressive or excessively destructive.

Despite all the above considerations, countless people still rehome Border Collies every day and make a wonderful success of it. They are often very special people. Many of the dogs can also be pretty special, too.

The following advice, however, is not for people who have experienced no problems, or have behavioural problems that have already been covered elsewhere in this section. It is for people who need more insight into what rehoming a rescued collie could involve, and for people who want to lower their chances of getting it wrong.

FACING REALITY

When considering a rescued collie, you must be mindful of some basic realities; the first being not to imagine that any dog you get will be problem-free from day one. Similarly, do not expect rescue centres, or foster carers, to always know, or successfully predict, how a dog might behave in a new home.

Some problems in rescued dogs only emerge, or re-emerge, over time, or will only occur in specific contexts. Many dogs who have come from rescue accommodation – particularly noisy kennels – may also be in a state of shock, which can have an inhibitory effect on their normal behaviour.

A common mistake new owners can make is to expect a dog from a rescue background to just *know* how you want him to behave when he comes to live in your home.

This may be the case with dogs who have had fairly normal domestic upbringings, and good early socialisation and training, prior to being rehomed, but many others may come from backgrounds that range from deprived and dysfunctional to virtually feral. As a result they can be nervous, wary or timid, or simply not know what the rules are when you live with human beings.

STARTING FROM SCRATCH

For all these reasons, it is best to begin your new life with a rescued dog much as if he were a puppy, i.e. do not assume he already knows anything you need him to know. Assume, instead, that you will have to teach him everything from scratch. Also start with a highly restricted regime (see below) which you can relax only when your dog's behaviour warrants it. This makes it much easier to keep less desirable behaviour in check and also better control what your dog learns.

As with a puppy, you will also need to build a working bond with your dog, and teach him to respect your authority, before you can begin any more formal training with him. His all round social training may also need a lot of work.

Most of all, try not to keep putting your rescued dog in situations where he can go on making mistakes, through poor judgement or experience, which anger or distress you. This will only sustain conflict between you and progressively undermine your growing new relationship.

THE RESCUED DOG REHABILITATION PROGRAMME

In general, proceed with your new rescued collie as follows:

Step One: **Setting up your dog's new quarters**
Before your rescued collie even comes home, set up some personal quarters for him. These are exactly the same kind of restricted quarters that you would set up for a puppy, as outlined in Part One (Chapter Four).

Your dog's quarters should be separated from the rest of your home by a dog gate. He should also have his own refuge zone in these quarters – e.g. an indoor kennel, covered on the top and three surrounding sides by a blanket, or some similarly enclosed peaceful and safe place. *Note:* If your dog gets into the habit of pulling this surrounding blanket through the bars of the kennel with his teeth, place a board on the top of the kennel which just overshoots its edges by around 7.5-10 cms cm (3-4 ins). You can then drape the blanket over this.

Would your dog be happier outside?
If your rescued dog has been used to being kennelled outside, being kennelled inside a new human home could initially prove too stressful for him. If this seems to be the case, try putting your dog's refuge zone outside, in a sheltered and quiet place. Make sure you also weatherproof it as best as possible. If being outside makes your dog calmer, it is likely he prefers this option.

Owners often find it hard to accept that a collie would

prefer living in outside accommodation, rather than inside the home with them. But it depends entirely on what the dog has previously been used to, and how much stressful activity and noise within the home is occurring of a kind that a less socially experienced/confident dog would prefer to escape or avoid.

Over time, as your dog grows more confident within the inside home environment, you could move his accommodation back indoors, providing this works well for both parties.

Step Two: Reducing feelings of stress and pressure

When rescued collies first go to new homes, they are often in a state of stress, shock and disorientation, so what they do not need is yet more stimulation or pressure piled on them from new owners.

It can be very tempting to make a great fuss of a new rescued dog when he first arrives, and to begin trying to interact with him as if he were any other normally raised dog you had known. But this can make timid dogs feel overly pressurised. It can also begin the process of turning insecure dogs into attention junkies and, thereafter, dogs who become increasingly dependent on your presence, emotionally and psychologically. Additionally, it can make dominant-minded dogs feel immediately more important in your household than they should be.

Much of the early fuss/attention lavished on new rescued dogs by owners can stem from their belief that the dogs should somehow be excited about their new home, or even feel grateful. But, in truth, a dog cannot know who you are at this earliest stage of rehabilitation, or what your shorter or longer term intentions may be, with regard to their welfare.

Also be aware that there may be lots of commonplace objects/sounds in your home that your rescued dog may never have experienced before – e.g. radio, doorbell, TV, washing machine, tumbler dryer. These may further increase his stress levels and render him generally more agitated and reactive.

Lowering sensory input
Due to the above considerations, the most important thing to do during your rescued collie's first days or weeks with you, is to totally lower the sensory input/stimulation levels within his living environment which, in turn, will lower his stress levels.

Put him in a restful environment where he is exposed to minimal bright light, visual movement and noise and, initially, totally ignore him as you move in and out or past his quarters, and get other household members to do the same.

Other than when hand feeding and employing other bond building measures (see page 186), do not keep trying to invite interactions with him during the early settling in period. This is particularly essential with timid dogs.

However contrary it seems to ignore your rescued dog during his initial days, or weeks, with you, you are giving him the best possible chance of adapting to his new surroundings with minimal pressure or stress.

Minimising future separation problems
By keeping all your early interactions with your new rescued dog pretty low key, and making him spend regular periods apart from you in his own quarters while you are still at home, you should also minimise the problem of him becoming excessively over-attached to you, emotionally and psychologically.

This can be a very common problem in rescued dogs who come from backgrounds of insecurity and uncertainty, and is also usually the trigger for destructive or other frustration/anxiety induced behaviours when they are left alone at home.

Step Three: Early assessment of your dog's character
After sufficient winding down time has passed, your rescued collie should let you know when he is ready to begin interacting with you; at which point you might get some early clues to his fundamental character.

If any time you approach your dog he backs away, particularly with his tail between his legs, he is not ready to interact with you. Do not push it; you could force him to behave in a more defensive way. Your dog is essentially pretty timid and/or anxious about interactions with less familiar people. He needs more time to feel more confident about you. He may also be a dog more prone to fear related problems (see *Fear and phobias*, page 170).

If your dog comes up confidently to you, wagging his tail, acknowledge and praise him for this, then immediately walk away again. If your dog stays where he is at this point, accepting that this is the end of the encounter, this is a good sign, because he is showing some early acknowledgement of your authority, as well as a level of psychological independence.

Manipulation and dependency
If, when you walk way from your dog, he insists on following you instead to prolong the encounter, or generally keeps pestering you for more attention, be aware that this can be an early sign of a dog with a more controlling nature, as detailed under *Manipulative behaviour* (page 177). This could also be the case if the dog, additionally, whines and protests each time you leave him in his own quarters. He could also be a dog more prone to becoming emotionally over dependent on you as just outlined (also see, *Emotional over dependency/attachment,* page 170).

Obviously, all the above, are just very basic early indications of a dog's potential character. It should still be said, however, that the real nature of a rescued dog often only emerges over greater time. The behaviour of most rescued dogs tends to improve with the steady development of greater confidence. With others, however, the reverse can sometimes apply, and it is wise to be mindful of this.

Step Four: Limit sources of early conflict

Many rescued collies can go through an initial honeymoon period of relatively good, or even ingratiating, behaviour when they first go to new homes. This is because the upheaval of the rehoming experience has lowered their normal confidence. They are also uncertain as to who rules their new pack and may take time to test the extent of other people's weakness before launching a challenge.

This, again, is why you should not be too complacent or over-indulgent towards your new rescued dog early on. You should also avoid initiating any kind of conflict scenario prior to building a much sounder and more respectful relationship with him (see, *Conflict preventing strategies*). Otherwise you could find your dog suddenly becoming aggressive when challenged over things such as these:

- A resource (e.g. food, toy, bone).
- Territory (e.g. access to front/back doors, or a certain room/space, piece of furniture).
- Access to his favoured household member.
- Status – i.e. you try to challenge the dog to stop doing something, or try to make him do something he does not want to do.

Situations like these with rehomed collies do not necessarily arise because the dog has an essentially bad character, but because the forces of stress and insecurity within him have compelled him to be more defensive and/or exploitative of weakness. Owners can then panic, or become very heavy handed in their retaliation/punishment, which can cause the problem to escalate as the dog becomes increasingly defensive towards people approaching or challenging him.

I have owned, and frequently seen, rescued collies who react aggressively (e.g. growling, teeth baring) at the slightest challenge during their initial weeks or months in a new home. But, very often, this is simply down to the level of stress they are under. Once these dogs' stress levels are reduced, and greater trust and confidence in their new owners was established, they never repeated the behaviour.

Dealing with early challenges

When challenged in this way, however, it is crucial for owners to keep their cool. Avoid eye contact with the dog and do not shout or get angry; either action could further provoke him. Also do not keep moving forward towards the dog.

Instead you must keep calm, stay still and stand your ground, as moving back or away in the face of your dog's

CONFLICT PREVENTING STRATEGIES

It is always better to prevent early conflicts with newly rehomed rescued dogs, through sticking to these guidelines:

- Do not pressure your dog into encounters/interactions with you he is not ready for.

- Do not give him food and then try to take it away.

- Do not allow him constant free access to certain household territories/items of furniture, and then suddenly challenge him to leave them. It is best not to give him access to them in the first place.

- Similarly, restrict access to any personal belongings of yours which your dog could then steal, and aggressively hold on to when you try to get them back.

- Do not suddenly grab your dog by the collar when he is not expecting it, or when you want to remove him from something/somewhere. Keep a length of line attached to his collar for this purpose.

- Do not let your dog own or monopolise a favoured household member/half of a couple. He may later try to guard this person as a personal resource. All household members must clearly be superior to your dog.

- Do not start laying down the law to a dog who is already under intense pressure, by shouting or using hostile body language and eye contact.

aggression will only show weakness and reward his behaviour.

Also understand that the controlling/intimidating dog is usually one under intense mental pressure or stress of some kind. Dogs like these can often react impulsively, and then be desperate for an escape route out of a confrontation they have initiated with an owner.

So give your dog that escape route. You can either:
a) Keep completely still and quiet (still avoiding any direct eye contact) until your dog eventually relaxes his aggressive stance and moves away, or
b) Call your dog to you, once he has relaxed, and then slowly and calmly walk away from him. Either way your authority has prevailed.

If, however, your rescue dog's aggression persists, or is more serious than just occasional growling/teeth baring, you must seek immediate expert advice. Also see *Aggression*, page 152.

Step Five: Building a bond

As previously stated, one of the biggest problems with rescued collies is that they have no established bond with you when they arrive, of a kind that will dictate not just the nature of their relationship with you, but also how much you can achieve with them, training-wise.

Many rescued collies – and non-rescued collies for that matter – who are deemed disobedient or unresponsive have simply never been given sufficient chance to find co-operating with people rewarding. Alternatively, they have had ample chance to discover many kinds of behaviour that are far *more* rewarding than co-operating with people.

It is often imagined, erroneously, that you can only get a collie to fully bond with you, and give you his maximum focus, during puppyhood. In fact, this can be achieved with a dog of any age, provided you go about it the right way.

Some dogs will always be easier to build bonds with than others, according to how dependent or independent their natural character leanings tend to be. But the key is to make yourself the gateway to everything your dog needs or finds rewarding in life.
Please note: the following strategies can work just as well for non-rescued collies, as rescued ones, when it comes to building or rebuilding that all important owner/dog bond.

Food

The bond building should begin with food. I am a great believer in feeding new rescued dogs entirely by hand, as now described. The beauty of this technique, if used properly, is that it forges an ever stronger bond with your dog, and steadily evolves more desired behaviour in him at the same time.

Timid dogs

Let us imagine, for instance, you have a very timid rescued dog. In cases like this, you would give your dog a piece of his daily food allowance each and every time he showed the confidence to approach you, or other people, of his own accord. Do not feed him any other time.

Switched off and non-responsive dogs

If you have a dog who completely switches off from you when you go out on a walk, keep him on a long line, initially, and only ever feed him for coming back to you, or even for just looking at you. Before feeding him, always praise him first for his 'right' behaviour.

If you have a dog who will not do anything you ask him to do at home – e.g. come in from the garden when called, stop barking or *sit* and *wait* – only ever give him a piece of food for complying with these requests/commands. By contrast, totally ignore his attempts to defy these commands; do not inadvertently reward his non-co-operation through giving this your attention.

Dogs with poor toilet training

If you have a dog with poor toilet training (also see *Toileting problems*, page 197), use some of his daily food allowance to reward him every single time he goes to the toilet in the right place – outside. Also praise him fulsomely just before you reward him. Use the rest of his food allowance to reward other desired behaviour, as just outlined.

Food as a currency for right behaviour

Eventually your dog should realise that when he does not focus on you, comply with one of your commands or do something 'right', he misses out on a chance to eat.

Of course, the greedier your collie, the faster he should learn these lessons. It is, however, important to measure out your dog's total food allowance for each day, and ensure that he never gets more than this during your daily training and bond building work.

Too many people grossly over-reward dogs with food/treats for relatively minor acts of co-operation, or actually bribe them; i.e. they will give them food to *stop* the dog doing something. Dogs see such events as signs of our over-indulgence and, thus, general weakness.

Keep remembering that the harder it is for a dog to get food from you, the harder he will have to work to earn it. Any food he earns will also acquire that much more value for him.

Toys

You can also use toys to keep 'buying' the behaviour you want from your rescued dog, and to keep strengthening your bond with him.

Some rescued collies may have had little previous

experience of playing with toys. Others may be mad about them. Even if your rescued collie initially seems uninterested in toys, it is often possible, through trial and error, to find one he really likes and becomes progressively more obsessed with.

If or once your collie has a favourite toy, again only ever let him have this in return for focusing on you, complying with a command and/or giving you some other desired behaviour. Always praise him just before you give him the toy.

A word of caution; a toy is *not* the right reward to give your collie if you want to encourage him to be quiet or settle. Praise, food and/or approving attention is better.

How your attention keeps rising in value to your dog
The more your collie associates focusing on you, and co-operating with you, with rewards, the more important your presence will become to him. Similarly, your attention will build up ever-greater value for him – to the extent where it becomes a reward for him in itself.

Step Six: Establishing your authority
Many owners of newly-rescued collies – or any collie for that matter – make the mistake of trying to lay the law down, in terms of telling their dog what he should and should not do, before he has developed sufficient trust in them and respect for their authority.

If your dog does not sufficiently trust you or respect your authority, or believe that your judgement in any situation will always be superior to his own, he is far less likely to accept your commands. It's as simple as that.

It is possible for a dog to be afraid of you, but not inherently trust or respect you. Similarly, it is possible for a dog to be incredibly fond of you, or highly attached to you emotionally, while still not respecting you as a higher authority. Both these scenarios can cause great frustration to owners, because they cannot understand what it is about their own approach to their dog which is sabotaging his ability to give them the behaviour they desire of him.

Respect for you and your authority is something you can never demand from any dog, and particularly not from collies. You have to *earn* your right to be respected instead, in ways outlined in Part One (Chapter Four to Six). These chapters outline how you should teach puppies to respect and co-operate with you, but the same approaches/exercises can work just as well with older dogs or rescued dogs.

MOVING ON
Hopefully the advice I have just outlined should help you settle in a rescued collie with maximum success. Once you get the essential early rehabilitation steps and strategies right, you should move on to sharing an ever more rewarding life with your new dog and be better placed to anticipate/prevent any budding problems.

SCENT MARKING
Scent marking – i.e. urinating in inappropriate places, such as inside the home – can be a sexually motivated behaviour, most commonly seen in entire male dogs. This is even more likely if they live with bitches, or with bitches and other entire males, as it is a way the dogs mark out their territory to other male rivals.

If the cause of this behaviour is entirely hormonal, castrating the offending male dog can often stop it.

But not all scent marking in dogs is fuelled purely by hormones. Sometimes it can become a more neurotic/obsessive habit that is triggered by anxiety, such as when the dog is left alone by an owner. For more advice on this, see *Separation distress*, page 189.

Dogs of either sex can also scent mark in the home, or other less appropriate places, when they suddenly feel threatened by the presence of other dogs on their patch.

Some dogs will use urinating or fouling to claim territory, not just from other dogs, but also from their owners. A dog urinating or defaecating on another dog's bed, or an owner's bed, is a classic example of this. Dogs like these should have their access to any area where they might inappropriately urinate/foul far more strictly controlled by owners.

SELF-MESMERISERS
Some collies self-stimulate (see page 188), and others will self-mesmerise; i.e. become addicted to staring at repetitive light and/or movement patterns, almost as if they were trying to hypnotise themselves.

Shadow chasing is a typical example of this. But collies can get equally addicted to staring, trance-like, at things like falling rain, or leaves blowing, or they may get behind you on a walk and become fixated on the movement of your legs going back and forward.

The behaviour probably stems from the strong eyeing instinct and intense levels of mental focus which are genetically programmed into the breed. Like other more neurotic collie habits, how much of a problem self-mesmerising is, or becomes, in your dog depends entirely on how often, and how obsessively, he pursues the behaviour and how easily, or not, you find it to interrupt it and stop it.

Either way, collies should never be actively encouraged to pursue and thereafter consistently ingrain this kind of behaviour. For more advice see *Obsessive compulsive behaviour patterns*, page 180.

CAN COLLIES SUFFER FROM ADHD?
Throughout this book I have repeatedly highlighted how more obsessive behaviour patterns in collies are reminiscent of the human condition, Obsessive Compulsive Disorder, which is now known to have some genetic factor involved.

Increasingly today, the possibility that dogs may suffer

from other mental disorders, previously associated only with humans, is being explored. These include conditions like autism or Attention Deficit Hyperactivity Disorder (ADHD). True hyperactivity, or hyperkinesis, in dogs, is deemed to be a relatively rare condition. Dogs suffering from it are constantly frantic, panting and restless. Their heart rates run high as they move endlessly, not stopping until they collapse with exhaustion.

Because, however, it can be hard to tell the difference between a truly hyperkinetic dog and one who is simply unruly, persistently over-aroused/excited or suffering from some obsessive-compulsive movement disorder such as tail-chasing, some vets may recommend trying your dog on a Ritalin-type stimulant medication.

Only genuinely hyperkinetic dogs will respond to this by slowing down. Normal dogs, by contrast, will either show no response or an increase in activity level.

SELF-STIMULATORS

Much like human gym junkies, or those who cannot stop exercising or taking drugs because of the high they get from such activities, many collies become addicted to the adrenaline and pleasure chemical buzz released when they physically exert themselves or hit an elevated state of mental arousal via other ways, such as obsessive activity or persistent barking.

Often owners will regard these dogs as manic when they are just constantly looking for ways to trigger arousal responses in themselves. The more they arouse themselves, the more addicted to the experience they can become, and the less they seem able to cope with the state of not being stimulated. This is why they so often find it hard to settle down quietly for any length of time, or sustain focus and concentration in training.

Self-stimulating dogs may also deliberately wind themselves up to displace feelings of frustration or anxiety, or to alleviate the discomfort caused by some physical condition – i.e. anything from itchy skin to arthritis.

When you go out on walks with persistent self-stimulators, they are not the dogs who trot happily by your heels and take time to quietly sniff and explore their environment. They are, instead, a continual whir of totally purposeless activity – eternally barking and whining and dashing hither and thither like some particularly demented strain of mosquito. Just watching them can be pretty exhausting in itself.

SELF STIMULATION AND STRESS

If you have never owned collies in whom a state of mental balance is persistently maintained – i.e. calm, focused, highly attuned to your presence and commands – then you might think that the aforementioned endlessly mad behaviour is fairly normal within the breed. But it isn't. It's just what happens when these dogs' arousal/excitement

mechanisms are allowed to spiral out of control.

It *is* normal, if not desirable, for collies to have episodes of exhilarating physical activity throughout the day, interspersed with much lengthier calmer activity. When things are persistently allowed to go the other way around, it just turns your dog's brain to mush, prompts him to make reckless decisions (including more aggressive reactions) and also puts his body under severe stress.

There can also be a misconception among owners that letting a collie tear madly about, non-stop, on a walk is a good thing because it will "tire him out." But, in fact, the more aroused your collie gets, the longer he will take to settle down again when he gets home.

RESTORING CALM

Once you realise how damaging persistent excitement/arousal in your collie can be, and the extent to which it prevents him attaining behaviour you may much prefer in him, the next step is to work on restoring him to a state of greater mental calm and balance. See *Winding down a collie*.

Be aware, however, that many collies' mental/metabolic arousal mechanisms are far stronger than their self-calming ones (a phenomenon more fully explained under *Stress and stress related problems*, page 194), thus, it can take more effort for them to master self-calming activity. The more often a dog has been allowed to self-stimulate, and the longer he has been stuck in a state of high mental arousal, the more time it can also take to wind him down again.

WINDING DOWN A COLLIE

If you have a collie who appears to be in a constant or near constant 'hyper' state, and the possibility of him suffering from the rarer clinical condition, hyperkinesis, has been ruled out (See, *Can collies suffer from ADHD?*, page 187) first try to establish whether there could be a direct stress source causing this; i.e. some immediate environmental concern/anxiety as outlined under *Stress and stress related problems*.

Additionally, or alternatively, your dog may have some source of physical pain/discomfort which he is seeking to alleviate through constant self-stimulation/mental arousal. This should be checked out.

If you have investigated the above factors and believe your dog has just become addicted to self-stimulation, proceed as follows:

• First, think about a time when your dog was last in the most ideal calm/responsive state. It always helps to have a picture in your mind of the mental state you most desire in your dog and then keep working to attain and sustain it.

• Second, establish a rigid daily routine for your dog of up time and down time. Your dog needs to learn that there are set times during the day/evening when he can be active, and times when he must settle and rest.

- Up times will be periods where you train your dog and physically exercise him. When you train your dog, constantly work on exercises that require focus and concentration – e.g. sit and watch me, down and stay, plus scent and search tasks. You may initially need great patience and determination to get your dog to do these exercises, as many hyper-aroused dogs can find it very difficult to focus, or will get very fidgety and whiney when asked to do something that requires them to stay still.

- When you take your dog out on a walk, do not take toys or make him do chase games. Instead, keep making him focus on you and regularly do the same above exercises that require concentration. Reward your dog with praise and a very tasty treat each time he complies with your commands.

- If your dog keeps trying to run off way ahead of you on a walk, in order to persistently self-stimulate, keep him on a long line. Also make him lie down and watch you each and every time he begins to get over-excited. Do the same every time he tries to pull ahead of you on the line. Refuse to carry on the walk until he calms down and shows you the behaviour you desire. Every time he looks calmer, praise him well.

- Walking your dog, side by side, with other very calm dogs should also help.

- Also understand that long, steady, distance exercise, and mental work will always tire your dog more than highly exciting/stimulating activity.

- Down time is when your dog should rest – but he may not want to. He may keep running round the garden or bringing you toys instead, to sustain the aroused mental state. If so, you must put him in an area of exceptionally low stimulation – i.e. low light/sound/movement levels – such as the indoor kennel or refuge zone repeatedly mentioned throughout this book.

- Once he is placed there, leave him totally undisturbed. Also place your dog in his refuge zone any time he gets excessively excited at home. Do not give his protests about this any attention whatsoever, no matter how long they carry on. Eventually your dog will settle down.

- If you undertake this settling down procedure at the same set times daily, it should eventually become a normal habit for your dog – although do note your dog should not be left in a closed kennel/confined space for more than a couple of hours, and only after he has had sufficient exercise. Otherwise you could cause him distress that will hamper any future attempts to get him to settle in these places.

DOGS AS OPTIMISTS OR PESSIMISTS

A very interesting study undertaken by researchers at Bristol University, in the UK, concluded that dogs may well be born with a more optimistic or pessimistic take on life. This revelation could well explain why some dogs are not only more inherently fearful of stranger things/experiences, but also why they become more anxious when left alone at home.

The researchers studied a large group of dogs – some of which were collies – in two specific tests. First, they gauged how anxious individual dogs became when separated from their owners for five minutes. In the second test, bowls of food were placed out for the dogs. When the bowls were placed at one end of a room they were empty, and when they were put at the other end they were full.

When the bowls were put in more ambiguous places – e.g. the centre of the room – the dogs who had been most anxious when separated from their owners were also those less inclined to approach the resituated bowl out of a belief that it would be empty. The dogs who had been less anxious, optimistically ran up to the bowl, regardless of where it was placed.

- All in all, the more you eliminate sources of ongoing stimulation for your dog, and make calm behaviour continually rewarding for him, the easier he will find it to enter and sustain a more wound down and focused mental state

SEPARATION DISTRESS

Not all dogs have a pack mentality, but I feel that collies generally do. They are also dogs with a tendency to emotionally over-attach to owners, if given the opportunity

KEY POINTS FOR RE-TRAINING SEPARATION-ANXIOUS DOGS

The key points for re-training separation-anxious dogs are as follows:

- Wean your dog off your presence very gradually, beginning while you are actually at home.
- Keep repeating the same separation routines and mock departure rituals in the same way.
- Always put your separation object in place (see page 191), in front of the dog gate, before leaving your dog.
- Never give attention to your dog while this object is in place.
- Never remove the object/go back to your dog while he is in an anxious/agitated state.
- Never make a fuss of your dog when you return to him, or allow him to make a fuss of you.

If this training is not working for your dog, either you are still rewarding his anxious/agitated behaviour in some way (e.g. with attention) or you are trying to push his separation tolerance too far, too fast, before he has had sufficient time to psychologically adjust to longer periods on his own.

personal impact of their dog's separation behaviour on *them* – i.e. persistent barking/whining which infuriates their neighbours, or destructiveness/household fouling that can be both time consuming and expensive to rectify.

Some owners even believe that a dog's destructiveness/fouling etc. is motivated by a desire to punish or seek revenge on them for departing which is, of course, total nonsense, and just leads to ever greater hostility towards a dog on an owner's part.

While anger and resentment may be understandable emotions to feel when you return to a trashed home, they do not take you any nearer to solving the problem of a dog who copes so badly when left alone.

THE MIND OF THE SEPARATED DOG

Canine separation problems can often be very tricky to tackle because they require us to better control how a dog thinks while we are not actually with him. A lot of this depends, in turn, on giving the dog the right psychological preparation when younger.

Each time we leave a dog, he needs to have the psychological/emotional resilience to cope with the experience of being alone (and often also confined), and the confidence to believe that we will soon be coming home again. If your dog has neither this psychological resilience, nor confidence, in place, that is when all your separation problems with him begin.

THE GENETIC COMPONENT

Throughout this book I have stressed how vital it is to teach your dog, from early puppyhood onwards, to cope with being separated from you for regular periods – beginning with when you are still at home. This lays down the foundations for greater emotional independence in him, and also makes your eventual departure from the home less of a shock for him. The same approach is also important for newly rehomed rescued dogs.

This said, I believe some collies will always be more prone to anxiety when left alone, because there is a genetic component behind this behaviour. Some dogs are not only more naturally needy emotionally, but also appear more likely to fear the worst when placed in uncertain situations. See *Dogs as optimists or pessimists, page 189.*

THE NEEDY DOG

To me, a more needy collie – and, thus, one far more likely to suffer from anxiety when separated from his owner – is usually very obvious. He is the dog continually checking on your whereabouts when you are at home. He finds it hard to remain in any room you have left without following you and loves to lie right by your feet, if not actually on top of them. He may also continually position himself in places like the hallway, stairway, or next to the front or back door,

to do so, and dogs who can react adversely when lengthily confined.

All these considerations explain why collies can so often be classic candidates for separation distress when left alone at home by an owner.

A lot of owners whose collies have separation problems do not focus enough on the emotional state their dog is in when they leave him. Instead, they concentrate more on the so that you cannot go anywhere without him knowing about it.

If you own a dog like this, try to see it less as flattering and more as psychologically unhealthy. Because the more you encourage or condone this kind of emotional dependency in your dog, the harder he will always find it when you eventually have to leave him on his own.

SOLVING THE SEPARATION PROBLEM IN NEEDY DOGS

If you have a classically needy collie, the key to solving his separation anxiety is to progressively wean him off his psychological dependency on you.

Begin, as previously highlighted in this book, by making him stay on his own for routine periods while you are still at home. Put him in his own quarters, which should be separated from the rest of your home by a dog gate.

Another tip is to get a symbolic object – e.g. a chair, a large vase, or a box – and always place it in front of the dog gate, for your dog to see, before you leave him on his own. Your dog needs to learn that while this object is in place, you will give him no attention whatsoever.

Start by leaving your dog alone in his quarters for a minute, while you are still at home; putting your symbolic/separation object in place first. No matter how much your dog whines, or protests, totally ignore him, as if he did not exist. *Only* once he is quiet and settled again, remove your symbolic object, then go back to your dog.

Each time you remove your separation object and go back to your dog, it is crucial that you acknowledge him only very casually, then walk immediately away from him. By making a big fuss of him, or allowing him to make a big fuss of you, you are reinforcing your dog's sense of relief at being reunited with you.

Continually work on this separation exercise, making your dog stay in his own quarters for progressively longer periods on his own in the day and evening, while you are still at home. Remember, always put your object in place before leaving your dog on his own, and never remove the object/go back to your dog until he is quiet and settled again. If you do not stick relentlessly to this regime, your dog will never gain greater emotional self-reliance.

GOING OUT

Once you have got your dog to settle on his own for lengthier periods, while you are still at home, next try the following.

Put your dog in his quarters and your separation object in place. Then do everything you would normally do if you were really going out; i.e. lock up, get your coat and keys etc. It is likely this will make your dog anxious, as he associates such rituals with your departure.

As before, totally ignore him. Then, while still ignoring him, put your coat, keys etc. back in their usual places and

unlock the house again. Then go and sit casually in another room/carry on with your normal routine, while still totally ignoring your dog. Go through this entire ritual around three or four times, until your dog eventually settles again.

Once you get to the point where you can get your keys etc. while your dog stays calm and settled, suddenly go out of the front door without acknowledging your dog at all, wait 10 seconds, then return. Totally ignore your dog when you return and go and sit in a separate room from him. Only remove your separation object and go back to your dog while he remains settled and quiet.

Work on the above kind of exercises relentlessly, until you can get your coat, keys etc. and go out of the home for five, ten minutes or more and come back while your dog is still settled. It is very important to keep doing the same separation exercises daily, in order to have a dog you can eventually leave more happily on his own for longer periods.. Also see *Key points for re-training separation-anxious dogs*.

MISTAKES

One of the most common mistakes owners make when leaving their dogs is to give them a treat, in the belief that this is some sort of consolation for their departure. In truth, it is just the cue for the dog that he is about to be left and as such, it marks the starting point of his anxiety.

Separation-anxious dogs never eat the treats you leave them when you go because they are too stressed. They only eat them once you come back home.

Similarly, owners will attempt to console dogs when they leave by saying something like: "I'll be back soon". These are words and a concept that a dog cannot possibly understand. What he does understand, however, is each time you say these specific words in a specific tone, and in a specific context, it means you are about to leave him. So once again, your attempt to be kind to your dog has simply proven to be the launchpad for his anxiety.

It is always best to leave separation-anxious dogs very casually, without acknowledging them, when you go out – as if you were simply popping outside, momentarily, to get something from your car. Similarly, never go overboard when you return.

Owners may find this goes against the grain but, ultimately, what is at stake here is the psychological wellbeing of your dog. You cannot encourage dogs to be overly devoted to you when it suits you, then expect them to switch straight back to self reliant mode when you leave them, as the psychological adjustment for the dog is just too great.

THE FRUSTRATED DOG

Not all collies who are destructive/noisy etc. when left alone are in a state of anxiety due to intense owner dependency.

They are in a state of frustration instead, because they resent being suddenly denied the owner attention they are used to, and have also had physical restrictions placed on their normal freedom of action/movement.

If you have a dog who exhibits few, if any, of the previously outlined emotionally needy symptoms and, instead, copes very badly with any attempt you make to physically restrict his behaviour, this is more likely. Such a dog may perpetually defy your commands to come in from the garden or get off furniture, whine and struggle madly when you hold him by the collar to stop him doing something, and/or try to nip/mouth your hands to get free again.

The problem can be most common in dogs who are used to having their every whim indulged by owners, and who have never been taught, in general, how to better cope psychologically when limits are placed on their expectations or desires.

It can also be quite a common problem in rescued dogs, for whom any sudden owner departure triggers past memories of lengthy confinement and abandonment. For this reason it is never wise to suddenly go out and leave a newly-rehomed rescued dog alone for a long period, especially not with the free run of your home, as the possibility for troubled behaviour, while you are out, is too great.

It is far better to see how the dog copes first with shorter separation periods away from you while you are still at home You can then build these up in length, according to how well he still continues to cope – much in the manner previously outlined for separation-anxious dogs.

Rescued dogs also need time to de-stress and develop a sense of confidence/security in their new living environment and general daily routine.

SHOULD YOU USE AN INDOOR KENNEL?

If you have a collie – rescued or not – who is particularly destructive when you go out, you may have been tempted to consider placing him in an indoor kennel. If you are going to go down this route, however, such enforced confinement should never be seen as a permanent solution to the problem. It is merely a way to initially stop the dog endlessly repeating wrong behaviour when you are out, until you can teach him better ways of behaving when left alone. You should also never leave your dog in a closed kennel for more than two hours maximum when you go out, and only after a good spell of exercise.

As outlined in Part One (Chapter Four, page 39), indoor kennels or crates are routinely abused by owners today, in a way that subjects dogs to intense psychological stress and suffering. Too many owners use kennels/crates much like straitjackets, to stop dogs releasing their emotional distress in more active/physical ways. This does not mean your dog's stress goes away; it means it just intensifies instead, then

turns inwards to cause ongoing physical and psychological harm.

If you cannot, yourself, stop your dog's destructiveness/barking etc., while you are out, seek professional help to steer you both through the right retraining. Don't just stick your dog in a cage all day and imagine this is okay, because it isn't.

THE FRIGHTENED DOG

Some collies become very anxious when owners depart less because they are madly attached to them, or frustrated, but more because they have come to associate their owner's departure with a scary experience.

The scary experience, which previously occurred when an owner was not present, could be anything from a backfiring car or thunderstorm, to noisy workmen nearby, or a stranger knocking on a window/coming to the front door. Alternatively, the scary experience could emanate from inside your home – e.g. noisy central heating system, or a telephone voicemail system suddenly kicking into action.

In cases like these, you need to try to identify what may be scaring your dog when you are out. Through being more observant, you may see him react adversely to the same particularly worrying noise/experience while you are at home. Thereafter, you need to work on gradually de-sensitising him to it. You may well need expert professional help to both pinpoint the relevant scary experience for your dog and then get him de-sensitised to it.

DIFFERENT CAUSES, DIFFERENT SOLUTIONS

Hopefully, this section will have made you aware that separation problems in collies are rarely straightforward. They can be motivated by different emotional factors in different dogs and the better you can identify these, the sooner you can work on improving the way your dog feels when left alone.

This said, owners should never underestimate the enormous leap of faith a dog has to make, in order to psychologically cope with being separated from them for any length of time – particularly if he is also restricted to a space he cannot readily escape from.

Ultimately, owners are seen by dogs as key to their survival, because they are the gateway to every resource in life they need – i.e. food, water, shelter, access to the outside world. Thus, a dog only has to doubt for a moment that an owner will return in order for his world to fall apart.

All the psychological preparation and training we give dogs, from puppyhood onwards, is aimed at keeping such doubts at bay in their heads. But there will still always be dogs who find it more natural to trust, dogs who find it more natural to doubt, and other dogs who find restriction and confinement of any kind, an intense emotional challenge. This is a reality every owner should bear in mind.

STEALING

There are two main kinds of stealing in collies, as in many other dogs. There is the opportunistic stealing of food, which owners have left in dog-accessible places. Then there is the deliberate snatching of other people's/dogs' possessions, in order for the dog to secure them as trophies and, thus, feel more superior/self-important.

FOOD

Let's start with food. Dogs are programmed to be opportunistic scavengers. Thus, if they see food around that no one else appears to be eating, and it is immediately accessible to them, the question you have to ask yourself is, why *wouldn't* they eat it? It makes perfect sense to them, if not you.

Over the years I have come to realise that, with this issue, there are basically three kinds of collie. There are the ones who will steal any food from anywhere any time. Then there are the ones who, genetically, have far greater inhibition about taking something they think might belong to you. Finally, there are collies who may be less naturally inhibited on this front, but have been taught, by their owners, to be more inhibited via consistent training and correction.

HIGHER AND LOWER FOOD-TAKING INHIBITION

Where you leave food is also highly significant. All my collies have high levels of inhibition when it comes to taking food off tables, kitchen surfaces, people's trays or plates etc., but if I left food on the floor – where they normally expect to find it – it would disappear pretty quickly.

Some dogs have high inhibition about eating ambiguously owned food in their owners' presence, but less inhibition about eating it when an owner is absent, or out of sight. Hence, the classic scenario of the dog sneaking into the kitchen to steal food while you are in another room.

If you are a person who regularly gives your dog food straight from your plate, you have the dual problem of a dog who steadily loses respect for you, and one who also becomes progressively less inhibited about where he takes food from. So whether or not you already have a food thieving dog, I would halt this unwisely indulgent practice straight away.

Dogs should be taught that all food comes to them, via you, in only two ways: first in return for co-operation (i.e. in training/rewarding good behaviour) and second, in a bowl at a set time.

DEALING WITH A FOOD THIEF

Obviously the simplest solution to a persistent canine food thief is to make sure no food is ever left out, in accessible places, for him to steal.

Alternatively or additionally, for dogs who steal things behind your back, you can try the booby trap technique.

This involves collecting lots of empty tin cans. Pierce a hole in the bottom of each can, run roughly a metre length of dark sewing thread through it, then tie/tape the end of the thread to secure it to the bottom of the can.

Once you have done this, tie a collection of cans to a bit of food left poking out on your kitchen surface – or any other place your dog has previously stolen from. Make sure your dog cannot easily see the tins attached to the food. Ideally, you want to place the food so that your dog will try to drag it off the higher surface and down to floor, with his teeth – setting off the booby trap.

With the trap set up, leave the room and wait for the inevitable clatter that will come when your dog tries to steal the food, and gets a big shock. It is very important that you are not there when this happens, because you want your dog to associate the shock with his stealing behaviour, rather than your presence.

If you do this enough times, you should solve the problem. Do not, however, leave particularly prized food in the booby trap – e.g. sausages, roast meat, cheese – because the pleasure he gets from these may outweigh the deterrent effect of the falling cans. Go, instead, for something like pieces of bread (e.g. end of a baguette) or a cooked potato; anything it is easy to tie thread to.

TROPHY STEALING

When dogs steal things from you, or other people, and run off with them as trophies and refuse to give them back, they are only doing so because you have made this so rewarding for them.

Imagine for a moment what it is like to be an average dog, in an average home, where the attention you get may sometimes be limited and where feelings of excitement and power are relatively few and far between. Then you discover that when you grab certain things, the whole house comes alive. Everybody is suddenly giving you attention, chasing you, and wanting what you have taken. The thrill of it all goes completely to your head and you just want to do it more and more.

Some dogs may go on to destroy items they have taken, or guard them aggressively from you.

If you had not given your dog access to your possessions when he was younger, he would not have been able to discover the joys of stealing them. Similarly, if you taught your dog, from day one, the high rewards of giving you things, on command, (as outlined in Part One, Chapter Five, page 55) he would not have learned the rewards of not giving them back to you instead.

Trophy stealing dogs should be taught the *give* command as soon as possible, beginning with the dog being placed on a long line if necessary. You must keep making this exercise incredibly rewarding, all the time. Simultaneously, at home or elsewhere, keep setting up items for your dog to 'steal' that are of no value to you whatsoever. As soon as he rushes off with them, as before, he must be totally ignored. Or even immediately walk away from him and leave him on his own.

The more no one wants what your dog has stolen, or even cares about it, the less and less appealing the trophy grabbing habit becomes for him. Also be aware that dogs who persistently steal toys from other dogs when out, and will not give them back, are a complete nuisance and aggravation to other owners. So if you have a dog like this, either retrain him as soon as possible, or keep him on a lead when other dogs are playing with their toys.

STRESS AND STRESS-RELATED PROBLEMS

All understanding of stress in dogs, and collies in particular, has to begin with a better appreciation of how animals' brains and bodies are programmed to work, in relation to their external environment.

The minds and bodies of dogs, much like our own, are governed by two counter-balancing 'upper' and 'downer' nervous systems; the sympathetic and the parasympathetic. These in turn are part of the autonomic nervous system, which lies at the heart of our responses to threat, and other environmental challenges.

The difference between the autonomic and the somatic nervous system is that while the somatic nervous system governs actions (e.g. muscle movement, bladder function) under an animal's conscious control, the effects of the autonomic one cannot for the most part be consciously controlled.

In other words, once external threat signals have been picked up by the senses and sent to an animal's brain, the autonomic nervous system is activated and an animal, thereafter, can't always control how much stress he registers as a result, or how much impact this will have on his mind and body.

This is such an important principle to appreciate, as it better explains why owners cannot make a dog consciously over-ride a stress process that has begun on a more sub-conscious level, and will thereafter run its course on much the same basis, as long as the dog is exposed to stimuli his senses register as threatening or challenging. Also see, *Sub-conscious stress* a little later.

STRESS AND YOUR DOG
The most important factors to consider when it comes to stress and your dog are as follows:
- A certain level of stress/mental and physical arousal is vital to maintaining optimum physical and mental health in a dog, and overall life quality
- Stress only becomes a problem when a dog is too persistently over-aroused or under-aroused.
- Whether a threat is real or just perceived/imagined by the senses, a dog's body/mind will mount exactly the same

stress response.
- Typical emotions triggering the stressed state in dogs are fear, anxiety, frustration and excitement.
- Every dog's perception of what is threatening can be different and, similarly, his way of responding to it. Much of this can have a genetic root, but it will also be down to the experiences a dog has been exposed to in life.
- The more naturally vulnerable your dog is to stress, the harder you will always have to work at keeping him in a more balanced state.

METABOLIC CHANGES
The sympathetic nervous system triggers the arousal response in animals, once a threat message has been sent to the brain. This causes the adrenal glands to release the stress hormones, adrenaline and cortisol, which prepare the body for a fight or flight reaction. Stress hormones cause immediate physical and metabolic changes; e.g. increased breathing and heart rate, to move oxygen-rich blood faster to the brain, and to the muscles needed for fighting or fleeing. The senses become sharper and the animal becomes less sensitive to pain.

This vital survival response, however, comes at a cost to other bodily processes – e.g. growth, reproduction, the immune and digestive systems and blood flow to the skin – whose optimum functioning gets put on hold while the hormonally induced crisis state is continuing. This crisis arousal state can also be highly destructive to cells within the body and brain.

All the above explains why persistently or chronically stressed animals are so prone to a wide range of health problems, particularly as they get older – e.g. cancers and other immune system-related disorders – as well as general premature physical and mental ageing. Persistent stress can also damage an animal's memory and ability to learn.

THE PARASYMPATHETIC SYSTEM
Because the state of hormonally induced high arousal can be so damaging, if prolonged, the parasympathetic nervous system will try to kick into action, as soon as possible, once a threat is judged to be over, in order to return the body back to normal functioning. This is done by flooding the body with tranquilising or self-calming chemicals, which suppress any further cortisol production.

The longer or more often a dog is stressed, the more adrenaline/cortisol remains in his body. This means his arousal responses are more easily triggered and he can find it ever harder to chemically self-calm or wind down again. This can be a problem with very many collies who are perpetually over-stimulated or regularly placed in highly frustrating, exciting or anxiety-inducing life situations.

A reverse problem can arise, however, in dogs who are perpetually under-stimulated, or in dogs whose arousal mechanisms get over-used then burn out, or when collies are older and their arousal mechanisms get weaker. In these situations they are suffering a different kind of stress induced by metabolic *under*-arousal – i.e. depression, lethargy.

SUB-CONSCIOUS STRESS

Earlier in this book, and in this section, I highlighted how stress gets triggered in animals on a sub-conscious level.

To better illustrate how this can happen, environmental psychologist, Gary Evans, of Cornell University in the USA – who is also an international expert on environmental stress – studied the effects of chronic low-level traffic noise on children. He focused on the type of noise that many of us, consciously, are unaware of even hearing or registering.

He found that levels of stress hormones in the children, as well as their blood pressure and heart rates, were all significantly raised, compared to those who were not exposed to the noise, and also that this kind of constant environmental stressor triggered more symptoms of anxiety and nervousness.

WHAT IS A HEALTHY LEVEL OF STRESS FOR YOUR DOG?

Establishing how much stress or mental/physical arousal a collie can be exposed to, before it stops being beneficial and risks harming him, is not always easy to quantify, because it can depend a lot on the individual dog.

Some collies are far more stress-vulnerable – in terms of the damaging impact it has on them – whereas others are more stress-resilient. Dogs who are more stress-vulnerable are usually quite obvious, in terms of how highly sensitive/responsive they are, how little it takes to provoke a fearful/anxious/excitable state in them, and how long they will remain aroused once this happens. They can also suffer from recurring stress-related skin and digestive problems.

Dogs who are more stress-resilient can often become quite excitable, too. However, they are able to return to a calm/balanced state far more quickly than stress-vulnerable dogs and also tend to be far less naturally fearful or anxious in nature.

Our assessments of dogs' true stress levels are often inaccurate, because we tend to base them only on overt physical signs, as outlined in *Classic stress symptoms in dogs*. But stress is not always the easiest thing to see or definitively rule out in a dog if the effects are more internal or subtle.

Many collies, for example, are able to master a look of intense focus, and outward stillness, on an owner's command, even when they are totally churning up inside.

THE BALANCED DOG

As mentioned previously, the most reliable way to gauge the amount of stress a dog is suffering is through measuring the cortisol levels in his body. But this is obviously not practical or possible for most owners on a regular basis.

CLASSIC STRESS SYMPTOMS IN DOGS

- Panting (not just when hot).
- Yawning.
- Shaking and shivering.
- Excessive scratching or licking.
- Glazed eyes, dilated pupils, constant blinking, avoiding eye contact.
- Tucked tail, low and slow wagging tail.
- Salivating.
- Persistently lowered head/lowered and held back ears.
- Persistent whining and barking.
- Persistent diarrhoea.
- Sudden onset of dandruff, shedding, loss of normal coat lustre.
- Muscle tension.
- Hyper-sensitivity, hyper-reactivity.
- General restlessness/inability to settle.

Personally, I think it can be more helpful to have a picture in your mind of how a collie should look and behave when he is in exactly in the right state of balance; i.e. neither too mentally/physiologically over-aroused or under-aroused. Over many years of owning and working with collies, I have devised my own criteria for recognising a perfectly balanced dog, which are as follows:

- He is alert but also calm and clear thinking.
- He happily and confidently follows commands without any sign of confusion, distraction, mental shut down or panic.
- There is no tension/tightness in his body.
- His body and tail posture are relaxed and confident – i.e. no head or body lowering or overly low/tucked in tail.
- His eyes are clear, bright and focused - i.e. no sign of glazing or persistently averted eye contact.
- He has a glossy, shiny coat and healthy skin.
- He has healthy, well-formed bowel movements.
- He does not indulge in excess whining, barking, or repeatedly manic or obsessive activity.

- He has a healthy thirst and appetite.
- He is socially outgoing/tolerant towards other dogs and people.
- He is not hyper-reactive/aggressive at the slightest provocation.
- He recovers swiftly from any sudden fright/episode of excitement to resume a state of balance again.
- In between training sessions and walks/physical exercise, he is happy to settle down quietly to rest and sleep.

STRESS AND BEHAVIOURAL PROBLEMS

Stress, of some kind, lies at the heart of a vast number of behavioural problems I see in dogs. It lurks like a persistent, debilitating fog, hampering their ability to see or master any better way of behaving, and slowly diminishing the overall quality of their lives.

Most dogs deemed to be badly behaved or even mad are just stressed. Either the stress is caused by the living environment/lifestyle imposed on the dog, or some deeper rooted psychological insecurities that date back to his earlier rearing and socialisation.

For example, inadequately socialised dogs tend to be far more fearful of change or new experiences, and can also be driven by a constant desire to control others. These feelings place them under persistent stress which is then so often released through aggression.

Whenever I am working with aggressive dogs, I know that as soon as I can reduce their mental stressloads, the level of aggression they use will start to wane or even stop altogether. The best way I can describe this process is like seeing a dog finally leaving a howling storm behind and stepping out into the warmth of the sun.

Owners should also understand that if a dog is anxious about situations like being left alone, or facing the world beyond his front door, he remains in a more or less persistent state of stress. This is because he never knows when these things are going to happen again. In other words, the additional stress caused to anxious dogs, through a sheer inability to exert any control over their lives, or predict when a scary thing is next going to happen, can be huge.

STRESS BEFORE BIRTH

Previously, I have mentioned how an individual collie's vulnerability to stress can have a genetic root. But it may also be that stress can affect dogs even before they are born. An interesting study, recently undertaken by the Institute of Psychiatry, Kings College London, in the UK, revealed that mothers experiencing high levels of stress during early pregnancy were far more likely to have children with ADHD, extreme anger issues and other behavioural problems. This was thought to be down to the effect of stress hormones on the unborn baby's developing brain.

Exactly the same process could well occur in dogs, and also help explain why so many dogs with more serious behavioural issues come from more deprived and stressful rearing environments, including puppy farms.

STRESS AND THE COMPETITION DOG

Collies who are used and trained to take part in different kinds of competitive pursuit can be exposed to higher levels of stress. The stress does not just come from the excitement of a pursuit, in itself, but all the additional pressure factors – i.e. noise, crowds, constant restriction of normal movement/behaviour – associated with the typical show environment.

Additional stress can also be inflicted on the competition dog via handler pressure. In fact, this can often be the last straw which causes a dog to mentally crack or shut down at a show.

For more information on stress in competition dogs, see Part One, Chapter Eleven, page 127.

REDUCING YOUR DOG'S STRESS LOAD

While it may be impossible to eliminate all sources of more harmful stress from our own lives, let alone those of our dogs, a high amount of canine stress could be reduced with better insight and consideration on an owner's part.

Rather than endlessly worrying about every little pressure scenario you expose your dog to, or which randomly comes his way (which will only make *you* more stressed), it is far better to focus on the biggest and most relentless sources of stress for collies (if not most dogs) as follows.

LACK OF ADEQUATE SOCIALISATION AND TRAINING

Dogs who are not adequately socialised and trained lack the basic mental tools to operate confidently in wider society or understand their owner's expectations of them at any given moment. This is all intensely stressful for them, as is being continually punished or chastised for reasons they do not understand. It is always possible to re-socialise and better train dogs like these, given the right expert help.

LIFESTYLE

Many dogs cannot cope with their lifestyles because they are totally unpredictable (i.e. lacking in set routine), or feature too many restrictions on their normal behaviour/freedom of action and movement (i.e. too much confinement/too little living space). Understand that the more your dog's lifestyle is at odds with his basic psychological needs/natural expectations of life, the more stressed he will always be. Dogs who live with other people or dogs who constantly threaten or bully them will also be highly stressed.

NOISE/VISUAL STIMULATION

Too many collies live in, or are exposed to, domestic environments that are too relentlessly noisy or visually stimulating; i.e. people or children constantly screaming/shouting/charging around, the TV or radio blaring full blast. This kind of endless sensory bombardment keeps their bodies in constant alert mode and makes it ever harder for them to regain a sense of inner calm and balance. As continually mentioned in this book, your dog must have his own special refuge zone, with very low surrounding noise/visual stimulation, where he can regularly wind down.

ACTIVITY LEVELS

The under-exercised, mentally under-stimulated collie will always be more stressed. So will the dog who is constantly over-stimulated by the wrong kind of highly exciting exercise that ramps up his adrenaline/cortisol levels to full thrust.

OWNER BEHAVIOUR

An owner's behaviour towards their dog has a massive bearing on his overall stress levels. Calm, kind but strong owners who always communicate what they want or desire, through good training, make a dog feel secure and protected. An owner who is more neurotic, hostile, aggressive or over-indulgent – or a scarily inconsistent mixture of all these things all the time, as is so often seen – does not. Ditto the owner who thinks that shouting aimless human words at their dog equals training.

EXTRA INDIVIDUAL FACTORS

In most collies' lives there can be one or more factors that push up their overall stressloads. These can include some specific environmental phobia, some compulsive/endlessly repeated behaviour pattern, an inappropriate diet – i.e. too rich/full of artificial additives – or some ongoing source of physical discomfort/pain. Wherever possible, you should try to better address these issues – with expert help if necessary – in order to own a calmer, happier dog.
Also see, *Winding down a collie*, page 188.

SUBMISSIVE BEHAVIOUR

It is pretty common, if not normal, for young puppies to exhibit overtly submissive behaviour towards less familiar people, dogs or visitors to your home; i.e., urinating, crawling on their bellies and/or rolling on their backs. Such actions are just a natural self-protection instinct. The puppy is basically advertising his helplessness/powerlessness to another individual who is likely to be higher ranking than him.

To be honest, I always worry far more about puppies who *don't* readily show submission, in any shape or form, because this is a vital starting tool for any young dog's successful integration into wider canine society later on.

Once dogs get older and more socially

confident/experienced, their submission signals tend to become more subtle – e.g. head lowering when approaching another person/dog and a low, slow, wag of the tail.

EXCESSIVE SUBMISSION IN OLDER DOGS

Many dogs are born to be more naturally submissive in nature than others – this is most obvious in puppyhood and tends to be most common in bitches. If a dog persists in showing highly submissive behaviour well beyond puppyhood, there could be several explanations for this.

If the acute submission persists towards people or some household members, it is likely that the behaviour is being continually reinforced in some way. The commonest way people do this is to make an intense fuss of a submissive dog, in order to make him feel more confident or at ease. In fact, this can have the reverse effect of making submissive behaviour more rewarding for the dog.

It is far better to totally ignore a highly submissive dog, as if he was not there, and only slowly return attention to him once he shows more confident behaviour. If a shy dog thinks people are always going to ignore him, initially, this also takes the pressure off him to use submission as a form of immediate self-defence.

Never forget how formidably big people can look to dogs, in relation to themselves, especially when people are standing over them and they are lying on their backs.

THE USE OF SUBMISSION IN FEAR-AGGRESSIVE DOGS

Many shy/submissive dogs only become fear-aggressive later on because submission, in itself, did not stop other people or dogs coming into their space and making them feel threatened.

As outlined earlier in the *Aggression* section, a typical pattern can emerge in fear-aggressive dogs where they are initially submissive towards other people/dogs, then suddenly switch, in panic, to more hostile behaviour. This is a sign of a dog in constant conflict as to how he should react because he is lacking the necessary degree of social confidence/experience to deal with the approach of new or strange individuals without feeling under pressure.

For more advice on these issues, once again, see *Aggression,* page 152, and also *Fear and phobias*, page 170.

TOILETING PROBLEMS

Anyone who has owned dogs will be aware of how strong a part habit plays in their toilet routines. Some dogs will favour particular surfaces, like grass, to relieve themselves on, and may also always choose to defaecate at a particular place on a walk. Similarly, some dogs may always choose to go to the toilet in their own gardens, rather than on a walk. With other dogs, it may be the other way around.

Either way, these habits exist due to persistent conditioning from puppyhood (i.e. toilet training undertaken by owners), and, thereafter, the mental associations individual dogs make between specific places/contexts and the activity of relieving themselves.

PROBLEMS

There are several different reasons why dogs develop inappropriate toileting habits; i.e. keep going to the toilet inside your home. When dogs are highly stressed/anxious, for example, they can lose their normal ability to control their bowel and bladder functions. This is why dogs with separation distress commonly foul in the home when left.

Dogs who have bowel/bladder disorders or infections can similarly lose their ability to control where they go to the toilet. A certain degree of urinary incontinence often occurs in spayed bitches, and a progressive loss of bowel/bladder control can also be a common problem in the ageing or elderly dog.

If none of the above reasons for inappropriate urinating/fouling in the home apply to your dog, and you do not think the behaviour is territorial (see *Scent-marking*, page 187), then, clearly, something has gone wrong with his earlier conditioning/training.

HOW DOGS LEARN INAPPROPRIATE TOILET HABITS

Whenever a dog's bladder or bowel is full, a message gets sent to his brain that he needs to go to the toilet. If a dog has been trained/conditioned since puppyhood that he should only 'go' outside, he will exert conscious control over his bowel/bladder until he gets outside.

If he has not had good enough early training/conditioning of this kind, he will just go wherever he happens to be, which will then become the norm. If, for example, when younger, he regularly urinated/defaecated inside the home, because no one properly trained/conditioned him to go outside instead, going to the toilet inside the home would become a normal

habit for him. This can be a common problem in rescued dogs coming from deprived, if not completely dysfunctional, early rearing backgrounds.

Similarly, dogs who have previously been kennelled outside often have poor toilet control within the home environment because they were never in a position to learn not to foul there earlier on.

Once you understand how dogs get into wrong habits like this, purely through inadequate early conditioning and training, you should also realise how pointless it is to punish them for it. This may make you feel better for a moment, but does nothing to solve the problem.

If you have problems with your dog fouling in the home through poor early conditioning, it is far better to go right back to scratch with him, and train him again much as if he were a young puppy. There are details on how you do this in Part One (Chapters Three and Four).

TRAINING PROBLEMS

See Part One (Chapter Seven).

WHINGEING/WHINING

See *Manipulative behaviour.*

X-CESSIVE, X-CITABLE, X-TREME BEHAVIOURS

Normal Border Collie.

YOU AND YOUR DOG: CONFLICTS AND RELATIONSHIP ISSUES

See, *Attention-seeking behaviour, Disobedience, Emotional incontinence/self-control, Emotional over-dependency/attachment, Manipulative behaviour, Rebuilding a bond* and *Separation distress.* Also see Chapter Five, Part One.

ZZZZzzzzzz....THE END

FINDING THE RIGHT HELP

Throughout this book I have constantly stressed the need for readers to find 'expert help', when it comes to issues concerning their dog's training or behaviour.

The traditional way of guiding readers to this help has always been through giving them lists of national/regional dog training or behavioural organisations. However, owners constantly tell me that the quality of knowledge and expertise offered by members of different organisations can be very mixed, particularly when it comes to a breed like the Border collie, which – as outlined a bit later – often calls for a more specialised level of understanding and experience.

It can thus be far more helpful to find yourself the right *individual,* rather than organisation. This may require an extra element of research on your part, or travelling further afield, but it will be well worth it if what your expert teaches you transforms your dog's performance in a particular pursuit, or solves some persistent behaviour problem in him.

Help with competition training

Let us imagine you are looking for someone to help you improve your collie's training in a particular competitive pursuit. The most obvious starting point would be to pick somebody who is currently doing well, and winning a lot, high up in this pursuit.

But would they necessarily be right for you and your dog? It's important to understand that a successful competitor and a good teacher aren't always one and the same thing. Some people, for instance, may do very well in competition with one particular dog, but aren't able to replicate similar success with other dogs they own.

This suggests they may only have one way of training a dog to do set tasks, rather than a range of different approaches and techniques that can be tailored to the nature of individual dogs. And maybe your dog is one who needs more imaginative or insightful handling to get the best out of him.

A high level of egotism can also drive some top competitors, whereas what you need in a good teacher is a greater degree of selflessness and a strong desire to inspire and help others. Competition trainers who constantly criticise you and/or pull your performance to pieces and then strut around with their own dogs to show you how clever *they* are, by comparison, are really putting the demands of their own egos first, and helping you a pretty poor second.

Why pay money to 'teachers' like this, just to get demoralised and insulted? It's totally absurd. Any owner/pupil deserves a lot better than this and better is always available.

Motivation and inspiration

You may have noticed that behind every top athlete or football team is the coach who has prompted them to achieve what they have achieved. The coach in question may not necessarily have been the most famed or acclaimed of competitors themselves, but they do know their sport inside out, in terms of its demands and technicalities, and most of all they know how to motivate and inspire others.

It is the job of the coach, first and foremost, to give people the self-belief required to be the best they can be. And I think the same should apply to any good competition trainer in the dog world, when they set themselves up as advisors to others.

If you are lucky enough, you can find a person like this via word of mouth. If not, begin your search by going to lots of competitions featuring your favoured dog pursuit and watch all the different handlers with their dogs very carefully; not just when they are in the ring, but also when they are outside it.

Desirable and less desirable role models

Look particularly for handlers who work more than one dog equally well, and who inject an extra level of style and accuracy into their performances. Most of all you should see a real bond of mutual respect and affection between the handler and each of his/her dogs. You also want to see someone who treats their dog with the same level of kindness and consideration, even when they don't do well, as every dog (and handler!) can have a day when things just go wrong, for many different reasons, regardless of how brilliant they normally are.

Someone, by contrast, who is harsher and less considerate to their dogs and who takes their own disappointment/frustration out on them, inside or outside the ring, is a far less desirable role model.

Keep questioning

It can be common for owners to stick to a certain way of training competition dogs, purely because this is all they know. In other words, they have begun training for a particular pursuit with a particular instructor, or club, who do things a specific way; using much the same methods for all dogs.

Because you have only ever trained for a pursuit one way,

however, this doesn't necessarily mean it is the *only* way to get the kind of results you desire, or that there aren't other people out there who have different methods that are better for both you and your dog.

Whether training or competing, never just blindly follow the pack; copying what everyone else does, or unquestioningly absorbing their set attitudes and views about dogs and their handling. The best trainers are always original thinkers; people who constantly question what you are doing with your dog and why you are doing it, and make you do the same. Look for someone like this if you can.

Above all, do not be bullied or pressurised into doing anything in training that you feel is wrong or unkind, because whatever an 'expert' says, no one ultimately knows your dog better than you.

Help with behaviour problems
When it comes to problems concerning your dog's behaviour, it is particularly important that the 'expert' you choose has considerable knowledge of the Border collie breed. This is because collies can have psychological instincts, sensitivities and complexities that are really quite unique, and if you not understand them or have extensive experience of working with them, finding answers to individual problems in these dogs will always be that much harder.

Sometimes a suitable collie behavioural advisor and a specialist trainer of these dogs (i.e. for sheepwork or competition) will be one and the same person; after all they should have considerable experience of working with collies one to one. You cannot, however, take this for granted; especially if the collie you have is owned as a social companion.

Competition and social behaviour skills
The expert you need is someone who is equally adept at managing both the working and social behaviour of collies; someone whose own dogs live with them and are not only highly trained but also socially bombproof wherever their owner takes them.

Some people may have vast expertise in training collies for set tasks within limited contexts (i.e. the home/training club/show or trials environment) but have little real feel for the social brain and behaviour of these dogs beyond their working function or role.

It is also not uncommon for competition trainers (and sheepdog owners/trainers) to kennel their dogs outside their immediate home environments. And if your dogs do not live intimately with you on a 24/7 basis, you will have less experience of observing, and dealing with, many of their

more challenging habits or neuroses at close quarters within a domestic setting. Similarly you will have less need to explore answers to these behaviours.

Limited experience of social handling
Many owners of competition dogs may not take them out daily for walks beyond their immediate home territory/kennel environment; their outings being principally limited to shows. The impact of this on the dogs concerned is to progressively undermine their levels of social tolerance and flexibility. Owners in turn get insufficient experience of managing collies, day in and day out, within a multitude of more challenging external social contexts.

If you have a problem collie, with some sort of social behaviour issue, this is exactly the kind of experience/expertise you will need to draw on in others. And if they haven't got it themselves then they can't help you.

In conclusion, when it comes to behavioural help, again use your own common sense, and keep looking and looking until you find what you really need and want. If you cannot find the expert you desire through word of mouth, or a national training/behavioural organisation, concentrate instead on individuals who could be the best possible role models for you. i.e:
- Someone who has had Border collies for many years
- Someone who lives with their dogs
- Someone who takes their dogs out on walks every day as a pack
- Someone skilled at managing the dynamics of a pack of collies, both outside and inside the home, so that they all live together in harmony
- Someone who seems to have calm, quiet authority
- Someone who clearly commands great respect, trust and affection from their dogs
- Someone who handles and trains their dogs with respect and compassion
- Someone who has trained their own dogs up to a high level
- Someone who can take all their collies anywhere, anytime, and they will all be brilliantly behaved.

You could find this person via other dog trainers or a friend, or just come across them at a competition, or even out on a walk. As soon as you do find them, grab their number; because even if they personally can't help you, they usually know someone who can.

Raw food diets
Raw food diets for dogs, comprising purely fresh meat and bones, vegetables and a host of other purely natural, non-

processed ingredients, have gained wide popularity among owners in recent years. There are owners who claim this diet has solved or cured a host of different problems in their dogs ranging from chronic skin and digestive disorders to aggressive behaviour.

Undoubtedly a large intake of fresh, as opposed to processed, food for your dog can only be good for him. Do be aware however that eating raw bones – particularly more brittle types which splinter easily – can also carry risks for dogs, such as broken teeth or sharp bone fragments piercing or damaging the throat or gut. It is therefore up to all owners to weigh up the benefits of this type of diet for their dog, which can often be immense, against the risks.

Meanwhile far more details on raw food diets can be found at: www.barfworld.com.

Working Trials

Readers – particularly those outside the UK – wishing to know far more about the discipline of Working Trials can do so by contacting Wendy Beasley through:
- www.borderdts.co.uk
- borderdts@aol.com

Working your dog with sheep

The best way to find out about courses where you can learn far more about working collies with sheep is via the International Sheep Dog Society in the UK and similar organisations in other countries catering for livestock working dogs. Contact details for these have already been listed at the beginning of this section (under *National Kennel Clubs and Border collie breed and working organisations*).

USEFUL ADDRESSES

NATIONAL KENNEL CLUBS AND BORDER COLLIE BREED AND WORKING DOG ORGANISATIONS

UK
The Kennel Club
www.thekennelclub.org.uk
Tel: 0844 463 3980

Border Collie Club of Great Britain
(national breed club of the UK)
www.bordercollieclub.com
Email: jwettern@btinternet.com
Phone: 01372 372229

East Anglian Border Collie Club
Email: eabcc.admin@blueyonder.co.uk
Phone: 01527 595820

Midlands Border Collie Club
www.midlandsbordercollieclub.com
Email: valerieearp@btinternet.com
Phone: 01162 869273

Southern Border Collie Club
www.southern-bcc.com
Email: angier@bilyara.wanadoo.co.uk
Phone: 01795 880410

Wessex Border Collie Club
www.freewebs.com/wessexbcc
Email: TARRYNDEN@aol.com
Phone: 02380 293258

North East Border Collie Club
Email: joan.tuffeigha@tiscali.co.uk
Phone: 01677 424296

North West Border Collie Club
Email: jeanrichardson06@tiscali.co.uk
Phone: 0161 703 8395

West Of England Border Collie Club
Email:margaret@icer.freeserve.co.uk
Phone: 01453 824903

Border Collie Club Of Wales
Email: claygar@btinternet.com
Phone: 01606 738078

The International Sheep Dog Society
(for enthusiasts of working dogs/dogs from working lines)
www.isds.org.uk
Email: office@isds.org.uk
Phone: 01234 352672

USA
The American Kennel Club
www.akc.org

Border Collie Society of America
www.bordercolliesociety.com

The American Border Collie Association
(for enthusiasts of livestock working dogs)
www.americanbordercollie.org

North American Sheep Dog Society
(for enthusiasts of livestock working dogs)
www.stockdog.com

CANADA
The Canadian Kennel Club
www.ckc.ca
Email: information@ckc.ca

The Canadian Border Collie Association
(for enthusiasts of working dogs)
www.canadianbordercollies.org
Email: secretary@canadianbordercollies.org

AUSTRALIA
Australian National Kennel Council
www.ankc.org.au
(website links to relevant local State or Territory controlling bodies, re breeder, training club or show/competition information)

The Australian Sheep Dog Workers' Association
(for enthusiasts of working dogs)
www.asdwa.org.au

Australian Working Border Collie Registry
www.awbcr.com/
(national registry for pure bred working border collies)

NEW ZEALAND
New Zealand Kennel Club
www.nzkc.org.nz
Email: secretary@nzkc.org.nz

New Zealand Sheep Dog Trial Association
(for enthusiasts of working dogs)
Email: NZSDTA@xtra.co.nz

SOUTH AFRICA
South African Sheep Dog Association
http://www.sasda.za.net/

BORDER COLLIE RESCUE ORGANISATIONS

UK
Specialist Border Collie rescue organisations in the UK

The Border Collie Trust (GB)
www.bordercollietrustgb.org.uk
Email: info@bordercollietrustgb.org.uk
Phone: 0871 560 2282

Border Collie Rescue
www.bordercollierescue.org
Email: hq@bordercollierescue.org
Phone: 0845 6044941

Valgrays Border Collie Rescue
www.valgraysbcrescue.org
Email: valgrays@hotmail.co.uk
(contact initially via email and appointment only)

Wiccaweys Rescued Border Collies and Working Sheepdogs
www.wiccaweys.co.uk
Email: wiccaweys@aol.com
Phone: **07905 203254**

Mainstream animal rescue organisations in the UK, that often need new homes for Border Collies:

The Dogs Trust
www.dogstrust.org.uk
Email: Direct via website. Website also lists all DT regional rehoming centres nationally.
Phone (Head Office): 0207 837 0006

Battersea Dogs' Home
www.battersea.org.uk
Email: info@battersea.org.uk
Phone: 0207 622 3626

The Blue Cross
www.bluecross.org.uk (lists regional rehoming centres in the UK)
Email: Contact via website
Phone: 01993 822651

USA
Specialist breed rescue organisations

Arizona Border Collie Rescue
www.azbordercollierescue.com

Border Collies In Need
(Has foster homes throughout Southern California and covers the following areas: Los Angeles, Orange, San Bernardino, San Diego, Riverside, Kern, Santa Barbara, Ventura, Imperial, and San Luis Obispo Counties)
www.bordercolliesinneed.org

Border Collie Rescue of Northern California
www.bcrescuenc.org

Border Collie Rescue Texas
www.bcrescuetexas.org

East Tennessee Border Collie Rescue
www.bordercollierescuetn.com

Border Collie Rescue of Minnesota
www.bcrmn.org

Mid-America Border Collie Rescue
(Serving Indiana, Illinois, Minnesota, Wisconsin, Michigan and Kentucky)
Email: midamericabcrescue@ yahoo.com

Mid-Atlantic Border Collie Rescue
www.mabcr.org

Midwest Border Collie Rescue
www.mwbcr.org

Pacific Northwest Border Collie Rescue
(Serving Washington, Oregon, Idaho and British Columbia)
www.pnwbcrescue.org

Wisconsin Border Collie Rescue
www.wibordercollierescue.com

CANADA
Border Collie Friends Rescue
www.bordercollie.ca

That'll Do Border Collie Rescue
www.bcbordercollies.com

Border Collie Rescue Canada
www.bordercollierescue.org (see links to Canadian rescue associations)

Canada Border Collie Rescue
www.bordercollie.rescueme.org/ca

Canada Border Collie Rescue Groups/Shelters
bordercollie.rescueshelter.com/ca

AUSTRALIA
Border Collie Rescue, Australia
(see links to different BC rescue organisations and shelters in different states/territories)
www.bcra.org.au

NEW ZEALAND
New Zealand Border Collie Rescue
Access your nearest rescue outlet in NZ via links from the following:
www.bordercollie.rescueme.org/sites
www.bordercollierescue.org

DNA RESEARCH PROJECTS
Readers might like to help with the following Border Collie DNA research projects:

Border Collie collapse
Collaborating researchers at the University of Saskatchewan in Canada and the University of Minnesota in the USA are looking into the syndrome of exercise intolerance in Border Collies known as Border Collie collapse (BCC). There are 4 aspects to their ongoing study: Namely, *questionnaires* from owners better describing their dogs BCC episodes and suspected triggers of these, as well as videotapes of these episodes if available; *pedigrees and registration details* from affected dogs; *DNA samples* from both affected and unaffected dogs and, finally, BCC affected dogs available to take part in strenuous exercise tests.
   More details on all the above are available via this link:
http://www.cvm.umn.edu/vbs/faculty/Mickelson/lab/home.html
   Then follow these steps:
• *Click on Exercise Induced Collapse under Canine Research*
• *Click on Border Collie Collapse*
• *Click on Sample Submission Form and Questionnaire*
• *Fill out the questionnaire online, print a copy for yourself and submit the questionnaire*
• *Addresses where you can send videotapes will also be listed*

Epilepsy
Those wishing to take part in research underway at the Animal Health Trust in the UK, investigating the possible genetic link with epilepsy in Border Collies, can obtain free cheek swab kits to obtain DNA samples from their dogs, plus further details on the project, via this email address: 'canine.genetics@aht.org.uk'

Hearing decline
Dr. Mark Neff at the University of California-Davis is currently studying non-congenital deafness in Border Collies. Non-congenital means that the deafness was not present at birth; rather, the deafness has a later onset, usually when the dog is between the ages of 4-6 years. Typically, dogs with this condition do not lose all of their hearing; instead, they seem to have an impaired hearing ability—much like a geriatric dog who is hard of hearing.
Dr. Neff's research has proven that the above-described hearing deficit is, in fact, inherited; but more information is needed to be able to develop a DNA test. Therefore, if you own a dog with this condition, or know someone who does, participate by sending in a cheek-swab sample from your affected dog.
   Participation is free, including postage. To request a collection kit, go to http://www.vgl.ucdavis.edu/cghg/kitreq.php. For further information, go to Dr. Neff's web page at: http://www.vgl.ucdavis.edu/cghg/index.php

EPILEPSY SUPPORT GROUPS
Help and advice for owners whose Border collies have epilepsy is available via the following sources:

UK
The Phyllis Croft Foundation for Canine Epilepsy
www.pcfce.org
Email: pcfce@btopenworld.com
01296 715829

USA
Canine Epilepsy Resource Center
www.canine-epilepsy.com
(Email via website)

INDEX